HAGGAI AND ZECHARIAH 1–8

BHHB
Baylor Handbook on the Hebrew Bible

General Editor

W. Dennis Tucker Jr.

HAGGAI AND ZECHARIAH 1–8
A Handbook on the Hebrew Text

Max Rogland

BAYLOR UNIVERSITY PRESS

© 2016 by Baylor University Press
Waco, Texas 76798

All Rights Reserved. No part of this publication may be reproduced, stored in a retrieval system, or transmitted, in any form or by any means, electronic, mechanical, photocopying, recording, or otherwise, without the prior permission in writing of Baylor University Press.

Cover Design by Pamela Poll
Cover photograph by Bruce and Kenneth Zuckerman, West Semitic Research, in collaboration with the Ancient Biblical Manuscript Center. Courtesy Russian National Library (Saltykov-Shchedrin).

Library of Congress Cataloging-in-Publication Data

Names: Rogland, M. F. (Max Frederick), 1968– author.
Title: Haggai and Zechariah 1–8 : a handbook on the Hebrew text / Max Rogland.
Description: Waco : Baylor University Press, 2016. | Series: Baylor handbook on the Hebrew Bible | Includes bibliographical references and index.
Identifiers: LCCN 2016013733| ISBN 9781602586741 (pbk. : alk. paper) | ISBN 9781481305631 (ebook-mobi/kindle)
Subjects: LCSH: Bible. Haggai. Hebrew—Criticism, interpretation, etc. | Bible. Zechariah, I–VIII. Hebrew—Criticism, interpretation, etc. | Hebrew language—Grammar.
Classification: LCC BS1655.52 .R64 2016 | DDC 224/.9704046—dc23
LC record available at https://lccn.loc.gov/2016013733

Printed in the United States of America on acid-free paper with a minimum of 30 percent post-consumer waste recycled content.

In memory of Eric Scott Wenger

Thus has YHWH Tsevaot said, "The fast of the fourth month and the fast of the fifth month and the fast of the seventh month and the fast of the tenth month will become exultation and joy and good appointed times for the house of Judah." (Zechariah 8:19)

TABLE OF CONTENTS

ACKNOWLEDGMENTS

As the Preacher of Ecclesiastes might have testified, the writing of this book has been both toilsome and full of joy. I am grateful to series editor Dennis Tucker not only for his patience with repeated delays in its completion but most especially for his suggestion to include Zechariah 1–8 along with my original proposal for a volume on Haggai. I did not realize exactly what I was getting into at the time when I agreed to take it on, but the additional labor proved to be more fascinating (and exhausting!) than I could have imagined.

Many hands have contributed in one way or another to this work. The library staff at Erskine College and Theological Seminary was extraordinarily helpful in handling my many requests for materials. It has been a pleasure to work alongside all of my colleagues at Erskine, but I am particularly grateful for the friendship and encouragement of Dr. Mark Ross.

The content of this book had its origin in my advanced Hebrew class at Erskine Theological Seminary, and I would be remiss not to mention those students who have taken that course and participated in many enjoyable discussions of the text of Haggai and Zechariah 1–8: Christian Crouch (whose remark that "Zechariah is a seriously trippy book" became a class mantra), Andrew DiIulio, Jonathan Harper, Martha Hill, Scott Hulstrand, Rod Johnson, Kristina Massey, Kent Suits, Jeremiah Thomas, Brooks Willet, and Chris Wilson. I especially wish to thank Rod Johnson, who provided valuable research assistance on some of the most puzzling passages in Zechariah. In addition, his comments on a draft of my manuscript came at a most opportune time.

There is a very real sense in which this book ought to be dedicated to my wife Lara. She has persevered with me through several arduous years on this volume. It is no exaggeration to say that, were it not for her, this handbook would never have been completed. "Let her deeds praise her in the gates!" (Prov 31:31)

As this project was coming to completion, the most gifted of my language students, and erstwhile teaching assistant, Eric Wenger, succumbed to a battle against aggressive and inoperable brain tumors. He is greatly missed by the Erskine community, and this book is affectionately dedicated to his memory.

Max Rogland
March 2016

LIST OF ABBREVIATIONS

AC	Arnold, Bill, and John H. Choi. 2003. *A Guide to Biblical Hebrew Syntax*. Cambridge: Cambridge University Press.
ANE	Ancient Near East
BDB	Brown, Francis I., S. R. Driver, and Charles A. Briggs. 1907. *A Hebrew and English Lexicon of the Old Testament*. Oxford: Clarendon.
BH	Biblical Hebrew
BHK	Kittel, Rudolf, and Paul Kahle. 1973. *Biblia Hebraica*. Stuttgart: Württembergische Bibelanstalt.
BHS	Elliger, Karl, and Wilhelm Ruldolph. 1977. *Biblica Hebraica Stuttgartensia*. Stuttgart: Deutsche Bibelgesellschaft.
BHQ	Gelston, Anthony. 2010. *The Twelve Minor Prophets*. Biblia Hebraica Quinta 13. Stuttgart: Deutsche Bibelgesellschaft.
CH	Classical Hebrew
DCH	Clines, David J. A. 1993–2011. *The Dictionary of Classical Hebrew*. 8 vols. Sheffield: Sheffield Academic.
DSS	Dead Sea Scrolls
Gibson	Gibson. John C. L. 1994. *Davidson's Introductory Hebrew Grammar: Syntax*. 4th ed. Edinburgh: T&T Clark.
GKC	Gesenius, Wilhelm, and Emil Kauzsch. 1910. *Gesenius' Hebrew Grammar*. Translated by A. E. Cowley. 2nd English ed. Oxford: Clarendon.
HAHAT	Gesenius, Wilhelm, and Frants Buhl. 1921. *Hebräisches und aramäisches Handwörterbuch über das alte Testament*. 17th ed. Leipzig: Vogel.
HALAT	Koehler, Ludwig, Walter Baumgartner, and Johann Jakob Stamm. 1967–1995. *Hebräisches und aramäisches Lexikon zum Alten Testament*. 5 vols. Leiden: Brill.

HALOT	Koehler, Ludwig, Walter Baumgartner, and Johann Jakob Stamm, 1994–2000. *The Hebrew and Aramaic Lexicon of the Old Testament.* Translated and edited under the supervision of M. E. J. Richardson. Leiden: Brill.
HB	Hebrew Bible
Jastrow	Jastrow, Marcus. 1886–1903. *Dictionary of the Targumim, Talmud Babli, Yerushalmi and Midrashic Literature.* 2 vols. New York: G. P. Putnam's Sons [1975 repr., New York: Judaica Press].
JM	Joüon, Paul, and Takamitsu Muraoka. 2006. *A Grammar of Biblical Hebrew.* 2nd ed. Rome: Pontifical Biblical Institute.
LBH	Late Biblical Hebrew
LXX	Septuagint
MH	Mishnaic Hebrew
MNK	Van der Merwe, Christo, Jackie A. Naudé, and Jan H. Kroeze. 1999. *A Biblical Hebrew Reference Grammar.* Sheffield: Sheffield Academic.
MT	Masoretic Text
NIDOTTE	*The New International Dictionary of Old Testament Theology and Exegesis*, edited by Willem Van Gemeren. 2006. 5 vols. Grand Rapids: Eerdmans.
QH	Qumran Hebrew
Rashi	Rashi's Commentary on the Bible, cited at the passage under discussion
RH	Rabbinic Hebrew
SBH	Standard Biblical Hebrew
Syr	Syriac
TDOT	*Theological Dictionary of the Old Testament*, edited by Johannes Botterweck, Helmer Ringgren, and Heinz-Josef Fabry. 1974–2006. Translated by John T. Willis, David E. Green, and Douglas W. Stott. 15 vols. Grand Rapids: Eerdmans.
Tg	Targum
TH	Transitional Hebrew
Vulg	Vulgate
WB	Williams, Ronald J., and John C. Beckman. 2007. *Williams' Hebrew Syntax.* 3rd ed. Toronto: University of Toronto Press.
WO	Waltke, Bruce K.m and Michael O'Connor. 1990. *An Introduction to Biblical Hebrew Syntax.* Winona Lake, Ind.: Eisenbrauns.

INTRODUCTION

The postexilic prophets Haggai and Zechariah, as well as the books bearing their names, have typically had a close association with one another. Biblical narrative connects the prophetic ministries of the two men (Ezra 5:1; 6:14) and gives the unmistakable impression that they together played a critical role in inspiring the completion of the second temple. The book of Haggai and the first six chapters of Zechariah are also tightly linked by their chronological proximity: dating formulae in the text place them in the second year of the Persian monarch Darius (Hag 1:1, 15; 2:1, 10, 20; Zech 1:1, 7), with Zech 7–8 being dated to his fourth year (Zech 7:1). In terms of their content, the books share an obvious and emphatic interest in issues pertaining to the temple, which fits remarkably well with the historical narrative of Ezra 5–6. It is hardly surprising, then, that a number of monographs, commentaries, and academic studies treat these two prophetic books together. Indeed, some redaction-critical studies allege that there were periods of time when earlier versions of the two books had been fused together as one united work (e.g., Hallaschka 2011). Such speculations can never be proven, of course, but the existence of these theories nevertheless testifies to the sense of connection between them.

Despite their historical and thematic links, Haggai and Zechariah stand in marked contrast to one another in other important respects. Apart from one brief section of historical narrative (Hag 1:12-15a), the book of Haggai consists of prophetic discourse, although beyond that general label the specific nature of Haggai's writing has been disputed: some assert that the language is prosaic, while others claim that it is poetic. This disagreement is evident in different editions of the Hebrew Bible (HB), with *BHK* presenting the text as prose but *BHS* and *BHQ* setting it forth in poetic form (see §2 below for further discussion). The literary style of Zechariah in turn differs from that of Haggai quite considerably. The centerpiece of Zech 1–8 is the fascinating series of visions written in narrative style, frequently referred to as the "Night Visions," which is preceded by a brief prologue (1:1-6) and capped by two more prosaic chapters (Zech 7–8), which serve to recapitulate and develop various themes from the visions. The bulk of Zech 1–8, therefore, is written in a style of biblical narrative that will seem reasonably familiar to the intermediate Hebrew student. On the other hand, Zech 9–14 displays considerable stylistic differences from Zech 1–8 and is manifestly more challenging to read. This handbook follows the common scholarly convention of treating the book of Haggai along with only the first eight chapters of Zechariah.

§1 "Early" and "Late" Biblical Hebrew and the Language of Haggai and Zechariah 1–8

Hebrew, like all human languages, has developed over time, both in terms of its lexicon, with words changing in meaning or disappearing and with new words emerging, and also in terms of its grammar, as certain grammatical forms became obsolete and new forms were developed. Hebrew grammarians have customarily distinguished between different historical phases of biblical Hebrew (BH), starting with its earliest (or "archaic") phase, primarily represented by poetic compositions such as Gen 49, Exod 15, and the like (Sáenz-Badillos, 56–62), to "early" or "standard" biblical Hebrew (SBH) found chiefly in preexilic compositions, and gradually developing into "late" biblical Hebrew (LBH) of the exilic and postexilic eras. LBH continued to evolve into what some have termed "transitional" Hebrew (TH), encompassing Qumran Hebrew (QH) and the extant Hebrew text of Ben Sira (cited here in the editions of Ben-Ḥayyim, as well as Beentjes), and on into the postbiblical era of Rabbinic Hebrew (RH). The entire range of Hebrew prior to the Rabbinic era can be conveniently termed "classical Hebrew" (CH). The studies of Ezekiel Kutscher and Avi Hurvitz have been particularly influential in developing this basic chronological framework for understanding the historical phases of the Hebrew language (for a more detailed discussion of specific lexical and grammatical developments in these different phases, see Kutscher 1982 and Sáenz-Badillos). Haggai and Zech 1–8 are acknowledged by all as postexilic compositions, and Hebraists have accordingly drawn attention to various lexical and grammatical features in these books which bear the marks of their linguistic milieu. This is not to say that there are no differences of opinion even within this shared framework; some scholars see the LBH elements in Haggai and Zech 1–8 as dominant (e.g., Rendsburg 2012), whereas others see more limited imprints of LBH on these books (e.g., Hurvitz, cited in Ehrensvärd 2003: 176).

In more recent times, however, this historical or "diachronic" framework has been strongly challenged by a vocal minority led by three scholars in particular: Ian Young, Robert Rezetko, and Martin Ehrensvärd. In a variety of publications and venues they have argued that the linguistic evidence does not support the notion that BH can be divided into SBH and LBH. Rather, they argue that what scholars have called "early" and "late" BH are to be understood instead as different literary styles of Hebrew which coexisted throughout the period during which the HB was produced (e.g., Young et al. 2008a: 361). A chief feature of this viewpoint is the denial that linguistic data can be used in any way as a criterion to confirm or deny the date of composition or final redaction of a biblical book. This perspective has been applied to Haggai and Zechariah, and in one study Ehrensvärd concludes that these books contain "no clear LBH features" (2003: 185; cf. Young et al. 2008b: 68). In another more detailed study of Zech 1–8, he examines thirteen linguistic features, which, he argues, indicate that the book's linguistic profile is more closely aligned with SBH than with LBH (Ehrensvärd 2006).

The arguments of Young et al. have provoked numerous responses, some positive and some negative (e.g., see the various essays in Young 2003). A full critical analysis of "the Young-Rezetko-Ehrensvärd thesis" is neither possible nor necessary here, however, since many such critiques are already available (see, e.g., Miller-Naudé and Zevit). One should take special note of the trenchant criticisms of Dresher, who demonstrates upon closer examination that many of their arguments are based upon poor linguistic methodology. Without overstating our ability to date biblical literature simply on the basis of linguistic data alone, this handbook follows the accepted division of BH into historical stages and the general validity of the diachronic description of SBH and LBH as articulated by Kutscher and others. Since the interest of this volume is in the actual linguistic data of Haggai and Zech 1–8, two points deserve particular emphasis.

First, it should be noted that Ehrensvärd's handling of the data in Haggai and Zech 1–8 is problematic at various places. These points will be noted in the course of the commentary; see, e.g., on Zech 6:15 and 8:21 regarding his assertions that the frequency of occurrence of the "paranomastic" infinitive absolute or of the "paragogic *nun*" in Zechariah reflects SBH rather than LBH (Ehrensvärd 2006: 181–82). As will be observed, the "early" features that he discerns in the texts are not as numerous as he alleges.

Second, LBH features are in fact more pervasive in Haggai and Zech 1–8 than Ehrensvärd is willing to admit. Shin (2007) and Rendsburg (2012) have analyzed an impressive collection of data bearing witness to LBH features in these books. While some of their particular readings of the data could be disputed (cf. Rogland 2013a: 74–77 with Rendsburg 2012: 331), the basic evaluation of Haggai and Zech 1–8 as LBH remains valid. In addition to the numerous examples collected and analyzed in these studies, additional LBH features will be mentioned in the course of the commentary here (see, e.g., on Hag 1:6; 2:19; Zech 1:1).

In sum, then, the general historical picture of the development of the Hebrew language as sketched out above is accepted as valid in this handbook, as well as the commonly accepted place of Haggai and Zech 1–8 within that framework. Both books display lexical and grammatical features indicative of a late, postexilic linguistic milieu, though admittedly not as many as some books in the LBH corpus. This general picture comports well with the widely accepted date of the books' composition as being relatively early in the Persian period. Shin's judicious conclusion for the Haggai-Zechariah-Malachi corpus at large applies here: "the language . . . is indeed part and parcel of LBH; yet, diachronically it must be located in an early stage of the LBH development" (160).

§2 The Language of Haggai: Prose or Poetry?

Zechariah's Night Visions can be identified as narrative (with oracular utterances occasionally interspersed) bounded on either side with more prosaic sections as bookends. As noted above, however, there is debate as to whether the language of Haggai is to be classified as prose or poetry. Many scholars argue for an in-between position and instead appeal to a scale or continuum between prose and poetry, characterizing the language of Haggai alternately as "poetic prose" (Ackroyd 1950–1951: 165–66), "rhythmic prose" (Verhoef 1987: 17), "oracular prose" or "elevated prose" (Meyers and Meyers, lxiv), and so on. Others prefer more discourse-analytical terminology and speak of distinctions between narrative and direct discourse rather than a prose versus poetry distinction (Petersen, 31–32). There is general agreement that Haggai is not to be considered prose narrative (apart from 1:12-15a), but beyond that opinions differ.

One attempt to establish more objective criteria for drawing the distinction between Hebrew prose and Hebrew poetry, with their relevance for the book of Haggai, is that of Meyers and Meyers (lxiii–lxvii), who employ the statistical methodology of Andersen and Freedman (59–66) of counting the number of "prose particles" used in a text. That is, by considering the statistical usage of the definite article and the particles אֲשֶׁר and אֵת, they conclude that Haggai–Zech 1–8 falls well within the realm of prose. However, to call it straightforward prose is too simplistic, and hence they label it "oracular prose":

> Clearly the language of our books by any statistical reckoning is prosaic in character, but it is difficult to deny the flair of the prophetic writer or editor when he breaks out in, or perhaps imitates, a poetic style. In such places it is probably best to use the term 'oracular prose' or even more simply 'elevated prose' to characterize the nature of these works. (Andersen and Freedman, lxvii)

Another attempt to establish objective criteria for distinguishing poetry from prose can be found in Wilfred Watson's manual *Classical Hebrew Poetry*. Watson acknowledges the difficulty of establishing such criteria but nevertheless compiles a significant number of features that do serve to distinguish poetry from prose (46–47). These features, along with the most evident ways in which Haggai does or does not meet them, can be seen in the following table adapted from Watson (46–47, 55):

Table I: Criteria for Distinguishing Poetry from Prose

A. Broad Criteria	**Presence/Absence in Haggai**
1. Established line-forms	
2. Ellipsis, esp. verb gapping	*Absence* of gapping when it could have been employed: Hag 1:10 כָּלְאוּ שָׁמַיִם מִטָּל וְהָאָרֶץ כָּלְאָה יְבוּלָהּ "the heavens *withheld* their dew and the earth *withheld* its produce."
3. Unusual (poetic, not merely technical) vocabulary	
4. Conciseness	
5. Unusual word order	n/a[1]
6, Archaisms	
7. Use of meter and rhythm	Uncertain[2]
8. Regularity and symmetry (cf. #14 below)	Hag 2:4 וְעַתָּה חֲזַק . . . וַחֲזַק . . . וַחֲזַק
B. Structural Criteria	
9. Use of parallelism	Hag 2:21-22 (?)
10. Word pairs	Hag 1:6, 9-11; 2:6, 8, 16-17, 19, 21-22, etc.
11. Chiastic patterns	Hag 1:6, 9-10; 2:23 (?)
12. Envelope figure/inclusion	
13. Break-up of stereotypical phrases	
14. Repetition (cf. #8 above)	עֵת (1:2, 4), שִׂים לֵב (1:5, 7; 2:15, 18), כֵּן (2:14)
15. Gender-matched parallelism	
16. Tricolon	
C. Other Criteria	
17. Rhyme	
18. Other sound patterns	Hag 1:10-11 wordplay חֹרֶב/חָרֵב

[1] Our understanding of Hebrew word order in poetry is still at a very rudimentary stage, and hence this criterion has not been considered here.

[2] Various metrical analyses of the book have been attempted (e.g., Bloomhardt; D. Christiansen 1993), though none can claim to hold a scholarly consensus.

Table I (cont.)

D. Negative Criteria	
19. Absence/rarity of prose elements	Use of "prose particles" is well attested (Meyers and Meyers, lxiv–lxvii)
Literary/nonformal criteria: figurative language, simile, metaphor, use of imagery, irony, allusion, hyperbole, etc.	Minimal usage

Even allowing for some debatable instances, in the end the number of potentially poetic features in Haggai is not especially impressive. What is more, Watson notes that the simple occurrence of *some* poetic features is not a decisive factor:

> [T]he mere presence of one or even of several of these indicators proves very little. Ultimately, the decision [whether a text is poetic or prosaic] owes a great deal to mature reflection which will consider content as well as form, with an eye on traditions both in Classical Hebrew and in ancient Near Eastern literature generally. (Watson, 55)

Indeed, certain poetic features are conspicuous by their *absence*. Most of the vocabulary of Haggai (criterion #3) is relatively ordinary and prosaic. In some instances a feature which would be expected in poetry is not attested; thus "ellipsis" or "verb gapping" (criterion #2) would have been expected in Hag 1:10 עַל־כֵּן עֲלֵיכֶם כָּלְאוּ שָׁמַיִם מִטָּל וְהָאָרֶץ כָּלְאָה יְבוּלָהּ, where the same verb occurs in what is arguably intended as an instance of grammatical parallelism.

Based on the data we have and our current state of knowledge regarding ancient Hebrew poetics, we must conclude that, as a whole, the book of Haggai makes only a very modest use of poetic structures and devices and is best classified as "prose" rather than "poetry" per se. This does not necessarily mean that the book ought to be viewed as "pedestrian" or "plain," however. As will be noted in the next section (§3), both Haggai and Zech 1–8 make significant use of intertextuality—that is, the intentional quotation of or allusion to a known work of literature or established tradition. The phenomenon has been examined before with respect to Zech 1–8 (e.g. Stead; Wenzel 2011a), but it is also pervasive in the book of Haggai as well; each oracle relies heavily upon intertextual argumentation to make its point. The significance of this observation to the point at hand is simply this: the widespread use of intertextuality marks Haggai out as a book with a very "literate" character. It assumes knowledgeable readers familiar with a shared literary tradition, who will be able to pick up on the author's cues which point toward his intended "intertexts." Thus, while we can fairly conclude that Haggai is not particularly "poetic" in form, a term such as "elevated prose" (Meyers and Meyers, lxiv) is indeed a fitting description of the book.

§3 Intertextuality and Intratextuality

"Intertextuality" has become a widely used term in contemporary biblical studies (for a brief survey of different approaches to the concept, see Stead, 19–27). Broadly defined it can be understood as the phenomenon of an author making use of another preexisting text or textual tradition. Such textual reuse can take a variety of forms, including a verbatim quote with source cited, an unattributed citation, and various types of allusion or "echo." Such textual "reuse" can serve a variety of purposes such as providing a "prooftext" to an argument or evoking textual coloring of some kind. "Intratextuality" is a related concept and refers to a text making reference to itself (Stead, 28–29).

As noted above, Zech 1–8 has been subjected to highly useful and detailed intertextual and intratextual analyses, and there are indications that Haggai has also made significant use of intertextuality (cf. Rogland 2007b and the commentary below). While these phenomena are typically examined with respect to their exegetical import, they also prove helpful for the philological analysis of texts. In his detailed study of Zech 1–8, Stead observes:

> One of the implications of a highly allusive text such as Zech 1–8 is that meaning cannot lie solely within that text alone, because the meaning is only produced by reading that text against its intertexts. With nothing but the bare text of Zechariah, in many places a reader cannot arrive at its sense, because it only makes sense when understood against the background of what (for example) Jeremiah or Ezekiel or Isaiah have already said. These other texts create a symbolic world, or frame of reference, for Zech 1–8. The meaning of Zech 1–8 is thus the product of the combination of the text

> of Zech 1–8 with those other texts, and this is a process which occurs in the mind of the reader. (25)

In other words, if the author of Zech 1–8 composed a passage which intentionally interacted with an outside text (an "intertext"), then the later composition can only be properly understood when that intertext is successfully identified and brought to bear in the process of interpretation. In some instances this is obvious. For example, the vision of the massive golden lampstand in Zech 4 presupposes some level of familiarity with the tabernacle lampstand of Exod 25:31-40. The failure to identify and appreciate an intended intertext will result in what Michael Riffaterre calls an "ungrammaticality." As Stead explains, an "ungrammaticality" is

> a word or phrase which, because of its awkwardness in the present context, points to another text which provides the key to its decoding, and so aids readers in the production of meaning: ". . . the dual sign works like a pun. We will see that the pun in poetic discourse grows out of textual 'roots.' It is first apprehended as a mere ungrammaticality, until the discovery is made that there is another text in which the word is grammatical; the moment the other text is identified, the dual sign becomes significant purely because of its shape, which alone alludes to that other code." (25, citing Riffaterre, 82)

There are a number of instances in Haggai and Zech 1–8 that have been perceived as "ungrammaticalities,"—that is, as grammatical or textual anomalies or problems. As will be seen, some of these problems can be given a philologically and exegetically satisfying analysis once the correct intertext has been identified (see, e.g., on Hag 2:5 and Zech 1:8). Although such intertextual uses will not be subjected to extensive exegetical treatment in this handbook, they will be regularly considered, particularly as they allow for an improved grammatical or lexical analysis of a text.

Features of This Handbook

This handbook was written to a large extent with intermediate to advanced Hebrew students in mind. In terms of their language, form, and style, Haggai and Zech 1–8 provide an excellent bridge for the student who wishes to progress from reading historical narratives to other literary genres. These texts are also admirably suited for this purpose as the Hebrew text is very well preserved, allowing the student to focus chiefly on grammatical and lexical analysis without becoming unduly caught up in text-critical problems. The text-critical data concerning Haggai and Zechariah can be conveniently found in the *BHQ* Minor Prophets fascicle, which is much less suspicious of the Masoretic Text (MT) than earlier editions. The text of Zechariah is not very well preserved at Qumran (Høgenhaven, 112), but a significant portion of the MT of Haggai (almost 50%) finds particularly strong confirmation in the Murabbaʿat text of the Minor Prophets (MurXII), displaying only miniscule variations from the Leningrad manuscript which forms the basis for *BHS* and *BHQ*. A few other Qumran fragments for Haggai and Zechariah also exist, and when they differ from the MT it is primarily with respect to orthography. As usual, the ancient versions such as the Septuagint (LXX) display more significant variants from the Hebrew manuscripts, but in general these are to be attributed to the translators' difficulty with the Hebrew text itself rather than to a different *Vorlage*. Thus, scholars increasingly acknowledge the general reliability of the MT (e.g., Meyers and Meyers, lxvii–lxviii), and it is notable that *BHQ* eschews many of the emendations proposed by its predecessors *BHK* and *BHS* as well as the extensive list of corrections proposed by Mitchell (30–35, 84–97). Most passages felt to be text-critically problematic are not due to textual uncertainty but simply to the difficulty of the Hebrew words and expressions used.

In terms of linguistic approach, this handbook is generally congenial to the definitions and framework set out by Holmstedt (2010: 1–16), with the exceptions that the Hebrew verbal system is understood here as expressing both tense and aspect (cf. Rogland 2003) instead of exclusively aspect (Holmstedt 2010: 8–9) and that a generally more agnostic stance is taken toward the question of BH word order (cf. Holmstedt 2010: 11, and much more emphatically Holmstedt 2011). A competent foundational knowledge of biblical Hebrew is assumed here, and grammatical terminology will be regularly employed (definitions of which can be found in the glossary). At the same time, this handbook is also guided by the assumption that the majority of its users are more interested in applied Hebrew linguistics than in theoretical linguistics for its own sake. Therefore it has sought to minimize distinctive jargon apart from the terminology encountered in the standard reference works on ancient Hebrew. The more advanced user of this volume should be able to incorporate the explanations in the commentary into his or her preferred linguistic framework.

Outline of Haggai

1. First Oracle (Haggai 1:1-11): Covenant Judgments and a Call to Rebuild the Temple
2. Narrative (Haggai 1:12-15a): The People's Response and YHWH's Reassurance
3. Second Oracle (Haggai 1:15b–2:9): The Latter Glory of YHWH's House
4. Third Oracle (Haggai 2:10-19): Uncleanness, Judgment, Rebuilding, and Blessing
5. Fourth Oracle (Haggai 2:20-23): A Message to Zerubbabel

Outline of Zechariah

1. Prologue (Zechariah 1:1-6): A Call to Return to YHWH
2. First Vision (Zechariah 1:7-17): A Rider Upon a Horse
3. Second Vision (Zechariah 2:1-4): Four Horns and Four Craftsmen
4. Third Vision (Zechariah 2:5-9): A Man with a Measuring Cord
5. Exhortation Based on the First Three Visions (Zechariah 2:10-17)
6. Fourth Vision (Zechariah 3:1-10): New High Priestly Clothes for Joshua
7. Fifth Vision (Zechariah 4:1-14): The Golden Lampstand and an Oracle for Zerubbabel
8. Sixth Vision (Zechariah 5:1-11): The Flying Scroll and the Flying Basket
9. Seventh Vision (Zechariah 6:1-8): Divine Chariots and God's Spirit
10. An Oracle (Zechariah 6:9-15): A Crown for Joshua, the Coming of *Ṣemaḥ*, and a Temple Memorial
11. Concluding Exhortation (Zechariah 7–8): The Past Judgment and Future Redemption of Zion

A HANDBOOK ON THE HEBREW TEXT OF HAGGAI AND ZECHARIAH 1–8

Haggai

First Oracle (Haggai 1:1-11)
Covenant Judgments and a Call to Rebuild the Temple

The basic thrust of Haggai's initial oracle is clear with its repeated exhortation for the people to "pay attention to their ways" (vv. 5, 7). Drawing attention to times of scarcity which they have been experiencing (vv. 6, 10-11), it summons them to acknowledge that these are acts of YHWH's judgment. The reason for such punishment is their neglect of YHWH's house (vv. 2, 4, 8-9) in favor of their own personal affairs (vv. 4, 6, 9). The solution presented in verse 8 is straightforward: the people need to get back to work rebuilding the temple so that YHWH may be honored!

The punishments mentioned bear the intertextual influence of both Lev 26 and Deut 28, the so-called covenantal judgments of the Torah (see vv. 10-11 below). The people's neglect of the temple is thus presented as constituting a fundamental failure in their relationship with YHWH. These references have a double-edged character in confirming the covenant relationship between the people and YHWH while at the same time challenging them to fulfill the obligations that that relationship entails. In addition, they highlight the crucial role the house of YHWH plays in establishing and maintaining the covenant relationship: without it, the intimate bond between YHWH and Israel is called into question.

[1]In the second year of Darius the king, in the sixth month, on the first day of the month, the word of YHWH came via Haggai the prophet to

Zerubbabel, son of Shealtiel, governor of Judah, and to Joshua, son of Jehozadaq, the high priest:

[2]*Thus has YHWH Tsevaot said, "This people have said, 'It is not a time to come, not a time for the house of YHWH to be rebuilt.'"*

[3]*And the word of YHWH came via Haggai the prophet:*

[4]*"Is it time for you yourselves to dwell in your houses which are paneled, while this house is desolate?"*

[5]*Now therefore, thus has YHWH Tsevaot said, "Pay attention to your ways.*

[6]*You have sown much, but brought in little; eaten, but could not be satisfied; drunk, but could not drink freely; gotten dressed, but could not warm yourself; and the one who earns wages earns wages going into a pierced pouch."*

[7]*Thus has YHWH Tsevaot said, "Pay attention to your ways.*

[8]*Go up to the hill country and then bring timber that you might build the house, and I will take pleasure in it and be honored"—YHWH has said.*

[9]*"You looked for much but behold, it turned out to be little. But bring [it] to the house and I will blow upon it. Why?"—oracle of YHWH Tsevaot—"On account of my house, which is a ruin, while each of you is guarding his own house.*

[10]*Therefore on account of you, the heavens withheld their dew, and the earth withheld its produce.*

[11]*And I summoned a drought upon the earth, and upon the hills, and upon the grain, and upon the fresh wine, and upon the fresh oil, and upon that which the ground brings forth, and upon man, and upon beast, and upon every product of hands."*

1:1 בִּשְׁנַ֤ת שְׁתַּ֙יִם֙ לְדָרְיָ֣וֶשׁ הַמֶּ֔לֶךְ בַּחֹ֙דֶשׁ֙ הַשִּׁשִּׁ֔י בְּי֥וֹם
אֶחָ֖ד לַחֹ֑דֶשׁ הָיָ֨ה דְבַר־יְהוָ֜ה בְּיַד־חַגַּ֣י הַנָּבִ֗יא אֶל־
זְרֻבָּבֶ֤ל בֶּן־שְׁאַלְתִּיאֵל֙ פַּחַ֣ת יְהוּדָ֔ה וְאֶל־יְהוֹשֻׁ֥עַ בֶּן־
יְהוֹצָדָ֛ק הַכֹּהֵ֥ן הַגָּד֖וֹל לֵאמֹֽר׃

בִּשְׁנַ֤ת שְׁתַּ֙יִם֙ לְדָרְיָ֣וֶשׁ הַמֶּ֔לֶךְ בַּחֹ֙דֶשׁ֙ הַשִּׁשִּׁ֔י בְּי֥וֹם אֶחָ֖ד לַחֹ֑דֶשׁ. The preposition לְ is commonly utilized to establish a variety of genitival relationships between nominals or nominal phrases (cf. BDB, 512–13, #5). In the phrase בִּשְׁנַ֤ת שְׁתַּ֙יִם֙ לְדָרְיָ֣וֶשׁ "the second year *to* Darius," the preposition indicates possession (JM §130b, §133d; GKC

§129; AC §4.1.10f-g; WB §270)—i.e., "the second year (belonging) to Darius," which is typically translated "the second year *of* Darius." The same is true of בְּיוֹם אֶחָד לַחֹדֶשׁ "in day one (belonging) to the month." Even though BH possesses both cardinal and ordinal numerals, it prefers to use cardinals with שָׁנָה "year" and יוֹם "day" but the ordinals with חֹדֶשׁ "month" (JM §142o). On the word order in date formulae, see the introductory remarks to 1:12-15a. The nouns in the phrase לְדָרְיָוֶשׁ הַמֶּלֶךְ "to Darius, the king" stand in grammatical apposition (JM §131; MNK §29; AC §2.4; WB §§61–71). In SBH, the typical word order is for הַמֶּלֶךְ to precede the proper name, whereas LBH prefers to have הַמֶּלֶךְ follow the proper name. The book of Esther is a significant exception to the pattern (Rendsburg 2012: 334–35), but Haggai's usage lines up with the general LBH pattern. It is common for prepositions or אֶת־ to be repeated in appositional structures and thus one might have expected *לְדָרְיָוֶשׁ לַמֶּלֶךְ, but exceptions do occur (JM §131i; WO §12.3f), particularly when the first member of an appositional pair is a name (WB §70), as is the case here.

הָיָה דְבַר־יְהוָה בְּיַד־חַגַּי הַנָּבִיא אֶל־זְרֻבָּבֶל בֶּן־שְׁאַלְתִּיאֵל. Qal *qatal* 3 m s √היה. Though typically classified as a stative verb, √היה often takes on the nature of a fientive verb or a verb of action in the sense of "to happen" or "to come to pass" (JM §111h–i), which is the case with the common prophetic formula found here. Often termed the "reception formula," this expression frequently serves to mark the beginning of an oracle. It does this particularly when, as in this instance, it occurs in conjunction with dating formulae (for further discussion, see Appendix §1). The prepositional phrase בְּיַד in בְּיַד־חַגַּי הַנָּבִיא means "*by the agency* or *instrumentality of*. . . esp. of 'י's speaking *by the agency* of prophets" (BDB, 391, #5d). Typically the reception formula utilizes the preposition אֶל rather than בְּיַד (the latter occurs only in 1 Kgs 16:7; Hag 1:1, 3; 2:1), but here it serves to distinguish the oracle's agent of transmission from its intended addressee.

פַּחַת יְהוּדָה. Strictly speaking this noun phrase could be in apposition to "Zerubbabel" or "Shealtiel," though certainly the former is intended (in 2:21 זְרֻבָּבֶל פַּחַת־יְהוּדָה the phrase is clearly appositional to "Zerubbabel"). פֶּחָה, an Akkadian loan-word, is grammatically masculine despite the ה-ending (JM §89b). It is attested in preexilic settings (e.g., 1 Kgs 20:24; 2 Kgs 18:24), but Rendsburg (2012: 332) suggests that its application to Jewish governors represents a LBH development. The data concerning regional administrative structure under the preexilic monarchy is limited, however, and it is not certain whether there would have been any occasion for such an application of the term prior to the exile.

וְאֶל־יְהוֹשֻׁעַ בֶּן־יְהוֹצָדָק הַכֹּהֵן הַגָּדוֹל. The preposition אֶל is repeated before the name "Joshua," and this is common with multiple prepositional objects (JM §132g; WB §238), though numerous exceptions occur. Like the preceding phrase פַּחַת יְהוּדָה, the phrase הַכֹּהֵן הַגָּדוֹל could be in apposition to the first name (Joshua) or to the last one (Jehozadaq), though the former is intended (cf. יְהוֹשֻׁעַ הַכֹּהֵן הַגָּדוֹל in Zech 3:1, 8). The name "Joshua" appears in SBH as יְהוֹשֻׁעַ but is steadily supplanted by יֵשׁוּעַ in LBH prose, TH, and Rabbinic texts (Shin, 141–44). This development did not affect the postexilic prophets Haggai and Zechariah, however, which consistently attest the form יְהוֹשֻׁעַ (Hag 1:1, 12, 14; 2:2, 4; Zech 3:1, 3, 6, 8, 9; 6:11).

לֵאמֹר. Qal inf cstr √אמר. The expected vocalization of this infinitive construct would be אֱמֹר, as occurs with the prepositions בְּ and כְּ (e.g., Deut 4:10 בֶּאֱמֹר and Josh 6:8 כֶּאֱמֹר), though other alternating forms of the infinitive construct of one and the same root are attested (e.g., Gen 20:6 לִנְגֹּעַ vs. 2 Sam 14:10 לָגַעַת; for discussion of the phenomenon, see Miller 1996: 167–68 n. 48). The phonology of לֵאמֹר is analogous to that of a noun such as אֱלֹהִים with prefixed preposition (→ לֵאלֹהִים), but this occurs uniquely with √אמר and is not attested with any other I-*alef* verb (Miller 1996: 168–69). However, there are cross-linguistic parallels for the use of morphologically unusual forms of verbs of speaking to introduce direct discourse (Miller 1996: 202–6), which is one of the most common functions of לֵאמֹר. This discourse-introducing function is often explained as an "explanatory" or "epexegetical" (or sometimes "gerundive") use of the infinitive construct that is to be translated as "by saying" (cf. WB §195), but Miller demonstrates that in cases such as these it is not functioning as a true gerundive but rather is simply a "complementizer" that introduces reported speech (Miller 1996: 179–85). As such, it can omitted in translation (similarly vv. 2, 3, 13; 2:1, 2, 10, 11, 20, 21).

1:2 כֹּה אָמַר יְהוָה צְבָאוֹת לֵאמֹר הָעָם הַזֶּה אָמְרוּ לֹא
עֶת־בֹּא עֶת־בֵּית יְהוָה לְהִבָּנוֹת׃ פ

כֹּה אָמַר יְהוָה צְבָאוֹת לֵאמֹר. Qal *qatal* 3 m s and Qal inf cstr √אמר. This so-called "messenger formula" is a common one in the HB with a variety of discourse-related functions (see Appendix §2). The divine name often occurs in the expanded form יהוה צְבָאוֹת "YHWH of hosts" (ca. 230×), which is typically assumed to be an ellipsis for the longer יהוה אֱלֹהֵי צְבָאוֹת "YHWH, God of hosts" (e.g., 2 Sam 5:10; see GKC §125h), though the latter appellation only occurs fifteen times. יהוה צְבָאוֹת is usually translated as a genitival construction, but typically a proper noun like יהוה does not occur in a construct relationship, although there are some inscriptions from ca. 800 BCE containing the phrases יהוה שמרן "YHWH of Samaria" and יהוה התמן "YHWH of Teman" (Emerton 1982: 2–3). Nevertheless, scholars have typically understood יהוה and צְבָאוֹת to be standing in grammatical apposition (JM §131o), suggesting that צְבָאוֹת came to be perceived as a proper name. This finds support in the fact that, in addition to the frequent construct phrase אֱלֹהֵי צְבָאוֹת "God of hosts" (e.g., 2 Sam 5:10), the appositional construction אֱלֹהִים צְבָאוֹת also occurs (e.g., Ps 80:5, 8, 15, 20). In light of these factors, צְבָאוֹת is best understood as a proper name just like יהוה (cf. Emerton 1982: 3–5), and thus is transliterated in this handbook as "YHWH Tsevaot" instead of translated as "YHWH of hosts."

הָעָם הַזֶּה אָמְרוּ. Qal *qatal* 3 c pl √אמר. The general rule is for a verb to agree with its subject noun in number and gender, though many exceptions occur (JM §150b; WB §§227–33; MNK §35), as here where the noun is singular but the verb is plural. Such fluctuation is particularly noticeable with collective nouns such as עָם, though there may be a general tendency to construe עָם as plural when it precedes the verb, as in this instance (Young 1999: 53–54). The *qatal* form is to be understood as a "global" past tense (JM §112d)—that is, as summarizing more than one instance of the people's making excuses for their inactivity with respect to the rebuilding of the temple.

לֹא עֶת־בֹּא עֶת־בֵּית יְהוָה לְהִבָּנוֹת. Qal inf cstr √בוא and Nifal inf cstr √בנה with לְ preposition. בֹּא is often revocalized to בָּא (see *BHS*), with עֵת "time, season" understood as the subject, resulting in the translation "the time has not come" (e.g., RSV). The noun עֵת often takes an infinitive construct, however (e.g., Qoh 3:1-8), obviating any need to repoint the form, and the phrase should be understood "(it is) not time to come." The same holds true for the following עֶת־בֵּית יְהוָה לְהִבָּנוֹת, which is syntactically similar to Gen 29:7 לֹא־עֵת הֵאָסֵף הַמִּקְנֶה "it is not time for the livestock to be gathered." The two infinitival phrases are coreferrential: "It is not a time to come, not a time for the house of YHWH to be built." Depending on the context, Nifal √בנה can refer either to something being "built" or "rebuilt."

1:3 וַיְהִי֙ דְּבַר־יְהוָ֔ה בְּיַד־חַגַּ֥י הַנָּבִ֖יא לֵאמֹֽר׃

Qal *wayyiqtol* 3 m s √היה and Qal inf cstr √אמר. For בְּיַד, see note on verse 1 above, and for this "reception formula," see verse 1 and Appendix §1. In this instance the formula indicates the giving of a prophetic revelation in response to the people's excuses (v. 2) and introduces the direct discourse that follows in verse 4.

1:4 הַעֵ֤ת לָכֶם֙ אַתֶּ֔ם לָשֶׁ֖בֶת בְּבָתֵּיכֶ֣ם סְפוּנִ֑ים וְהַבַּ֥יִת הַזֶּ֖ה חָרֵֽב׃

הַעֵ֤ת לָכֶם֙ אַתֶּ֔ם לָשֶׁ֖בֶת בְּבָתֵּיכֶ֣ם סְפוּנִ֑ים. Qal inf cstr √ישב with לְ preposition, Qal pass ptc m pl √ספן. לָשֶׁ֖בֶת serves as an infinitival complement to the noun עֵת (see v. 2). For a similarly phrased question utilizing עֵת, see 2 Kgs 5:26 הַעֵ֞ת לָקַ֤חַת אֶת־הַכֶּ֙סֶף֙ וְלָקַ֣חַת בְּגָדִ֔ים "Was it a time to take silver and to take garments?" Not only does the noun עֵת utilize infinitival phrases, it can also take לְ to indicate the subject of the infinitive, as in Ps 119:126 עֵת לַעֲשׂוֹת לַיהוה "it is time for YHWH to act." In light of this, Hag 1:4 would easily be rendered as "Is it time for you to dwell . . . ?" if it simply read *הַעֵת לָכֶם לָשֶׁבֶת. The addition of the independent personal pronoun אַתֶּם, however, complicates the analysis. Even though it represents a different grammatical case (nominative vs. oblique), אַתֶּם is nevertheless to be understood as standing in apposition to the pronoun suffix on לָכֶם, which is a phenomenon encountered elsewhere in BH (JM §146d; Muraoka 1985: 62; GKC §135d, g). It is pleonastic or grammatically unnecessary, raising the question as to its function here. Although "emphasis" is too easily invoked by scholars (Muraoka 1985), the occurrence of three forms indicating the 2mpl in rapid succession (לָכֶם, אַתֶּם, בְּבָתֵּיכֶם) can legitimately be considered emphatic in this instance (JM §146d; WO §16.3.4a; GKC §135g), which is often rendered in translation here as "you *yourselves.*" The phrase בְּבָתֵּיכֶ֣ם סְפוּנִ֑ים is grammatically challenging insofar as the common rendering "in your paneled houses" would require the participle to have the definite article, seeing that it follows the grammatically definite בָּתֵּיכֶם. Therefore we are to understand סְפוּנִים to be subordinated to לָשֶׁ֖בֶת בְּבָתֵּיכֶ֣ם as a type of "indirect accusative," specifically a "predicative accusative of state" (JM §126a1), and בְּבָתֵּיכֶם סְפוּנִים should be rendered "in your houses (which are) paneled." The effect of the construction is to indicate that the problem is not that the people are dwelling "in houses" but that they are dwelling in houses that are סְפוּנִים ("paneled") while YHWH's house is "desolate" (חָרֵב). The precise meaning of סְפוּנִים has been a matter of much discussion: Is it indicative of luxuriously paneled homes or does it simply refer to houses that have been "finished," roofs and all? The philological data for √ספן is scanty and does not definitively settle the matter, but the general context suggests that in this instance it most likely refers to ornate, rather than merely functional, architecture. The clause as a whole establishes an antithesis between the people's dwelling in well-maintained houses versus YHWH's dwelling in a "desolate" house (cf. the following phrase).

וְהַבַּיִת הַזֶּה חָרֵב. The *vav* introducing this circumstantial clause could arguably be understood as concessive ("even though"), adversative ("but"), or concomitant ("while"). In light of the discussion of אַתֶּם in the previous note, the notion of concomitant circumstances seems most fitting: "*while* this house (where I am dwelling) is a ruin?"

1:5 וְעַתָּה כֹּה אָמַר יְהוָה צְבָאוֹת שִׂימוּ לְבַבְכֶם עַל־
דַּרְכֵיכֶם׃

וְעַתָּה כֹּה אָמַר יְהוָה צְבָאוֹת. Qal *qatal* 3 m s √אמר. The "messenger formula" (see v. 2) sometimes occurs with inferential particles such as וְעַתָּה, which is often used for drawing a conclusion (MNK §44.6). In such instances, the logical relationships between the clauses are to be analyzed without taking into the formula into account (see Appendix §2B)—that is, the main proposition is וְעַתָּה . . . שִׂימוּ לְבַבְכֶם עַל־דַּרְכֵיכֶם, with כֹּה אָמַר יְהוָה צְבָאוֹת being, in a sense, an "intrusion" into the flow of the sentence. In this case the messenger formula appears to have a more rhetorically motivated function for the purpose of "validating" the divine origin of the message (see Appendix §2F).

שִׂימוּ לְבַבְכֶם עַל־דַּרְכֵיכֶם. Qal impv 2 m pl √שׂים. The expression √שׂים plus לֵב means "to pay attention" (see, e.g., Exod 9:21; Deut 32:46; 1 Sam 9:20; 21:13; 25:25; etc.). According to Rendsburg (2012: 331), the use of עַל (instead of לְ or אֶל) in this collocation represents a shift from SBH to LBH.

1:6 זְרַעְתֶּ֨ם הַרְבֵּ֜ה וְהָבֵ֣א מְעָ֗ט אָכ֤וֹל וְאֵין־לְשָׂבְעָה֙
שָׁת֣וֹ וְאֵין־לְשָׁכְרָ֔ה לָב֖וֹשׁ וְאֵין־לְחֹ֣ם ל֑וֹ וְהַמִּשְׂתַּכֵּ֕ר
מִשְׂתַּכֵּ֖ר אֶל־צְר֥וֹר נָקֽוּב׃ פ

זְרַעְתֶּ֨ם הַרְבֵּ֜ה וְהָבֵ֣א מְעָ֗ט. Qal *qatal* 2 m pl √זרע, Hifil inf abs √רבה, Hifil infinitive absolute √בוא. וְהָבֵ֣א . . . זְרַעְתֶּ֨ם is the first of several examples in this pericope of an infinitive absolute continuing a finite verb, which is one of its common uses in BH and particularly so in LBH (JM §123x; WB §208, §210; AC §3.4.2d). Since וְהָבֵ֣א follows the *qatal* form זְרַעְתֶּ֨ם, it is to be translated as a past tense. הַרְבֵּה is often used adverbially in the sense of "greatly, exceedingly" (BDB, 915, #1e3), in which case זְרַעְתֶּ֨ם הַרְבֵּ֜ה would mean that the people had done much sowing. On the other hand, הַרְבֵּה can also be used as a substantival adjective, which may be preferable here (BDB, 915, #1e4; Rendsburg 2012: 331–32; see v. 9 below). In that case then the substantive would indicate "many *things*" (referring to many seeds or crops) and would function as the direct object of the verb. מְעָט likewise displays both adjectival and adverbial functions, although the latter is infrequent and sometimes questionable (see Hag 2:6).

אָכ֤וֹל וְאֵין־לְשָׂבְעָה֙. Qal inf abs √אכל and Qal inf cstr √שׂבע with the feminine ending ־ה plus לְ-preposition. Infinitive construct forms ending with ־ה occur a number of times in BH, primarily with stative verbs (JM §49d; GKC §45d). As in the preceding clause, the infinitive absolute functions as a finite verb. The negated infinitive construct (the first of several in this verse) indicates possibility or permission (JM §160 j), thus: "one could not find satisfaction." In SBH the infinitive construct is typically negated by לְבִלְתִּי, while the use of אֵין instead is a feature of LBH (Hurvitz).

שָׁת֣וֹ וְאֵין־לְשָׁכְרָ֔ה לָב֖וֹשׁ וְאֵין־לְחֹ֣ם ל֑וֹ. Qal inf abs √שׁתה, Qal inf cstr √שׁכר with the feminine ending ־ה with לְ preposition, Qal inf abs √לבשׁ, and Qal inf cstr √חמם with לְ preposition. On the function of the infinitive absolute and infinitive construct, and on the form of לְשָׁכְרָה, see above. The spelling of the infinitive absolute of III-*he* verbs with ־וֹ instead of ־ֹה occurs regularly. Yet even though the infintive absolute is often spelled *plene*, e.g., קָטוֹל, with the III-*he* infinitive absolute we only encounter forms such as שָׁתוֹ and שָׁתֹה but never *שָׁתוֹה. In RH the verb √שׁכר can mean "to fill, saturate, drink freely" (Jastrow, 1576), which best suits the context. וְאֵין־לְחֹ֣ם ל֑וֹ is an instance of the so-called *dativus ethicus* or *dativus commodi* (JM §133d; MNK

§39.11.5iii; GKC §119s, §135i)—that is, the suffix of לוֹ refers to the subject of the action and basically serves to express a reflexive notion (Van der Merwe 2003: 16). In this instance it could be rendered, "one could not get oneself warm," but since the sentence has a second person addressee (זְרַעְתֶּם) it is rendered here as, "you could not warm yourself."

As stated in the introduction to the unit, this pericope contains a number of intertextual references to the "covenant judgments" of Lev 26 and Deut 28 (Kessler, 132, 139, 154–56), and the former is particularly influential on this verse. If the people are faithful, YHWH promises in Lev 26:5 וַאֲכַלְתֶּם לַחְמְכֶם לָשֹׂבַע, "and you shall eat your bread to satiation." On the other hand, if they are disobedient, Lev 26:16 threatens וּזְרַעְתֶּם לָרִיק זַרְעֲכֶם וַאֲכָלֻהוּ אֹיְבֵיכֶם, "And you shall sow your seed in vain, for your enemies shall eat it" and verse 26 states וַאֲכַלְתֶּם וְלֹא תִשְׂבָּעוּ, "and you shall eat, and not be satisfied."

וְהַמִּשְׂתַּכֵּר מִשְׂתַּכֵּר אֶל־צְרוֹר נָקוּב. Hitpael ptc m s √שׂכר (with metathesis), with and without the definite article. These are the only occurrences of this Hitpael verb form in CH but it is attested in RH (cf. Jastrow, 1576), which would comport with the book's linguistic profile as LBH. Substantival and attributive participles do not express time or aspect (JM §121i), and therefore הַמִּשְׂתַּכֵּר could be understood as "the one who earns, earned, will earn." The statement expresses a general or habitual present tense analogous to a proverb. We often encounter proverbial statements in BH headed by a substantival participle (e.g., Prov 10:9, 10a; 11:27, 28, 29), but typically it would be followed by a *yiqtol* form expressing the general present, rather than a participle. Over time the participle took over this function and *yiqtol* became purely a future-referring form, a trend which can be observed in LBH, the Hebrew text of Ben Sira (Van Peursen, 216–19), and is fully developed in RH (Rogland 2003: 10 n. 54), again aligning Haggai with LBH (see Introduction §1). מִשְׂתַּכֵּר אֶל־צְרוֹר נָקוּב is an instance of a "pregnant" use of the preposition אֶל (cf. BDB, 39, #1)—that is, the compact expression implies another verbal idea. In this case, the notion of *putting* the wages earned "into" the bag is to be understood.

1:7 **כֹּה אָמַר יְהוָה צְבָאוֹת שִׂימוּ לְבַבְכֶם עַל־דַּרְכֵיכֶם׃**

כֹּה אָמַר יְהוָה צְבָאוֹת. Qal *qatal* 3 m s √אמר.

שִׂ֥ימוּ לְבַבְכֶ֖ם עַל־דַּרְכֵיכֶֽם. Qal impv 2 m pl √שׂים. See verse 5 regarding the meaning of the expression.

1:8 עֲל֥וּ הָהָ֛ר וַהֲבֵאתֶ֥ם עֵ֖ץ וּבְנ֣וּ הַבָּ֑יִת וְאֶרְצֶה־בּ֥וֹ
וְאֶכָּבְד֖ה אָמַ֥ר יְהוָֽה׃

עֲל֥וּ הָהָ֛ר. Qal impv 2 m pl √עלה. There is no preposition such as לְ or אֶל linked with הָהָ֛ר, but verbs of movement such as √עלה often take an "accusative of local determination" (JM §126h; WB §54a-b; AC §2.3.2a) indicating direction or destination. The noun הַר has a collective sense, i.e., "the hill (country)" or "the mountain (range)" (BDB, 250, #1b or #2).

וַהֲבֵאתֶ֥ם עֵ֖ץ. Hifil *weqatal* 2 m pl √בוא. It is common to continue an imperative with *weqatal* (JM §119l). As with הַר in the preceding clause, עֵץ is functioning as a collective, indicating either "trees" or "pieces of wood" (BDB, 781, #1b or #2)

וּבְנ֣וּ הַבָּ֑יִת. Qal impv 2 m pl √בנה with *vav*. Instead of continuing with another *weqatal* form, the speaker shifts to an "indirect volitive,"—that is, *vav* prefixed to an imperative, cohortative, or jussive (JM §116; WB §181a, §188; Driver, §§59–65; AC §3.5.3; MNK §21.5; WO §34.5.2). Such indirect volitives often express a notion of purpose or consecution, and the former is best suited here (Rogland 2014d: 158): "*that* you might build the house."

וְאֶרְצֶה־בּ֥וֹ. Qal *yiqtol* or cohortative 1 c s √רצה + *vav*. There is no distinctive cohortative form for III-*he* verbs (JM §79o): the same form will be used for indicative and cohortative functions, and it is therefore a contextual decision how it is to be analyzed. See further the following note on וְאֶכָּבֵד/וְאֶכָּבְדָה. The verb √רצה often governs its object via the preposition בְּ (BDB, 953) and can have a cultic nuance, referring to YHWH's acceptance of sacrifices (Rogland 2014d: 159). In light of this, there is a certain ambiguity as to whether וְאֶרְצֶה־בּ֥וֹ means to say "and I will take pleasure in it" or rather "and I will accept it."

וְאֶכָּבְד֖. The *Ketiv* reads Nifal *yiqtol* 1 c s √כבד plus *vav*, but the *Qere* has וְאֶכָּבְדָה, which is Nifal cohortative 1 c s √כבד plus *vav*. The *Ketiv* would indicate an indicative future interpretation of both verbs ("and I will take pleasure in it and I will be honored"), whereas the *Qere* would signify indirect volitives, again expressing purpose or consecution ("*so that* I may take pleasure in it and be honored"; see וּבְנוּ above). Either analysis is possible, but in light of the book's later promises of future glory to fill the "house" (Hag 2:7, 9), a futuristic interpretation seems preferable here (cf. Rogland 2014d: 158).

אָמַר יְהוָה. Qal *qatal* 3 m s √אמר. This is a shorter form of the messenger formula כֹּה אָמַר יהוה (see Appendix §2).

1:9 פָּנֹה אֶל־הַרְבֵּה וְהִנֵּה לִמְעָט וַהֲבֵאתֶם הַבַּיִת וְנָפַחְתִּי בוֹ יַעַן מֶה נְאֻם יְהוָה צְבָאוֹת יַעַן בֵּיתִי אֲשֶׁר־הוּא חָרֵב וְאַתֶּם רָצִים אִישׁ לְבֵיתוֹ׃

פָּנֹה אֶל־הַרְבֵּה וְהִנֵּה לִמְעָט. Qal inf abs √פנה and Hifil inf abs √רבה. The clause is parallel to זְרַעְתֶּם הַרְבֵּה וְהָבֵא מְעָט in verse 6 (Verhoef 1987: 69). As in that verse, we find an infinitive absolute (פָּנֹה) being used as the equivalent of a finite verb form, with a past tense interpretation being the only realistic translation option (Rogland 2014d: 159). √פנה often occurs with the preposition אֶל (BDB, 815) and in light of the parallel with verse 6 communicates a sense of expectant waiting for the growth of what was "sown." On the adjectival/substantival versus adverbial use of הַרְבֵּה and מְעַט, see verse 6 above. Several ancient versions (e.g., LXX) and modern commentators (e.g., Meyers and Meyers, 3, 29) have found the syntax of וְהִנֵּה לִמְעָט to be difficult, and some emend וְהִנֵּה to a verbal form, but the MT is supported by the Murraba'at manuscript's והנה. The difficulty is presented by the preposition לְ. Verhoef (1987: 70) explains this to be an "emphatic *lamed*," but this is problematic (Muraoka 1985: 113–23). BDB (512, #4a) lists a number of analogous examples of verbless clauses with a prepositional phrase headed by לְ, which indicate a change of state or condition, in effect implying a form of היה. While not all of their examples are convincing, the basic analysis remains valid, and hence we can supply an expression of being or becoming in translation: "and behold, *it turned out to be* little."

וַהֲבֵאתֶם הַבַּיִת וְנָפַחְתִּי בוֹ. Hifil *weqatal* 2 m pl √בוא and Qal *weqatal* 1 c s √נפח. הַבַּיִת is another "accusative of local determination" (see v. 8): "*to* the house." The verbs are typically analyzed as non-converted *weqatal* forms ("*vav*-copulative" perfects) indicating the simple past (JM §115; WB §182): "and when you brought it home, I blew it away" (RSV). In many forms it is impossible to distinguish between inverted and *vav*-copulative *weqatals*, though "inverted" *weqatals* display an accent shift in certain forms such as the 1 c s, with the typical *mil'el* accent (קָטַ֫לְתִּי) shifting to the ultima (וְקָטַלְתִּ֫י; see JM §117). In this instance, however, the *mil'el* accent on וְנָפַ֫חְתִּי does not necessarily indicate that the form is a *vav*-copulative perfect, since the following monosyllabic בוֹ prevents the expected accent shift to the final syllable (Driver, §100). What is more, a past tense interpretation of these verbs is problematic on several counts (see Rogland 2014d for a more expansive discussion): First, in the context, הַבַּיִת certainly refers to God's house—that is, the temple, just as the same form did in verse 8 (in this pericope the people's homes have pronominal suffixes: see the following לְבֵיתוֹ and בְּבָתֵּיכֶם in verse 4). Yet it is clear from the context that the people have *not* been bringing goods to the temple. Second, the identical form וַהֲבֵאתֶם in verse 8 continues the imperative עֲלוּ and is to be interpreted as an injunctive ("bring it to the house!"), making a similar interpretation of this form likely. The rapid shift from a past-referring form (פָּנֹה) to an injunctive (וַהֲבֵאתֶם) is attested in BH (Rogland 2014d: 160–61). Third, the interpretation of וְנָפַחְתִּי בוֹ in a negative sense of judgment is questionable (Rogland 2014d: 162). Though often taken in a derisive sense of "snort," the only certain instance of √נפח with this meaning occurs in Mal 1:13 in the Hifil, rather than the Qal. Most often the verb is used with reference to blowing on coals or fire, and this sense is perfectly fitting here when one recalls that fire played a critical role in the ritual of the temple complex: sacrifices were burned, some in whole and some in part, in the fires of the altar, to create a "pleasing aroma" to YHWH. Thus, verse 9a enjoins the people to bring what "little" they have to offer at the temple, and promises cultic acceptance (see note on רצה in v. 8).

יַ֣עַן מֶ֔ה נְאֻ֖ם יְהוָ֣ה צְבָא֑וֹת יַ֗עַן בֵּיתִי֙ אֲשֶׁר־ה֣וּא חָרֵ֔ב. The syntagm יַ֣עַן מֶ֔ה "on account of what?" can be translated as "why?" The vocalization מֶה is sometimes encountered instead of the more common מָה (JM §37). Contrary to many scholarly assertions, the so-called "oracle formula" נְאֻ֖ם יְהוָ֣ה צְבָא֑וֹת does not necessarily mark the closure of an oracle, and in this instance appears to interrupt the flow of the sentence. In this case the formula serves a more rhetorical function of validating the divine authenticity of the message (see Appendix §2). יַ֗עַן בֵּיתִי֙ אֲשֶׁר־ה֣וּא חָרֵ֔ב provides the first explicit explanation for YHWH's judgment of sending poor harvests (see also vv. 10-11).

וְאַתֶּ֥ם רָצִ֖ים אִ֥ישׁ לְבֵיתֽוֹ. Qal ptc m pl √רוץ. וְאַתֶּם introduces a circumstantial clause (JM §159) and can be translated as "while you. . . ." The scholarly consensus is that √רוץ "to run (after)" means "to busy oneself with" or "to concern oneself with" in this instance (see *HALOT*, 1208, #4c [incorrectly printed as #4a, cf. *HALAT*]). While this certainly suits the context, it lacks clear parallels in BH, though Steck (370 n. 45) suggests some possible instances in Isa 59:7 רַגְלֵיהֶם לָרַע יָרֻצוּ, "their feet run to evil" (similarly Prov 1:16; 6:18) and Sir 11:11 (MsA) יש עמל ויגע ורץ וכדי כן הוא מתאחר, "There is one who labors and toils and runs and all the more he stays behind" (Van Peursen, 23). An interpretive option with better philological support is suggested by the frequent substantival use of the participle √רוץ for "guard, royal escort" (e.g., 1 Sam 22:17; 2 Sam 15:1; 1 Kgs 1:5; 14:27-28; etc.; see BDB, 930, #2). This is more in keeping with the general theme of the book, namely, the need to rebuild the temple, which featured שֹׁעֲרִים ("gatekeepers") who guarded the complex (see, e.g., 1 Chron 9:21ff.; 26:1, 12, 19; 2 Chron 23:4, 19; Ezra 2:70; Neh 7:73). Thus the people are faulted for "guarding" their own homes exclusively rather than the house of YHWH. In the phrase אִישׁ לְבֵיתוֹ, the noun אִישׁ has a distributive sense meaning "each, every" (JM §147d).

1:10 עַל־כֵּן עֲלֵיכֶם כָּלְאוּ שָׁמַיִם מִטָּל וְהָאָרֶץ כָּלְאָה יְבוּלָהּ׃

עַל־כֵּן עֲלֵיכֶם כָּלְאוּ שָׁמַיִם מִטָּל. Qal *qatal* 3 c pl √כלא. עֲלֵיכֶם is to be understood as "because of you" or "on account of you" in this instance (BDB, 754). The preposition מִן is often employed with verbs of keeping or withholding (BDB, 577–78) and need not be rendered in translation. The withholding of טַל ("dew" or perhaps "light rain": Futato, 93–94), rather than one of the other many terms for "rain," could indicate the most severe type of drought (e.g., 1 Kgs 17:1). The general context does not indicate such extreme conditions, however, and hence it seems better to understand it as a withholding of YHWH's richest blessings (Gen 27:28; Deut 33:13, 28).

וְהָאָרֶץ כָּלְאָה יְבוּלָהּ. Qal *qatal* 3 f s √כלא. The clause is parallel to the preceding one and omits the preposition מִן. Such omissions from parallel lines occur frequently in poetic texts, but it should be noted that if the verse were truly poetic then the verb כָּלְאָה could have also been omitted. As discussed in the Introduction (§2), Haggai's writing displays only a modest use of poetic devices and is best understood as literate prose rather than poetry. The context of covenantal judgment and the reference to the land's "yield" (יְבוּל) appears to be reflective of Lev 26:4, 20 (cf. also Deut 11:17; 32:22).

1:11 וָאֶקְרָ֨א חֹ֜רֶב עַל־הָאָ֣רֶץ וְעַל־הֶהָרִ֗ים וְעַל־הַדָּגָן֙
וְעַל־הַתִּירֹ֣ושׁ וְעַל־הַיִּצְהָ֔ר וְעַ֕ל אֲשֶׁ֥ר תֹּוצִ֖יא
הָאֲדָמָ֑ה וְעַל־הָֽאָדָם֙ וְעַל־הַבְּהֵמָ֔ה וְעַ֖ל כָּל־יְגִ֥יעַ
כַּפָּֽיִם׃ ס

וָאֶקְרָ֨א חֹ֜רֶב עַל־הָאָ֣רֶץ וְעַל־הֶהָרִ֗ים. Qal *wayyiqtol* 1 c s √קרא. The verb is well attested with the sense of "to summon" (BDB, 895, #5). There is an apparent wordplay between חֹרֶב in verse 11 and חָרֵב in verses 4 and 9. Moreover, וָאֶקְרָא חֹרֶב possibly evokes the use of חָרְבָּה "desolation" in Lev 26:31, 33.[1] On the repetition of prepositions, see verse 1.

וְעַל־הַדָּגָן֙ וְעַל־הַתִּירֹ֣ושׁ וְעַל־הַיִּצְהָ֔ר. A dual mention of "grain and wine" is often observed in the HB (e.g. Gen 27:28, 37; Num 18:27; Deut 33:28), but the trio of "grain, fresh wine, and fresh oil" occurs repeatedly in Deuteronomy (7:13; 11:14; 12:17; 14:23; 18:4), including the covenant judgments in Deut 28:51.

וְעַ֕ל אֲשֶׁ֥ר תֹּוצִ֖יא הָאֲדָמָ֑ה וְעַל־הָֽאָדָם֙ וְעַל־הַבְּהֵמָ֔ה. Hifil *yiqtol* 3 f s √יצא. The nouns "man" (הָאָדָם) and "beast" (הַבְּהֵמָה) are functioning as collectives here (JM §135c). It is common for such nouns, in representing classes or species of beings, to have the definite article (JM §137i), and they can be left anarthrous in translation.

וְעַ֖ל כָּל־יְגִ֥יעַ כַּפָּֽיִם. The noun יְגִיעַ can refer both to "toil" and to the "product" achieved by toil, and the latter is preferable here: "every product of hands." כַּף is used only once of animals in Lev 11:27 (BDB, 496, #1c), and hence this phrase refers to human labors (e.g., "all human endeavor"; Kessler, 106). In light of other intertextual references to Deut 28 in this chapter, it is plausible to view this as evoking Deut 28:33: "a nation which you have not known shall eat up the fruit of your ground and of *all your produce* (וְכָל־יְגִיעֲךָ)."

[1] It could be a reference to Deut 28:22 if one revocalizes "sword" in Deut 28:22 to "drought," as some have suggested (e.g., McConville, 400).

Narrative (Haggai 1:12-15a)
The People's Response and YHWH's Reassurance

Unlike Zech 1–8, which utilizes extensive sections of narrative (albeit of a visionary nature), the prophecies of Haggai consist primarily of oracular discourse. Apart from some interchange of dialogue in Hag 2:12-14 as a lead-in to the oracle of 2:15-19, this brief pericope recounting the people's response to Haggai's initial oracle is the only narrative portion in the book. Under the leadership of Zerubbabel and Joshua, the people first respond with "fear," or reverent worship of YHWH (v. 12). In turn, YHWH assures them that he is "with" them (v. 13; cf. 2:4). This reffirmation of YHWH's presence evokes earlier divine promises to the patriarchs, Moses, Solomon, and others (e.g., Gen 26:3, 24; 31:3; Exod 3:12; 1 Kgs 11:38; Isa 43:5; Jer 30:11; 42:11; 46:28; etc.), and is particularly needed at this juncture, given that the first oracle highlighted the people's failure with regard to their covenant relationship with YHWH (see Hag 1:6, 10-11). Having provided this comfort and encouragement to the people, YHWH subsequently "stirs up" the spirits of the leaders and the remnant of the people to work on his house (v. 14; cf. Ezra 1:1, 5).

A note must be made here regarding the dating formulae of the book of Haggai (see Verhoef 1988; Kessler, 41–51; Shin, 134–37), as they are attested with various combinations of the year, month, or day in the MT as currently organized by the scribal divisions. Pre–seventh-century texts were content to provide only the year, but by the early to mid-sixth century more precise formulae were utilized which included the month and/or the day. These are attested in BH as well as in inscriptions (Kessler, 42–43). The following formulae occur in Haggai:

Year-Month-Day	1:1 (2nd Year, 6th Month, 1st Day, [= 29 August])
Day-Month-Year	1:15 (24th Day, 6th Month, 2nd Year [= 21 Sept])
	2:10 (24th Day, 9th Month, 2nd Year [= 18 Dec])
Month-Day	2:1 (7th Month, 21st Day [= 17 Oct])
Day-Month	2:18 (24th Day, 9th Month [= 18 Dec])
Day	2:20 (24th Day of the Month)

It would be misleading to treat the singular occurrence in 2:20 mentioning the day alone as a separate formula, however, since the text specifies that this is the "second" (שֵׁנִית) oracle delivered on the same date as 2:10. This is simply a special case and is best omitted from the list:

Year-Month-Day	1:1
Day-Month-Year	1:15; 2:10
Month-Day	2:1
Day-Month	2:18

According to Kessler (47), the older Judaean formula was Year-Month-Day or, when an element was omitted, either Month-Day or Year-Month. Persian-period texts clearly favor the combination of Day-Month-Year, or either Day-Month or Month-Year. Haggai, it thus appears, utilizes both the older order (e.g., 1:1) as well as the pattern more typical of Persian-period compositions. Kessler (48) suggests that this could be a sign of a transitional period in the development of dating formulae, or possibly that older formulae were used for literary effect to make it "sound" more like the oracles of preexilic prophets.

In the current pericope, the MT of verse 15 attests the structure Day-Month-Year, while the formula of 2:1 consists of Month-Day, which is otherwise unattested in Haggai and stands in contrast to 2:18, where the formula is Day-Month. The fact that no other dating formula commences with the month has led many scholars to suggest, with a great deal of plausibility, that the traditional scribal verse divisions were incorrectly placed in this instance and that the pericope ends with verse 15a (Hallaschka 2011: 15–16). Thus, verse 15b בִּשְׁנַ֣ת שְׁתַּ֔יִם לְדָרְיָ֖וֶשׁ הַמֶּֽלֶךְ would initiate the following pericope (2:1-9). This is not to propose a textual emendation; rather, it simply redraws the scribal pericope markings so that the narrative concludes at 1:15a, with Haggai's second oracle commencing with 1:15b. Thus the dating formulae would be:

Year, Month, Day	1:1; 1:15b–2:1
Day, Month, Year	2:10
Day, Month	1:15a; 2:18

As such, 1:15a indicates the date on which the people set to work in response to Haggai's initial oracle (viz., 21 Sept), and 1:15b initiates the dating formula of the second oracle (17 Oct).

A diachronic shift has also been discerned in the designation of dates from the eleventh to thirtieth of a month. As Shin has noted, three formulae are attested in BH (134–37; Rendsburg 2012: 335):

1. ב-X יום לחדש
2. ב-X לחדש
3. (ב)יום X לחדש

Formula #1 occurs in about 80 percent of SBH formulae (e.g., Gen 7:11; Num 28:17; 1 Kgs 12:32) but does not occur in postexilic texts. Formula #2 occurs three times in SBH and primarily in exilic and postexilic books (e.g., Ezek 29:1; 32:17; Esth 3:13; 8:12; Ezra 6:19; 8:31; 2 Chron 30:15; 35:1) as well as the DSS (Qimron, 90) and RH. Formula #3 appears once in Exod 12:18 and primarily in LBH prose (e.g., Esth 9:15, 17, 19, 21; Dan 10:4; Neh 9:1; 2 Chron 7:10; 29:17). Rendsburg (2012: 335) classifies Formula #3 as LBH and Formula #2 as belonging to the transitional stage of SBH to LBH, both of which are attested in Haggai and Zech 1–8 (Hag 1:15a; 2:1, 20; Zech 1:7).

[12]*And Zerubabbel, son of Shealtiel, and Joshua, son of Jehozadaq, the high priest, and all of the remnant people obeyed the voice of YHWH their God and yielded to the words of Haggai the prophet, when YHWH their God sent him, and the people worshiped before YHWH.*

[13]*And Haggai the messenger of YHWH said, by the messenger's commission of YHWH to the people, "I am with you"—oracle of YHWH.*

[14-15a]*And YHWH stirred up the spirit of Zerubbabel son of Shealtiel, governor of Judah, and the spirit of Joshua son of Jehozadaq, the high priest, and the spirit of all the remnant people, and they came and they did work in the house of YHWH Tsevaot, their God, on the twenty-fourth day of the sixth month.*

1:12 וַיִּשְׁמַע זְרֻבָּבֶל ׀ בֶּן־שַׁלְתִּיאֵל וִיהוֹשֻׁעַ בֶּן־יְהוֹצָדָק
הַכֹּהֵן הַגָּדוֹל וְכֹל ׀ שְׁאֵרִית הָעָם בְּקוֹל יְהוָה
אֱלֹהֵיהֶם וְעַל־דִּבְרֵי חַגַּי הַנָּבִיא כַּאֲשֶׁר שְׁלָחוֹ יְהוָה
אֱלֹהֵיהֶם וַיִּירְאוּ הָעָם מִפְּנֵי יְהוָה׃

וַיִּשְׁמַע זְרֻבָּבֶל ׀ בֶּן־שַׁלְתִּיאֵל וִיהוֹשֻׁעַ בֶּן־יְהוֹצָדָק הַכֹּהֵן הַגָּדוֹל. Qal *wayyiqtol* 3 m s √שמע. It is not uncommon for a singular verb to be used with a plural subject, particularly when the verb precedes the subject (JM §150b; cf. on 1:2). Zerubbabel's title פַּחַת־יְהוּדָה is sometimes included (Hag 1:1, 14; 2:2, 21), but it is omitted here and occasionally elsewhere (2:4, 23), while Joshua's title הַכֹּהֵן הַגָּדוֹל is always included (1:1, 12, 14; 2:2, 4). One wonders whether the omission was due to a certain discomfort at the frequent reminder that the Davidic heir was "merely" a governor rather than a king.

וְכָל | שְׁאֵרִ֣ית הָעָ֔ם. In contrast to the noun שְׁאָר, which can refer to a surviving number of either animate or inanimate objects, the noun שְׁאֵרִית refers almost exclusively to human beings, with only two exceptions out of its sixty-six attestations (Isa 44:17; Ps 76:10). The term שְׁאֵרִית does not specifically imply returned exiles here (contra, e.g., Park, 17) but simply indicates the surviving portion of the people, whether returnees or nonexiled Judeans who had somehow avoided deportation. The noun is used in both positive and negative contexts and can focus attention either upon the aspect of continued survival or upon a state of decimation after the removal of a portion of the group (cf. Hasel). The addition of כֹּל here and in verse 14, as well as the use of הָעָם alone in the final clause of the verse, makes it clear that the Judean community as a whole is in view (cf. Kessler, 141 n. 270). In this instance, then, the construct phrase שְׁאֵרִ֣ית הָעָ֔ם should be understood not as a partitive genitive ("a remnant *out of* the people") but rather as a genitive of genus or an "explicative genitive" (JM §129f3; WB §43; AC §2.2.12; GKC §128l–m; WO §9.5.3g–h): "a remnant of people" = "a remnant people." (Cf., e.g., Ezek 36:38 צֹאן אָדָם "flock of man" = "human flock" and Prov 15:20 כְּסִיל אָדָם "fool of a man" = "foolish man.")

בְּקוֹל֙ יְהוָ֣ה אֱלֹֽהֵיהֶ֔ם וְעַל־דִּבְרֵי֙ חַגַּ֣י הַנָּבִ֔יא. Kessler (106 n. 32) argues that the conjunction on וְעַל־דִּבְרֵי֙ חַגַּ֣י is a *vav-explicativum* (GKC §146f), making the phrase epexegetical of בְּקוֹל֙ יְהוָ֣ה: "the voice of Yahweh their God, *that is to say*, the words of Haggai." Petersen, on the other hand, argues that the phrase is causal: "heeded Yahweh their God, *because of* Haggai the prophet" (55). In fact, neither suggestion is satisfying here, as we are dealing with two separate prepositional complements to the verb √שׁמע. The syntagm √שׁמע plus בְּקוֹל indicates not merely auditory cognition but rather obedient responsiveness (BDB, 1034, #1m). The prepositions אֶל and עַל are also used with שׁמע with the meaning "to listen to, yield to" (BDB, 1034, #1k) and can refer to a welcoming reception (e.g., 2 Kgs 20:13). The translation above reflects this, though admittedly in many instances these syntagms could serve as functional equivalents. In this case it seems likely that the second prepositional phrase was added not so much to bring out a unique semantic nuance of the verb as to highlight the asymmetry in the prepositional objects: The first phrase indicates that it is *YHWH* who is being obeyed, whereas the second phrase expresses that it is Haggai's *words* which are being heeded, not Haggai himself. The different phrasings forestall any unintended impression of parity between the role and authority of YHWH and of his prophet, who simply remains a "messenger" (v. 13 מַלְאָךְ).

כַּאֲשֶׁר שְׁלָחוֹ יְהוָה אֱלֹהֵיהֶם. Qal *qatal* 3 m s √שׁלח with 3 m s pronoun suffix. כַּאֲשֶׁר can mean "according as, as," "as if," "because" or "when" (*HALOT*, 455); in this instance, a temporal interpretation of "when" fits best.

וַיִּירְאוּ הָעָם מִפְּנֵי יְהוָה. Qal *wayyiqtol* 3 m pl √ירא. The noun עָם is construed collectively here, and thus the verb is plural (see 1:2). Van der Merwe (1992: 181–83) contends that the use of √ירא with מִפְּנֵי indicates that the subject of the verb experiences a fear involving what is perceived as an immediate threat or adversary. The only other instance of the syntagm with YHWH as the object of the verb is Exod 9:30, however, which Van der Merwe admits has the sense of honoring or reverencing the deity. This is sufficient for the present context, which refers to cultic worship.

1:13 וַיֹּאמֶר חַגַּי מַלְאַךְ יְהוָה בְּמַלְאֲכוּת יְהוָה לָעָם
לֵאמֹר אֲנִי אִתְּכֶם נְאֻם־יְהוָה׃

וַיֹּאמֶר חַגַּי מַלְאַךְ יְהוָה בְּמַלְאֲכוּת יְהוָה לָעָם לֵאמֹר. Qal *wayyiqtol* 3 m s and Qal inf cstr √אמר. This is a clear use of מַלְאַךְ יהוה with a human referent (so also Mal 2:7; cf. Lopez, 3, 12). The *–ut* sufformative of מַלְאֲכוּת typically indicates an abstract noun (JM §88Mj; GKC §86k), and although it is attested in SBH, its usage there is rare, being much more common in MH and Aramaic (Shin, 72). מַלְאֲכוּת, often glossed as "message" (e.g., RSV), is a *hapax* in CH (*DCH*, 5: 290) but is attested in RH with the meaning "messenger's function, angeldom" (Jastrow, 786). It is attested by the ancient versions except for the LXX, where its absence is most likely due to homoteleuton (*BHQ*, 114)—that is, a scribal omission caused by words with similar appearance. In light of the Rabbinic attestation, it is glossed above as "messenger's commission," which is supported particularly by the Targum's שְׁלִיחוּת ("message, agency, commission") and by ἐν ἀποστολῇ κυρίου in some manuscripts of the Lucianic recension, as well as by a number of commentators (e.g. Wolff, 28, 31; Kessler, 107 n. 37; Verhoef 1987: 84). Unless one accepts a textual error of בְּ־ for כְּ־, the attempt of Verhoef (1987: 84) to explain the preposition בְּ־ as "according to" is unconvincing. It is translated above in an instrumental sense, though בְּ־ could also be taken in a temporal sense of "when" or "of a state or condition, whether material or mental, *in* which an action takes place" (BDB, 88, #I5 and #I6).

אֲנִי אִתְּכֶם נְאֻם־יְהוָה. The important divine promise אֲנִי אִתְּכֶם also occurs with the preposition עִם (e.g., Gen 28:15; Isa 41:10) without a discernible difference in meaning (cf. Isa 41:10 עִמְּךָ־אָנִי and 43:5 אִתְּךָ־אָנִי). On the function of the "oracle formula" נְאֻם־יְהוָה, see 1:9 and Appendix §3.

1:14 וַיָּעַר יְהוָה אֶת־רוּחַ זְרֻבָּבֶל בֶּן־שַׁלְתִּיאֵל פַּחַת
יְהוּדָה וְאֶת־רוּחַ יְהוֹשֻׁעַ בֶּן־יְהוֹצָדָק הַכֹּהֵן הַגָּדוֹל
וְאֶת־רוּחַ כֹּל שְׁאֵרִית הָעָם וַיָּבֹאוּ וַיַּעֲשׂוּ מְלָאכָה
בְּבֵית־יְהוָה צְבָאוֹת אֱלֹהֵיהֶם׃ פ

וַיָּעַר יְהוָה אֶת־רוּחַ זְרֻבָּבֶל בֶּן־שַׁלְתִּיאֵל פַּחַת יְהוּדָה. Hifil *wayyiqtol* 3 m s √עור. Cf. Ezra 1:1, 5.

וְאֶת־רוּחַ יְהוֹשֻׁעַ בֶּן־יְהוֹצָדָק הַכֹּהֵן הַגָּדוֹל. Like prepositions, the particle אֵת is generally repeated for each object. See Hag 1:1.

וְאֶת־רוּחַ כֹּל שְׁאֵרִית הָעָם. On שְׁאֵרִית, see verse 12 above.

וַיָּבֹאוּ. Qal *wayyiqtol* 3 m pl √בוא. The verb is so common in the HB as rarely to require comment, but in this instance it is worth noting how it forms an exegetical counterpart to לֹא עֶת־בֹּא "it is not time to come" in verse 2 (see 1:2 for this rendering). Previously the people had denied that it was time "to come" and work on the temple, but now they are doing precisely that.

וַיַּעֲשׂוּ מְלָאכָה בְּבֵית־יְהוָה. Qal *wayyiqtol* 3 m pl √עשׂה. The context may suggest an inceptive nuance to the verb, i.e., "they *began* to do work" (cf. Verhoef 1987: 87). There is possibly an intentional wordplay between מְלָאכָה "work" and מַלְאֲכוּת and מַלְאָךְ in verse 11. It should be noted that מְלָאכָה occurs frequently in the tabernacle construction sections of Exodus (e.g., Exod 35–36), which form an obvious parallel to the second temple rebuilding project and supply important intertexts for the book of Haggai (see Hag 2:5). Translations often render בְּ as "on," indicating the indirect object of the verb, but the preposition could just as well be spatial or locative in nature, expressing that the work was carried out "in" the temple.

1:15a בְּי֛וֹם עֶשְׂרִ֧ים וְאַרְבָּעָ֛ה לַחֹ֖דֶשׁ בַּשִּׁשִּׁ֑י

See the discussion of dating formulae and the pericope's textual divisions in the introductory remarks above. BH prefers to use cardinal numbers for days and years but the ordinals for months (JM §142o; WO §15.3.2a). As in this instance, sometimes the ordinal stands alone, without the noun חֹ֫דֶשׁ (e.g., Ezek 1:1; 8:1; 20:1; 31:1; 45:25; Hag 2:1, 10, 18; Zech 7:5; 8:19).

Second Oracle (Haggai 1:15b–2:9)
The Latter Glory of YHWH's House

Haggai's second oracle comes seven weeks after the first (1:1-11) and almost a month after the people's initial response (1:12-15a). As the temple rebuilding has progressed, unfavorable comparisons with the Solomonic temple have begun to surface, creating a sense of disappointment and discouragement (v. 3). Nevertheless, the people are urged to remain strong in their task (v. 4). Echoing the directives of the book of Exodus (see Rogland 2007b), the people are urged to give generously to the rebuilding project (v. 5), just as the Israelites had been commanded to make offerings in order to build the tabernacle where YHWH would dwell in their midst (Exod 25:8; 29:45, 46). The people should feel no hesitation about this because YHWH will sovereignly cause the precious things of the nations to fill the temple (vv. 6-8). The end result will be that the latter glory of the temple will exceed the former, and it will become a center of peace (v. 9).

[1.15b–2.1]*In the second year of Darius the king, in the seventh month, on the twenty-first day of the month, the word of YHWH came via Haggai the prophet:*

[2]*"Please speak to Zerubbabel son of Shealtiel, governor of Judah, and to Joshua son of Jehozadaq, the high priest, and to the remnant people:,*

[3]*Who among you is the survivor who saw this house in its former glory? And how do you see it now? Isn't it nothing in your eyes?*

[4]*And now, be strong, O Zerubbabel"—oracle of YHWH—"and be strong, O Joshua, son of Jehozadaq, the high priest, and be strong, all you people of the land"—oracle of YHWH—"so that you can work, for I am with you"—oracle of YHWH Tsevaot.*

[5]*"Do not fear the thing which I covenanted with you when you came out from Egypt, while my Spirit was abiding in your midst."*

[6]*For thus has YHWH Tsevaot said, "One more thing is a small matter, namely: I am going to shake the heavens and the earth and the sea and the dry ground.*

[7]*And I will shake all the nations and the desirable things of all the nations will come and I will fill this house with glory," YHWH Tsevaot has said.*

[8]*"The silver is mine, and the gold is mine"—oracle of YHWH Tsevaot.*

[9]*"Greater will be the latter glory of this house than the former"—YHWH Tsevaot has said—"and in this place I will grant peace"—oracle of YHWH Tsevaot.*

1:15b בִּשְׁנַ֥ת שְׁתַּ֖יִם לְדָרְיָ֥וֶשׁ הַמֶּֽלֶךְ׃

2:1 בַּשְּׁבִיעִ֕י בְּעֶשְׂרִ֥ים וְאֶחָ֖ד לַחֹ֑דֶשׁ הָיָה֙ דְּבַר־יְהוָ֔ה
בְּיַד־חַגַּ֥י הַנָּבִ֖יא לֵאמֹֽר׃

בִּשְׁנַ֥ת שְׁתַּ֖יִם לְדָרְיָ֥וֶשׁ הַמֶּֽלֶךְ. See the introductory comments on 1:12-15b for a discussion of the pericope division. On the use of לְ and the word order of מֶ֫לֶךְ with a proper name, see 1:1.

הָיָה֙ דְּבַר־יְהוָ֔ה בְּיַד־חַגַּ֥י הַנָּבִ֖יא לֵאמֹֽר. Qal *qatal* 3 m s √היה and Qal inf cstr √אמר. On this prophetic "reception formula," see the Appendix (§1). In this instance it indicates the giving of a new revelation from YHWH to Haggai, and in conjunction with the dating formula also serves to mark the beginning of a new textual unit. The prepositional phrase בְּיַד־חַגַּ֥י indicates the agent transmitting YHWH's message (see 1:1).

2:2 אֱמָר־נָ֗א אֶל־זְרֻבָּבֶ֤ל בֶּן־שַׁלְתִּיאֵל֙ פַּחַ֣ת יְהוּדָ֔ה
וְאֶל־יְהוֹשֻׁ֥עַ בֶּן־יְהוֹצָדָ֖ק הַכֹּהֵ֣ן הַגָּד֑וֹל וְאֶל־שְׁאֵרִ֥ית
הָעָ֖ם לֵאמֹֽר׃

אֱמָר־נָ֗א אֶל־זְרֻבָּבֶ֤ל בֶּן־שַׁלְתִּיאֵל֙ פַּחַ֣ת יְהוּדָ֔ה. Qal impv 2 m s √אמר. The particle of entreaty and exhortation נָא is often used with imperatives and other volitional forms (JM §105c; MNK §19.4.1). It is typically translated as "please" and occurs not only in requests made from an inferior to a superior or between equals but also in requests and directives from a superior to an inferior (Shulman, 68). It is used not only with human entreaties (e.g., Abraham to his servant in Gen 24:2) but also, as here and elsewhere, in divine commands (e.g., Gen 13:14; 22:2; Exod 4:6; 11:2; Isa 7:3; Hag 2:11, 15, 18; Zech 1:4; 3:8; 5:5). This indicates that social status alone does not account for the use or non-use of נָא. There does not seem to be any pattern with respect to the recipient of the command in the book of Haggai; YHWH sometimes employs the particle with imperatives addressed to the prophet (2:2, 11) but sometimes not (2:21), and likewise employs it occasionally when addressing the people (2:15, 18) but not at other times (1:5, 7; 2:4, 18), and thus we even encounter both types in the same verse (2:18 שִׂימוּ־נָא לְבַבְכֶם . . . שִׂימוּ לְבַבְכֶם).

Waltke and O'Connor's proposal (WO §34.7a) that the imperative + נָא marks the request as a logical consequence is hardly fitting in Hag 2:2, since אֱמָר־נָא occurs at the beginning of its pericope and the problem to be addressed (viz., the people's disappointment and discouragement) has not yet been mentioned. Shulman argues that, in all of its occurrences, נָא in some way marks an utterance as a "polite, personal, or emotional request of the addressee," possibly utilized to avoid an impression of forcefully commanding another (67; cf. Wilt 1996). Drawing upon the sociolinguistic analysis of Wilt (esp. 1996: 241–42), Bent Christiansen notes that politeness can indeed be one implicature of making a proposition utilizing נָא, which "redresses" a straight, "bald" command in order to make it in some way more appealing and less threatening to the addressee. However, Christiansen (1999: 385) also points out that the frequent use of נָא with cohortatives cannot be fully explained by the factor of "politeness," and thus he argues it is better termed a "propositive particle." That is, נָא "functions to signal that the speaker is *proposing* a course of action with which the addressee may or may not agree or choose to accommodate."

וְאֶל־יְהוֹשֻׁעַ בֶּן־יְהוֹצָדָק הַכֹּהֵן הַגָּדוֹל וְאֶל־שְׁאֵרִית הָעָם לֵאמֹר. Qal inf cstr √אמר. On the repetition of the preposition אֶל in this appositional structure, see 1:1. On the noun שְׁאֵרִית, see 1:12. In this instance the construct phrase שְׁאֵרִית הָעָם is not prefaced by כֹּל־ (cp. 1:12, 14).

2:3 מִי בָכֶם הַנִּשְׁאָר אֲשֶׁר רָאָה אֶת־הַבַּיִת הַזֶּה
בִּכְבוֹדוֹ הָרִאשׁוֹן וּמָה אַתֶּם רֹאִים אֹתוֹ עַתָּה
הֲלוֹא כָמֹהוּ כְּאַיִן בְּעֵינֵיכֶם׃

מִי בָכֶם הַנִּשְׁאָר אֲשֶׁר רָאָה. Nifal ptc m s √שׁאר with def art, Qal *qatal* 3 m s √ראה. The interrogative pronoun מִי can function as a collective (e.g., Exod 10:8), referring to a group of people (JM §144a), although the singular forms of the participle הַנִּשְׁאָר and the *qatal* verb רָאָה which follow speak against this. For בְּ as "among," see BDB (88, #I2). The definite article on הַנִּשְׁאָר could be interpreted in different ways: it could be a "generic article" (JM §137i; AC §2.6.5; WB §92) that refers to a class rather than an individual and could be translated anarthrously: "who among you is *a survivor* who saw this house." On the other hand, the root √שׁאר provides an etymological link between הַנִּשְׁאָר and שְׁאֵרִית (cf. Hasel, 168), and thus it would perhaps be possible to consider the def art as "anaphoric" (JM §137f I3; AC §2.6.1; WB §83)—that is, as referring to something already mentioned in the text, namely the שְׁאֵרִית of 1:12, 14 and 2:2. As such, it is querying those, out of all of the "remnant people" (see 1:12), who were survivors that had actually seen the temple prior to its destruction.

אֶת־הַבַּיִת הַזֶּה בִּכְבוֹדוֹ הָרִאשׁוֹן. The position of הַזֶּה indicates that it is modifying בַּיִת, thus: "*this* house in its former glory" (JM §143h), not "this former house in its glory." The adjective רִאשׁוֹן requires the definite article because it modifies the determinate בִּכְבוֹדוֹ. For discussion of the noun כָּבוֹד, see Verhoef (1987: 105) and C. J. Collins.

וּמָה אַתֶּם רֹאִים אֹתוֹ עַתָּה. Qal ptc m pl √ראה. The interrogative pronoun מָה can function adverbially for "how?" (WB §126; BDB, 553, #2a), and this is contextually required here: "*How* do you see it now?" Interrogatives frequently utilize the *yiqtol* form due to its largely modal nature (Joosten 2002: 54; 1997: 58 n. 26); the participle is also regularly employed in interrogatives but it does not possess modal functions. It is possible that the usage of רֹאִים here represents the developing trend in LBH and post-BH for the participle to take over the function of expressing the "general present" in place of the *yiqtol* form (see 1:6). Yet in other instances of questions utilizing the participle of √ראה the speaker is asking what the hearer is seeing at the moment of inquiry (Jer 1:11,13; 24:3; Amos 7:8; 8:2; Zech 4:2; 5:2), in accord with the participle's use for the "actual present" (Rogland 2003: 10–11

n. 54)—that is, to refer to what is actually occurring at the moment of speaking. Thus, רֹאִים should be understood as referring to the actual present, indicating that the conversation between Haggai and his audience is taking place at the temple site as they are observing the ruin.

הֲלוֹא כָמֹהוּ כְּאַיִן בְּעֵינֵיכֶם. The repeated use of the preposition -כְּ indicates that two entities are identical in some respect (JM §174i; BDB, 454, #2a). From the observers' perspective, the temple as it was being rehabilitated was not merely "like" nothing, it *was* nothing.

2:4 וְעַתָּה חֲזַק זְרֻבָּבֶל | נְאֻם־יְהוָה וַחֲזַק יְהוֹשֻׁעַ בֶּן־
יְהוֹצָדָק הַכֹּהֵן הַגָּדוֹל וַחֲזַק כָּל־עַם הָאָרֶץ נְאֻם־
יְהוָה וַעֲשׂוּ כִּי־אֲנִי אִתְּכֶם נְאֻם יְהוָה צְבָאוֹת׃

וְעַתָּה חֲזַק זְרֻבָּבֶל | נְאֻם־יְהוָה. Qal impv 2 m s √חזק. On וְעַתָּה as a logical marker, see 1:5. It is curious that Zerubbabel's lineage as "son of Shealtiel" is not listed here (nor in v. 21), as it is elsewhere (1:1, 12, 14; 2:2, 23) and as is consistently done with Joshua's (1:1, 12, 14; 2:2, 4). Perhaps the omission in this instance is due to the "interruption" created by the phrase נְאֻם־יְהוָה (on which, see below).

וַחֲזַק יְהוֹשֻׁעַ בֶּן־יְהוֹצָדָק הַכֹּהֵן הַגָּדוֹל וַחֲזַק כָּל־עַם הָאָרֶץ נְאֻם־יְהוָה. Qal impv 2 m s √חזק with *vav*. In this instance the *vav* plus imperative syntagm is not to be taken as an "indirect volitive" (cf. on 1:8) but as a simple *vav* with a volitive (JM §115a, d). The repetition of the imperative is striking and, in a sense, grammatically unnecessary, since one imperative in the singular can be used with multiple addressees, as in fact occurs in verse 2 above. In this case the speaker wished to address the command to each of the different participants in the discourse, perhaps as a means of heightening the sense of individual obligation and responsibility. The phrase עַם הָאָרֶץ has been much discussed, as it displays a number of distinct usages in the Bible, the DSS, and Rabbinic literature, some positive and others derogatory (see, inter alia, Meyers and Meyers, 50–51; Kessler, 168–69), and each instance should be evaluated on its own terms. There is nothing in the text to distinguish these addressees from the "people" (עַם) already mentioned (Hag 1:2, 12, 14; 2:2), and thus it appears to be an inclusive reference to the entire Judean community (Verhoef 1987: 98).

וַעֲשׂוּ כִּי־אֲנִי אִתְּכֶם. Qal impv 2 m pl √עשׂה with *vav*. The speaker shifts from a series of singular imperatives to a plural imperative, and this corresponds with a shift to the indirect volitive: "so that you might work" (see 1:8). On כִּי־אֲנִי אִתְּכֶם, see 1:13.

נְאֻם יְהוָה צְבָאוֹת. This verse is striking for its thrice-repeated "oracle formula," which can hardly be delineating the structure of the text; such repetition is rather, as Wilt (1999: 303) observes, "obtrusive." Even Parunak's helpful description of the formula as a "low level focus marker" does not easily fit here, as the points where it is located in the text seem somewhat arbitrary (see Appendix §3). In this case, the repeated use of the formula appears to be motivated rhetorically. As Wilt suggests, "the original audience would have perceived the repetition as a means of heavily underlining the source and reliability of the message" (1999: 303). This would function both to confirm the necessity of persevering in the rebuilding project (cf. v. 5) as well as to provide added strength to the promises shortly to be made in verses 6-9. For further discussion of the formula, see the Appendix (§3).

2:5 אֶת־הַדָּבָר אֲשֶׁר־כָּרַתִּי אִתְּכֶם בְּצֵאתְכֶם מִמִּצְרַיִם
וְרוּחִי עֹמֶדֶת בְּתוֹכְכֶם אַל־תִּירָאוּ׃ ס

אֶת־הַדָּבָר אֲשֶׁר־כָּרַתִּי אִתְּכֶם בְּצֵאתְכֶם מִמִּצְרַיִם. Qal *qatal* 1 c s √כרת, Qal inf cstr √יצא with prefixed בְּ and 2 m pl pronoun suffix. √כרת is the verb for covenant-making par excellence, and it often omits the object בְּרִית (BDB, 503, #4). Infinitival phrases such as בְּצֵאתְכֶם are a very common means for forming a temporal clause (WB §504§ ,241; AC §3.4.1b; MNK §39.6.2; JM §166l): "*when* you came out from Egypt."

The great challenge with this verse is presented by the initial אֶת־הַדָּבָר, which is frequently emended. It has been proposed that אֶת־ here is the preposition "with," that it marks the direct object of a verb to be supplied or the verb וַעֲשׂוּ from verse 4, that it is an adverbial accusative (to be translated as "according to the word"), and that it is a rare use of the particle to mark the grammatical subject of a sentence. Each of these options involves serious grammatical problems, and none has been able to command the majority of scholarly opinion (see discussion in Rogland 2007b: 410–11). Nonetheless, the difficulty of the verse can be alleviated if one understands אֶת־הַדָּבָר to be the head of a lengthy direct object clause governed by אַל־תִּירָאוּ, thus reading it as the common BH syntagm ירא plus אֵת. As such, it can be translated as given above, "Do not fear the thing which I covenanted with you when you came out from Egypt, while my Spirit was abiding in your midst." In other instances in BH we find a considerable distance between a verb and the head of an object clause (e.g., 1 Sam 8:16; Amos 6:14), and we likewise encounter examples of direct objects modified by lengthy relative clauses (e.g., Gen 24:48; 26:18; see examples in Rogland 2007b: 412–13). The statement is to be understood as an intertextual reference to the tabernacle building portions of the book of Exodus (see 1:14; and Rogland 2007b: 413–15). In passages such as Exod 25:1ff. and 35:4ff., the people are summoned to contribute silver and gold for the construction of the tabernacle so that YHWH might dwell in their midst (e.g., Exod 25:8 וְעָשׂוּ לִי מִקְדָּשׁ וְשָׁכַנְתִּי בְּתוֹכָם). What is more, the Israelites responded in such an overwhelmingly generous fashion that Moses had to restrain their giving (Exod 36:3ff.). With regard to rebuilding the second temple, YHWH summons the people to again give sacrificially, but he assures them that there will be abundant gold and silver for the project (vv. 6-8).

וְרוּחִי עֹמֶדֶת בְּתוֹכְכֶם. Qal ptc f s √עמד. The verb can have various nuances of "to continue, abide" (BDB, 764, #3c). This is a circumstantial clause expressing action concomitant with the preceding clause (WB §494).

אַל־תִּירָאוּ. Qal jussive 2 m pl √ירא (a pausal form instead of תִּירְאוּ). As noted above, this is the primary verb in the sentence, and אֶת־הַדָּבָר is the head of its object clause.

2:6 כִּי כֹה אָמַר יְהוָה צְבָאוֹת עוֹד אַחַת מְעַט הִיא
וַאֲנִי מַרְעִישׁ אֶת־הַשָּׁמַיִם וְאֶת־הָאָרֶץ וְאֶת־הַיָּם
וְאֶת־הֶחָרָבָה׃

כִּי כֹה אָמַר יְהוָה צְבָאוֹת. Qal *qatal* 3 m s √אמר. On the use of this "messenger formula" with inferential particles, see 1:5. The formula itself does not affect the logical relationships of the propositions, and thus the basic structure to be analyzed is כִּי . . . עוֹד אַחַת מְעַט הִיא. See the Appendix (§2B).

עוֹד אַחַת מְעַט הִיא. This "cryptic phrase" (Ackroyd 1968: 153) is widely taken as adverbial in nature, modifying וַאֲנִי מַרְעִישׁ, e.g., "once again, in a little while, I will shake" (RSV) or the LXX's ἔτι ἅπαξ ἐγὼ σείσω (influential due to its citation in Heb 12:26, though it omits the final phrase מְעַט הִיא). An adverbial interpretation faces insuperable objections, however. First, on a prosodic level (i.e., pertaining to the intonation, stress, and rhythm of an utterance), it should be observed that the *athnach* in הִ֑יא provides a major disjunction, which argues against linking עֹ֥וד אַחַ֖ת מְעַ֣ט הִ֑יא with the following וַאֲנִ֗י מַרְעִישׁ. As a general rule, adverbial עוֹד stands as close to the verb as possible (MNK §46.3.ii.a). Second, the various suggested meanings of עֹ֥וד אַחַ֖ת מְעַ֣ט הִ֑יא do not correspond with the actual behavior of the lexemes involved (cf. Kessler, 160 n. 11; 173–75); עוֹד is never followed by the numeral 1 elsewhere to indicate "once more." As already observed, most of the time in BH מְעַט is functioning as an adjectival substantive for "little" (see 1:6). There are a handful of temporal uses of מְעַט in BH (BDB 590a, #1e*b*), some indeed involving the particle עוֹד and having the meaning "a little while yet," but in all these instances we encounter עוֹד מְעַט without an intervening element, unlike the present verse (a point not sufficiently acknowledged by Richter, 180) (e.g., Jer 51:33 עֹ֣וד מְעַ֔ט וּבָ֥אָה עֵֽת־הַקָּצִ֖יר לָֽהּ, "yet a little while and the time of harvest will come to her"; Hos 1:4 כִּֽי־עֹ֣וד מְעַ֗ט וּפָֽקַדְתִּ֞י, "for yet a little while and I will visit . . ." [see also Exod 17:4; Isa 10:25; 29:17; Ps 37:10]). Meyers and Meyers (52) conclude it to be a neologism communicating a temporally imminent event ("*In only a moment* I will shake . . ."), but this too is open to the objections mentioned above.

In light of these difficulties, עֹ֥וד אַחַ֖ת מְעַ֣ט הִ֑יא is best understood as follows: עוֹד is to be taken as a substantive (cf. BDB, 728) and עֹ֥וד אַחַ֖ת as a nominal phrase meaning "yet one more (thing)." The following מְעַט should be taken as a substantival adjective, i.e., "a little (thing)," rather than as a substantive acting adverbially (cf. Richter, 180), with the pronoun הִיא functioning as an equivalent of the copula. The somewhat wooden translation "yet one more thing is a little thing" (cf. Ackroyd 1968: 153–54) can be smoothed out as "one more thing is a small matter." The idea is that the "shaking of the nations" about to be mentioned in the following clause is considered a trifling, easy thing. In the context, it is being implicitly compared to the Exodus event just referenced (see v. 5), which represented the pinnacle of YHWH's saving power hitherto in the HB. YHWH is asserting, with a kind of boastful statement meant to inspire confidence in his hearers, that "yet one more thing"—namely, the shaking of the cosmos in order to provide precious items for the temple—will not be difficult for him.

וַאֲנִי מַרְעִישׁ אֶת־הַשָּׁמַיִם וְאֶת־הָאָרֶץ וְאֶת־הַיָּם וְאֶת־הֶחָרָבָה. Hifil ptc m s √רעשׁ. The use of the participle to indicate the imminent future (*futurum instans*) is very common in prophetic utterances, and in the HB more generally, as an extension of its use for referring to the actual present (JM §121e; MNK, 162; WB §214; WO §37.6f; GKC §116p). The *vav* conjunction attached to the personal pronoun אֲנִי can be rendered as an explicative or epexegetical "namely" (WB §434; AC §4.3.3.d; MNK §40.8.2.vii), thus specifying what the "little thing" is, though it could also have a logical force of "therefore" (cf. BDB, 254, #4) or simply be pleonastic (WB §435; MNK §40.8.3).

2:7 וְהִרְעַשְׁתִּי אֶת־כָּל־הַגּוֹיִם וּבָאוּ חֶמְדַּת כָּל־הַגּוֹיִם
וּמִלֵּאתִי אֶת־הַבַּיִת הַזֶּה כָּבוֹד אָמַר יְהוָה צְבָאוֹת׃

וְהִרְעַשְׁתִּי אֶת־כָּל־הַגּוֹיִם. Hifil *weqatal* 1 c s √רעשׁ. The ptc-*weqatal* sequence in a future time sphere often indicates sequential events (Kessler, 160 n. 12), but the use of *weqatal* without an idea of succession is also common (JM §119f), and it seems unlikely that וַאֲנִי מַרְעִישׁ . . . וְהִרְעַשְׁתִּי in verses 6-7 is meant to suggest two successive "shakings," one of the cosmos and the other of the nations. Possibly the universal cataclysm of verse 6 is intended as a summary statement, with verse 7 focusing on some specific results of this "shaking," and how they will affect human affairs. On the other hand, we find other instances of a repeated verbal form that seem to have the sense of "to continue to do something" (see Zech 2:14-15 and 6:12-13).

וּבָאוּ חֶמְדַּת כָּל־הַגּוֹיִם. Qal *weqatal* 3 c pl √בוא. The problems with interpreting חֶמְדַּת כָּל־הַגּוֹיִם as a messianic title ("Desire of Nations") are well known and have been thoroughly discussed elsewhere (Kessler, 161 n. 14; Verhoef 1987: 103–4). The plural verb form indicates that the feminine noun חֶמְדָּה ("desirable thing") is being understood collectively (see 1:8), which speaks decisively against a messianic interpretation.

וּמִלֵּאתִי אֶת־הַבַּיִת הַזֶּה כָּבוֹד. Piel *weqatal* 1 c s √מלא. The Piel of מלא often occurs with a double accusative (BDB, 570, #2), one indicating the object filled (הַבַּיִת) and the other indicating the object used to fill (כָּבוֹד).

אָמַר יְהוָה צְבָאוֹת. Qal *qatal* 3 m s √אמר.

2:8 לִ֥י הַכֶּ֖סֶף וְלִ֣י הַזָּהָ֑ב נְאֻ֖ם יְהוָ֥ה צְבָאֽוֹת׃

לִ֥י הַכֶּ֖סֶף וְלִ֣י הַזָּהָ֑ב. Possessive clauses (see 1:1): "The silver is mine, and the gold is mine." Since verse 7 had already mentioned "desirable things," the "silver" and "gold" of this verse can be considered the "topic" or information already known; the new information here is represented by the prepositional phrase לִי, which forms the predicate of both clauses and is "fronted" or clause-initial. As such it highlights YHWH's claim to ownership of the nations' wealth, which undergirds his promise to fill the temple with it. Shin (126–29) notes that the syntax of כֶּ֫סֶף preceding זָהָב represents the SBH word order, which in fact is more common in the Haggai–Zechariah–Malachi corpus than the LBH word order of זָהָב preceding כֶּ֫סֶף (attested in Zech 14:14; Mal 3:3).

2:9 גָּד֣וֹל יִֽהְיֶ֡ה כְּב֞וֹד הַבַּ֤יִת הַזֶּה֙ הָאַֽחֲר֔וֹן מִן־הָ֣רִאשׁ֔וֹן אָמַ֖ר יְהוָ֣ה צְבָא֑וֹת וּבַמָּק֤וֹם הַזֶּה֙ אֶתֵּ֣ן שָׁל֔וֹם נְאֻ֖ם יְהוָ֥ה צְבָאֽוֹת׃ פ

גָּד֣וֹל יִֽהְיֶ֡ה כְּב֞וֹד הַבַּ֤יִת הַזֶּה֙ הָאַֽחֲר֔וֹן מִן־הָ֣רִאשׁ֔וֹן. Qal *yiqtol* 3 m s √היה. מִן־הָ֣רִאשׁ֔וֹן represents the "comparative מִן" (JM §141g–h; WB §317). Since BH lacks comparative forms of adjectives (e.g., good → *better*), it instead utilizes מִן with an adjective. הָאַֽחֲר֔וֹן modifies "glory," not "house" (contra Petersen, 61; and the KJV), for that would require *כְּבוֹד הַבַּ֫יִת הָאַחֲרוֹן הַזֶּה (JM §139a, §143h; cf. v. 3), that is, it should be translated "the latter glory of this house," not "the glory of this latter house." The clause is concerned not with different houses but with the former versus latter glory of one and the same house. In terms of information structure and pragmatics (Holmstedt 2010: 9–10; cf. also MNK §46), the fronted adjective גָּד֣וֹל is the "focus" ("information contrasted with possible alternatives"). While the present state of YHWH's house may be unimpressive (v. 3), in the future it will have great glory.

אָמַ֖ר יְהוָ֣ה צְבָא֑וֹת. Qal *qatal* 3 m s √אמר.

וּבַמָּק֤וֹם הַזֶּה֙ אֶתֵּ֣ן שָׁל֔וֹם נְאֻ֖ם יְהוָ֥ה צְבָאֽוֹת. Qal *yiqtol* 1 c s √נתן. Joüon (419 n. 1) takes the *vav* as explicative, "because, for."

Third Oracle (Haggai 2:10-19)
Uncleanness, Judgment, Rebuilding, and Blessing

Haggai's third oracle is fraught with textual and linguistic difficulties, particularly in verses 15-19 (Rogland 2013a; Clark 1983), although the pericope's overall message is reasonably clear. In this passage Haggai is instructed to make legal inquiries of the priests regarding ritual sanctity and uncleanness (vv. 11-13). As Fishbane (296–98) has noted, the questions posed are based upon the laws of Leviticus (Lev 6:20 [ET: v. 27]; 7:19; 22:4; cf. Num 19:22). Such uncleanness is applied analogously to the people's status during the temple's state of disrepair (v. 14); they have an infectious impurity (Taylor and Clendenen, 178 and n. 39). YHWH asserts that the people's neglect of the temple has resulted in divine judgment, expressed particularly in meager harvests (vv. 16-17, 19; cf. 1:6, 9-10). The revival of the building project marks a change that demands special attention (vv. 15, 18), however. Now that the people have renewed their interest in YHWH's house, he intends to bless them (v. 19).

10 *On the twenty-fourth day of the ninth month in the second year of Darius the word of YHWH came to Haggai the prophet:*

11 *Thus has YHWH Tsevaot said, "Please ask the priests for a ruling:*

12 *If a man carries holy meat in the corner of his garment, and with his corner touches some bread or some stew or some wine or oil or any food, will it become holy?" And the priests answered and they said, "No."*

13 *And Haggai said, "If one unclean from a dead person touches any of these things, will it become unclean?" The priests answered and they said, "It will become unclean."*

14 *And Haggai answered and he said, "Thus is this people and thus is this nation before me"—oracle of YHWH—"and thus is all that they do, and where they offer is unclean.*

15 *Now therefore please pay attention, from this day forward: Before*
the placing of stone against stone in the temple of YHWH 16 *(so that they*
would not be going to a heap of twenty and it would turn out to be ten
and going to a wine vat to skim off fifty purah and it would turn out to be
twenty), 17 *I struck you and all the work of your hands with blight and with*
mildew and with hail, since you had nothing directed toward me."—oracle
of YHWH.

18 *"Please pay attention from this day forward, from the twenty-fourth of the ninth month; pay attention from the day when the temple of YHWH was refounded.*

[19]Is there yet seed in the storehouse? It has not yielded even as much as a vine or fig tree or pomegranate or olive tree. From this day I will bless you."

2:10 בְּעֶשְׂרִ֤ים וְאַרְבָּעָה֙ לַתְּשִׁיעִ֔י בִּשְׁנַ֥ת שְׁתַּ֖יִם לְדָרְיָ֑וֶשׁ
הָיָה֙ דְּבַר־יְהוָ֔ה אֶל־חַגַּ֥י הַנָּבִ֖יא לֵאמֹֽר׃

בְּעֶשְׂרִ֤ים וְאַרְבָּעָה֙ לַתְּשִׁיעִ֔י בִּשְׁנַ֥ת שְׁתַּ֖יִם לְדָרְיָ֑וֶשׁ. See the introductory remarks to 1:12-15a on dating formulae. On the use of לְ, see Hag 1:1. On the use of ordinal numbers alone (without the noun חֹ֫דֶשׁ) for indicating the month, see 1:15a.

הָיָה֙ דְּבַר־יְהוָ֔ה אֶל־חַגַּ֥י הַנָּבִ֖יא לֵאמֹר. Qal *qatal* 3 m s √היה and Qal inf cstr √אמר. This "reception formula" often occurs at the beginning of an oracle (see 1:1 and Appendix §1). In this instance the word comes "to" (אֶל) Haggai, not "via" (בְּיַד) the prophet as in 1:1, 3 and 2:1, but the distinction in meaning has little exegetical significance here. Although Haggai is the recipient of divine revelation in this verse, his task is then to communicate it to others.

2:11 כֹּ֤ה אָמַר֙ יְהוָ֣ה צְבָא֔וֹת שְׁאַל־נָ֧א אֶת־הַכֹּהֲנִ֛ים
תּוֹרָ֖ה לֵאמֹֽר׃

כֹּ֤ה אָמַר֙ יְהוָ֣ה צְבָא֔וֹת. Qal *qatal* 3 m s √אמר. In a number of instances the "messenger formula" follows the "reception formula" (for details, see Appendix §2).

שְׁאַל־נָ֧א אֶת־הַכֹּהֲנִ֛ים תּוֹרָ֖ה לֵאמֹר. Qal impv 2 m s √שאל and Qal inf cstr √אמר. The verb √שאל takes a double accusative here, which is a common phenomenon in BH (WO §10.2.3; JM §125u–w; MNK §33.2.2; AC §2.3.1e). In this occurrence, תּוֹרָה refers to a casuistic priestly ruling (BDB, 436, #1e; Meyers and Meyers, 55), since the priests were charged with applying the Law and making rulings regarding ceremonial cleanness and sanctity (Lev 10:10-11). YHWH again uses the particle נָא in issuing a command to Haggai (see v. 2).

2:12 הֵ֣ן ׀ יִשָּׂא־אִ֞ישׁ בְּשַׂר־קֹ֗דֶשׁ בִּכְנַ֣ף בִּגְד֔וֹ וְנָגַ֣ע בִּ֠כְנָפוֹ
אֶל־הַלֶּ֨חֶם וְאֶל־הַנָּזִ֜יד וְאֶל־הַיַּ֧יִן וְאֶל־שֶׁ֛מֶן וְאֶל־
כָּל־מַאֲכָ֖ל הֲיִקְדָּ֑שׁ וַיַּעֲנ֧וּ הַכֹּהֲנִ֛ים וַיֹּאמְר֖וּ לֹֽא׃

הֵ֣ן | יִשָּׂא־אִ֞ישׁ בְּשַׂר־קֹ֗דֶשׁ בִּכְנַ֣ף בִּגְדוֹ. Qal *yiqtol* 3 m s √נשׂא. הֵ֣ן, an allomorph of the more common הִנֵּה, is attested as a hypothetical particle (WB §514; WO §38.2d), possibly due to the influence of Aramaic (JM §167l; GKC §155w; Rendsburg 2012: 330–31). בְּשַׂר־קֹ֗דֶשׁ "holy meat" is an "attributive genitive" (WB §41; JM §129f), in which the absolute noun (the *nomen rectum*) provides an adjectival attribute for the construct noun (the *nomen regens*), as in הַר־קָדְשִׁי "mountain of my holiness" = "my holy mountain." The noun כָּנָף can be used for the "extremity, corner, or skirt" of a garment as in Num 15:38 and 1 Sam 15:27 (BDB, 489, #2a). By folding over a garment it could be used to transport food, as in Ruth 3:15. The exegetical question in this instance is whether the אִישׁ carrying "holy meat" is a layperson (so Petterson 2015: 76–77) or a priest (Hill, 87). If referring to a layperson, the case deals with the worshipper's handling of his portion of a votive or freewill offering which, unlike the thanksgiving offering, may be eaten on the day following the sacrifice (Lev 7:15-17; cf. 19:5-8). If referring to a priest, it would deal with one who has received his due portion of the temple sacrifices (Lev 7:35; 22:7) and is sharing these "holy things" (קֳדָשִׁים) with members of his household (Lev 22:10-13), which would have necessitated their transport out of the temple precincts. It is difficult to be certain and, in the end, the transport of "holy meat" was a matter of interest to all, both priests and laypeople alike (Petersen, 77). The fact that the Law did not explicitly address these details meant that a priestly "ruling" (v. 11 תּוֹרָה) was needed to deal with such circumstances as are envisioned in verses 12-13.

וְנָגַ֣ע בִּ֠כְנָפוֹ אֶל־הַלֶּ֨חֶם וְאֶל־הַנָּזִ֜יד וְאֶל־הַיַּ֧יִן וְאֶל־שֶׁ֛מֶן וְאֶל־כָּל־מַאֲכָ֖ל. Qal *weqatal* 3 m s √נגע. This clause adds a subcondition to the protasis (cf. JM §167e), thus addressing not merely the transport of "holy meat" but particularly the resulting situation should it come into contact with other items. The *vav* conjunctions in אֶל־הַלֶּ֨חֶם וְאֶל־הַנָּזִ֜יד וְאֶל־הַיַּ֧יִן have the sense of "or" (JM §175b; WB §433; BDB, 252, #1d). Strangely, some but not all of the foodstuffs mentioned are definite. Verhoef (1987: 117) asserts that the definite article denotes the specific kind of bread, stew, and wine in view, but then it is hard to explain its absence from שֶׁ֛מֶן (though the anarthrous state of כָּל־מַאֲכָ֖ל "any food" is not surprising in any event; cf. JM §139g–h; MNK §36.5.1). One could view these as instances of the "generic article" (see 2:3), but its omission with שֶׁ֛מֶן would nevertheless remain puzzling. It is probably best to classify this as an instance of "imperfect determination," in which a thing "which is not perceived as determinate by the writer or by the person who is addressed is sometimes specifically determinate by itself" (JM §137m). Joüon and Muraoka further explain that this occurs with some objects that "are specifically determinate because they are *taken* or *used* for some specific purpose" (cf. MNK §24.4.4iic). In this regard, it should be noted that bread, wine, and oil were staple elements at the temple and utilized in its ritual, and while the rare word נָזִיד ("stew") does not itself occur in cultic contexts, passages such as Num 6:19 and 1 Sam 2:13-16 suggest that boiling meat was standard practice at least with regard to certain offerings (cf. also Exod 29:31; Lev 8:31; Deut 16:7; Ezek 46:20, 23, 24; Zech 14:21). Joüon and Muraoka note that with imperfect determination the article is sometimes best rendered as "a certain," hence the rendering offered above: "*some* bread, or *some* stew, or *some* wine. . . ."

הֲיִקְדָּשׁ. Qal *yiqtol* 3 m s √קדשׁ (pausal form with *qameṣ* instead of *pataḥ*) with an interrogative *he*. For a similarly phrased conditional question (הֵן . . . הֲ), see Jer 3:1 (cf. Lev 10:19d).

וַיַּעֲנוּ הַכֹּהֲנִים וַיֹּאמְרוּ לֹא. Qal *wayyiqtol* 3 m pl √ענה and √אמר. For the next few verses the text shifts into narrative dialogue, even though it has only indicated the command for Haggai to speak and has not reported him doing it. It is common for biblical authors to omit such details when they can be readily assumed from the context.

2:13 וַיֹּאמֶר חַגַּי אִם־יִגַּע טְמֵא־נֶפֶשׁ בְּכָל־אֵלֶּה הֲיִטְמָא
וַיַּעֲנוּ הַכֹּהֲנִים וַיֹּאמְרוּ יִטְמָא׃

וַיֹּאמֶר חַגַּי אִם־יִגַּע טְמֵא־נֶפֶשׁ בְּכָל־אֵלֶּה. Qal *wayyiqtol* 3 m s √אמר and Qal *yiqtol* 3 m s √נגע. This conditional statement is introduced with the more common אִם instead of הֵן, but there does not appear to be any semantic or syntactical significance to the variation here. The phrase אִם־יִגַּע . . . בְּכָל־אֵלֶּה is grammatically parallel to the case envisioned in verse 12 and is to be understood as a separate scenario, not a further subcondition of the first. Both cases inquire as to what will happen to foodstuffs when brought into contact with items in a different cultic state, verse 12 dealing with consecrated meat and verse 13 with ritually unclean people. The general principles of the Levitical laws of purity and sanctity determine the priests' answers: sanctity is nontransferrable by contact, while many types of defilement are. The particular defilement addressed in verse 13 is that of a person termed טְמֵא־נֶ֫פֶשׁ. The noun נֶ֫פֶשׁ is amply attested in BH with the sense of "deceased person" or "corpse" (BDB, 660, #4c5), and טְמֵא־נֶ֫פֶשׁ refers to someone who is "unclean (from) a dead person" (cf. Lev 22:4; Num 5:2; 9:6, 7, 10; 19:13)—i.e., by having come into physical contact with a dead body.

הֲיִטְמָ֑א. Qal *yiqtol* 3 m s √טמא with the interrogative *he*. On this use of הֲ in a conditional question, see verse 12.

וַיַּעֲנ֧וּ הַכֹּהֲנִ֛ים וַיֹּאמְר֖וּ יִטְמָֽא. Qal *wayyiqtol* 3 m pl √ענה and √אמר and Qal *yiqtol* 3 m s √טמא. Like the adjective טָמֵא, the cognate verb √טמא belongs to the semantic field of ritual purity, defilement, sanctity, and the like (cf. Averbeck 2007a: 365–76). In this instance the verb יִטְמָֽא displays an active or dynamic sense of "will become unclean" (cf. JM §113a). This legal ruling by the priests is the "punch line" of verses 12-13, which will form the basis of the charge to be made in verse 14. In other words, the question about holy items potentially sanctifying other items through contact (v. 12) was, in fact, a "set up" for this verse's question regarding profanation and defilement (cf. Fishbane, 297). The complex ritual for cleansing from corpse defilement in Num 19 indicates that this is one of the most serious forms of uncleanness to contract. However, it should be observed that most forms of ritual uncleanness would have also resulted in the defilement of the foodstuffs under discussion in these verses. This indicates that טְמֵא־נֶ֫פֶשׁ is the real focus of verse 13, with the verse seeking to highlight the severity of the people's sin of omission: they have been, so to speak, guilty of corpse defilement due to their neglect of the temple.

2:14 וַיַּ֫עַן חַגַּ֫י וַיֹּ֫אמֶר כֵּ֣ן הָֽעָם־הַ֠זֶּה וְכֵן־הַגּ֨וֹי הַזֶּ֤ה לְפָנַי֙
נְאֻם־יְהוָ֔ה וְכֵ֖ן כָּל־מַעֲשֵׂ֣ה יְדֵיהֶ֑ם וַאֲשֶׁ֥ר יַקְרִ֛יבוּ
שָׁ֖ם טָמֵ֥א הֽוּא׃

וַיַּ֫עַן חַגַּ֫י וַיֹּ֫אמֶר. Qal *wayyiqtol* 3 m s √ענה and √אמר. The verb √ענה does not always indicate a reply to a specific inquiry but can indicate a more general notion of "to respond" (cf. BDB, 773, #2a).

כֵּ֣ן הָֽעָם־הַ֠זֶּה וְכֵן־הַגּ֨וֹי הַזֶּ֤ה לְפָנַי֙ נְאֻם־יְהוָ֔ה וְכֵ֖ן כָּל־מַעֲשֵׂ֣ה יְדֵיהֶ֑ם. A copula ("is") must be supplied for these comparative clauses likening the Judean community to the corpse-uncleanness discussed in the previous verse. The noun עַם has been used several times already in referring to the Judean community (1:2, 12, 13, 14; 2:2, 4), but here we also find the term גּוֹי used in tandem. This word can be used for Israel or Judah in the HB (BDB, 156, #1b), sometimes in conjunction with עָם, and is not inherently derogatory (e.g., Exod 33:13; Zeph 2:9; Ps 33:12). Thus, any pejorative tone here is due to the criticism of the people being made in the context, not to the word גּוֹי itself. The phrase מַעֲשֵׂה יָד is common in the HB and refers to all manner of human endeavor. The lexical sense of the phrase is all encompassing, but in verse 17 it is used to refer more specifically to agricultural labor.

נְאֻם־יְהוָה. In this instance the oracle formula interrupts the natural structure of the utterance, and hence can hardly be marking textual structure or the "climax/peak" of the discourse. Rather, it should probably be taken in its "validating" function of reminding the addressees that they are hearing revelation from YHWH (see Appendix §3). Perhaps such a reminder was needed at this juncture due to the back-and-forth dialogue that had been taking place between Haggai and the priests. The oracle formula prevents the mistaken impression that Haggai's legal inquiry was motivated by his own curiosity and indicates that it has served as YHWH's heuristic device to drive home the seriousness of the people's uncleanness due to neglect of the temple.

וַאֲשֶׁר יַקְרִיבוּ שָׁם טָמֵא הוּא. Hifil *yiqtol* 3 m pl √קרב. The RSV is typical of most translations: "and what they offer there is unclean." The LXX's καὶ ὃς ἐὰν ἐγγίσῃ ἐκεῖ ("and whoever comes near there") takes the אֲשֶׁר-clause not as referring to the objects of sacrifice but rather to the worshippers or ministrants: "and those who draw near there." One point in favor of the LXX's rendering is that terms for ritual purity and cleanness are almost never applied to a sacrifice or offering, with perhaps the sole exception of Mal 1:11 (מִנְחָה טְהוֹרָה), but are regularly used to describe people (Lev 5:2; 13; 15:2, 25; Num 9:7; 19:20). On the other hand, several factors weigh against this option. The LXX is so expansive in this instance that its reliability for text-critical matters is dubious (*BHQ*, 116, 132*; cf. Haupt). The Hifil of קרב typically takes an accusative object and only rarely occurs absolutely (Num 7:2, 18; 2 Chron 35:12; cf. BDB, 898, #2b7). The LXX's rendering also implies a lack of grammatical concord between the singular טָמֵא הוּא and the plural verb יַקְרִיבוּ, though this phenomenon is certainly attested in BH (see 1:2). Finally, the expression "those who offer" could have been more clearly expressed with the substantival participle הַמַּקְרִיבִים (cf. Lev 7:18, 29, 33; Num 7:12; 15:4). Joüon (418–19) argues that אֲשֶׁר

refers to the location, with שָׁם being a retrospective element pointing back to the relative particle (JM §158j): "and (the place) where they offer is impure." This would most often be expressed with הַמָּקוֹם to head the clause (e.g., Gen 13:3), but we do encounter cases where it is omitted and the clause begins with the relative particle (e.g., Exod 32:34; Josh 1:16; Ruth 1:16; see BDB, 82, #4bβ–γ). Buildings and places can indeed be classified as טָמֵא (BDB, 379–80), and hence this proposal does the best justice to the grammar and semantics of the clause, as well as to the exegetical context.

2:15 וְעַתָּה֙ שִֽׂימוּ־נָ֣א לְבַבְכֶ֔ם מִן־הַיּ֥וֹם הַזֶּ֖ה וָמָ֑עְלָה
מִטֶּ֧רֶם שֽׂוּם־אֶ֛בֶן אֶל־אֶ֖בֶן בְּהֵיכַ֥ל יְהוָֽה׃

Verses 15b-17 are notoriously difficult. The commentary will analyze the individual lexemes and clauses, with the interclausal relationships being addressed in the note following verse 17.

וְעַתָּה֙ שִֽׂימוּ־נָ֣א לְבַבְכֶ֔ם. Qal impv 2 m pl √שׂים. וְעַתָּה marks a logical inference: "now therefore" (see 1:6). For the meaning of שִׂים לֵב, see 1:5, and on the particle נָא, see 2:2. In this case, נָא might have the sense of an insistent "*please!*"

מִן־הַיּ֥וֹם הַזֶּ֖ה וָמָ֑עְלָה. There has been extensive scholarly discussion regarding whether מָעְלָה is retrospective or prospective—that is, does מִן־הַיּוֹם הַזֶּה וָמָעְלָה mean "from this day *and before*" or "from this day *onward*"? The use of מָעְלָה in 1 Sam 16:13 and 30:25 clearly favors the latter, but many nevertheless understand this verse and verse 18 (where the phrase is repeated) as having the past in view, thus leading to a retrospective interpretation of the phrase. Yet there seems to be a gradually developing consensus in favor of the prospective interpretation (Clark 1983: 432–33; Kessler, 198 n. 7; 206–7), and this is contextually suitable when it is recognized that מִן־הַיּוֹם הַזֶּה וָמָעְלָה is an adverbial modifier of the imperative ("consider *from this day onward*") and not an object clause for the verb ("consider *this day and before*").

מִטֶּ֧רֶם שֽׂוּם־אֶ֛בֶן אֶל־אֶ֖בֶן בְּהֵיכַ֥ל יְהוָֽה. Qal inf cstr √שׂים. This is the only known attestation of מִטֶּרֶם; normally we find בְּטֶרֶם or טֶרֶם alone, but it is evident that the syntagms are equivalent in meaning. The preposition מִן can be used with a temporal force of "since, after," which BDB (583, #7c) notes is "chiefly late."

2:16 מְהְיוֹתָם בָּא אֶל־עֲרֵמַת עֶשְׂרִים וְהָיְתָה עֲשָׂרָה בָּא אֶל־הַיֶּקֶב לַחְשֹׂף חֲמִשִּׁים פּוּרָה וְהָיְתָה עֶשְׂרִים׃

מְהְיוֹתָם בָּא אֶל־עֲרֵמַת עֶשְׂרִים וְהָיְתָה עֲשָׂרָה. Qal inf cstr √היה with 3 m pl pronoun suffix plus מִן, Qal ptc m s √בוא (for reasons to become clear below, it should not be parsed as Qal *qatal* 3 m s), Qal *weqatal* 3 f s √היה. The noun עֲרֵמָה is a lexeme possibly indicative of an LBH milieu, as its biblical occurrences are primarily exilic or postexilic (Ruth 3:7; 2 Chron 31.6-9; Neh 3.34; 13:15; Cant 7:3; Jer 50:26) and it is attested in RH. מְהְיוֹתָם is very difficult and is frequently emended (e.g. *BHQ*, 132–33*). When מִן is prefixed to this infinitive construct, the vocalization is always with *hireq* rather than the expected *ṣere* (JM §79s), modeled after the form of the other inseparable prepositions. The use of מִן with the infinitive construct of √היה expresses nonexistence as either the purpose or result of some act or situation (cf. BDB, 583, #7b*b*) (e.g., Jer 33:24 וְאֶת־עַמִּי יִנְאָצוּן מִהְיוֹת עוֹד גּוֹי לִפְנֵיהֶם "and they kept despising my people *so that they were no longer* a nation in their sight"; see also Lev 26:13; 1 Sam 2:31; Jer 33:21, 24). מְהְיוֹתָם בָּא should be taken as the periphrastic construction consisting of a form of √היה plus a participle, which draws attention to the durative nature of the situation (JM §121e–h). Such periphrastic constructions occur with infinitival forms of √היה, and the pronoun suffixes, when present, indicate the subject of the verb (e.g., 1 Sam 25:16 כָּל־יְמֵי הֱיוֹתֵנוּ עִמָּם רֹעִים הַצֹּאן, "all the days *when we were with them keeping* the sheep"; 2 Chron 29:11 כִּי־בָכֶם בָּחַר יְהוָה לַעֲמֹד לְפָנָיו לְשָׁרְתוֹ וְלִהְיוֹת לוֹ מְשָׁרְתִים וּמַקְטִרִים, "For YHWH has chosen you to stand before him, to minister to him, and *to be ministering* for him and making offerings"). Based on these considerations, מְהְיוֹתָם בָּא אֶל־עֲרֵמַת עֶשְׂרִים would be best translated, "*so that they were not going* to a heap of twenty" (see further Rogland 2013a: 72). The *weqatal* וְהָיְתָה marks repeated action in the past (JM §119v), which fits well with the periphrastic construction as they overlap in expressing the iterative past: "so that *one was not going* to a heap of twenty *and it would turn out to be* ten." The past-iterative usage of *weqatal* declined in LBH, as Joosten (2006) has documented, culminating in its disappearance from RH.

בָּא אֶל־הַיֶּקֶב לַחְשֹׂף חֲמִשִּׁים פּוּרָה וְהָיְתָה עֶשְׂרִים. Qal ptc m s √בוא, Qal inf cstr √חשׂף, and Qal *weqatal* 3 f s √היה. The participle בָּא continues the periphrastic construction of the previous clause and is followed by another past-iterative וְהָיְתָה (see the preceding comment):

"(so that they were not) *going* to a wine vat to skim off fifty purah *and it would turn out to be* twenty." יֶ֫קֶב refers to an entire winepress or vat, while פּוּרָה refers specifically to the trough of a winepress (Foulkes, 591–92) and is used as a term of measurement. In its only other occurrence in BH (Isa 63:3) פּוּרָה indeed *refers* to a full winepress, but this is to be understood as a *pars pro toto*. The verb √חשׂף is used for stripping something bare, and refers to "skimming off" a liquid here and in Isa 30:14 (*HALOT,* 359, #3; cf. Reymond, 205–7).

2:17 הִכֵּ֨יתִי אֶתְכֶ֜ם בַּשִּׁדָּפ֤וֹן וּבַיֵּרָקוֹן֙ וּבַבָּרָ֔ד אֵ֖ת כָּל־
מַעֲשֵׂ֣ה יְדֵיכֶ֑ם וְאֵין־אֶתְכֶ֥ם אֵלַ֖י נְאֻם־יְהוָֽה׃

הִכֵּ֨יתִי אֶתְכֶ֜ם בַּשִּׁדָּפ֤וֹן וּבַיֵּרָקוֹן֙ וּבַבָּרָ֔ד אֵ֖ת כָּל־מַעֲשֵׂ֣ה יְדֵיכֶ֑ם. Hifil *qatal* 1 c s √נכה. There are reasons to question whether this is a gloss on Amos 4:9, as has often been supposed (see Rogland 2007a: 553–54). In light of other intertextual echoes of Deut 28 in the book of Haggai (see Introduction §3 and *passim* on 1:6, 10-11), it seems more probable that this is a reference to the covenant judgments of Deuteronomy, particularly Deut 28:22 יַכְּכָה֩ יְהוָ֨ה בַּשַּׁחֶ֜פֶת . . . וּבַשִּׁדָּפ֖וֹן וּבַיֵּרָק֑וֹן, "May YHWH strike you with consumption . . . and with blight and with mildew." The presence of the definite article on בַּשִּׁדָּפ֤וֹן וּבַיֵּרָקוֹן֙ וּבַבָּרָ֔ד is simply due to the intertext, whether that is viewed as Deut 28:22 or Amos 4:9. The second direct object clause (אֵ֖ת כָּל־מַעֲשֵׂ֣ה יְדֵיכֶ֑ם) can strike the reader as awkward, since there was already one immediately following the verb (הִכֵּ֨יתִי אֶתְכֶ֜ם) with an intervening string of prepositional phrases. Probably this is to be interpreted as a case of verbal ellipsis, a regular phenomenon in BH (Miller 2003), with הִכֵּיתִי to be understood with אֵ֖ת כָּל־מַעֲשֵׂ֣ה יְדֵיכֶ֑ם (Kessler, 199 n. 18; Meyers and Meyers, 62).

וְאֵין־אֶתְכֶ֥ם אֵלַ֖י נְאֻם־יְהוָֽה. This clause has proven difficult, but יֵשׁ and אֵין occur with the particle אֵת in possessive clauses (e.g., 2 Kgs 3:12 יֵ֥שׁ אוֹת֖וֹ דְּבַר־יְהוָ֑ה, "he has the word of YHWH" and 1QS 6:13 יש אתי דבר לדבר לרבים, "I have a word to speak to the many"; for more extensive discussion and additional examples, see Rogland 2007a). Thus, וְאֵין־אֶתְכֶם should be understood as "and you had nothing," with the following אֵלַ֖י indicating direction "toward" an object: "and you had nothing directed towards me." As will be argued below, this should be understood as a causal clause, which can simply be introduced with a *vav* (JM §170c).

To make sense of verses 15b-17, it is important to grasp the syntactical relationship between the different statements (for a more detailed version of this analysis, see Rogland 2013a). The primary verbal clause is in verse 17 הִכֵּיתִי אֶתְכֶם, to which verse 15b's מִטֶּרֶם שׂוּם־אֶבֶן אֶל־אֶבֶן בְּהֵיכַל יְהוָה is a subordinate temporal clause:

> v. 15b Before the placing of stone against stone in the temple of YHWH . . .
> v. 17 *I struck you* . . .

The final clause of verse 17 adds an explanatory element, thus:

> v. 15b Before the placing of stone against stone in the temple of YHWH . . .
> v. 17 *I struck you* . . .
> *because* you had nothing directed toward me.

The statement recalls the indictment of the first chapter (1:1-11) and the poor harvests that had resulted from the people's neglect of the temple.

Verse 16 is to be understood as a parenthetical statement subordinate to verse 15b, explaining the purpose or motivation for the "placing of stone against stone." In other words, it explains the reason why the people recommenced the building program: to escape the times of scarcity that had maintained during that period of prior neglect. Thus:

> v. 15b Before the placing of stone against stone in the temple of YHWH . . .
> v. 16 (so that they would not be going to a heap of twenty and it would turn out to be ten . . .)
> v. 17 *I struck you* . . .
> *because* you had nothing directed toward me.

The interclausal relationships are indeed more complex than one typically encounters elsewhere in the HB; coupled with some philologically challenging expressions, it is no wonder that these verses have proven so puzzling to interpreters. As analyzed here, however, they are well suited to the immediate context and to the overall message of Haggai's prophecy.

2:18 שִׂימוּ־נָ֣א לְבַבְכֶ֔ם מִן־הַיּ֥וֹם הַזֶּ֖ה וָמָ֑עְלָה מִיּוֹם֩ עֶשְׂרִ֨ים וְאַרְבָּעָ֜ה לַתְּשִׁיעִ֗י לְמִן־הַיּ֛וֹם אֲשֶׁר־יֻסַּ֥ד הֵיכַל־יְהוָ֖ה שִׂ֥ימוּ לְבַבְכֶֽם׃

שִׂימוּ־נָ֣א לְבַבְכֶ֔ם מִן־הַיּ֥וֹם הַזֶּ֖ה וָמָ֑עְלָה. Qal impv 2 m pl √שׂים. See verse 15 regarding this identical clause. On the use of נָא with an imperative, see verse 2.

מִיּוֹם֩ עֶשְׂרִ֨ים וְאַרְבָּעָ֜ה לַתְּשִׁיעִ֗י. This clause provides further explanation of "from this day forward" by specifying "this day" as the twenty-fourth day of the ninth month. On the use of לְ, see note on 1:1. On the use of ordinal numbers alone for marking the month (as in v. 10), see 1:15a.

לְמִן־הַיּ֛וֹם אֲשֶׁר־יֻסַּ֥ד הֵיכַל־יְהוָ֖ה. Pual *qatal* 3 m s √יסד. This clause has triggered a great deal of exegetical discussion regarding the temporal references of the text. As argued above, YHWH is calling the people to "consider their ways *from this day onward*" (see v. 15), which the preceding clause specified to be the twenty-fourth day of the ninth month (see also v. 10). Yet the present clause, referring to the day of the "founding" (√יסד) of the temple, is often understood as hearkening back to an earlier time such as the initial rebuilding of the altar (e.g., Ezra 3:10-12). Various attempts have been made to account for this (cf. Clark 1983: 435–36), but probably the simplest explanations are either to note that the verb √יסד can refer to repairing or reestablishing something, rather than brand new construction (e.g. Ezra 3:10; see BDB, 413–14; *DCH* 4, 231–32; cf. Meyers and Meyers, 420–21), or to acknowledge that more than one "foundation-laying ritual" was not unheard of in antiquity (Clark 1983: 436). The former approach is taken here, understanding this to refer to the renewed building attempts of 520 BCE. The combination of לְ and מִן occurs occasionally and is identical in function to מִן (see Rogland 2010: 13–14, with references to additional literature).

שִׂ֥ימוּ לְבַבְכֶֽם. Qal impv 2 m pl √שׂים. See 1:5.

2:19 הַע֤וֹד הַזֶּ֙רַע֙ בַּמְּגוּרָ֔ה וְעַד־הַגֶּ֨פֶן וְהַתְּאֵנָ֧ה וְהָרִמּ֛וֹן וְעֵ֥ץ הַזַּ֖יִת לֹ֣א נָשָׂ֑א מִן־הַיּ֥וֹם הַזֶּ֖ה אֲבָרֵֽךְ׃ ס

הַע֤וֹד הַזֶּ֙רַע֙ בַּמְּגוּרָ֔ה. This is generally taken as a rhetorical question ("Is the seed still in the storehouse?"), but the nature of the rhetoric is disputed. It is possible that the interrogative *he* is being used to create an exclamation (JM §161b): "Surely, the seed is still in the storehouse!" On the other hand, Clark (1983: 436–39) has made a convincing case from the agricultural background to the pericope (specifically, the growing seasons of Syro-Palestine) that this is a rhetorical question expecting a negative answer. Thus, it is asserting by means of the question that the seed is no longer in storage because it has been planted. מְגוּרָה ("storehouse, storeroom, bin") is a *hapax* in CH but is attested in the Rabbinic period, and thus comports with the linguistic profile of the book as LBH (see Introduction §1).

וְעַד־הַגֶּ֫פֶן וְהַתְּאֵנָה וְהָרִמּוֹן וְעֵץ הַזַּיִת לֹא נָשָׂא. Qal *qatal* 3 m s √נשׂא. This clause has proven challenging, but if זֶרַע is understood as the subject of לֹא נָשָׂא then a grammatically acceptable sentence emerges: "it (viz., the seed) has not yielded" (cf. BDB, 671, #2g; for more extensive discussion see Rogland 2013a: 74–77). With a negative, the particle עַד can express "not even as much as" (BDB, 724 #I3), and thus one can smoothly translate, "(The seed) has not yielded even as much as a vine or a fig tree or a pomegranate or an olive tree." The definite articles are generic (see Hag 2:3).

מִן־הַיּוֹם הַזֶּה אֲבָרֵךְ. Piel *yiqtol* 1 c s √ברך. When God is the subject the verb can denote either a declarative act (a promise to bless) or a fulfillment of such a promise (Aitken, 113, 116); in this case, the declarative sense is intended.

Fourth Oracle (Haggai 2:20-23)
A Message to Zerubbabel

Haggai's fourth oracle occurs on the same date as the third (vv. 10, 20). It consists of a message directed personally to Zerubbabel the governor and speaks of a coming cosmic upheaval. Verse 21 refers intratextually (cf. Introduction §3) to Haggai's second oracle delivered nearly two months prior by repeating verse 6 in an only slightly abbreviated form. Although this serves to strengthen the literary coherence of the book as a whole it does not necessarily mean that the two oracles are referring to one and the same future event (cf. Kashow, 388 n. 14). The language of "shaking" nations and kingdoms is an established prophetic idiom that occurs in other oracles (e.g. Isa 13:13; 14:16; 23:11; Ezek 26:15; 27:28; 31:16) with a variety of historical referents. Moreover, the subject matter of the two oracles is entirely different. In 2:1-9 YHWH's "shaking" of the cosmos has the effect of bringing the "treasured things of the nations" to the people of God for the purpose of glorifying the temple (vv. 7-9), with no indication of this being a violent or catastrophic event. In contrast, the "shaking" of verse 21 echoes the casting of Pharaoh's army into the sea in Exod 14–15 (Petersen, 101; see v. 22) and is calamitous in nature, causing widespread destruction (v. 22). It is in this context that YHWH utters a promise to protect and preserve Zerubbabel as his חוֹתָם (v. 23), often rendered "signet ring" (but see v. 23).

For the most part, the language and syntax of this brief oracle is fairly simple. Nevertheless, it has garnered considerable attention due to the potential historical problem it presents: Haggai's oracle is often understood as a promise of the political ascendancy of Zerubbabel or the Davidic House in the postexilic era. As such it is viewed as a reversal of Jer 22:24-30, in which Jehoiachin (Coniah) is "removed" as YHWH's "signet ring" (e.g. Stead, 146–48). The fact that Zerubbabel never actually became "king" has thus been viewed by many as a historical or theological problem, with some asserting that Haggai's prophecy was mistaken or simply failed. Several other alternate explanations have been proposed as well, for example, that the oracle predicts a socio-political leadership role for Zerubbabel similar (but not identical) to that of a king (Schreiner, 164), that the oracle (like much prophecy in the HB) was contingent in nature and that the people's failure prevented its eventual fulfillment (Kashow), or that the oracle is not speaking of political leadership at all (Rose, 208–47). This handbook will not attempt to critique these positions, though of course they are not all mutually exclusive.

20And the word of YHWH came a second time to Haggai on the twenty-fourth of the month:

21"Say to Zerubbabel, governor of Judah, 'I am going to shake the heavens and the earth.

22And I will overturn thrones of kingdoms. And I will destroy the strength of the kingdoms of the nations. And I will overturn each chariot with its riders, and horses and their riders will go down by one another's sword.

23In that day'—oracle of YHWH Tsevaot—'I will take you, Zerubbabel son of Shealtiel, my servant'—oracle of YHWH—'and I will make you as a signet ring, for I have chosen you'—oracle of YHWH Tsevaot."

2:20 וַיְהִ֨י דְבַר־יְהוָ֤ה ׀ שֵׁנִית֙ אֶל־חַגַּ֔י בְּעֶשְׂרִ֥ים וְאַרְבָּעָ֛ה
לַחֹ֖דֶשׁ לֵאמֹֽר׃

Qal *wayyiqtol* 3 m s √היה and Qal inf cstr √אמר. Feminine ordinal numerals such as שֵׁנִית can be used adverbially to express how many times something occurs (JM §101f). Wolff (98–99) finds it problematic that אֶל is used both for Haggai as mediator (v. 20) and for Zerubbabel as recipient (v. 21) since the prophetic intermediary is indicated by בְּיַד elsewhere (1:1, 3; 2:1), but the double use of אֶל is attested several times in similar contexts (e.g. 2 Sam 7:4-5; 24:11-12; 1 Kgs 12:22-23; 13:20-21; 2 Kgs 20:4-5; Jer 37:6-7). On dating formulae, see the introductory remarks to 1:12-15a. In this case, the month does not need to be mentioned since it is specified that this is "the second time" (שֵׁנִית) an oracle was given on this day.

2:21 אֱמֹ֕ר אֶל־זְרֻבָּבֶ֥ל פַּֽחַת־יְהוּדָ֖ה לֵאמֹ֑ר אֲנִ֣י מַרְעִ֔ישׁ
אֶת־הַשָּׁמַ֖יִם וְאֶת־הָאָֽרֶץ׃

אֱמֹ֕ר אֶל־זְרֻבָּבֶ֥ל פַּֽחַת־יְהוּדָ֖ה לֵאמֹ֑ר. Qal impv 2 m s and Qal inf cstr √אמר. On the noun פֶּחָה, see 1:1. Zerubbabel's role as "governor" is mentioned here, in contrast to its omission in 1:12 and 2:4 (see 1:12).

אֲנִ֣י מַרְעִ֔ישׁ אֶת־הַשָּׁמַ֖יִם וְאֶת־הָאָֽרֶץ. Hifil ptc m s √רעשׁ. The participle indicates the imminent future (see v. 6) and is followed in verse 22 by *weqatal* forms, which is a very common verbal sequence in prophetic oracles. The MT citation in verse 21 is shorter than verse 6, lacking the introductory עוֹד אַחַת מְעַט הִיא and stating only the shaking of "the heavens and the earth," thereby omitting the mention of "the sea and the dry land" in verse 6. The LXX has brought the two into line with each other by rendering τὸν οὐρανὸν καὶ τὴν γῆν καὶ τὴν θάλασσαν καὶ τὴν ξηρὰν in both verses.

2:22 וְהָֽפַכְתִּי֙ כִּסֵּ֣א מַמְלָכ֔וֹת וְהִ֨שְׁמַדְתִּ֔י חֹ֖זֶק מַמְלְכ֣וֹת
הַגּוֹיִ֑ם וְהָפַכְתִּ֤י מֶרְכָּבָה֙ וְרֹ֣כְבֶ֔יהָ וְיָרְד֤וּ סוּסִים֙
וְרֹ֣כְבֵיהֶ֔ם אִ֖ישׁ בְּחֶ֥רֶב אָחִֽיו׃

וְהָפַכְתִּי כִּסֵּא מַמְלָכוֹת. Qal *weqatal* 1 c s √הפך. The phrase refers to a political overthrow, whereas the following clause speaks more explicitly of a military one. Kessler (219 n. 4) rightly notes that the singular כִּסֵּא of the construct phrase כִּסֵּא מַמְלָכוֹת "throne of kingdoms" does not mean that the author has a single empire (e.g., the Persian) in mind, for with genitive phrases expressing a compound idea the plural absolute noun is sufficient to indicate the notion of plurality (GKC §124p, r; cf. LXX's θρόνους βασιλέων). The phrase could perhaps be rendered as determinate if one understands מַמְלָכוֹת as an elliptical form either of the following phrase מַמְלְכוֹת הַגּוֹיִם "the kingdoms of the nations" (see also 2 Chron 20:6; Isa 13:4) or the even more common expression מַמְלְכוֹת הָאָרֶץ "the kingdoms of the earth" (Deut 28:25; 2 Kgs 19:15, 19; 2 Chron 36:23; Ezra 1:2; Ps 68:33; Isa 23:17; 37:16, 20; Jer 15:4; 24:9; 29:18; 34:1, 17). כִּסֵּא occurs in tandem with מַמְלָכָה (2 Sam 3:10; 7:16; Isa 9:6) and sometimes in the same construct phrase encountered here (Deut 17:18; 2 Sam 7:13; 1 Kgs 9:5; 2 Chron 23:20), but כִּסֵּא also occurs with מַלְכוּת (1 Kgs 2:12; 1 Chron 17:14; Pss 45:7; 103:19), including the construct phrase כִּסֵּא מַלְכוּת (1 Chron 22:10; 28:5; 2 Chron 7:18; Esth 1:2; 5:1). The meaning and usage of the two idioms appears to be identical, but the distribution suggests that כִּסֵּא מַלְכוּת is favored in LBH whereas כִּסֵּא מַמְלָכָה is in SBH.

וְהִשְׁמַדְתִּי חֹזֶק מַמְלְכוֹת הַגּוֹיִם. Hifil *weqatal* 1 c s √שׁמד. BH contains a number of etymologically related nouns for "strength" (חֵזֶק, חֶזְקָה, חָזְקָה), none of which are particularly frequent (cf. BDB, 305–6), and it is somewhat unclear if or how they differ in meaning from חֹזֶק. Half of the biblical occurrences of חֹזֶק occur in the context of the Exodus narrative (Exod 13:3, 14, 16). The occurrence of the noun in this verse is possibly due to the intertextual influence of the Exodus narrative on this oracle (see the introductory comments above).

וְהָפַכְתִּי מֶרְכָּבָה וְרֹכְבֶיהָ. Qal *weqatal* 1 c s √הפך. מֶרְכָּבָה could be functioning as a collective in this instance (cf. JM §135c) as in 1 Sam 8:11 and Mic 1:13. On the other hand, one might object that it is the related noun רֶכֶב, not מֶרְכָּבָה, which is used much more commonly as a grammatical collective for "chariots" or "chariotry" in the HB. It might be preferable, then, to take the phrase as a "universal distributive expression" (WO §15.6c) in which a singular predicate has a plural referent in the sense of "all who" or "each one who" (cf. e.g. Exod 31:14; Prov 3:18). In that case the clause can be rendered, "and I will overturn each chariot with its riders" (see also the following comment). The Exodus narrative also contains references to “chariots” (Exod 14:25; 15:4) and “riders” (subst ptc of √רכב in Exod 15:1, 21) and is most probably an intended intertext here (cf. Introduction §3 and on Zech 1:7-17 *passim*).

וְיָרְד֤וּ סוּסִים֙ וְרֹ֣כְבֵיהֶ֔ם אִ֖ישׁ בְּחֶ֥רֶב אָחִֽיו. Qal *weqatal* 3 c pl √ירד, Qal ptc m pl √רכב with 3 m pl pronoun suffix. The phrase אִ֖ישׁ בְּחֶ֥רֶב אָחִֽיו expresses reciprocity (e.g., “each other, one another”; JM §147c; WB §§131–32).

2:23 בַּיּ֣וֹם הַה֣וּא נְאֻם־יְהוָ֣ה צְבָא֡וֹת אֶ֠קָּחֲךָ זְרֻבָּבֶ֨ל בֶּן־שְׁאַלְתִּיאֵ֤ל עַבְדִּי֙ נְאֻם־יְהוָ֔ה וְשַׂמְתִּ֖יךָ כַּֽחוֹתָ֑ם כִּֽי־בְךָ֣ בָחַ֔רְתִּי נְאֻ֖ם יְהוָ֥ה צְבָאֽוֹת׃

בַּיּ֣וֹם הַה֣וּא נְאֻם־יְהוָ֣ה צְבָא֡וֹת אֶ֠קָּחֲךָ. Qal *yiqtol* 1 c s √לקח with 2 m s pronoun suffix. The verb √לקח is a general one and should not be invested with an overly technical sense here (cf. Rose, 216–18). אֶקָּחֲךָ simply forms the lead-in to the following וְשַׂמְתִּ֖יךָ כַּֽחוֹתָ֑ם, which is the main point of interest in the oracle (see below). The adverbial phrase בַּיּ֣וֹם הַה֣וּא “in that day” occurs frequently with different verb tenses, referring to the past or future. In this instance the verbal phrase is interrupted by the “oracle formula” נְאֻם־יְהוָה צְבָאוֹת, a phenomenon observed elsewhere in Haggai; see 2:4 and the Appendix (§3).

זְרֻבָּבֶ֨ל בֶּן־שְׁאַלְתִּיאֵ֤ל עַבְדִּי֙ נְאֻם־יְהוָ֔ה. These phrases are in apposition to the pronoun suffix on the preceding אֶקָּחֲךָ and are to be understood as vocatives: “O Zerubbabel, son of Shealtiel, my servant.” See 1:12 and 2:21 regarding the use or non-use of Zerubbabel’s title “governor.”

וְשַׂמְתִּ֖יךָ כַּֽחוֹתָ֑ם. Qal *weqatal* 1 c s √שׂים with 2 m s pronoun suffix. As noted in the introductory comments above, this pericope is often viewed as a promise of political ascendancy for Zerubabbel and as a reversal of Jer 22:24. Rose (237) has persuasively shown, however, that such a view treats the imagery and philological details of Jer 22:24 as well as of Hag 2:23 in a superficial way. Both instances employ the broader term חוֹתָם “seal” rather than the more specific טַבַּעַת “signet ring,” and Rose (224–43) has assembled an impressive array of evidence from material culture, ANE literature (Egyptian poetry, Assyrian royal correspondence), and biblical usage for interpreting וְשַׂמְתִּ֖יךָ כַּֽחוֹתָ֑ם as a symbol of preciousness and protection. A precise syntactical parallel is found in Cant 8:6 שִׂימֵנִי כַחוֹתָם עַל־לִבֶּךָ כַּחוֹתָם עַל־זְרוֹעֶךָ "Place me *as a seal* upon your heart, *as a seal* upon your arm," a statement that communicates safety and security. In the context of a catastrophic political and military judgment upon the nations, YHWH promises to shield and protect Zerubbabel. While one may wish to argue for political implications to the oracle nonetheless, this would have to be done based on broader historical or theological factors rather than strictly philological ones (cf. Kashow, 387 n. 11).

כִּי־בְךָ בָחַרְתִּי נְאֻם יְהוָה צְבָאוֹת. Qal *qatal* 1 c s √בחר. The verb typically utilizes the preposition ־בְּ for its object complement (BDB, 103–4, #1).

Prologue (Zechariah 1:1-6)
A Call to Return to YHWH

Zechariah's introductory pericope falls in the eighth month of Darius' second year, and thus within the period between Haggai's initial messages to the citizens of Judea (the sixth month: Hag 1:1–2:9) and his final two oracles (the ninth month: Hag 2:20-23). This opening unit functions programmatically in the book (cf. Wenzel 2011a), summoning the people in verse 3 to "return" (שׁוּבוּ) to YHWH, even as YHWH promises to "return" to them (וְאָשׁוּב). The exhortation to "return" is the same one issued by previous prophets, which their forefathers rejected (v. 4), resulting in divine judgment (vv. 5-6a). According to the interpretation followed here, however, Zechariah's hearers show themselves to be different from their ancestors and respond by "returning" to YHWH (see וַיָּשׁוּבוּ in v. 6). It is evident that the verb שׁוב serves as a thematic word for this unit (Stead, 79–80) and, indeed, for Zech 1–8: YHWH twice assures them "I have returned" (שַׁבְתִּי), an utterance that functions as bookends for the Night Visions (1:16; 8:3).

In this unit there is an especially pervasive use of the three basic prophetic formulae encountered frequently in Haggai:

v. 1 The word of YHWH came to Zechariah . . . saying
v. 3 Thus has YHWH Tsevaot said
Oracle of YHWH Tsevaot
YHWH Tsevaot has said
v. 4 Thus has YHWH Tsevaot said
Oracle of YHWH Tsevaot

The density of usage of these formulae seems cumbersome here (Meier, 321; cf. Clark 1994: 531–33) and they cannot be explained strictly as structural markers. In these instances they appear to have a "validating" function, with an overall effect of attesting to the divine origin of Zechariah's (and the earlier prophets') summons to the people. For further discussion, see the Appendix.

[1]In the eighth month, in the second year of Darius, the word of YHWH came to Zechariah, the son of Berekiah, the son of Iddo, the prophet:
[2] "YHWH was exceedingly wrathful against your forefathers.
[3]And you will say to them: Thus has YHWH of hosts said, 'If you return to me'—oracle of YHWH Tsevaot—'then I will return to you,' YHWH Tsevaot has said.
[4]Do not be like your forefathers, unto whom the earlier prophets called, 'Thus has YHWH Tsevaot said, Please return from your evil ways and your evil deeds.' But they did not hear and they did not give attention to me"—oracle of YHWH.
[5]"Your forefathers—where are they? And as for their prophets, could they live forever?
[6]Surely, my words and my statutes which I commanded my servants the prophets overtook your forefathers."
And they returned and they said, "As YHWH Tsevaot purposed to do to us according to our ways and according to our deeds, so has he dealt with us."

1:1 בַּחֹ֙דֶשׁ֙ הַשְּׁמִינִ֔י בִּשְׁנַ֖ת שְׁתַּ֣יִם לְדָרְיָ֑וֶשׁ הָיָ֣ה דְבַר־
יְהוָ֗ה אֶל־זְכַרְיָה֙ בֶּן־בֶּ֣רֶכְיָ֔ה בֶּן־עִדּ֥וֹ הַנָּבִ֖יא לֵאמֹֽר׃

בַּחֹ֙דֶשׁ֙ הַשְּׁמִינִ֔י בִּשְׁנַ֖ת שְׁתַּ֣יִם לְדָרְיָ֑וֶשׁ. The dating formula used here is exceptional in that it omits the day of the month, which is included elsewhere in Zechariah (1:7; 7:1) and in Haggai (see the introductory remarks to Hag 1:12-15a). The Peshitta does indeed insert "the first day" between the month and year, but the MT is supported by MurXII (Benoit et al., 205) and other ancient versions, indicating that this is a secondary expansion (*BHQ*, *133). Given that there is no single consistent pattern of dating formulae in the books (cf. Kessler, 44), there is no compelling reason to emend the text. On the use of לְ and of cardinal and ordinal numerals in dating formulae, see Hag 1:1.

הָיָה דְבַר־יְהוָה אֶל־זְכַרְיָה בֶּן־בֶּרֶכְיָה בֶּן־עִדּוֹ הַנָּבִיא לֵאמֹר. Qal *qatal* 3 m s √היה and Qal inf cstr √אמר. It is possible that הַנָּבִיא could be standing in grammatical apposition either to the name "Iddo" or to "Zechariah" (see Hag 1:1), but the latter option is best suited to the present context. The name "Berechiah" is spelled בֶּרֶכְיָה in this verse while in verse 7 it is spelled בֶּרֶכְיָהוּ. Other names display this sort of spelling variation between ־יה and ־יהו endings and are extensively discussed by Shin (101–14), who demonstrates that the former represents LBH spelling whereas the latter represents SBH. The ־יה spelling is used almost exclusively in the postexilic prophets Haggai, Zechariah and Malachi (Shin, 107). While the name "Zechariah" is attested in both spellings in the HB, only the ־יה spelling occurs in the book of Zechariah.

1:2 קָצַף יְהוָה עַל־אֲבוֹתֵיכֶם קָצֶף׃

קָצַף יְהוָה עַל־אֲבוֹתֵיכֶם קָצֶף. Qal *qatal* 3 m s √קצף represents the "cognate accusative" or "accusative of internal object" which is so common in BH (JM §125q; AC §2.3.1c; WB §51; MNK §33.2.1ic; GKC §117p–r; WO §10.2.1f–g). קָצֶף is a pausal form due to the heavy *silluq* accent, and thus displays *qameṣ* instead *segol* (קֶ֫צֶף). When Qal √קצף occurs with a prepositional complement it typically takes עַל, though אֶל occurs once (Josh 22:18). Petersen's suggestion (127) that עַל indicates cause or ground here ("*on account of* your forefathers": see BDB, 754, #II1f*b*) is not impossible, but in a number of occurrences of קָצַף with עַל the preposition indicates the object of anger (e.g., Gen 40:2; 41:10; Exod 16:20; etc.), which would favor the rendering, "YHWH was wroth with wrath *against* your forefathers." The word "father" can refer to a more distant ancestor (BDB, 3, #4) and not one's direct parent.

1:3 וְאָמַרְתָּ אֲלֵהֶם כֹּה אָמַר יְהוָה צְבָאוֹת שׁוּבוּ אֵלַי
נְאֻם יְהוָה צְבָאוֹת וְאָשׁוּב אֲלֵיכֶם אָמַר יְהוָה
צְבָאוֹת׃

וְאָמַרְתָּ אֲלֵהֶם כֹּה אָמַר יְהוָה צְבָאוֹת. Qal *weqatal* 2 m s and Qal *qatal* 3 m s √אמר. The *weqatal* verb has an injunctive or imperatival force, which is perfectly grammatical even in the absence of a preceding volitive form (see Driver, §119β; contra, e.g., Stead, 76–78; Petersen, 129; Wenzel 2011a: 52 n. 27). Obviously, Zechariah is not being directed to speak to the now-deceased "forefathers" of verse 2, but that does not mean that there is no antecedent for the pronominal suffix on אֲלֵהֶם ("to them"), as Tigchelaar (72) suggests. Rather, the antecedent is supplied by the 2 pl pronoun suffix on אֲבוֹתֵיכֶם (v. 2) and refers to the prophet's contemporaries (cf. Meyers and Meyers, 92–93; Clark 1994: 531). On the treatment of צְבָאוֹת as a name "Tsevaot," see Hag 1:2.

שׁוּבוּ אֵלַי נְאֻם יְהוָה צְבָאוֹת וְאָשׁוּב אֲלֵיכֶם. Qal impv 2 m pl √שׁוב and Qal *yiqtol* 1 c s √שׁוב with *vav* conjunction. A smattering of manuscripts read ואשובה instead of וְאָשׁוּב (Kennicott, 290), but the manuscript evidence for the MT is so strong that the variant is not even mentioned in *BHQ*. The imperative שׁוּבוּ "return!" has a sense of moral return, i.e., to seek penitently or "repent" (BDB, 997, #6c). Given the nation's long history of disobedience (cf. vv. 4-6a) the exhortation is not superfluous, even though the people have in fact already begun to respond to Haggai's earlier preaching by commencing the rebuilding project.

The verbal form וְאָשׁוּב requires comment: Is this to be understood as a future tense ("*and I will* return to you"; Meyers and Meyers, 89) or as an expression of purpose ("*so that I may* return to you"; Petersen, 127)? The former option is to be preferred, because in the case of the latter reading, one would expect either an "indirect volitive" utilizing the cohortative form וְאָשׁוּבָה (JM §116b) as in Mal 3:7 or one of the other means for expressing purpose in BH such as the conjunction לְמַעַן. The use of a *weyiqtol* form וְאָשׁוּב instead of the more common *weqatal* (e.g., וְשַׁבְתִּי) is noteworthy. It must first be observed that we are dealing with a conditional statement expressed simply by the juxtaposition of two clauses, with the imperative שׁוּבוּ forming the protasis and וְאָשׁוּב the apodosis: "(If) you return to me . . . (then) I will return to you" (see JM §162a2, which contains grammatically similar examples). The use of *weyiqtol* instead of *weqatal* is to be attributed to diachronic development, as LBH shows a decreasing usage of *weqatal* in the apodosis of conditional sentences following a *yiqtol* or an imperative (Eskhult 2000: 88–89; 2005: 361–62).

אָמַר יְהוָה צְבָאוֹת. Qal *qatal* 3 m s √אמר. This abbreviated form of the "messenger formula" occurs regularly in Haggai-Zechariah (see Appendix §2).

1:4 אַל־תִּהְיוּ כַאֲבֹתֵיכֶם אֲשֶׁר קָרְאוּ־אֲלֵיהֶם הַנְּבִיאִים הָרִאשֹׁנִים לֵאמֹר כֹּה אָמַר יְהוָה צְבָאוֹת שׁוּבוּ נָא מִדַּרְכֵיכֶם הָרָעִים וּמַעַלְלֵיכֶם הָרָעִים וְלֹא שָׁמְעוּ וְלֹא־הִקְשִׁיבוּ אֵלַי נְאֻם־יְהוָה׃

אַל־תִּהְיוּ כַאֲבֹתֵיכֶם. Qal jussive 2 m pl √היה. Wenzel (2011b) argues for the translation "Beware of being like your fathers" ("Hört auf zu sein wie eure Väter!") rather than "Don't be like your fathers" ("Seid nicht wie eure Väter!"). However, such a translation in no way supports his claim that Zechariah's hearers had the same attitude of pessimism, cynicism, and resignation as previous former generations (2011b: 200–1). Indeed, his proposed translation could just as easily be interpreted as an indication that Zechariah's hearers had not yet fallen into such a mindset. It will be argued below that the text in fact indicates that Zechariah's audience responded differently than former generations to the prophetic summons to "return" to YHWH (see v. 6b).

אֲשֶׁר קָרְאוּ־אֲלֵיהֶם הַנְּבִיאִים הָרִאשֹׁנִים לֵאמֹר. Qal *qatal* 3 c pl √קרא and Qal inf cstr √אמר. The phrase הַנְּבִיאִים הָרִאשֹׁנִים occurs only here and in 7:7, 12 and has been much discussed (e.g., Wenzel 2011a: 59–61). In the post-biblical era this became a canonical designation referring to the books of Joshua through Kings. Zechariah is referring to the prophets who spoke to previous generations, however, and hence it is rendered above as "earlier prophets" so as to avoid potential confusion with this more specific usage. As frequently occurs with אֲשֶׁר clauses, a retrospective pronoun suffix is found on אֲלֵיהֶם, referring back to "your forefathers" אֲבֹתֵיכֶם, which can be omitted in English translation.

כֹּה אָמַר יְהוָה צְבָאוֹת. Qal *qatal* 3 m s √אמר.

שׁוּבוּ נָא מִדַּרְכֵיכֶם הָרָעִים וּמַעַלְלֵיכֶם הָרָעִים. Qal impv 2 m pl √שׁוב. The particle נָא quite often occurs with an imperative (see Hag 2:2). The call to repent issued to Zechariah's hearers (v. 3 שׁוּבוּ) was also issued to the forefathers by the prophets of previous generations. It may be that we are dealing with a specific intertextual reference to Jer 25:5-7 שׁוּבוּ־נָא אִישׁ מִדַּרְכּוֹ הָרָעָה וּמֵרֹעַ מַעַלְלֵיכֶם, as some have argued (e.g., Wenzel 2011a: 62; Stead, 31–32). Due to the parallel with מִדַּרְכֵיכֶם, BHQ (133*) argues that a מִן preposition has been dropped from מַעַלְלֵיכֶם due to haplography. Emendation is unnecessary, however, for although prepositions are often repeated with enumerated objects, this is not always the case (JM §132g), and they can be understood on the basis of parallelism. Instead of the Ketiv's וּמַעֲלִילֵיכֶם, most scholars adopt the Qere reading of וּמַעַלְלֵיכֶם in accordance with the usage of the noun מַעֲלָל in verse 6. Petersen (127) attempts to read the Ketiv as מִן plus the noun עֲלִילָה, which is similar in meaning to מַעֲלָל, but this does not commend itself as the plural form would be עֲלִילוֹת. Appealing to the principle of lectio difficilior, BHQ (133*) argues that מעליל is "most likely a genuine byform of the more common מעלל," but this would be the only certain occurrence of the form anywhere in premodern Hebrew (on its possible restoration in the fragmentary 4Q370 i 2 and 4Q381; cf. Broshi et al., 91–93 and Eshel, 136–37, respectively). דֶּרֶךְ and מַעֲלָל frequently occur together (Jdg 2:19; Jer 4:18; 7:3, 5; 17:10; 18:11; 23:22; 25:5; 26:3, 13; 32:19; 35:15; Ezek 36:31; Hos 4:9; 12:3). On the whole, then, it is safest to assume that the Ketiv represents a scribal error, which the Qere seeks to correct.

וְלֹא שָׁמְעוּ וְלֹא־הִקְשִׁיבוּ אֵלַי נְאֻם־יְהוָה. Qal *qatal* 3 c pl √שמע and Hifil *qatal* 3 c pl √קשׁב. These two verbs form a common word pair: 1 Sam 15:22; Job 13:6; 33:31; Pss 10:17; 17:1; 61:2; etc.

1:5 אֲבוֹתֵיכֶם אַיֵּה־הֵם וְהַנְּבִאִים הַלְעוֹלָם יִחְיוּ׃

אֲבוֹתֵיכֶם אַיֵּה־הֵם. The interrogative אַיֵּה occurs often (48×) but never takes a verb, in contrast to אֵיפֹה (BDB, 32).

וְהַנְּבִאִים הַלְעוֹלָם יִחְיוּ. Qal *yiqtol* 3 m pl √חיה. Although the lexical meaning of הַנְּבִאִים is not problematic, the referent is debated in this instance since it stands in parallelism to a group that falls under condemnation (אֲבוֹתֵיכֶם). Some maintain that it has the same referent as "the earlier prophets" of verse 4 and "my servants the prophets" in verse 6 and thus expresses either that both the righteous and the wicked suffered the effects of the exile or the more general reality that all men are mortal (cf. Petersen, 133–34). Yet it is difficult to see how either point would serve the prophet's exhortation to his contemporaries, and others argue on the basis of the parallelism that הַנְּבִאִים must refer to "*false* prophets." Stead (82) appeals to intertextual factors in favor of this second option. He argues that this pericope has been influenced by Jeremiah (see v. 4), in which the common term "prophets" (43×) without qualification has a negative connotation in contrast to the positive connotation of the phrase "my servants the prophets." On the whole, this approach seems to create the fewest problems. In this case, then, the definite article on הַנְּבִאִים may be equivalent to a possessive pronoun (JM §137I2; WB §85; WO §13.5.1e), "(their) prophets."

The verb יִֽחְיֽוּ could have different temporal or modal nuances. Petersen (127, 133), e.g., translates it as a past tense: "Did they live forever?" Probably it is best to understand a modal nuance in this instance, indicating impossibility: "Could they live forever?"

1:6 אַ֣ךְ ׀ דְּבָרַ֣י וְחֻקַּ֗י אֲשֶׁ֤ר צִוִּ֙יתִי֙ אֶת־עֲבָדַ֣י הַנְּבִיאִ֔ים
הֲל֖וֹא הִשִּׂ֣יגוּ אֲבֹתֵיכֶ֑ם וַיָּשׁ֣וּבוּ וַיֹּאמְר֗וּ כַּאֲשֶׁ֨ר זָמַ֜ם
יְהוָ֤ה צְבָאוֹת֙ לַעֲשׂ֣וֹת לָ֔נוּ כִּדְרָכֵ֙ינוּ֙ וּכְמַ֣עֲלָלֵ֔ינוּ כֵּ֖ן
עָשָׂ֥ה אִתָּֽנוּ׃ ס

אַ֣ךְ ׀ דְּבָרַ֣י וְחֻקַּ֗י אֲשֶׁ֤ר צִוִּ֙יתִי֙ אֶת־עֲבָדַ֣י הַנְּבִיאִ֔ים הֲל֖וֹא הִשִּׂ֣יגוּ אֲבֹתֵיכֶ֑ם. Piel *qatal* 1 c s √צוה and Hifil *qatal* 3 c pl √נשׂג. The adverb אַךְ has "asseverative-emphatic" and "restrictive-adversative" functions, the former being translated by, e.g., "without a doubt, surely, truly" and the latter by, e.g., "howbeit, yet, but, only" (see Muraoka 1985: 129–30; cf. JM §164a; BDB, 36; Van der Merwe 1991: 304–9). The asseverative sense emerges when it is appreciated that the following question (הֲל֖וֹא הִשִּׂ֣יגוּ אֲבֹתֵיכֶ֑ם) is rhetorical and is to be taken as fully exclamatory (JM §161a–b): "*Surely/without a doubt*, my words and statutes . . . overtook your forefathers." The language of "words" and "decrees" (חֻקִּים) "overtaking" (Hifil √נשׂג) evildoers is drawn from the "covenant curses" of Lev 26:3, 15, 43 and Deut 28:15, 45 (cf. Meyers and Meyers, 95; Petersen, 134).

וַיָּשׁ֣וּבוּ וַיֹּאמְר֗וּ. Qal *wayyiqtol* 3 m pl √שׁוב and √אמר. The verb √שׁוב again has the sense of "repent" (see v. 3). Some take this as continuing the reference to the actions of the forefathers in verses 4-6a (e.g., Wolters 2014: 39), describing the repentance of a previous generation. In light of what has been said of the forefathers already (e.g., 1:2, 4-5), however, this seems most unlikely. Instead, this is to be taken as a narrative comment indicating the penitent response of Zechariah's audience (cf. Meyers and Meyers, 96). It is on account of this "return" that YHWH will shortly announce his own "return" to Jerusalem (1:16). As such it indicates that Zechariah's hearers are indeed taking care "not to be like their fathers" (see v. 4).

כַּאֲשֶׁר זָמַם יְהוָה צְבָאוֹת לַעֲשׂוֹת לָנוּ כִּדְרָכֵינוּ וּכְמַעֲלָלֵינוּ כֵּן עָשָׂה אִתָּנוּ. Qal *qatal* 3 m s √זמם, Qal inf cstr √עשׂה with לְ preposition, and Qal *qatal* 3 m s √עשׂה. The verb √זמם "to devise, plan, purpose" takes an infinitive construct as a complement in a number of instances (Gen 11:6; Deut 19:19; Ps 31:14; Zech 8:14-15; 1QpHab 12:6; 4Q171 f1_2 ii 14; 4Q381 f45 a-b 2; 11Q19 61:10). It occurs with the construction כֵּן . . . כַּאֲשֶׁר here and in Zech 8:14-15, though in the latter passage there is a temporal contrast of YHWH's past and future "purposes," while in this verse the temporal reference is only past. According to the structure of the sentence, כִּדְרָכֵינוּ וּכְמַעֲלָלֵינוּ is to be linked with the infinitival phrase לַעֲשׂוֹת לָנוּ, rather than the following עָשָׂה אִתָּנוּ (contra Petersen, 127), as rendered in the translation above. The verb עשׂה can take a variety of prepositions, including אֵת "with."

First Vision (Zechariah 1:7-17)
A Rider upon a Horse

Zechariah's hortatory prologue placed the book in the second year of King Darius (1:1). This initial vision further specifies the precise date and nocturnal setting (v. 7), and the lack of later dating markers has widely been taken to mean that the visions of chapters 1–6 occurred on the same night (Schöpflin, 190; Petersen, 111). In this unit the prophet sees a rider upon a horse, with other horsemen standing at the ready behind him. Having patrolled the earth, they report that all is quiet (v. 11), whereupon the angel of YHWH begs him to show compassion on Jerusalem and the cities of Judea. YHWH responds with "good, comforting words" (v. 13), affirming his "zeal" for Jerusalem (v. 14), which will be expressed in part by his "great wrath" against the nations (v. 15). YHWH further declares that he has "returned" to Jerusalem (v. 16), a result of which being that his house will be rebuilt and the people will experience prosperity again (v. 17). YHWH's "return" to Jerusalem is in accord with the promise of verse 3 and the people's repentance in verse 6a.

Angelic intermediaries feature prominently in this vision as they do elsewhere in the cycle. One must always bear in mind that the term מַלְאָךְ in the HB can refer to purely human "messengers" (e.g., Haggai is called the מַלְאַךְ־יהוה "messenger of YHWH" in Hag 1:13), but one regularly encounters supernatural beings in Second Temple visionary literature, and this is clearly the intent of מַלְאָךְ here. The appearance of different מַלְאָכִים in this pericope creates some interpretive perplexity and has caused some to allege the presence of redactional layers in the text (e.g., Hallaschka 2010). The mention of the "angel of YHWH" (מַלְאַךְ־יהוה) in verses 11-12 raises the perennial question as to whether (and how) this angel is distinct from YHWH himself (see the instructive debate between Lopez and Malone; cf. also Paul). Some distinction between the two is implied in verse 10, where the angel reports YHWH's actions, and is made explicit in verse 12 when the angel calls out to YHWH. The number of angelic figures present in the pericope has been a point of contention. A full interaction with the different scholarly views on the subject is not possible here, but the present handbook follows the "two angel" analysis of Clark (1982: 214–15; cf. Schöpflin, 192) as the simplest explanation of the participants in the text. Specifically, the rider on the red horse "between the myrtles" (vv. 8, 10) is to be identified with the "angel of YHWH" in light of verse 11 (מַלְאַךְ יְהוָה הָעֹמֵד בֵּין הַהֲדַסִּים) and is distinct from הַמַּלְאָךְ הַדֹּבֵר בִּי "the angel who spoke with me" (vv. 9, 13, and 14). This latter figure, the so-called "Interpreting Angel," appears repeatedly in the night visions (2:2 [ET: 1:19], 7 [ET: 2:3]; 4:1, 5; 5:5, 10; 6:4) to help explain them to the prophet, and thus has a distinct identity. Analogous examples of "interpreting angels" are found elsewhere in the HB and in Second Temple apocalypses and have been the subject of much scholarly study (see, e.g., Schöpflin). In addition to these two angelic figures, YHWH appears as one of the text's participants in verse 13 by addressing the "interpreting angel." Whether this took place as a theophany or as a purely auditory phenomenon is left indeterminate.

7*On the twenty-fourth day of the eleventh month, which is the month of Shevat, in the second year of Darius, the word of YHWH came to Zechariah, the son of Berekiah, the son of Iddo, the prophet:*

8*Last night I saw, and behold a man, a rider upon a copper red horse, and he was waiting between the myrtles by the ocean deep, and behind him were copper red, dapple-grey, and white horses.*

9*And I said, "What are these, my lord?" And the angel who was speaking with me said to me, "I shall let you see what these are."*

10*And the man sitting between the myrtles answered and he said, "These are the ones whom YHWH sent to go about in the earth."*

11*And they answered the angel of YHWH who was standing between the myrtles and they said, "We have gone about in the earth, and behold, all the earth is inhabited and quiet."*

[12]*And the angel of YHWH answered and said, "O YHWH Tsevaot, how long will you not show mercy on Jerusalem and the cities of Judah, which you have denounced for these seventy years?"*

[13]*And YHWH answered good, comforting words to the angel who was speaking with me.*

[14]*And the angel who was speaking with me said to me, "Call out: 'Thus has YHWH Tsevaot said: I am exceedingly zealous for Jerusalem and for Zion.*

[15]*And I am growing exceedingly wrathful against the complacent nations; for I was wrathful a little, but they assisted with harmful intent.*

[16]*Therefore,'—thus has YHWH said—'I have returned to Jerusalem with mercy. My house shall be built in it'—oracle of YHWH Tsevaot—'and a line shall be stretched over Jerusalem.'*

[17]*Keep calling out: 'Thus has YHWH Tsevaot said, My cities shall again overflow from prosperity, and YHWH shall again comfort Zion and shall again choose Jerusalem.'"*

1:7 בְּיוֹם֩ עֶשְׂרִ֨ים וְאַרְבָּעָ֜ה לְעַשְׁתֵּֽי־עָשָׂ֥ר חֹ֙דֶשׁ֙ הוּא־
חֹ֣דֶשׁ שְׁבָ֔ט בִּשְׁנַ֥ת שְׁתַּ֖יִם לְדָרְיָ֑וֶשׁ הָיָ֣ה דְבַר־יְהוָ֗ה
אֶל־זְכַרְיָה֙ בֶּן־בֶּ֣רֶכְיָ֔הוּ בֶּן־עִדּ֥וֹא הַנָּבִ֖יא לֵאמֹֽר׃

בְּיוֹם֩ עֶשְׂרִ֨ים וְאַרְבָּעָ֜ה לְעַשְׁתֵּֽי־עָשָׂ֥ר חֹ֙דֶשׁ֙ הוּא־חֹ֣דֶשׁ שְׁבָ֔ט בִּשְׁנַ֥ת שְׁתַּ֖יִם לְדָרְיָ֑וֶשׁ. On the use of לְ in dating formulae, see Hag 1:1. Meyers and Meyers (108) find it "curious" that the day and month are mentioned before the year, but the same order occurs in Hag 2:10 (see the introductory remarks to Hag 1:12-15a). שְׁבָט is the name for the eleventh month in the Babylonian calendar; it is a *hapax* in BH, though it occurs in RH and in various inscriptions and papyri from the Second Temple period (see Shin, 117–18). The explanatory phrase הוּא־חֹ֣דֶשׁ שְׁבָ֔ט may seem like an odd or unnecessary intrusion, but the preexilic system of designating months with numbers or with Canaanite names was becoming obsolete, and the names of months were in the process of being replaced by their Babylonian names (Shin, 119).[1]

[1] Ehrensvärd (2006: 186) denies that this is a linguistic feature relevant to diachronic dating of language, but if so then his definition of what constitutes a "linguistic feature" is most unclear. Calendrical names pertain to the lexicon of a given language and thus are of potential value in diachronic analysis.

הָיָה דְבַר־יְהוָה אֶל־זְכַרְיָה בֶּן־בֶּרֶכְיָהוּ בֶּן־עִדּוֹא הַנָּבִיא לֵאמֹר. Qal *qatal* 3 m s √היה and Qal inf cstr √אמר. On the use of היה with אֶל, see Hag 1:1. הַנָּבִיא could be understood as standing apposition either to "Iddo" or to "Zechariah" (see 1:1). On the spelling of "Berechiah" with the ending ־יהו instead of ־יה, see 1:1. "Iddo" is spelled עִדּוֹא here, in contrast to עִדּוֹ in 1:1. Shin (96–97) argues that the spelling with *alef* is part of an orthographical trend in LBH texts. Wolters claims that the use of the infinitive construct לֵאמֹר is "anomalous," since "its normal usage would imply that it is the Lord himself who speaks the words that follow" (2014: 48), instead of the prophet speaking in his own voice, as in this instance. Yet this evaluation is based on an overly wooden understanding of this prophetic formula (and even if it were an anomaly, it would pertain to the use of the formula as a whole, not to the infinitive construct לֵאמֹר specifically). Naturally, when the formula introduces direct discourse it is most often a quotation from YHWH himself rather than a prophet. However, one of the main functions of the formula is simply to indicate that divine communication has occurred, and it is the vision about to be reported by the prophet that constitutes the revelation or message from YHWH. The fact that the prophet describes it from the standpoint of his own experience, rather than presenting it as the *ipsissima verba Dei*, is in accord with this basic function. For further discussion, see the Appendix (§1).

1:8 רָאִיתִי ׀ הַלַּיְלָה וְהִנֵּה־אִישׁ רֹכֵב עַל־סוּס אָדֹם
וְהוּא עֹמֵד בֵּין הַהֲדַסִּים אֲשֶׁר בַּמְּצֻלָה וְאַחֲרָיו
סוּסִים אֲדֻמִּים שְׂרֻקִּים וּלְבָנִים׃

רָאִיתִי ׀ הַלַּיְלָה. Qal *qatal* 1 c s √ראה. The verb √ראה can occur without a direct object in the sense of "to receive revelation" (BDB, 906–7, #1 b). Petersen (138) calls רָאִיתִי ׀ הַלַּיְלָה an "awkward formulation" since it lacks a preposition, but indirect or adverbial accusatives are common in BH, and this is easily explained as a temporal accusative or an "accusative of temporal determination" (JM §126i; WB √56a–b; AC √2.3.2b; MNK §33.3i; WO §10.2.2c; GKC §118i, k). Although many understand הַלַּיְלָה as a general adverbial idea of "at night," its use in conjunction with the precise dating formula of verse 7 favors the rendering "last night" (Petersen, 136–37; cf. BDB, 539).

וְהִנֵּה־אִישׁ רֹכֵב עַל־סוּס אָדֹם. Qal ptc m s √רכב. Many have perceived a difficulty in that the man is here described as "riding" but in the following clause as "standing" (cf. Tiemeyer 2015: 70–71). Yet it should be recalled that not only can the participle be verbal in nature, indicating an action in process, but also substantival as well. In this case, it is more fitting to understand רֹכֵב as a substantive indicating a "rider," as it does frequently (e.g., Gen 49:17; Exod 15:1, 21; Jdg 5:10; 2 Kgs 9:18-19; 18:23; Esth 8:10, 14; Job 39:18; Isa 36:8; Jer 51:21; Ezek 23:6, 12, 23; 38:15; Amos 2:15; Hag 2:22; Zech 10:5; 12:4), thus standing in apposition to אִישׁ. In Zechariah some "I saw" statements are followed by verbal clauses (5:9; 6:1) and others by verbless clauses (2:1 [ET: 1:18], 5 [ET: 2:1]; in 5:1 the participle עָפָה "flying" is functioning as an adjectival modifier of the noun מְגִלָּה). Thus the clause should be translated "behold, a man, *a rider* upon a copper-red horse" rather than "behold, a man *was riding* upon a copper-red horse" (so most translations). Regarding סוּס אָדֹם, Clark (2005; 1982: 216–17) notes that when speaking of horses, the color "red" must refer to a less vivid shade with more of a brownish hue, hence the rendering "copper red" above. On the other colors, see below.

וְהוּא עֹמֵד בֵּין הַהֲדַסִּים אֲשֶׁר בַּמְּצֻלָה. Qal ptc m s √עמד. The subject of וְהוּא עֹמֵד could be either the man or the horse, but in verse 10 the participle is in apposition to "the man" (הָאִישׁ הָעֹמֵד), making the former option the most probable. In that case the verb √עמד does not refer to standing physically (since the man is mounted upon the horse) but rather to stopping or standing still (BDB, 764, #2).

בֵּין הַהֲדַסִּים. The LXX reads "the mountains" instead of הַהֲדַסִּים ("the myrtles") here and in verses 10-11, which is either an intentional attempt to assimilate the verse to 6:1 (so *BHQ*, 119) or else a copyist's misreading of ההדסים as ההרים (though not ההררים as suggested by Wolters [2014: 50], since the triliteral form never occurs in the absolute state). The word הָדָס itself is not very common in BH (Neh 8:15; Isa 41:19; 55:13; Zech 1:8, 10, 11) or in the DSS,[2] though it is attested in RH (Jastrow, 334) and there is little doubt over its meaning of "myrtle." It is the word's exegetical significance, not its lexical meaning, that is debated in this instance. The phrase "among the myrtles" possibly indicates myrtle branches strewn as a sign of welcome for a triumphant conqueror (cf. Matt 21:8; Mark 11:8; John 12:3; Rev 7:9). See also the following on the noun מְצֻלָה.

[2] There is only one reconstructed form in 4Q219 2:7.

אֲשֶׁר בַּמְּצֻלָה. In contrast to the preceding הַהֲדַסִּים, not only is the exegetical significance of מְצוּלָה hotly disputed but so is its lexical meaning. The biblical attestation of מְצוּלָה quite clearly demonstrates it to mean "ocean deeps" (cf. BDB, 846–47), and this is amply supported by its DSS occurrences as well (1QH[a] 11:7, 15; 16:20; 4Q158 14 i 7; 4Q286 5 a–c 9; 4Q418 119 2–3), yet many scholars find this inappropriate to the context and argue that here it means "valley" or "glen," possibly indicating a kind of Edenic setting (e.g. Petersen, 139). The LXX reads τῶν κατασκίων (similarly Peshitta), causing *BHS* to suggest a reading of אשר בַּמְּצִלָּה, indicating a place of shade (Meyers and Meyers, 110; Wolters 2014: 52). In fact, מְצוּלָה represents an "ungrammaticality" (see Introduction §3) alerting the reader to an intertext necessary for interpreting the speaker's meaning. In light of the references to "horses," "riders," and particularly the "deep," it seems highly likely that we are dealing with an intertextual echo of Exod 15 (cf. Kline, 7), which likewise contains pervasive references to "horses" and "riders" (nominalized participles of √רכב; see vv. 1, 19, 21 and on Hag 2:22) being thrown into the "deeps" (v. 5 מְצוֹלֹת). Notably, the same term מְצוֹלֹת also occurs in an echo of Exod 15 in Neh 9:11. For discussion of the intertextual influence of Exod 15 on a variety of biblical texts, see Russell. In conjunction with the preceding reference to "myrtles," the text is suggestive of a victory that has just taken place.

וְאַחֲרָיו סוּסִים אֲדֻמִּים שְׂרֻקִּים וּלְבָנִים. The colors of the horses have persistently vexed commentators (e.g., Petersen, 141–43; Meyers and Meyers, 111–13; Clark 2005; Wolters 2014: 5354; Tiemeyer 2015: 62–67). The term לְבָנִים "white" is relatively straightforward, and on אֲדֻמִּים, see above. The meaning of שְׂרֻקִּים, however, is most uncertain. It is often glossed as "sorrel" in the lexica of BH and RH (e.g., BDB, 977; Jastrow, 1629), indicating a reddish-brown color. It is difficult to know what distinction this would then have from the preceding אֲדֻמִּים, though multiple shades of brown are used to describe horses both in ancient Mesopotamian records and in modern equine classification systems (Petersen, 141). But there is little firm data to support this sense, apart from some possible Arabic cognates (see BDB, 977). Some uses of Hifil √שרק (Sir 43:9 [M, B margin]; 50:7 [MsB]) could arguably indicate a reddish color (so *DCH* 8, 198) but need not refer to a color at all, and "sparkle" or "shine brightly" would also be possible glosses. The only other occurrence of the adjective שָׂרֹק in pre-RH is in Isa 16:8, where it refers to a "vine-tendril" and may be a separate lexeme altogether (so BDB, 977; *DCH* 8, 198). Though there are some textual variants (Ziegler, 292), the LXX uses two words for MT's שְׂרֻקִּים, namely ψαρός "dapple-grey" and ποικίλος "multi-colored" (Muraoka 2009: 741 and 571), and this option finds some support in the medieval Jewish tradition (Wolters 2014: 53). The LXX rendering is often thought to be an attempt to harmonize the number of horse teams in this vision to that of 6:1-8 (so *BHQ*, 134*; Tiemeyer 2015: 65), but all the same it seems to provide the only substantive guidance on the matter, and thus this handbook has opted for the rendering "dapple-grey" above (similarly Lowe, 19–20).

1:9 וָאֹמַר מָה־אֵלֶּה אֲדֹנִי וַיֹּאמֶר אֵלַי הַמַּלְאָךְ הַדֹּבֵר
בִּי אֲנִי אַרְאֶךָּ מָה־הֵמָּה אֵלֶּה׃

וָאֹמַר מָה־אֵלֶּה אֲדֹנִי. Qal *wayyiqtol* 1 c s √אמר. Several times in the Night Visions the prophet asks מָה־אֵלֶּה (2:2, 4; 4:4, 13; 6:4), inquiring into the significance of what is being viewed, not the content of the vision (cf. Rogland 2014e: 79). Thus the question is asking, "What do these things *mean*?" rather than "What *are* these things?" See also Ezek 17:12; 24:19; 37:18; Zech 6:3.

וַיֹּאמֶר אֵלַי הַמַּלְאָךְ הַדֹּבֵר בִּי. Qal *wayyiqtol* 3 m s √אמר and Qal ptc m s √דבר with def art. On the Interpreting Angel, see the introductory remarks to this pericope. Except for one instance of the infinitive construct (Ps 51:6), the only usage of √דבר in the Qal *binyan* is in the participle (39×, 11 of which are comprised by this Zecharian expression). On the temporal and aspectual significance of attributive ptcs, see Hag 1:6.

אֲנִי אַרְאֶךָּ מָה־הֵמָּה אֵלֶּה. Hifil *yiqtol* 1 c s √ראה with 2 m s pronoun suffix. Ehrlich (326) draws attention to the use of Hifil √ראה as opposed to, e.g., Hifil √נגד. The answer to the prophet's question will come not from the Interpreting Angel but from the rider on the horse/angel of Yahweh in verse 10. The Interpreting Angel is allowing the prophet's question to be answered by the participants in the vision, and the Hifil has a permissive-tolerative sense here of "to let someone see something" (Creason 246–48, 283–84; WO §27.5; AC §3.1.6e). The use of אֲנִי with a finite verb already indicating the first person singular is noteworthy since it is not necessary from a grammatical standpoint. In a careful study of emphatic structures in BH, Muraoka notes that this often occurs in responses and promises—both of which are the case here—since a speaker is especially self-conscious when making such utterances (1985: 53–54; cf. JM §146a3).

מָה־הֵ֫מָּה אֵ֫לֶּה. As noted above, the prophet asks מָה־אֵ֫לֶּה a number of times. The angel's response in in the form of an indirect question and utilizes the 3 pl personal pronoun הֵ֫מָּה. In fact, there is some variation in such direct and indirect questions: sometimes the independent personal pronoun is included (1:9; 4:5) and other times it is not (4:13; Ezek 7:12). The inclusion of the pronoun alongside a grammatical predicate (which can be an interrogative pronoun: JM §154j) and subject (here: אֵ֫לֶּה) creates what is termed a "tripartite nominal clause" (cf. JM §154i). As it turns out, the question of the tripartite nominal clause has provoked sharp debate among grammarians of Hebrew and other Semitic languages, particularly as to whether the personal pronoun adds a distinguishable semantic force (so Muraoka 1985: 67–82) or whether it sometimes serves as a pure copula ("is/are") in such constructions (so Holmstedt and Jones, with references to recent literature). With the word order here (subject–personal pronoun–predicate) the pronoun gives some prominence to the preceding clause constituent (JM §154j). Thus the angel's reply is not "I will show you what *these* are," as if the prophet is unclear as to what he is seeing, but rather "I will show you *what* these are," i.e., what they signify (see above).

1:10 וַיַּ֜עַן הָאִ֨ישׁ הָעֹמֵ֤ד בֵּין־הַהֲדַסִּים֙ וַיֹּאמַ֔ר אֵ֚לֶּה אֲשֶׁ֣ר שָׁלַ֣ח יְהוָ֔ה לְהִתְהַלֵּ֖ךְ בָּאָֽרֶץ׃

וַיַּ֜עַן הָאִ֨ישׁ הָעֹמֵ֤ד בֵּין־הַהֲדַסִּים֙ וַיֹּאמַ֔ר. Qal *wayyiqtol* 3 m s √ענה, Qal ptc m s √עמד with def art, and Qal *wayyiqtol* 3 m s √אמר. On √ענה in the sense of "to respond," see Hag 2:14 (so also in vv. 11-12). Even though the prophet posed his question to the interpreting angel, the rider on the horse responds. On הֲדַס, see verse 8.

אֵ֚לֶּה אֲשֶׁ֣ר שָׁלַ֣ח יְהוָ֔ה לְהִתְהַלֵּ֖ךְ בָּאָֽרֶץ. Qal *qatal* 3 m s √שלח and Hitpael inf cstr √הלך with לְ preposition. The particle אֲשֶׁר is often used to create substantival clauses in any of the grammatical cases, thus in this instance: "(the ones) whom YHWH sent to walk around in the earth." The verb √שלח frequently takes an infinitive construct as a complement (e.g., Gen 3:23; 8:8; 19:13; etc.). In general the Hitpael of √הלך conveys more than the simple action of walking but instead typically indicates "walking about" or "walking to and fro," sometimes in the sense of "traversing" or "patrolling" (BDB, 235–36). The terminology of "walking to and fro in the earth" seems to be an intertextual echo of Job 1–2 (Stead, 87).

1:11 וַיַּעֲנ֞וּ אֶת־מַלְאַ֣ךְ יְהוָ֗ה הָעֹמֵד֙ בֵּ֣ין הַהֲדַסִּ֔ים וַיֹּאמְר֖וּ
הִתְהַלַּ֣כְנוּ בָאָ֑רֶץ וְהִנֵּ֥ה כָל־הָאָ֖רֶץ יֹשֶׁ֥בֶת וְשֹׁקָֽטֶת׃

וַיַּעֲנ֞וּ אֶת־מַלְאַ֣ךְ יְהוָ֗ה הָעֹמֵד֙ בֵּ֣ין הַהֲדַסִּ֔ים וַיֹּאמְר֖וּ. Qal *wayyiqtol* 3 m pl √ענה, Qal ptc m s √עמד with def art, and Qal *wayyiqtol* 3 m pl √אמר. On הַהֲדַסִּים see verse 8. As noted in the introduction to this pericope, the description of the angel of YHWH as "the one who was standing between the myrtles" indicates his identity with the "rider on the copper red horse" of verse 8.

הִתְהַלַּ֣כְנוּ בָאָ֑רֶץ. Hitpael *qatal* 1 c pl √הלך. On the meaning of the verb, see verse 10.

וְהִנֵּ֥ה כָל־הָאָ֖רֶץ יֹשֶׁ֥בֶת וְשֹׁקָֽטֶת. Qal ptc f s √ישב and Qal ptc f s √שקט (pausal form with *qameṣ* instead of *segol*). The verb √ישב is used in speaking of a land or city to indicate that it is inhabited (BDB, 443, #4; Stead, 90 n. 56); cf. 7:7 בִּהְי֤וֹת יְרוּשָׁלַ֙ם יֹשֶׁ֙בֶת֙ וּשְׁלֵוָ֔ה "when Jerusalem was inhabited and peaceful." Petersen (145) notes that √שקט "is regularly used to describe geographic areas" such as cities (2 Chron 23:21), nations (Josh 11:23; Jer 48:11), and "all the earth" (Isa 14:7), and suggests that here the expression refers to "regions not involved in military activity or civil strife." The report sounds positive at first, but it will provoke an impassioned response from the angel of YHWH in the following verse. It appears, then, that a contrast is being drawn on the one hand between the "earth" at large, which is at peace but under pagan domination (cf. v. 15), and Jerusalem and the cities of Judea on the other, which are still experiencing ruin and hard times.

1:12 וַיַּ֣עַן מַלְאַךְ־יְהוָה֮ וַיֹּאמַר֒ יְהוָ֣ה צְבָא֔וֹת עַד־מָתַ֗י
אַתָּה֙ לֹֽא־תְרַחֵ֣ם אֶת־יְרוּשָׁלַ֔͏ִם וְאֵ֖ת עָרֵ֣י יְהוּדָ֑ה
אֲשֶׁ֣ר זָעַ֔מְתָּה זֶ֖ה שִׁבְעִ֥ים שָׁנָֽה׃

וַיַּ֣עַן מַלְאַךְ־יְהוָה֮ וַיֹּאמַר֒ יְהוָ֣ה צְבָא֔וֹת. Qal *wayyiqtol* 3 m s √ענה and Qal wayyiqtol 3 m s √אמר. יְהוָ֣ה צְבָא֔וֹת is to be understood as a vocative: "O YHWH Tsevaot."

עַד־מָתַ֗י אַתָּה֙ לֹֽא־תְרַחֵ֣ם אֶת־יְרוּשָׁלַ֔͏ִם וְאֵ֖ת עָרֵ֣י יְהוּדָ֑ה. Piel *yiqtol* 2 m s √רחם. On its own, the interrogative particle מָתַי asks "when?"

but when preceded by עַד the syntagm means "until when?" or "how long?" The only other instance of עַד־מָתַי followed by a negated verb is Hos 8:5 עַד־מָתַי לֹא יוּכְלוּ נִקָּיֹן, "How long will they be incapable of innocence?" Since אַתָּה is not grammatically necessary in עַד־מָתַי אַתָּה לֹא־תְרַחֵם it is legitimate to ask what its significance here might be (cf. on v. 9). Mitchell (130) says that it is not for emphasis but rather for "rhythmical effect" (GKC §135a), but Muraoka (1985: 48) disputes such an explanation, and observes that the personal pronoun is often found with a finite verb when "a situation is described in which strong emotional heightening is involved" (1985: 50, 58). Such is certainly the case here, as the angel of YHWH pleads for compassion upon Jerusalem. The name יְרוּשָׁלִָם is a case of "Qere perpetuum,"—that is, the standard consonantal written form is not what is regularly pronounced, but being such a commonly occurring word, the marginal notes do not indicate the desired reading of יְרוּשָׁלַיִם (JM §16f4).

אֲשֶׁר זָעַמְתָּה זֶה שִׁבְעִים שָׁנָה. Qal *qatal* 2 m s √זעם. The Qal of √זעם can take an accusative object, which can be a nation such as Israel (Num 23:7) or a "people" (עַם) as in Mal 1:4. The verb is glossed both as "to be angry, indignant" as well as "to curse, scold, denounce" (BDB, 276; *HALOT*, 276–77). These are potentially widely divergent notions, one relating to an emotional state and the other to a speech act, and either sense could possibly overlap significantly with many other BH terms in the semantic field of either "anger" or "cursing." The analysis of Kotzé (2004: 107; 2005: 121) which argues that √זעם, √חמה, and √קצף are fundamentally rooted in a metonymy of anger expressed by "foaming at the mouth," possibly as the result of an epileptic seizure is most unlikely. The evidence for such an origin is slim at best, at least as far as √זעם is concerned; the verb certainly does not indicate this, and the noun זַעַם is only rarely linked with the "mouth/lips" (Isa 30:27) or "tongue" (Hos 7:16). Kruger derives the biblical understanding of anger chiefly from the notion of "heat," though he does not address the √זעם word-group specifically. Van Wolde (8 n. 11) argues that the verb √זעם "designates 'be angry' or 'express anger in speech,'" which is true as far as it goes, but her analysis (following BDB, 276) becomes speculative when she appeals to an Arabic cognate meaning "roar of a camel" and claims that "noise" and "the stammering of the tongue" are the conceptual base of anger for this root (8; see Aitken 135–36). It should be observed that forms of the verb √זעם occur in conjunction with Hebrew terms for "cursing" such as √ארר or √קבב in BH (Num

23:7-8; Prov 24:24) and in most of the clear contexts in the DSS (1QS 2:7; 1QM 13:1, 4, 5; 4Q280 2:5; 4Q286 7 ii 1, 3, 4, 5), though there are a number of occurrences in BH in which the notion of a verbal "curse" is not absolutely necessary (Ps 7:12; Prov 22:14; Isa 66:14; Dan 11:30; Mic 6:10; Mal 1:4; see also Sir 3:16 [MsC]). Taking these factors together, the most fitting sense of the verb √זעם appears to be "to denounce," a speech act which, depending on the pragmatic context, easily lends itself to being employed as a formal "curse" or act of repudiation. The historical referent of זָעַמְתָּה in verse 12 is the destruction of Jerusalem and the ensuing exile, and while these events were indeed to be understood as the fulfillment of YHWH's "covenant curses" of Lev 26 and Deut 28, it seems that in this instance זָעַמְתָּה is referring to them as an act of public censure or repudiation; by allowing the destruction and exile seventy years prior, YHWH had formally "repudiated" his people. For a more extensive semantic analysis of √זעם, see Aitken (144–50).

זֶה שִׁבְעִים שָׁנָה. Temporal accusative or an accusative of time (see v. 8). The same phrase occurs in 7:5, and the use of the singular זֶה instead of the plural אֵלֶּה is standard with the noun שָׁנָה "year," e.g., Gen 31:38 זֶה עֶשְׂרִים שָׁנָה "these twenty years"; Josh 14:10 זֶה אַרְבָּעִים וְחָמֵשׁ שָׁנָה "these forty-five years." On the phrase as an intertextual reference to Jer 25 and Jer 29, see Stead (93–95).

1:13 וַיַּעַן יְהוָה אֶת־הַמַּלְאָךְ הַדֹּבֵר בִּי דְּבָרִים טוֹבִים דְּבָרִים נִחֻמִים׃

וַיַּעַן יְהוָה אֶת־הַמַּלְאָךְ הַדֹּבֵר בִּי. Qal *wayyiqtol* 3 m s √ענה and Qal ptc m s √דבר with def art.

דְּבָרִים טוֹבִים דְּבָרִים נִחֻמִים. While the construction דְּבָרִים טוֹבִים "good words" is unexceptional, דְּבָרִים נִחֻמִים has proven more complicated, since נִחוּם "comfort, compassion" is not an adjective but a rare noun occurring only in Isa 57:18 and Hos 11:8 (its occurrence in 4Q417 is too fragmentary to provide any clarification). Wolters (2014: 64) proposes understanding דְּבָרִים as a construct plural דברי with an "enclitic *mem*," thus reading דְּבָרִים נִחֻמִים as a construct chain, claiming that this "makes for smoother Hebrew." Despite the enthusiasm of many for identifying possible examples of the "enclitic *mem*" in the HB (e.g., Cohen; Hummel; WO §9.8), the more cautious approach of others is advisable (e.g., Emerton 1996; JM §103g n. 22, §129u; Barr,

31–33). It seems highly unlikely that two occurrences of דְּבָרִים in rapid succession would be understood in such different ways, and the expression can easily be understood as an appositional construction (Mitchell, 130). It should be noted that the noun נִחוּם is only attested in the plural, and this is one of the common means for expressing an abstract idea or quality (JM §136g; WB §7; MNK §24.3.3vi; GKC §124d–f; WO §7.4.2). In addition, appositional structures are well attested for expressing concrete or abstract qualities of the noun modified (see the plentiful examples in JM §131c). The full phrase דְּבָרִים טוֹבִים דְּבָרִים נִחֻמִים can thus be translated "good, comforting words."

1:14 וַיֹּאמֶר אֵלַי הַמַּלְאָךְ הַדֹּבֵר בִּי קְרָא לֵאמֹר כֹּה אָמַר יְהוָה צְבָאוֹת קִנֵּאתִי לִירוּשָׁלִַם וּלְצִיּוֹן קִנְאָה גְדוֹלָה׃

וַיֹּאמֶר אֵלַי הַמַּלְאָךְ הַדֹּבֵר בִּי. Qal *wayyiqtol* 3 m s √אמר and Qal ptc m s √דבר with def art.

קְרָא לֵאמֹר. Qal impv 2 m s √קרא and Qal inf cstr √אמר. Having experienced the vision, the prophet is instructed to proclaim its message to others. Meyers and Meyers (119) suggest that קְרָא might indicate "reading" a written oracle, and while this is a possible meaning of √קרא, it is not contextually required here. The infinitive construct לֵאמֹר often introduces direct discourse following the verb √קרא (e.g., Exod 19:3; Num 22:5; Jdg 7:3; 16:18; etc.) and can be omitted in translation.

כֹּה אָמַר יְהוָה צְבָאוֹת. Qal *qatal* 3 m s √אמר.

קִנֵּאתִי לִירוּשָׁלִַם וּלְצִיּוֹן קִנְאָה גְדוֹלָה. Piel *qatal* 1 c s √קנא. On the "cognate accusative" קִנֵּאתִי . . . קִנְאָה, see verse 2. Wolters (2014: 64) rightly notes the wide semantic range of the verb √קנא, which denotes an admirable type of protective relational "jealousy" in addition to "zeal" for a particular purpose or goal. The statement is repeated almost verbatim in 8:2 but with the omission of לִירוּשָׁלִַם, even though references to "Jerusalem" greatly outnumber references to "Zion" in Zech 1–8 (17 vs. 6 occurrences). In this pericope, it seems likely that the combined reference to "Jerusalem and Zion" forms an *inclusio* with "Zion and Jerusalem" in verse 17.

1:15 וְקֶ֣צֶף גָּד֗וֹל אֲנִ֤י קֹצֵף֙ עַל־הַגּוֹיִ֣ם הַשַּׁאֲנַנִּ֔ים אֲשֶׁ֤ר
אֲנִי֙ קָצַ֣פְתִּי מְּעָ֔ט וְהֵ֖מָּה עָזְר֥וּ לְרָעָֽה׃

וְקֶ֣צֶף גָּד֗וֹל אֲנִ֤י קֹצֵף֙ עַל־הַגּוֹיִ֣ם הַשַּׁאֲנַנִּ֔ים. Qal ptc m s √קצף. The participle marks the actual present, indicating an action currently in process: "I *am growing* exceedingly wrathful." The statement creates a contrast with verse 14b, likewise utilizing a cognate accusative (see v. 14b): "I am exceedingly jealous for Jerusalem . . . I am growing exceedingly wrathful against the nations" (cf. Stead, 96 n. 85, 98). As in verse 2, the question arises as to whether עַל־הַגּוֹיִם indicates the prepositional object of the verb √קצף or "on account of" (see v. 2), though the former option is more likely.

הַשַּׁאֲנַנִּ֔ים. With the exception of Isa 32:18 and 33:20, the adjective שַׁאֲנָן "at ease, secure, complacent" is used in the HB in negative contexts indicating a presumptuous self-confidence that takes no heed of YHWH (2 Kgs 19:28; Job 12:5; Ps 123:4; Isa 32:9, 11; 37:29; Amos 6:1; cf. *HALOT*, 1375; *DCH* 8, 217). Stead (98–99) correctly notes that this statement is thematically linked with verse 11: וְהִנֵּ֥ה כָל־הָאָ֖רֶץ יֹשֶׁ֥בֶת וְשֹׁקָֽטֶת "and behold, all the earth is inhabited and quiet." The statement makes explicit that the quiet and peaceful state of the pagan world is displeasing to YHWH.

אֲשֶׁ֤ר אֲנִי֙ קָצַ֣פְתִּי מְּעָ֔ט וְהֵ֖מָּה עָזְר֥וּ לְרָעָֽה. Qal *qatal* 1 c s √קצף and Qal *qatal* 3 c pl √עזר. Some seek to translate אֲשֶׁר as a relative pronoun here (e.g., Meyers and Meyers: ". . . the nations . . . *with whom* I felt but little wrath" [107]), thus understanding "the nations" (הַגּוֹיִם) as the objects of God's wrath in this instance, with the point being to draw some kind of contrast between the "little" (מְעָט) anger expressed previously and the "great anger" (קֶצֶף גָּדוֹל) to come. Understood in this way it indicates a great increase in YHWH's wrath against the nations. Yet most commentators understand אֲנִי קָצַפְתִּי מְעָט to be speaking of YHWH's wrath against his own people. Thus a preferable alternative is to understand אֲשֶׁר as a causal conjunction (cf. GKC §158b; AC §5.2.5; WB §468; MNK §40.6.5; WO §38.4a; JM §170e; BDB, 83, #8c); the "little wrath" would then refer to YHWH's punishment of his own people, which, of course, is assumed to be perfectly just. The fact that the nations "assisted" in bringing calamity upon YHWH's people, however, is blameworthy and provokes him to "great wrath" (see below).

אֲנִי קָצַפְתִּי. The use of what appears to be a grammatically "unnecessary" personal pronoun with a finite verbal form (which already indicates the person and number of the subject) raises the question as to the pronoun's function (see v. 12). There can be a variety of reasons for this, but in this case it is being used to create a contrast or antithesis with וְהֵמָּה in the following clause (cf. Muraoka 1985: 54–57): "*I* was a little wrathful, but *they* . . ."

מְּעָט. The *dagesh* is a particular type of *dagesh forte* known as the *dagesh dirimens* or "separating *dagesh*" (JM §18k; GKC §20h). When certain consonants (such as *mem*) have a *sheva*, it is sometimes strengthened with a *dagesh forte* to make the letter more audible. The lexical question is whether מְעָט indicates the *duration* of YHWH's wrath or rather its *degree*. In other words, does it mean "I was angry *for a little while*" or "I was angry *a little*"? The former option is taken by Wolters (2014: 65), in which case it would be indicating that the "seventy years" of verse 12 are to be understood—at least from the divine perspective—as a "short time." However, it seems more likely that it is intended to indicate degree and to stand in contrast to the "great wrath" (קֶצֶף גָּדוֹל) of the preceding clause.

וְהֵמָּה עָזְרוּ לְרָעָה. This is often translated as "they furthered the disaster" (RSV) or "they helped the evil" (cf. Stead, 99), but an abstract entity as the object of this verb would be unparalleled, for when √עזר takes an object, whether a direct accusative or a prepositional object, the object is either a person or location (e.g., a city). Various interpretations and emendations have been proposed (see the extensive discussion by Wolters 2014: 65–67), but the simplest solution is to interpret the verb intransitively here (BDB, 740), with לְרָעָה indicating "for harm," as it does frequently (e.g., Gen 31:52; Deut 29:20; Jdg 2:15; Jer 21:10; Amos 9:4; Eccl 5:12; see BDB, 949, #2). The clause then indicates that the nations "assisted" in the execution of God's judgment against his people, but they did so with harmful intent, in contrast to YHWH's own righteous purposes.

1:16 לָכֵ֞ן כֹּֽה־אָמַ֣ר יְהוָ֗ה שַׁ֤בְתִּי לִירוּשָׁלִַ֙ם֙ בְּֽרַחֲמִ֔ים
בֵּיתִי֙ יִבָּ֣נֶה בָּ֔הּ נְאֻ֖ם יְהוָ֣ה צְבָא֑וֹת וְקָוֶה יִנָּטֶ֖ה עַל־
יְרוּשָׁלִָֽם׃

לָכֵ֞ן כֹּה־אָמַ֣ר יְהוָ֗ה. Qal *qatal* 3 m s √אמר. On the use of this "messenger formula" with inferential particles such as לָכֵן, see Hag 1:5 and the Appendix (§2B). The textual evidence for reading צְבָאוֹת after יהוה is not compelling (cf. *BHQ*, 122).

שַׁ֤בְתִּי לִירוּשָׁלִַ֙ם֙ בְּֽרַחֲמִ֔ים. Qal *qatal* 1 c s √שׁוב. There is no need to take שַׁבְתִּי as a "prophetic perfect" (so, e.g., Wolters 2014: 67–68), even though the following clause has a future tense (cf. Rogland 2003: 108); the past tense value of שַׁבְתִּי indicates that YHWH has already started to respond to the people's "repentance" just as he had promised (see vv. 3 and 6b). A similar statement is made in 8:3 though with a different (but semantically equivalent) preposition (שַׁבְתִּי אֶל־צִיּוֹן).

רַחֲמִים. "compassion, mercy" is either a plural of intensification (JM §136f; so BDB, 933) or, more likely, an abstract plural (JM §136g; so HALOT, 1218–19) of רֶ֫חֶם/רַ֫חַם. רַחֲמִים represents an older and rarer form of the masculine plural of segolate nouns built on the primitive singular form, as opposed to younger masculine plural forms such as סְפָרִים and מְלָכִים (see JM §96Ab). Kutscher (1959: 433) draws attention to the addition of the phrase ברחמים at 52:8 in the Great Isaiah Scroll of Qumran (thus יראו בשוב יהוה ציון ברחמים as opposed to the MT's יִרְאוּ בְּשׁוּב יְהוָה צִיּוֹן) and suggests that the idiom שׁוּב בְּרַחֲמִים is a late liturgical expression, seeing that it occurs in prayer formulae originating in the late Second Temple period, though a good deal of caution is in order (cf. Shin, 132–33). YHWH's return "with mercy" stands in contrast to his earlier anger against Jerusalem (v. 15) and provides the response to the angel of YHWH's question in verse 12: "How long *will you not show mercy* (אַתָּה לֹא־תְרַחֵם)?"

בֵּיתִי֙ יִבָּ֣נֶה בָּ֔הּ נְאֻם֙ יְהוָ֣ה צְבָא֔וֹת. Nifal *yiqtol* 3 m s √בנה. In this context the verb refers to "rebuilding" YHWH's house (see Hag 1:2).

וְקָוה יִנָּטֶ֖ה עַל־יְרוּשָׁלִָֽם. Nifal *yiqtol* 3 m s √נטה. For a similar variant of *Qere* (וְקָו) versus *Ketiv* (וקוה), see 1 Kgs 7:23 and Jer 31:39. The effects of YHWH's return begin with the temple rebuilding, but will expand to encompass Jerusalem in the following clause and the cities of Judea in verse 17. The term קָו is amply attested in BH and other corpora (1× in Sir and 10× in the DSS). It refers here to a "line" used either for measuring length or for checking alignment. A different term is encountered in Zech 2:1 [ET v. 5] חֶבֶל מִדָּה, but it seems to have the same function (Wolters 2014: 68); note that Jer 31:39 combines the terminology of Zech 1:16 and 2:1 with קָו הַמִּדָּה.

1:17 עֹ֣וד ׀ קְרָ֣א לֵאמֹ֗ר כֹּ֤ה אָמַר֙ יְהוָ֣ה צְבָא֔וֹת ע֛וֹד
תְּפוּצֶ֥ינָה עָרַ֖י מִטּ֑וֹב וְנִחַ֨ם יְהוָ֥ה עוֹד֙ אֶת־צִיּ֔וֹן
וּבָחַ֥ר ע֖וֹד בִּירוּשָׁלִָֽם׃

עֹ֣וד ׀ קְרָ֣א לֵאמֹ֗ר. Qal impv 2 m s √קרא and Qal inf cstr √אמר. On the imperative קְרָא, see verse 14. The infinitive construct לֵאמֹר simply introduces direct discourse, that is, what is to be proclaimed. The adverb עוֹד occurs four times in this verse and is clearly a key word. With the verbs תְּפוּצֶינָה, וְנִחַם, and וּבָחַר it indicates that something will happen "again." However, with the imperative קְרָא this notion does not fit as well, since there has been no indication of a break since the identical imperative קְרָא in verse 14. It must be remembered that the particle can express continuance, hence in this case it might be preferable to translate "*keep* calling out."

כֹּ֤ה אָמַר֙ יְהוָ֣ה צְבָא֔וֹת. Qal *qatal* 3 m s √אמר.

ע֛וֹד תְּפוּצֶ֥ינָה עָרַ֖י מִטּ֑וֹב. Qal *yiqtol* 3 f pl √פוק. There is disagreement whether there are two homonymous but distinct verbs, namely √פוק I "to spread, disperse, scatter" and √פוק II "to flow, overflow." Some lexica list both meanings under one lemma (e.g., *HALOT*, 918–19) whereas others provide separate lemmata (e.g., BDB, 806–7; *DCH* 6, 667–68), and Wolters (2014: 68) draws attention to the existence of two analogous cognates in Arabic, *faḍḍa* "to disperse" and *fāḍa* "to overflow." In any event, the sense of "overflow" is clearly attested in Prov 5:16 יָפוּצוּ מַעְיְנֹתֶיךָ חוּצָה בָּרְחֹבוֹת פַּלְגֵי־מָיִם, "Shall your springs overflow (LXX: ὑπερεκχείσθω) outside, (your) streams of water in the streets?" and is the most fitting here. This imagery is picked up in 2:8, where Jerusalem is presented as a "city without walls because of the multitude of people and livestock within it" (Stead, 101–2). The noun טוֹב here indicates "prosperity" (BDB, 375, #1). The preposition מִן has a range of uses and can indicate either the source of something or a cause or ground (BDB, 579–80); thus, מִטּוֹב could indicate that the cities will overflow "*from* prosperity" or "*on account of* good." The basic meaning would be very similar in either case.

וְנִחַ֨ם יְהוָ֥ה עוֹד֙ אֶת־צִיּ֔וֹן. Piel *weqatal* 3 m s √נחם. *BHS* suggests reading וְרִחַם instead of וְנִחַם, based on the LXX's καὶ ἐλεήσει, but *BHQ* (135*) notes that √נחם is rendered by ἐλεέω elsewhere (e.g. Isa 12:1; 49:13; 52:9; Ezek 24:14) and that the MT is supported by Tg and

Vulg. The change of subject from YHWH speaking in the first person to speaking in the third person may seem odd but is in fact not unusual in the HB, for it is not uncommon in BH for a speaker to refer to himself or herself in the third person (e.g., Gen 18:3, 5; 19:19; Ruth 3:9; 1 Sam 1:11). The particular combination of weak and guttural letters in the root √נחם has the effect of blurring the morphological distinctions between the Nifal and Piel *binyanim*, which are the most frequent ones for this verb. וְנִחַם could therefore be parsed either as Nifal or Piel *weqatal* 3 m s. The Nifal has a range of meanings such as "to be sorry, relent, repent, comfort oneself, be comforted," while the Piel's range is narrower: "to comfort, console." We do find some instances of √שׁוב and Nifal √נחם used together in a context of "(not) relenting" (Joel 2:14; Jer 4:28; 31:19), which may suggest that this was an established collocation, and the verb's occurrence in 8:14 is to be analyzed as Nifal. Yet Nifal does not govern an object with אֶת, but either occurs absolutely or with prepositions such as עַל or אֶל. Thus, the analysis as Piel is to be preferred. Thematically this is linked to דְּבָרִים נִחֻמִים "comforting words" in verse 13.

וּבָחַר עוֹד בִּירוּשָׁלִָם. Qal *weqatal* 3 m s √בחר. The verb commonly, though not exclusively, uses the בְּ preposition to govern an object (BDB, 103–4). As noted above, this statement forms an *inclusio* with verse 14. The identical phrase occurs in 2:16 [ET v. 12], and a similar one in 3:2 הַבֹּחֵר בִּירוּשָׁלִָם "(YHWH), who chooses Jerusalem . . . ," indicating the importance of the theme in the Night Visions. Here it suggests the reversal of YHWH's "denunciation" of his people mentioned in verse 12. For further discussion of YHWH's "choosing" Zion/Jerusalem, see Schreiner (155–58) and Boda (2004: 201–2).

Second Vision (Zechariah 2:1-4)
Four Horns and Four Craftsmen

Zechariah's second vision consists of four horns, which represent the hostile nations (v. 4 הַגּוֹיִם) responsible for scattering God's people. After seeing these horns the prophet then observes four "craftsmen" who are God's agents of judgment upon them (on the disputed term חָרָשִׁים, see v. 3). The brevity of the vision, coupled with some difficult philological problems, has proven a challenge to scholars (see Rogland 2014a), though the general notion of the suppression of Israel's enemies is clear enough.

[1]And I lifted up my eyes and I looked, and behold, four horns.

[2]And I said to the angel who was speaking with me, "What are these?" And he said to me, "These are the horns that scattered Judah, Israel and Jerusalem."

[3]And YHWH showed me four craftsmen.

[4]And I said, "What are these coming to do?" And he said, "These are the horns that scattered Judah as a man who had not been numbered, so that these [craftsmen] have come to terrify them, to lay hands on the horns of the nations that lifted up a horn against the land of Judah in order to scatter her." [ET: 1:18-21]

2:1 וָאֶשָּׂא אֶת־עֵינַי וָאֵרֶא וְהִנֵּה אַרְבַּע קְרָנוֹת׃

וָאֶשָּׂא אֶת־עֵינַי וָאֵרֶא. Qal *wayyiqtol* 1 c s √נשׂא and √ראה. "To lift up the eyes and see" is a frequent idiom in BH (ca. 35×; e.g., Gen 13:10; 18:2) and in the Night Visions (2:5 [ET v. 1]; 5:1, 5, 9; 6:1).

וְהִנֵּה אַרְבַּע קְרָנוֹת. In Hebrew the numbers 3-10 can occur after the noun in the absolute state or before the noun in either the absolute state or, as here with אַרְבַּע קְרָנוֹת, the construct state (JM §142d; MNK §37.2.2iii). Moreover, these numbers display dissymmetry in that feminine forms are used with masculine nouns and vice versa (JM §100d; GKC §97a; WO §15.2.2; WB §95b). The noun קֶ֫רֶן is attested a number of times in dual form (both קַרְנַ֫יִם and קְרָנַיִם, see JM §91b), but the plural form קְרָנוֹת is more common and is used here because four horns are explicitly mentioned (Wolters 2014: 70–71). The lexical sense of קֶ֫רֶן is "horn," so there is no dispute regarding the translation of the clause, but what is uncertain in this instance is the term's *referent*: Are these קְרָנוֹת those of animals, altars, or demons, or are they purely symbols of political/military power? The exegetical interpretation of the קְרָנוֹת is affected to a large extent by how other terms in the unit are understood (see below).

2:2 וָאֹמַר אֶל־הַמַּלְאָךְ הַדֹּבֵר בִּי מָה־אֵלֶּה וַיֹּאמֶר אֵלַי אֵלֶּה הַקְּרָנוֹת אֲשֶׁר זֵרוּ אֶת־יְהוּדָה אֶת־יִשְׂרָאֵל וִירוּשָׁלִָם׃ ס

וָאֹמַר אֶל־הַמַּלְאָךְ הַדֹּבֵר בִּי. Qal *wayyiqtol* 1c s √אמר and Qal ptc m s √דבר with def art. See 1:9 regarding the use of √דבר in the Qal stem, and on the Interpreting Angel see the introductory remarks to 1:7-17.

מָה־אֵ֫לֶּה. "What are these?" As has been noted previously (see 1:9), this question is not purely informational, since the content of the vision was just indicated in verse 1, but is inquiring as to the significance of what has been seen.

וַיֹּ֣אמֶר אֵלַ֔י אֵ֚לֶּה הַקְּרָנוֹת֙ אֲשֶׁ֣ר זֵר֣וּ אֶת־יְהוּדָ֔ה אֶת־יִשְׂרָאֵ֖ל וִירוּשָׁלָֽם. Qal *wayyiqtol* 3 m s √אמר and Piel *qatal* 3 c pl √זרה. The verb √זרה "to scatter" is used elsewhere to refer to the Diaspora (e.g., Lev 26:33; Jer 31:10). On the name "Jerusalem" as an instance of *Qere perpetuum*, see 1:12.

The phrase אֶת־יְהוּדָ֔ה אֶת־יִשְׂרָאֵ֖ל וִירוּשָׁלָֽם is an "apparent redundancy" (Stead, 105 n. 119), which is undoubtedly responsible for the omission of either "Israel" or "Jerusalem" in various LXX mss (cf. *BHQ*, 120). In fact, this trifold reference to "Judah, Israel, and Jerusalem" is unique in the HB, which speaks to its originality here. The inconsistent use of the object marker אֶת־ is somewhat peculiar, but the particle is rarely obligatory, even though its use is extremely frequent with proper nouns (ca. 97 percent of the time; see Malessa, 33). Kropat (34) notes that the Chronicler will use the particle with the first of a series of accusatives but omit it with those that follow, as in the very similar 1 Chron 5:41 [ET 6:14] בְּהַגְל֣וֹת יְהוָ֔ה אֶת־יְהוּדָ֖ה וִירוּשָׁלִָ֑ם "when YHWH exiled Judah and Jerusalem" and 2 Chron 34:3 לְטַהֵ֣ר אֶת־יְהוּדָ֔ה וִ֣ירוּשָׁלִַ֔ם "to purify Judah and Jerusalem." On the other hand, it appears that the proper noun "Jerusalem" is fairly resistant to prefixing by the particle אֶת־, which only occurs twenty-two times in the entire HB.

2:3 וַיַּרְאֵ֣נִי יְהוָ֔ה אַרְבָּעָ֖ה חָרָשִֽׁים׃

Hifil *wayyiqtol* 3 m s √ראה with 1 c s pronoun suffix. A pronominal suffix on a verb does not necessarily indicate a direct object (cf. Muraoka 1979), and in this case it indicates the indirect object, since the direct object is אַרְבָּעָ֖ה חָרָשִֽׁים. The previous occurrence of Hifil √ראה in 1:9 had the Interpreting Angel as its subject rather than YHWH. On the use of numerals with a phrase such as אַרְבָּעָ֖ה חָרָשִׁים, see verse 1. Like גַּנָּב "thief" or טַבָּח "butcher," חָרָשׁ is a *qattāl* formation used for professions (JM §88Ha), with compensatory lengthening of the initial *pataḥ* due the rejection of the *dagesh forte*. As noted in the introduction to this unit, there is disagreement over the meaning of this term: It is clear that these חָרָשִׁים will perform some kind of judgment on the horns (v. 4), but this and other key terms have been felt to be opaque, with the result that the overall imagery of the vision is disputed. Most commonly the חָרָשִׁים have been interpreted as "craftsmen" of some kind (e.g., Petterson 2015: 123–24). Some object to this since craftsmen engage in constructive, rather than destructive, work. The chief alternate proposal is that the imagery is "bucolic" and that the term חָרָשִׁים is to be understood as "ploughmen." Good (56) arrives at this conclusion partly by appeal to comparative Semitic evidence, while Boda (2005: 25) proposes a revocalization to חֹרְשִׁים and draws attention to the following clause's use of √החריד, which can be used for "driving" a group of animals (e.g., Isa 17:2; Deut 28:26; Jer 7:33). Yet the proposal is unpersuasive, above all since the noun חָרָשׁ consistently refers to a "craftsman" or "artisan" in BH, TH (1QM 5:6, 9, 10, 11; fragmentary context in 4Q491 1_3:7; 4Q167 11_13:3),[3] and RH (Jastrow, 507). This understanding of חָרָשִׁים is also reflected in the ancient versions (LXX: τέκτων; Vulg: *faber*; Tg: אוּמָּן). It is possible to make sense of the vision by understanding the חָרָשִׁים as "artisans, craftsmen," since we find חָרָשׁ used in a metaphor for agents of judgment in Ezek 21:36: "I will deliver you into the hands of brutish men, *craftsmen of destruction* (חָרָשֵׁי מַשְׁחִית)" (possibly also Isa 54:16; cf. Stead, 107). Regardless of whether the קְרָנוֹת are understood as altar horns or military-political symbols, the point is that these artisans possess mastery over their craft, and therefore will be able to exert their will upon the objects of their attention.

2:4 וָאֹמַר מָה אֵלֶּה בָאִים לַעֲשׂוֹת וַיֹּאמֶר לֵאמֹר
אֵלֶּה הַקְּרָנוֹת אֲשֶׁר־זֵרוּ אֶת־יְהוּדָה כְּפִי־אִישׁ
לֹא־נָשָׂא רֹאשׁוֹ וַיָּבֹאוּ אֵלֶּה לְהַחֲרִיד אֹתָם לְיַדּוֹת
אֶת־קַרְנוֹת הַגּוֹיִם הַנֹּשְׂאִים קֶרֶן אֶל־אֶרֶץ יְהוּדָה
לְזָרוֹתָהּ׃ ס

וָאֹמַר מָה אֵלֶּה בָאִים לַעֲשׂוֹת. Qal *wayyiqtol* 1 c s √אמר, Qal ptc m pl √בוא, and Qal inf cstr √עשה. The use of the participle indicates

[3] The text of Sir 38:27 (MsB) is fragmentary, though the initial ḥet is visible according to Ben-Ḥayyim's edition (40), in contrast to Beentjes (67). The LXX rendering of makes Ben-Ḥayyim's restoration אף עשה ח[רש והו]שב highly plausible.

that the prophet is watching the חָרָשִׁים approaching as he is speaking (on the participle indicating the "actual present" in questions, see Hag 2:3). The infinitive construct לַעֲשׂוֹת functions here as a complement to בָּאִים. Having established what the horns signify (v. 2), the prophet seeks information concerning what they are coming to do.

וַיֹּאמֶר לֵאמֹר אֵלֶּה הַקְּרָנוֹת אֲשֶׁר־זֵרוּ אֶת־יְהוּדָה. Qal *wayyiqtol* 3 m s, Qal inf cstr √אמר, Piel *qatal* 3 c pl √זרה.

כְּפִי־אִישׁ לֹא־נָשָׂא רֹאשׁוֹ. Qal *qatal* 3 m s √נשׂא. Though often emended, this troubling clause is capable of a grammatically acceptable explanation as it stands (see Rogland 2014a). כְּפִי is to be understood here as functionally equivalent to the simple preposition כְּ־ "as, like," e.g., Job 33:6 הֶן־אֲנִי כְפִיךָ לָאֵל, "Behold, I am as you toward God"; Sir 6:7 [MsB] כי יש אוהב כפי עת ואל יעמוד ביום צרה, "For there is a friend who is like a season, but he will not endure in a day of tribulation." Comparative statements are frequently modified by asyndetic relative clauses (JM §174c), and כְּפִי־אִישׁ is best translated "as a man who" (cf. *BHQ*, 135*; Hallaschka 2011: 168 n. 145). The expression נָשָׂא רֹאשׁ is typically understood here as "to act with boldness" (e.g., Jdg 8:28), and while this is one possible meaning of the syntagm, much more frequently it refers to "counting heads" in the sense of numbering people for the purpose of taking a census (Exod 30:12; Num 1:2, 49; 4:2, 22; 26:2; 31:49; etc.). The pronoun suffix of רֹאשׁוֹ refers back to אִישׁ, but in this instance אִישׁ is not to be understood as the subject of the verb לֹא־נָשָׂא. Rather, this is best interpreted as an impersonal use of the verb: "as a man whom one had not numbered." Impersonal uses of the verb are often best rendered in the passive voice (cf. JM §155), hence the translation offered above: "who scattered Judah *as a man who had not been numbered*." The statement implies that the people who were exiled had not been properly "numbered" among the legitimate citizenry of the land of Judah; they were, in a sense, "illegal aliens" dwelling in the land and were therefore subject to displacement. For other similes involving "scattering," see 1 Kgs 22:17; Isa 30:22; Jer 13:24; Ps 147:16.

וַיָּבֹאוּ אֵלֶּה לְהַחֲרִיד אֹתָם לְיַדּוֹת אֶת־קַרְנוֹת הַגּוֹיִם. Qal *wayyiqtol* 3 m pl √בוא, Hifil inf cstr √חרד, Piel inf cstr √ידה. In this instance the *wayyiqtol* form וַיָּבֹאוּ could well have a notion of logical consecution (JM §118h; AC §3.5.1b): "*with the result that/so that* these (craftsmen) have come. . . ." Even though קַרְנוֹת is feminine, we find the masculine אֹתָם since the "horns" are horns of the "nations" (קַרְנוֹת הַגּוֹיִם). Good (58–59) alleges, without any external evidence whatsoever, that הַגּוֹיִם

is a late interpretative gloss, but there is no reason to be suspicious of the MT here. Hifil √חרד means "to frighten, terrify" (BDB, 353; *DCH* 3, 312; Jastrow, 498) and does not by itself suggest "driving on" flocks of animals (cf. on v. 2); for example, it can occur in explicitly militaristic contexts (Jdg 8:12; 2 Sam 17:2; Ezek 30:9; 2Q22 1:3). Most frequently we encounter the phrase וְאֵין מַחֲרִיד "and there will be none to terrify" speaking of God's people living unthreatened in the Promised Land (Lev 26:6; Deut 28:26; Jer 30:10; 46:27; Ezek 34:28; 39:26; Mic 4:4; Zeph 3:13). The infinitive construct לְהַחֲרִיד indicates the purpose for which the craftsmen are coming.

The infinitive construct לְיַדּוֹת has occasioned much discussion, since the Piel of √ידה is only attested one other time in BH (Lam 3:53) and is not attested in post-BH, either in TH (*DCH* 4: 97) or RH (Jastrow, 564). Contra Lowe (21), the phrase יַדּוּ גוֹרָל "they threw the lot" (Joel 4:3; Obd 11; Nah 3:10) is from the geminate verb √ידד according to the Masoretic vocalization (GKC §69u). Some view the form as suspect (e.g., Good, 57), though the MT should be accepted as the *lectio difficilior*. The rarity of the verb has led to considerable debate over its meaning. Tigchelaar (50–55), who suggests that the "horns" of Zech 2:1-4 represent demonic entities, appeals to Ugaritic *ydy* "to expel, cast out" and argues that the scene is one of demonic exorcism. While it is a stimulating proposal, it cannot apply to the other occurrences of √ידה and thus appears to be a case of semantic special pleading. Moreover, the evidence from the HB for understanding the "horns" as representative of demons is weak. Most often Piel √ידה is explained by reference to the equally rare Qal, which only occurs in Jer 50:14 כָּל־דֹּ֣רְכֵי קֶ֔שֶׁת יְד֣וּ אֵלֶ֔יהָ אַֽל־תַּחְמְל֖וּ אֶל־חֵ֑ץ "All you who draw the bow, *cast* (= shoot) at her; do not spare the arrow!"—a textually problematic example, with some codices reading the verb √ירה (cf. *DCH* 4: 97; Meyers and Meyers, 142)—and Sir 14:15 (MsA) ליודי גורל "to those who *cast* the lot." Applied to the Piel √ידה in Lam 3:53, it is most often understood as referring to an act of throwing: וַיַּדּוּ־אֶ֖בֶן בִּֽי, "And they **cast** a stone at me" (on וַיַּדּוּ instead of *וַיְיַדּוּ, see GKC §69u). The result of these considerations is that the infinitive construct לְיַדּוֹת is often translated in Zech 2:4 as "to cast down"; Qimchi, for example, glosses the verb as להשליך "to throw" in his *Sefer Ha-Shorashim*.

It is evident that the textual data concerning √ידה is extremely thin. It seems preferable to view the verb as denominative of יַד "hand," as some have suggested (e.g., *HAHAT*, 285; Jastrow, 564). In this case it would mean "to put one's hand to" or "to lay one's hand on." Not only would this suit the instances mentioned above, it would also be particularly appropriate to the image of "craftsmen" who "work with their hands." In this case, the craftsmen will "lay hands" on the nations to exert their will upon them, with the contextual implication being that it is for the purposes of judgment (cf. 1:15). Subtle support for this line of interpretation is found in the LXX's τοῦ ὀξῦναι αὐτὰ εἰς χεῖρας αὐτῶν "to sharpen them for their hands," which, while not correctly reading לידות as a verbal form, nonetheless sensed a link between the τέκτονες and their χεῖρες. The infinitive construct לְיַדּוֹת could be understood as an "epexegetical" infinitive (cf. JM §124o), explaining how the smiths will "terrify" the horns: "to terrify them, *by laying hands on them*." Alternately, it could also be understood as an additional statement of purpose parallel to the preceding infinitive construct לְהַחֲרִיד: "these have come (in order) to terrify them, to lay hands on . . ."

הַנֹּשְׂאִים קֶרֶן אֶל־אֶרֶץ יְהוּדָה לְזָרוֹתָהּ. Qal ptc m pl √נשׂא with def art, Piel inf cstr √זרה with 3 f s pronoun suffix. Substantival and attributive participles such as הַנֹּשְׂאִים can have a past reference (see Hag 1:6), which is required by the context here (Lowe, 22): "the nations which *raised* a horn." The expression "to raise a horn" utilizes the Hifil √רום, and the collocation with Qal √נשׂא is unique in the HB. It is possible that √נשׂא was used as some kind of wordplay with the same verb in the preceding clause. However, a syntactical explanation is more likely. With Hifil √רום the subject is almost always used for exalting the horn of another (Ps 75:5-6 is exceptional), whereas in this instance Qal √נשׂא refers to the subjects' raising of their own horn. It is standard for הֵרִים קֶרֶן to utilize the singular "horn" (קֶרֶן) as opposed to the plural "horns" (1 Sam 2:10; 1 Chron 25:5; Pss 75:5-6; 89:18 *Ketiv*; 92:11; 148:14; Lam 2:17). In this instance, as often, אֶל has the sense of עַל "against" (BDB, 41, n. 2).

Third Vision (Zechariah 2:5-9)
A Man with the Measuring Cord

The third Night Vision (ET: 2:1-5) consists of a man with a measuring cord who intends to measure the dimensions of Jerusalem (vv. 5-6). This picks up the promise of 1:16, which stated, "the measuring line will be stretched out over Jerusalem" (Stead, 109). The Interpreting Angel prepares to follow this man but is intercepted by "another angel" (v. 7), who directs him to deliver a brief prophecy (v. 8a). The message is that the populace of Jerusalem will eventually become so numerous that walls will be unable to contain it, forcing people to live in "unwalled villages" (v. 8b). This will not pose a danger, however, since YHWH will be a wall of fire surrounding them (v. 9).

One particularly confusing feature of the sparse narrative is the number of participants in the text (Schöttler, 72). In addition to Zechariah, there are at least two angels involved, but with another two possible actors depending upon the interpretation of various details. Some attribute the confusion to redaction-critical factors (e.g., Hallaschka 2011: 186), but such a solution seems altogether too convenient. One issue that has contributed to the confusion is the failure of commentators to appreciate fully the movement of the vision's participants as narrated in verse 7, which is typically passed over with little comment, and to integrate its significance into the interpretation of the text. Although her interpretation is not adopted here, Tiemeyer (2015: 106) is correct in asserting, "The extant text is not incoherent or contradictory, merely complex and otherworldly."

[5]And I lifted up my eyes and I looked and behold, a man, and in his hand was a cord of measurement.

[6]And I said, "Where are you about to go?" And he said to me, "To measure Jerusalem to see how much is her width and how much is her length."

[7]And behold, the angel who was speaking with me was going out, but another angel was coming out to meet him

[8]and he said to him [viz., the Interpreting Angel], "Run, speak to that young man: In unwalled villages shall Jerusalem dwell on account of the abundance of man and beast in her midst.

[9]And as for me, I myself will be for her"—oracle of YHWH—"a wall of fire all around, and I will be the Glory in her midst." [ET: 2:1-5]

2:5 וָאֶשָּׂא עֵינַי וָאֵרֶא וְהִנֵּה־אִישׁ וּבְיָדוֹ חֶבֶל מִדָּה׃

וָאֶשָּׂא עֵינַי וָאֵרֶא. Qal *wayyiqtol* 1 c s √נשׂא; Qal *wayyiqtol* 1 c s √ראה. On this idiom, see 2:1.

וְהִנֵּה־אִישׁ וּבְיָדוֹ חֶבֶל מִדָּה. אִישׁ denotes a humanoid figure who may, as in the first vision (1:7-17), turn out to be an angelic being, but in this vision the nature of this "man" is less clear (Tiemeyer 2015: 107). חֶבֶל is a common term for "cord" or "rope" used for a variety of functions, one of which is to take measurements. It often occurs without additional modification (BDB, 286, #2), but in this case the noun מִדָּה "measure, measurement" makes its function explicit (see also the use of the infinitive construct from the cognate verb √מדד in v. 6). Thematically this takes up the promise concerning the "measuring line" of 1:16, as חֶבֶל מִדָּה and קָו appear to be functional equivalents (Wolters 2014: 75). For similar instances of "measuring" taking place in a visionary experience, see Ezek 40:3 and 47:3 (cf. Amos 7:7-9).

2:6 וָאֹמַ֕ר אָ֖נָה אַתָּ֣ה הֹלֵ֑ךְ וַיֹּ֣אמֶר אֵלַ֗י לָמֹד֙ אֶת־
יְר֣וּשָׁלַ֔ם לִרְא֥וֹת כַּמָּה־רָחְבָּ֖הּ וְכַמָּ֥ה אָרְכָּֽהּ׃

וָאֹמַ֕ר אָ֖נָה אַתָּ֣ה הֹלֵ֑ךְ. Qal *wayyiqtol* 1 c s √אמר, Qal ptc m s √הלך. Verse 5 had not indicated that the אִישׁ was in motion, and therefore it is best to understand the participle as indicating the imminent future (JM §121e): "Where are you *about to go*?" The particle אָ֫נָה represents a contraction of אַ֫יִן to אָן with the addition of the *he locale* or directional *he* (BDB, 33). Since the man responds with an infinitival phrase, Wolters argues that in this instance אָ֫נָה indicates "for what end" or "to what purpose" rather than "whither/to what place," appealing to 5:10 and Ruth 2:19 (2014: 75–76, following Stinespring). Rather than explaining such usages in terms of the semantics of אָ֫נָה, however, it is preferable to explain them in terms of pragmatics: to ask a person where s/he is going is often to *imply* a second question, namely, "Why are you going *there*?" It is for this reason that the reply to an inquiry about one's destination might provide not only the location but also, anticipating the follow-up question, the purpose for going (so here and in 5:11). For example, if someone asks, "Where are you going?" there is nothing unusual about replying "To the store to buy milk."

וַיֹּ֣אמֶר אֵלַ֗י לָמֹד֙ אֶת־יְר֣וּשָׁלַ֔ם לִרְא֥וֹת כַּמָּה־רָחְבָּ֖הּ וְכַמָּ֥ה אָרְכָּֽהּ. Qal *wayyiqtol* 3 m s √אמר, Qal inf cstr √מדד with לְ-preposition, Qal inf cstr √ראה with לְ-preposition. Qal √מדד is used both for measuring quantities (e.g., Exod 16:18; Ruth 3:15; Isa 40:12) as well as for measuring distances or dimensions (Num 35:5; Deut 21:2; Ezek 41–47 *passim*). As Shin (130–31) notes, measurements of length always precede measurements of width except in this instance and in the book of Ezekiel (40:11; 41:2, 12; 45:6; 48:8, 10).

2:7 וְהִנֵּה הַמַּלְאָךְ הַדֹּבֵר בִּי יֹצֵא וּמַלְאָךְ אַחֵר יֹצֵא לִקְרָאתוֹ׃

וְהִנֵּה הַמַּלְאָךְ הַדֹּבֵר בִּי יֹצֵא. Qal ptc m s √דבר with def art, Qal ptc m s √יצא. Some (e.g., Rashi) identify the Interpreting Angel as the "man" from verse 5, but the Interpreting Angel maintains a distinct identity throughout the Night Visions, and hence it is best to understand these as separate *dramatis personae* (cf. Mitchell, 136). Thus the Interpreting Angel intends to follow the man with the cord to Jerusalem, thereby becoming a more direct participant in the events of the visionary scene (cf. Tiemeyer 2015: 110).

וּמַלְאָךְ אַחֵר יֹצֵא לִקְרָאתוֹ. Qal ptc m s √יצא, Qal inf cstr √קרא with לְ preposition and 3 m s pronoun suffix (an infinitive construct per BDB, 896, though JM §78k treats לִקְרַאת as a verbal noun). The verb √קרא II is an alternate form of √קרה (BDB, 896; JM §78k) and can mean "to befall" in a more general sense but more often means "to meet, encounter," always in the infinitive construct and almost always used with a verb of motion. Wolters (2014: 76) notes the frequent use of Qal √יצא in the Night Visions (5:3, 5, 9; 6:1, 5, 6, 7) and argues that it means "to emerge" in the sense of "to appear on the scene" or "to enter the prophet's field of vision." While this is certainly fitting in some contexts (e.g., 6:1), in the present verse this would suggest that the Interpreting Angel had somehow disappeared between the second and third visions, which is an unnecessary assumption. Qal √יצא can be translated as "to go out" or "to come out" (BDB, 422), with the particular translational choice depending on the speaker's viewpoint and whether the motion described is away from or toward the speaker. Given the fact that the Interpreting Angel is typically found accompanying the prophet (the speaker), the first occurrence of יֹצֵא in this verse should be rendered "was going out," since he is moving away from the speaker (Zechariah). On the other hand, the second occurrence of יֹצֵא introduces a new character, "another angel" (מַלְאָךְ אַחֵר), coming toward Zechariah, and hence it should be translated "was coming out."

This second angel comes forth to intercept the Interpreting Angel and to redirect him from his intended course to Jerusalem (see v. 8), and thus the *vav* which introduces the clause is best understood as adversative: "*But* another angel was coming forth. . . ." It seems unlikely that this is the angel of YHWH from chapter 1, given that he is a distinct entity in the HB in general and in Zechariah's surrounding visions in chapters 1 and 3 (Mitchell, 137–38). In any event, at this point it is reasonably clear that there are four actors on the stage (Tiemeyer 2015: 110): the man with measuring cord, the Interpreting Angel, the "other angel" and, of course, Zechariah himself.

It is important to note the use of the participles in this verse. Wolters (2014: 75–76) translates both occurrences of יֹצֵא as simple past tenses, but this cannot be justified grammatically. While they could possibly mark the imminent future as הֹלֵךְ in verse 6, יֹצֵא is best interpreted as an action in process. In BH it is very common to use the participle to set up a situation or condition in a dependent clause, with a finite verb in an independent clause providing the primary action (cf. JM §166c, f). What is not common is for two participial clauses to occur side by side if one of them is intended to be understood as the primary action in a main clause (for some rare possible examples, see JM §166e). To make sense of this, it must be recognized that verse 7 contains multiple dependent, subordinate clauses, with the main clause commencing with וַיֹּאמֶר in verse 8: "The angel who spoke with me was going out, but another angel was coming out to meet him, *and he said . . .*"

2:8 וַיֹּאמֶר אֵלָו רֻץ דַּבֵּר אֶל־הַנַּעַר הַלָּז לֵאמֹר פְּרָזוֹת
תֵּשֵׁב יְרוּשָׁלַם מֵרֹב אָדָם וּבְהֵמָה בְּתוֹכָהּ׃

וַיֹּאמֶר אֵלָו. Qal *wayyiqtol* 3 m s √אמר. In 1 Sam 22:13 and Ezek 9:4 the *Ketiv* אֵלָו is corrected to אֵלָיו by the *Qere*, but somewhat inexplicably the MT is left alone in this instance. The grammatical subject of וַיֹּאמֶר has been much disputed (Schöttler 72–73) and, as a corollary, there is uncertainty regarding the object of אֵלָו: Is the Interpreting Angel speaking or is it the "other angel"? Meyers and Meyers claim that the closest grammatical antecedent is the pronoun suffix on לִקְרָאתוֹ (v. 7), understood as the Interpreting Angel. Thus they argue (152) that the Interpreting Angel is the subject of וַיֹּאמֶר, who is commanding the "other angel" to run with a message. While this possibility cannot be absolutely excluded, lacking other contextual indicators one would rather assume that the subject of וַיֹּאמֶר is the same as the subject of the preceding verbal form, viz. the second יֹצֵא of verse 7. In other words, it is in fact the "other angel" who is the one speaking and urging the Interpreting Angel to "run" (so Tiemeyer 2015: 110).

רֻ֗ץ דַּבֵּ֞ר אֶל־הַנַּ֤עַר הַלָּז֙ לֵאמֹ֔ר. Qal impv 2 m s √רוץ, Piel impv 2 m s √דבר, Qal inf cstr √אמר. The rare demonstrative pronoun הַלָּז (7× in the HB; JM §36b; GKC §34f), which can be used with masculine or feminine nouns, represents a shortening of the still rarer הַלָּזֶה (masc: only Gen 24:65; 37:19) and הַלֵּזוּ (fem: only Ezek 36:35). Though some instances are open to interpretation, several examples strongly suggest that it has a "far demonstrative" function—that is, "*that one* (over there)" (e.g., Gen 24:65; 37:19; 1 Sam 14:1; 17:26; 2 Kgs 4:25; Ezek 36:35), a nuance confirmed by the LXX's consistent rendering with forms of ἐκεῖνος rather than οὗτος. Contrary to Tiemeyer (2015: 111), however, הַלָּז does not necessarily refer to something already mentioned in the context, as shown by cases such as Jdg 6:20 and 2 Kgs 23:17. According to the interpretation of וַיֹּאמֶר advocated here, the "other angel" has intercepted the Interpreting Angel (see v. 7) in order to give him a message for "that young man." The reference to "that young man" has produced a significant amount of exegetical confusion: Does it refer to the man with the measuring line of verse 5, to Zechariah, to one of the angels, or does it introduce another character entirely? The term נַעַר itself does nothing to settle the question. Wolters (2014: 76) argues that it refers to a surveyor's assistant, since the use of a measuring cord would require two people at each end of the line. While this is not implausible in itself, the introduction of a hitherto unmentioned assistant, who plays no further role in the text, would serve no purpose for the vision's overall message (cf. Meyers and Meyers, 153). Many scholars understand הַנַּעַר הַלָּז to refer to the man with the measuring cord from verse 5 (e.g., Boda 2004: 223; Mitchell, 138). According to this approach, the man with the cord is being stopped from going to measure Jerusalem, either because it will no longer be needed (so Rashi; cf. vv.8b-9) or because it might even be against the divine will (so Tiemeyer 2015: 111). Neither option can square with the promise of 1:16 וְקָו יִנָּטֶה עַל־יְרוּשָׁלָם, upon which the vision clearly builds.

On the whole, the view that "that young man" refers to Zechariah himself (so Rashi and other rabbinic commentators) is the simplest and has the most to commend it. Tiemeyer's objection that it is unlikely that the narrator would refer to himself as "that young man" (2015: 112–13) lacks force, since in the context of the vision it is not the narrator who says these words but rather the "other angel." In sum, the Interpreting Angel is being directed back to the prophet with a message of restoration; he assists as a mediating figure, but the task of proclamation belongs to the prophet (cf. the use of קָרָא in 1:14, 17). The fact that he is prevented from accompanying the man with the measuring cord but instead is told to "run" to transmit this message to Zechariah implies its urgency.

פְּרָזוֹת תֵּשֵׁב יְרוּשָׁלִַם מֵרֹב אָדָם וּבְהֵמָה בְּתוֹכָהּ. Qal *yiqtol* 3 f s √ישׁב. Jerusalem is the subject of the verb, but it refers by metonymy to the population of Jerusalem. פְּרָזוֹת is an "accusative of local determination" (JM §126h) or "directive accusative/accusative of place" (WB §54a–b; AC §2.3.2a; MNK §33.2.3i; GKC §118d–g; WO §10.2.2b). Compare a similar example with √ישׁב in Gen 18:1 וְהוּא יֹשֵׁב פֶּתַח־הָאֹהֶל, "while he was sitting *at the entrance* to his tent." פְּרָזָה refers to a "hamlet" (BDB, 826); Ezek 38:11 notes that these lack walls, precisely as the פְּרָזוֹת in this instance (cf. v. 9). The question of word order in BH is a highly complex and disputed subject, and there is little consensus whether Hebrew is a "verb-first" or "subject-first" language, but it is generally acknowledged that an object-first clause such as this is less common. In terms of information structure (see discussion in Holmstedt 2010: 9–16), the object introduces new information ("focus") relevant to the subject, Jerusalem, which is the "topic" already known from the context (v. 6).

מֵרֹב אָדָם וּבְהֵמָה. The preposition מִן has a causal sense, as reflected in most translations (BDB, 580, #2e–f), and the singular nouns אָדָם and בְּהֵמָה are used as collectives (JM §135b–c).

2:9 וַאֲנִי אֶהְיֶה־לָּהּ נְאֻם־יְהוָה חוֹמַת אֵשׁ סָבִיב וּלְכָבוֹד אֶהְיֶה בְתוֹכָהּ׃ פ

וַאֲנִי אֶהְיֶה־לָּהּ נְאֻם־יְהוָה חוֹמַת אֵשׁ סָבִיב. Qal *yiqtol* 1 c s √היה. It has been suggested that אֶהְיֶה is to be rendered as the personal name "Ehyeh" in light of Exod 3:14 and Hos 1:9 (cf. Meyers and Meyers, 156; Stead, 113 n. 146), but this is excluded by the syntax of the full clause (וַאֲנִי אֶהְיֶה־לָּהּ . . . חוֹמַת אֵשׁ סָבִיב). The use of the personal pronoun with a finite verb is noteworthy since it is, strictly speaking, grammatically unnecessary here (see 1:12). וַאֲנִי does not appear to be used for contrast or juxtaposition (cf. JM §146a1–2) but rather is a genuine case of emphasis intended to strengthen a promissory utterance (JM §146a3–4). Such an analysis is further confirmed by the use of the oracle formula (נְאֻם־יְהוָה) which, due to its "intrusive" appearance here, is not to be explained as a structural marker but must be rhetorically motivated, serving to "reinforce" or "validate" what is being said (see Appendix §3). In this particular instance it also seems highly likely that וַאֲנִי אֶהְיֶה is intended to add intertextual coloring: With only two exceptions (Jdg 11:9; 1 Sam 23:17), the only times we encounter אֲנִי or אָנֹכִי followed by אֶהְיֶה are with YHWH as the speaker (Exod 4:12, 15; Deut 31:23; 2 Sam 7:14; 1 Chron 17:13; 28:6), most often in the divine promise "I will be your God" (Jer 11:4; 24:7; 30:22; 32:38; Ezek 11:20; 14:11; 36:28; 37:23; Zech 8:8).

The verb √היה, which can have the sense of "to become," occurs here with the noun phrase חוֹמַת אֵשׁ סָבִיב as predicate (BDB, 226, #II2a). The expression "wall of fire" is unique in the HB.[4] The prepositional phrase לָהּ in the clause וַאֲנִי אֶהְיֶה־לָּהּ . . . חוֹמַת אֵשׁ סָבִיב could be analyzed as a complement of the verb אֶהְיֶה or could be linked with סָבִיב. The former option is how Zech 2:9 is commonly understood, e.g., "I will be *to her* a wall of fire round about" (RSV). In this case √היה with nominal predicate is complemented with a לְ indicating the indirect object or beneficiary (BDB, 226, #II2d), as in Gen 24:51 וּתְהִי אִשָּׁה לְבֶן־אֲדֹנֶיךָ "And let her become wife to the son of your lord."[5] On the other hand, the second option is possible since סָבִיב לְ־ is a standard prepositional phrase (BDB, 687, #1c*b*)—e.g., Nah 3:8 מַיִם סָבִיב לָהּ "(with) water surrounding her," Ps 125:2 יְרוּשָׁלַםִ הָרִים סָבִיב לָהּ וַיהוָה סָבִיב לְעַמּוֹ "Jerusalem—mountains surround her, and YHWH surrounds his people." Hence אֶהְיֶה־לָּהּ . . . חוֹמַת אֵשׁ סָבִיב could also translated, "I will be . . . a wall of fire surrounding *her*" (cf. Tiemeyer 2015: 113). That לָהּ precedes סָבִיב does not preclude this option (e.g., Exod 25:25; 28:32; 37:12; 39:23). However, when סָבִיב is used with the noun חוֹמָה, we rarely find לְ, and when it does occur it is not in the סָבִיב לְ־ syntagm but rather indicates possession: Lev 25:31 וּבָתֵּי הַחֲצֵרִים אֲשֶׁר אֵין־לָהֶם חֹמָה סָבִיב, "But the houses of the villages which *have no wall* around"; Ezek 42:20 חוֹמָה לוֹ סָבִיב | סָבִיב, "*it had a wall* round about." All things considered, the common understanding

[4] Perhaps the closest analogies are 2 Kgs 6:17 וָרֶכֶב אֵשׁ סְבִיבֹת אֱלִישָׁע "and chariotry of fire was surrounding Elisha" and Ps 34:8 חֹנֶה מַלְאַךְ־יְהוָה סָבִיב לִירֵאָיו "the angel of YHWH encamps around those who fear him" (Stead 2009: 112 n. 114).

[5] The notion easily extends into the indication of possession or ownership (BDB, 226, #II2h).

of לָּהּ as linked with אֶהְיֶה rather than סָבִיב appears to be correct. The *dagesh* in the *lamed* of לָּהּ is an instance of "euphonic" gemination due to *dḥiq* or "compression" of two words together (on the conditions under which this occurs, see JM §18i).

וּלְכָבוֹד אֶהְיֶה בְתוֹכָהּ. Qal *yiqtol* 1 c s √היה. Unlike the preceding clause, the predicate of Qal √היה does not occur as a noun phrase but rather is marked by the לְ-preposition, a common syntagm in BH (BDB, 226, #II2e): "and I will be(come) glory in her midst." As it does frequently in the HB, כָּבוֹד serves as "a technical term for God's manifest presence" (C. J. Collins, 581–82). The noun is anarthrous, though it is typically translated here with the definite article ("*the* glory"), and this is not unheard of with this particular usage of כָּבוֹד, see 1 Sam 4:22 גָּלָה כָבוֹד מִיִּשְׂרָאֵל "(The) Glory has departed from Israel"; Isa 24:23 וְנֶגֶד זְקֵנָיו כָּבוֹד "and before his elders he will manifest (his) glory" (RSV); possibly also Isa 4:5 and Ps 85:9.

Exhortation Based on the First Three Visions *(Zechariah 2:10-17)*

The boundary between this pericope and the preceding one is disputed since the vision of 2:5-9 [ET: 2:1-5] concluded with exhortation (vv. 8-9) and 2:10-17 is hortatory rather than narrative in nature. Both passages, moreover, address Jerusalem's future (vv. 6, 8-9; vv. 15-16). Therefore some scholars treat all of verses 5-17 [ET vv. 1-13] together (e.g., Stead, 109–27), whereas others view verses 10-17 as a separate pericope (e.g., Petersen, 174). Themes and keywords from each of the preceding visions recur in this unit, however, suggesting that it is a summarizing appeal based upon all of 1:7–2:9 (cf. Meyers and Meyers, 172). For example:

Vision 1 (1:7-17)	**Exhortation of 2:10-17**
1:10 "These are the ones whom *YHWH sent* to go about in the earth."	2:12-13 "*He sent* me behind the Glory to the nations . . . and you will know *that YHWH Tsevaot has sent me.*"
1:17 "*And he shall again choose Jerusalem.*"	2:16 "*And he shall again choose Jerusalem.*"
Vision 2 (2:1-4)	
2:1-2, 4 "And behold, *four* horns . . . 'These are the horns that *scattered* Judah . . .' "	2:10 "I have *spread you out* as the *four* winds of heaven . . ."
Vision 3 (2:5-9)	
2:9 "And I will be *the Glory in her midst.*"	2:12, 14-15 "He sent me behind *the Glory* to the nations . . . And I will dwell *in your midst* . . ."

The exhortation contains the announcement that YHWH will settle in the midst of his people in order to claim possession of Judah (vv. 14-16). This represents the fulfillment of the promises of restoration in the first and third visions (1:7-17; 2:5-9), which stand in contrast to the people's present state of dispersion (v. 10; cf. 2:1-4). Nevertheless, YHWH summons them to return from exile (vv. 10-11), assuring them of their continued special status in his eyes (v. 12) and promising judgment upon their plunderers (v. 13). Moreover, it is prophesied that the populace of Jerusalem will be supplemented by foreign nations aligning themselves with YHWH (v. 15). The scope of YHWH's plan thus involves both Judeans and foreign nations, and accordingly, "all flesh" (כָּל־בָּשָׂר) is called to reverent silence before him (v. 17).

An especially complex issue in this pericope relates to the confusing switches between first and third person speakers and the identity of the speakers in the pericope (e.g., prophet, YHWH, and potentially one or more angels). This will be addressed at various points in the commentary and in the Excursus following verses 12-13.

[10]"Ho! Ho! Then flee from the land of the north"—oracle of YHWH—"for I have spread you out as the four winds of the heavens"—oracle of YHWH.

11 *"Ho! O Zion, escape! O inhabitant of Daughter Babylon!"*

12 *For thus has YHWH Tsevaot said, He has sent me behind the Glory to the nations who plundered you, for the one who touches you touches the pupil of his eye.*

13 *For behold, I am about to shake my hand against them, and they will become plunder for their slaves, and then you will know that YHWH Tsevaot has sent me.*

14 *Cry out and rejoice, O Daughter Zion! 'For behold, I am coming and I will settle down to dwell in your midst'—oracle of YHWH.*

15 *'And many nations will join themselves to YHWH on that day, and they will become to me a people, and I will continue to dwell in your midst,' and you will know that YHWH Tsevaot has sent me to you.*

16 *And YHWH will take possession of Judah as his portion upon the holy ground, and he will again choose Jerusalem.*

17 *Keep silence, all flesh, before YHWH! For he has roused himself from his holy habitation." [ET: 2:6-13]*

2:10 הֹ֣וי הֹ֗וי וְנֻ֛סוּ מֵאֶ֥רֶץ צָפֹ֖ון נְאֻם־יְהוָ֑ה כִּ֗י כְּאַרְבַּ֞ע
רוּחֹ֧ות הַשָּׁמַ֛יִם פֵּרַ֥שְׂתִּי אֶתְכֶ֖ם נְאֻם־יְהוָֽה׃

הֹ֣וי הֹ֗וי וְנֻ֛סוּ מֵאֶ֥רֶץ צָפֹ֖ון נְאֻם־יְהוָ֑ה. Qal impv 2 m pl √נוס with *vav*. With the exception of 1 Kgs 13:30, הוֹי occurs exclusively in the prophetic books, and this is the only instance of the interjection being repeated in immediate succession. In contrast to אוֹי, the interjection הוֹי is not necessarily an expression of woe (WO §40.2.4a; cp. MNK §45.4i), though Rashi overstates the matter when he asserts that הוֹי "is only an expression of proclamation and an announcement of assembly." וְנֻסוּ is by no means difficult to understand, but it is rare to begin an utterance with *vav* plus imperative; typically this follows some type of volitive verb form. The grammar of Gesenius maintains that a protasis has been suppressed in this instance "due to passionate excitement or haste, which does not allow time for full expression" (GKC §154b). This is a possible analysis, but a highly subjective one, and it is more prudent to note that הוֹי serves as a summons to action (WO §40.2.4a; *HALOT*, 242) and thus takes on a quasi-volitional or imperatival force. As such it can be understood as an "indirect volitive" (see Hag 1:8) indicating a sense of logical consecution: "Flee then/therefore!" In the HB, most of Israel's enemies, including Babylon, were viewed as coming from the "north" (Petersen, 174–75). On the repeated use of the "oracle formula" נְאֻם־יְהוָה throughout this pericope, see Hag 2:4 and the Appendix (§3).

כִּי כְּאַרְבַּע רוּחוֹת הַשָּׁמַיִם פֵּרַשְׂתִּי אֶתְכֶם נְאֻם־יְהוָה. Piel *qatal* 1 c s √פרשׂ. On the "four winds of heaven," cf. Jer 49:36; Dan 7:2 (Aramaic); 8:8; 11:4; Zech 6:5. Previous verses spoke of the Judeans being "scattered" using Piel √זרה (2:2, 4). Piel √פּרשׂ typically means "to spread (out)," most often speaking of spreading out one's hands (Ps 143:6; Isa 1:15; 25:11; 65:2; Jer 4:31; Lam 1:17), but the verb does occur in Ps 68:15 with reference to YHWH dispersing people, which is the sense here. Contra Tiemeyer (2004: 353), it cannot be assumed that the oracle formula נְאֻם־יהוה always introduces first person divine speech (see Appendix §3).

2:11 הוֹי צִיּוֹן הִמָּלְטִי יוֹשֶׁבֶת בַּת־בָּבֶל׃ ס

Nifal impv 2 f s √מלט; Qal ptc f s √ישׁב. See הוֹי in the previous verse. The use of √מלט along with √נוס in the previous verse may be the result of the intertextual influence of Jer 51:6 (Stead, 113–14). Many translations take צִיּוֹן as locative, e.g., "escape *to* Zion" (cf. RSV; LXX: εἰς Σιων), which is possible in light of an example such as 2 Kgs 19:37 וְהֵמָּה נִמְלְטוּ אֶרֶץ אֲרָרָט "and they escaped *to* the land of Ararat." However, it is not very common, and הוֹי is often followed by a vocative (WO §40.2.4a), suggesting that "Zion" is to be understood as the form of direct address (Vulg: *o Sion fuge*). The shift from the masculine plural imperative of verse 10 to the feminine singular imperative in verse 11 is due to the fact that "Zion" is being personified here. In this instance צִיּוֹן is symbolic of the entire people, not necessarily those living in Judea, and thus can stand in parallelism to יוֹשֶׁבֶת בַּת־בָּבֶל "O inhabitant of Daughter Babylon" (cf. Mitchell, 140–41). On the meaning of Qal √ישׁב as "to inhabit," see 1:11.

Construct phrases such as "daughter of Babylon" or "daughter of Zion" in verse 14 used as epithets are frequent in the HB (BDB, 123, #3). Typically these are understood as a type of appositional genitive and thus translated as "Daughter Babylon" or "Daughter Zion" (cf. GKC §128k; JM §129f7, r; WB §42a–b; MNK §25.4.4; AC §2.2.12), since the point is not that Zion *has* a "daughter" but rather Zion *is* the "daughter." This analysis has been challenged in recent years, however. Based on comparative Semitic parallels for the use of titles of goddesses with locations, Dobbs-Allsopp (1995: 451) argued that the Hebrew construction is to be understood as a divine epithet with the proper name of the city, country, or location in question as a genitive of location. He subsequently moderated his emphasis on the divine nature of the epithet but maintained his basic analysis of the construct phrase as a genitive of location (2009: 128–30, esp. n. 16). Floyd is dogmatic that a phrase such as בַּת־צִיּוֹן "cannot be grammatically analyzed as an appositional genitive" (504; cf. 490–92) and contends that the expression is intended figuratively to indicate that Zion has a daughter (or daughters) and that it is linked with the personification of Jerusalem/ Zion as a "mother" (Floyd, 492, 499, 502, 504). Regardless of the possible religious, socio-cultural, or literary backgrounds to the expression, however, both of these alternative proposals founder on the phrase בַּת־עַמִּי "daughter of my people" (e.g., Isa 22:4; Jer 4:11; etc.), which Dobbs-Allsopp (2009: 131 n. 21) rightly views as analogous to such constructions but Floyd (498 n. 34) arbitrarily excludes from consideration. It is clear that עַמִּי cannot function as a genitive of location, nor is it suitable as a genitive of possession or ownership when used with the singular בַּת, though such an analysis could plausibly be applied to the plural "daughters of X" in referring to the citizenry or populace of a location, e.g., Jdg 11:40 בְּנוֹת־יִשְׂרָאֵל "daughters of Israel," Isa 16:2 בְּנוֹת מוֹאָב "daughters of Moab," Isa 3:16 בְּנוֹת צִיּוֹן "daughters of Zion." In the end, the analysis of singular בַּת with the name of a location as an appositional genitive remains the best analysis.

2:12 כִּי כֹה אָמַר֮ יְהוָ֣ה צְבָאוֹת֒ אַחַ֣ר כָּב֔וֹד שְׁלָחַ֕נִי אֶל־הַגּוֹיִ֖ם הַשֹּׁלְלִ֣ים אֶתְכֶ֑ם כִּ֚י הַנֹּגֵ֣עַ בָּכֶ֔ם נֹגֵ֖עַ בְּבָבַ֥ת עֵינֽוֹ׃

Verses 12-13 are some of the most puzzling in the Night Visions (O'Kennedy 2013: 1). The commentary will focus first on grammatical and textual issues, and exegetical issues will be discussed below in the Excursus following verse 13.

כִּי כֹה אָמַר֮ יְהוָ֣ה צְבָאוֹת֒. Qal *qatal* 3 m s √אמר. It should be noted that this "messenger formula" does not always introduce a quotation of direct speech from YHWH, hence this does not necessarily determine who the speaker is in the following clause (see Appendix §2E).

אַחַ֣ר כָּב֔וֹד שְׁלָחַ֕נִי אֶל־הַגּוֹיִ֖ם הַשֹּׁלְלִ֣ים אֶתְכֶ֑ם. Qal *qatal* 3 m s √שלח with 1 c s pronoun suffix, Qal ptc m pl √שלל with def art. Since the participle is a verbal adjective, הַשֹּׁלְלִים can take a direct object such as אֶתְכֶם (WO §37.3b; JM §121k), even when it is functioning attributively, as in this instance. Attributive and substantival participles are unmarked for time reference (see Hag 1:6), and הַשֹּׁלְלִים need not be understood as referring to a "plundering" going on at the moment of speaking; in this instance, rather, it refers to past events and can be translated as such: "the nations which plundered you."

The verb √שׁלח is a key word in the passage, occurring in verses 12, 13, and 15. Some have suggested that שְׁלָחַנִי should be understood as a "prophetic perfect" referring to the future (Tiemeyer 2004: 369; Stead, 115 n. 153), but this usage of *qatal* is much less frequent than is typically supposed (Rogland 2003: 113–14). Moreover, a future-referring interpretation is most unlikely in light of the repeated use of the identical form שְׁלָחַנִי in the phrase וִידַעְתֶּם כִּי־יְהוָה צְבָאוֹת שְׁלָחָנִי "and you will know that YHWH Tsevaot *has sent me*" in verses 13 and 15 (see also 4:9 and 6:15). The identity of the subject and object of the verb are much disputed, as is the referent of the noun כָּבוֹד, e.g., "honor," "(vision of) glory," God's manifest presence, etc., and will be discussed in the Excursus below. The preposition אֶל could be understood as "to," "among," "concerning," or depending on one's overall interpretation of the clause, in a more antagonistic sense of "against" (Tiemeyer 2004: 362–63).

The most difficult grammatical challenge is the usage of אַחַר, which has been surveyed several times (e.g., Petitjean, 109–19; Tiemeyer 2004: 364–70; O'Kennedy 2013: 2–4; Wolters 2014: 80–82). It can mean "after" or "afterwards," functioning temporally as an adverb, preposition, or conjunction, though for the latter two uses the plural construct אַחֲרֵי is more common (BDB, 30). It is often alleged that אַחַר has some sort of final force, indicating purpose (see esp. Kloos and WO §11.2.1a), but despite the popularity of this suggestion it is very questionable philologically (Mitchell, 146; cf. JM §103a; BDB, 29–30; *HALOT*, 35–36). אַחַר often functions as a locative or spatial preposition ("behind"), and others have alleged that it can also mean "with" (e.g., Wolters 2014: 84), but this latter sense is dubious. It should be particularly noted that אַחַר occurs as a locative or spatial preposition with verbs of motion, e.g., Gen 37:17 וַיֵּלֶךְ יוֹסֵף אַחַר אֶחָיו "and Joseph went *after* his brothers," Num 25:8 וַיָּבֹא אַחַר אִישׁ־יִשְׂרָאֵל "and he went *after* the man of Israel" (BDB 29, #2a). Moreover, the construct plural form occurs with the verb √שׁלח, e.g., 2 Sam 3:26

וַיִּשְׁלַח מַלְאָכִים אַחֲרֵי אַבְנֵר "and he sent messengers *after* Abner," 2 Kgs 7:14 וַיִּשְׁלַח הַמֶּלֶךְ אַחֲרֵי מַחֲנֵה־אֲרָם "and the king sent (them) *after* the camp of Aram." The most straightforward syntactical analysis, then, is to take אַחַר כָּבוֹד as a prepositional complement to the verb √שׁלח, with the pronoun suffix indicating the direct object and אֶל־הַגּוֹיִם the indirect object. For further discussion, see the Excursus below.

כִּי הַנֹּגֵעַ בָּכֶם נֹגֵעַ בְּבָבַת עֵינוֹ. Qal ptc m s √נגע, with and without def art. The verb √נגע regularly utilizes בְּ to mark its object (Gen 3:3; 26:11; etc.). The noun בָּבָה is a *hapax* in CH, but it does occur in RH in a similar construction glossed as "pupil" (Jastrow, 136). Finley understands Hebrew בָּבָה to mean "gate" and claims that it is a wordplay with "Babylon" based on an Akkadian cognate, but this is a very tenuous suggestion (Wolters 2014: 85). An Aramaic origin is much more likely based on the Targumim, DSS, and Rabbinic sources (Shin, 65–67; cf. also BDB, 93; *HALOT*, 107). Elsewhere in CH we find what appears to be the functionally equivalent expressions אִישׁוֹן עַיִן (Deut 32:10; Prov 7:2; 4Q274 A 3:i:1) and אִישׁוֹן בַּת־עָיִן (Ps 17:8), or sometimes just אִישׁוֹן (Sir 3:25 [MsA] באין אישון יחסר אור "Without a pupil, one lacks light"), with no obvious difference in meaning from בָּבַת עָיִן. Some claim that אִישׁוֹן is a diminutive form of אִישׁ ("the little man of the eye": GKC §86d; *HALOT*, 44), but an instance such as Prov 7:9 בְּאִישׁוֹן לַיְלָה "in the middle of the night" (also 4Q184 1:6) suggests that "center (of the eye)" is preferable. In any event, the meaning "pupil" for אִישׁוֹן has disappeared in RH (Jastrow, 60), so perhaps we are simply dealing with a case of בָּבָה replacing an equivalent term (אִישׁוֹן) over time, with Zech 2:12 being the first CH attestation of this process.

MT's עֵינוֹ "his eye" is an instance of the *tiqqune sopherim* or "corrections of the scribes," who allegedly emended an original עֵינִי "my eye" for theological reasons (see *BHQ*, 136*; Tiemeyer 2004: 356). In a thorough analysis of this example, however, Fuller argues that the earliest Rabbinic discussions did not speak of this as a "correction" (תִּיקּוּן) but rather as a "euphemism" (כִּינּוּי, related to Piel √כנה), indicating that their comments were originally exegetical rather than text-critical in nature (Fuller, 24, 27). The earliest Hebrew manuscript evidence is found in the DSS (4Q12[e]) and, contrary to some claims otherwise, reads עינו rather than עיני (Fuller, 26–27; Ego et al., 175). This reading is supported by Targum Jonathan, the Peshitta, and most LXX manuscripts. Yet the possibility of scribal confusion of ו and י is well known, and there is evidence from some Latin and Greek witnesses supporting the reading "my eye" (Fuller, 25), indicating that the two readings existed at an early stage. On the whole, the weight of the textual data clearly favors the reading עֵינוֹ, a point granted even by those who accept the scribal correction to עֵינִי (e.g., Tiemeyer 2004: 357). The text-critical decision is typically made for exegetical rather than textual reasons; for example, Fuller (27–28) ultimately finds עֵינִי to be the preferable reading, since he believes that YHWH is the speaker in verse 12. See the Excursus below for further discussion of this point.

2:13 כִּ֣י הִנְנִ֨י מֵנִ֤יף אֶת־יָדִי֙ עֲלֵיהֶ֔ם וְהָי֥וּ שָׁלָ֖ל לְעַבְדֵיהֶ֑ם
וִֽידַעְתֶּ֕ם כִּֽי־יְהוָ֥ה צְבָא֖וֹת שְׁלָחָֽנִי׃ ס

כִּ֣י הִנְנִ֨י מֵנִ֤יף אֶת־יָדִי֙ עֲלֵיהֶ֔ם. Hifil ptc m s √נוף. The participle indicates the imminent future (see Hag 2:6). The preposition עַל could indicate "over" (Vulg: *super eos*) or "against" (LXX: ἐπ' αὐτούς), but the latter is to be preferred here due to the context of judgment. Hifil √נוף is most often used of worshippers or priests with reference to making a "wave offering" (Exod 29:24, 26; 35:22; Lev 8:27; etc.). When the HB refers to YHWH "raising" or "shaking" his hand at evildoers, typically the verb √נטה is used—e.g., Exod 7:5 בִּנְטֹתִ֥י אֶת־יָדִ֖י עַל־מִצְרָ֑יִם "when I stretch out my hand against Egypt"; Isa 5:25 וַיֵּ֨ט יָד֤וֹ עָלָיו֙ "and he stretched out his hand against him"; only twice in such contexts do we find YHWH as the subject of Hifil √נוף (Isa 11:15; 19:16).

וְהָי֥וּ שָׁלָ֖ל לְעַבְדֵיהֶ֑ם. Qal *weqatal* 3 c pl √היה. The verb √היה often indicates a change of state ("to become") and, as here, can occur with a predicate plus a לְ-phrase indicating the indirect object or beneficiary of a situation (BDB, 226, #II2d).

וִֽידַעְתֶּ֕ם כִּֽי־יְהוָ֥ה צְבָא֖וֹת שְׁלָחָֽנִי. Qal *weqatal* 2 m pl √ידע, Qal *qatal* 3 m s √שׁלח with 1 c s pronoun suffix. Similar "validation" formulae occur elsewhere in Zechariah (2:15; 4:9; 6:15), though other instances add the prepositional complement "to you" (cf. Stead, 122) and there is variation in the verbal form used (2:15 וְיָדַ֫עַתְּ; 4:9 וְיָדַעְתָּ֫) corresponding to the addressee. For the identity of the one who is "sent," see the following Excursus.

Excursus
Exegetical Analysis of Zechariah 2:12-13 [ET: vv. 8-9]

This Excursus cannot hope to summarize, let alone interact with, all of the detailed scholarly attempts to explain these verses (for a concise summary of the different interpretive options, see Wolters 2014: 80–82). Nevertheless, some brief exegetical remarks are in order by way of integrating the philological and grammatical issues discussed above. Various emendations are regularly proposed in order to make the text easier to comprehend, but these remarks will seek to explain the MT as the *lectio difficilior*.

One of the most pressing exegetical questions in these verses is that of the different participants: Who is the speaker in verses 12-13 (or elsewhere in vv. 10-17, for that matter)? Who or what is the subject, and who is the object, of שְׁלָחַ֫נִי in verses 12-13, and who is the subject of וִידַעְתֶּם and הִנְנִי מֵנִיף in verse 13? Throughout the pericope there is clearly *some* amount of switching between the voice of YHWH and the voice of the prophet, but some suggest the presence of other voices as well such as the Interpreting Angel, the angel of YHWH, or the Rider on the Red Horse from 1:7-17 (see the discussion in Tiemeyer 2004; Stead, 121–22; Wolters 2014: 84).

It is easiest to begin with the subject of וִידַעְתֶּם in verse 13 (and of וְיָדַ֫עַתְּ in v. 15) as there is the greatest amount of agreement here. It is widely acknowledged, despite the grammatical variation in gender and number (see v. 12), that the subject is God's people, either viewed as a feminine personification in verse 15 ("Daughter Zion") or as a plural group in verse 13 (cf. Wolters 2014: 86–87).

With regard to שְׁלָחַ֫נִי in verse 13, which has an explicit subject (YHWH), there is a fairly widespread consensus that understands the object suffix to be referring to the prophet. As Tiemeyer states, the purpose of the clause "is to verify the fact that Zechariah was sent by God to the Judahites and accordingly, the prophet's words are God's words" (2004: 355; see also Stead, 121; Wolters 2014: 86–87). The consensus is not shared by all, however. Von Orelli (186) takes the object to be the angel of YHWH; similarly, Van der Woude (1988a: 239) argues that Zechariah was never sent to the nations as verse 12 says, and therefore he identifies the "sent" one as the Interpreting Angel, which he also identifies with the angel of YHWH. Both views are problematic, however, since הַמַּלְאָךְ הַדֹּבֵר בִּי is distinct from מַלְאַךְ־יהוה in 1:7-17 (see the introductory remarks on 1:7-17), and the text gives no reason to view either one as speakers in this pericope (particularly as the angel of YHWH was last mentioned in 1:12). Besides, it is difficult to imagine what need there would be to validate that an angel had been sent by YHWH! Van der Woude's objection to taking the prophet as the object of שְׁלָחַנִי lacks force, for it must be borne in mind that this exhortation is given in the context of Zechariah's visionary experience, and therefore the question of what he may or may not have experienced in reality is irrelevant. Moreover, Stead (121) rightly notes that the prophet's initial commission was to proclaim a double message of YHWH's anger at the nations (1:14-15) and his return to his people (1:16-17). Historically, many Christian exegetes have understood the object of שְׁלָחַנִי (also in v. 12) to be Christ (Jerome, *PL* 25: 1433; Augustine, *De civitate Dei* 20:30; Luther, 571–74) or the angel of YHWH interpreted christologically (Calvin), though the latter view is open to the criticisms mentioned above (see also Wolters 2014: 84 and Tiemeyer 2004: 360). Furthermore the fact that this validation formula refers to the sending of the prophet in all of its other occurrences (2:15; 4:9; 6:15) speaks against either option. The consensus view is adopted here, according to which verse 13 speaks of YHWH sending the prophet.

Turning to the analysis of שְׁלָחַנִי in verse 12, scholarly opinions begin to part ways more dramatically. Some of the problems have just been noted with the notion that Christ or the angel of YHWH could be the object of the verb. Some analyze the form precisely as the identical שְׁלָחַנִי in verses 13 and 15, namely, that YHWH is the subject and the prophet the object (e.g., Stead, 121; Wolters 2014: 83, 86–87), and that is the understanding followed here (the formula כֹּה אָמַר יְהוָה does not require that the following words be understood as direct speech from YHWH; see v. 12). Tiemeyer (2004: 355) avers, claiming that the clauses in question are dissimilar inasmuch as שְׁלָחַנִי in verse 12 is part of a more complex clause and involves different addressees (v. 12 הַגּוֹיִם vs. v. 13 God's people). Moreover, she argues that verse 12 is surrounded by verses in which God speaks in the first person singular, and finds it unlikely that verse 12 would be an exception. Thus she believes that YHWH is the object of שְׁלָחַנִי in verse 12 (which she understands as a future-referring prophetic perfect). Interpreting אַחַר as a temporal adverb ("afterwards") understood in relation to the preceding verse, she takes כָּבוֹד in the sense of "honor" as the subject of the verb שְׁלָחַנִי. Tiemeyer's proposal, then, is that a sense of honor will "send" or compel YHWH to go against the despoiling nations (2004: 370–72). This interpretation requires several questionable assumptions, however, such as reading שְׁלָחַ֫נִי as a prophetic perfect and the "emended" reading of עֵינִי instead of the better-attested עֵינוֹ (see v. 12). Moreover, despite her claims to the contrary, there is a great deal of *prima facie* plausibility for interpreting the verbal form שְׁלָחַ֫נִי in verses 12, 13, and 15 in a similar fashion, according to which YHWH is the subject and the prophet is the object.

How then is the difficult אַחַר כָּבוֹד שְׁלָחַנִי אֶל־הַגּוֹיִם הַשֹּׁלְלִים אֶתְכֶם of verse 12 to be understood? It was argued above (see v. 12), in light of the use of אַחַר/אַחֲרֵי with verbs of movement and sending, that the most straightforward syntactical explanation is to take אַחַר כָּבוֹד as a prepositional complement to the verb √שׁלח: YHWH sent the prophet אַחַר כָּבוֹד. In the immediate context of Zech 2, the most plausible understanding of כָּבוֹד is in line with its previous occurrence just a few verses earlier, namely, as "the manifest presence of YHWH" (see v. 9). Thus the clause should be translated, "After (behind, following) the Glory he sent me to the nations who plundered you." The statement is to be understood as picking up the Pentateuchal theme of YHWH (or his angel) "going before" (לִפְנֵי) Moses and the Israelites (Exod 14:19; 22:30; 23:23; 32:34; 33:2; Deut 1:30; 31:8; cf. Exod 23:27-28; 32:1, 23) in a pillar of smoke and fire (Exod 13:21-22; Num 9:15-33; 10:34-36; 11:25; 12:5, 10; 14:14; Deut 1:33; 4:11; 5:22; 31:15; cf. Exod 14:19-20, 24), which was the manifestation of the כְּבוֹד־יהוה (Exod 16:7, 10; 24:16-18; 33:9-10, 18, 22; 40:34-38; Num 10:11-14; 17:7; Deut 5:24; cf. Exod 19:9, 16; 29:43; 34:5; Num 14:21-22; 16:19; 20:6). Instead of speaking of God's glorious presence "going before" the prophet, it is just as legitimate to speak of the prophet as being "sent after" it or following it. The prophet has been sent "to the nations who plundered" God's people, the apple of "his" eye (עֵינוֹ), yet he is not going alone: he is preceded by "the Glory," that is, the powerful presence of YHWH.

One possible objection to this proposal is that the identity of the speaker appears to shift without warning in the next verse. (This is not unique to the interpretation proposed here; however, it is one of the chief sources of confusion for any exegetical analysis.) כִּי הִנְנִי מֵנִיף אֶת־יָדִי עֲלֵיהֶם וְהָיוּ שָׁלָל לְעַבְדֵיהֶם in verse 13 is typically understood as YHWH's promise to punish the nations hostile to his people, spoken in the first person. Despite the general agreement on this point, however, there are reasons to question this assumption. As noted above (see v. 13), YHWH's "stretching out his hand" as an act of judgment typically employs different terminology (e.g., √נטה), whereas the subject of the verb √נוף is almost always a human agent and is only very rarely used of YHWH in a context of judgment. A smoother reading results if we maintain that the prophet is the speaker in verse 13, as he is in verse 12. One might further object that this wrongly attributes divine power to the prophet's gesture, but such an objection creates a false dichotomy between prophetic actions and YHWH's deeds. In 2 Kgs 5:11, for example, Naaman grumbles about having to wash in the Jordan River, since he was expecting a prophetic sign-act to accompany a miraculous cleansing: יֵצֵא יָצוֹא וְעָמַד וְקָרָא בְּשֵׁם־יְהוָה אֱלֹהָיו וְהֵנִיף יָדוֹ אֶל־הַמָּקוֹם וְאָסַף הַמְּצֹרָע "He will surely come and stand and call on the name of YHWH his God *and wave his hand* over the spot and he will remove the leprous one." Similarly, in the Exodus narrative, Moses and Aaron are given a series of "signs" by which YHWH brings the plagues on the Egyptians (Exod 4; 7–10). It is noteworthy that divine judgments are frequently initiated by the hand motions of Moses and Aaron (Exod 7:19; 8:1; 9:22; 10:12, 21; 14:16, 26; cf. 8:2, 13; 10:22; 14:21, 27; 17:11). There is thus no need to create a disjunction between a prophetic sign-gesture and YHWH's acts of power.

This proposed reading of verse 13 finds intertextual confirmation as well. If one casts a glance back over the first two chapters of Zechariah, one can observe a number of significant intertextual references to the book of Exodus. It was argued above that the "rider on the red horse" standing by "the deep" in chapter 1 was an allusion to the events at the *Yam Suf* in Exod 14–15 (see 1:8), and the vision of the man with the measuring cord also contained possible references to Exod 3–4 (see 2:9). As proposed above, the prophet's being sent "behind" the manifest glory of YHWH draws upon themes from the Pentateuch, most profoundly from Exodus (see above). The reference in verse 13 to a prophetic sign-gesture as an instrument of YHWH's judgment likewise draws upon similar themes from the Exodus narrative of Moses' call and the plagues upon Egypt. This convergence of probable references to the book of Exodus suggests that it was a productive source of intertexts for the Night Visions. This in turn helps to explain the somewhat unexpected occurrence of the "prophetic validation" theme in verses

13 and 15. Wolters (2014: 87) remarks, "The repeated use of this formula seems to suggest that Zechariah initially encountered some skepticism about his legitimacy as a נָבִיא who could claim to speak on behalf of the Lord." This appears unlikely in view of the people's receptive response to the initial prophetic summons (see 1:6). Rather, its presence in verses 13 and 15 is more likely to be attributed to the intertextual influence of Exodus, for it must be recalled that Moses was given prophetic signs that would validate him as one to whom YHWH had "appeared" (Exod 3:16; 4:1, 5) and whom he had "sent" (√שׁלח: Exod 3:12-15; 7:16; cf. 5:22). The prophet in Zech 2 is thus being presented as a kind of "new Moses," performing "signs" which both confirm his prophetic credentials and also initiate YHWH's judgment on those who had made "slaves" (עֲבָדִים) of God's people. Indeed, just as the Israelites "plundered the Egyptians" before (Exod 12:36), so it is promised that once again the enemies of God's people "will become plunder for their slaves" (v. 13 וְהָיוּ שָׁלָל לְעַבְדֵיהֶם).

2:14 רָנִּי וְשִׂמְחִי בַּת־צִיּוֹן כִּי הִנְנִי־בָא וְשָׁכַנְתִּי בְתוֹכֵךְ נְאֻם־יְהוָה׃

רָנִּי וְשִׂמְחִי בַּת־צִיּוֹן. Qal impv 2 f s √רנן, Qal impv 2 f s √שׂמח with prefixed *vav*. The two verbs are used in parallelism several times (Pss 5:12; 32:11; 35:27; 67:5; 90:14; Prov 29:6; Zeph 3:14). On the construct phrase בַּת־צִיּוֹן "Daughter Zion," see verse 11.

כִּי הִנְנִי־בָא וְשָׁכַנְתִּי בְתוֹכֵךְ נְאֻם־יְהוָה. Qal ptc m s √בוא, Qal *weqatal* 1 c s √שׁכן. On the frequent use of the participle-*weqatal* sequence in the prophets, see Hag 2:7. The theme of YHWH "dwelling" (√שׁכן) among his people is common in the HB (see discussion in Wolters 2014: 234–36), being applied to the tabernacle (e.g., Exod 25:8; 29:45-46; Num 5:3), Solomonic temple (1 Kgs 6:13), and Ezekelian (eschatological) temple (Ezek 43:7, 9), and occurs elsewhere in Zechariah (8:3, cf. v. 8). The verb is typically translated as "to dwell" but can have a more inceptive sense of "to settle down to abide" (BDB, 1015, #1; e.g., Jdg 5:17 גִּלְעָד בְּעֵבֶר הַיַּרְדֵּן שָׁכֵן "Gilead settled across the Jordan"), which seems to be the sense here (see the identical statement in the following verse).

2:15 וְנִלְווּ֩ גוֹיִ֨ם רַבִּ֤ים אֶל־יְהוָה֙ בַּיּ֣וֹם הַה֔וּא וְהָ֥יוּ לִ֖י לְעָ֑ם וְשָׁכַנְתִּ֣י בְתוֹכֵ֔ךְ וְיָדַ֕עַתְּ כִּֽי־יְהוָ֥ה צְבָא֖וֹת שְׁלָחַ֥נִי אֵלָֽיִךְ׃

וְנִלְווּ֩ גוֹיִ֨ם רַבִּ֤ים אֶל־יְהוָה֙ בַּיּ֣וֹם הַה֔וּא. Nifal *weqatal* 3 c pl √לוה. The verb is used in a similar context of Gentiles "joining themselves" to the people of God in Esth 9:27; Isa 14:1; 56:3, 6 (cf. Stead, 119–20).

וְהָ֥יוּ לִ֖י לְעָ֑ם וְשָׁכַנְתִּ֣י בְתוֹכֵ֔ךְ. Qal *weqatal* 3 c pl √היה, Qal *weqatal* 1 c s √שׁכן. The verb √היה can occur with two לְ-complements (BDB, 226, #II2f), one indicating the predicate (i.e., what something is *becoming*) and the other indicating the indirect object or beneficiary (BDB, 226, #IIf), e.g., Gen 11:3 וַתְּהִי לָהֶם הַלְּבֵנָה לְאָבֶן "and the brick was (as) stone for them." It is striking that this portion of the common covenantal formula (see, e.g., Jer 31:33) is applied to "many nations" who have joined themselves to YHWH (for the full formula, see 8:8). On וְשָׁכַנְתִּ֣י בְתוֹכֵ֔ךְ, see verse 14. It is possible that the verbatim repetition of the phrase from verse 14 is simply intended to reinforce the point being made, but as noted above, וְשָׁכַנְתִּ֣י in verse 14 follows the promise of YHWH's "coming" to Zion (הִנְנִי־בָא) and appears to have an inceptive sense of "settling down" to take up residence among the covenant community (see v. 14). The present statement, in contrast, implies continued dwelling there.

וְיָדַ֕עַתְּ כִּֽי־יְהוָ֥ה צְבָא֖וֹת שְׁלָחַ֥נִי אֵלָֽיִךְ. Qal *weqatal* 2 f s √ידע, Qal *qatal* 3 m s √שׁלח with 1 c s pronoun suffix. On the variations of this "validation formula," see v. 13. On the identity of the speaker as Zechariah, see the Excursus above.

2:16 וְנָחַ֨ל יְהוָ֤ה אֶת־יְהוּדָה֙ חֶלְק֔וֹ עַ֖ל אַדְמַ֣ת הַקֹּ֑דֶשׁ וּבָחַ֥ר ע֖וֹד בִּירוּשָׁלִָֽם׃

וְנָחַ֨ל יְהוָ֤ה אֶת־יְהוּדָה֙ חֶלְק֔וֹ עַ֖ל אַדְמַ֣ת הַקֹּ֑דֶשׁ. Qal *weqatal* 3 m s √נחל. YHWH is said to "take possession" or "inherit" his people (Exod 34:9 וּנְחַלְתָּנוּ "and take possession of us"; cf. Ps 82:8 כִּי־אַתָּה תִנְחַל בְּכָל־הַגּוֹיִם), who are elsewhere called his נַחֲלָה "inheritance" (Deut 32:9 חֵלֶק . . . נַחֲלָתוֹ; Isa 19:25). In this instance, the reference to "Judah" is probably not intended as a metonymy for the Judean populace (cf. on v. 8) but is rather as a geographical-territorial designation, since it is specified that YHWH will take possession of Judah "as his portion upon the holy ground," with חֶלְקוֹ "his portion" to be understood as an indirect accusative (JM §126c; WB §57a–b; MNK §33.3iii; AC §2.3.2d; WO §10.2.2d–e). אַדְמַת הַקֹּדֶשׁ (cf. Exod 3:5) represents a "genitive of quality." BH regularly uses such construct relationships involving abstract nouns in the place of an adjective in grammatical apposition to a noun (JM §129f; AC §2.2.5; WB §41; MNK §25.4.6iii; WO §9.5.3a–b).

וּבָחַר עוֹד בִּירוּשָׁלִָם. Qal *weqatal* 3 m s √בחר. See 1:17.

2:17 הַס כָּל־בָּשָׂר מִפְּנֵי יְהוָה כִּי נֵעוֹר מִמְּעוֹן קָדְשׁוֹ׃ ס

Nifal *qatal* 3 m s √עור. According to *HALOT* (253), the interjection הַס "be silent!" resulted in a denominative verb √הסה, attested in Num 13:30 וַיַּהַס כָּלֵב אֶת־הָעָם "and Caleb quieted the people" and found in the DSS (1QH 18:15) and RH (Jastrow, 359). כָּל־בָּשָׂר "all flesh" is a common epithet in the HB for "every creature/ all living creatures," and depending on the context can have a specifically human referent or can include animals as well as human beings. Nifal √עור suggests being roused from a state of inactivity, including sleeping and death (BDB, 735). Most occurrences of the noun מָעוֹן occur either in the idiom מְעוֹן תַּנִּים "lair of jackals" (Jer 9:10; 10:22; 49:33; 51:37) or else refer to YHWH's "habitation" in heaven (e.g., Deut 6:15; 2 Chron 30:27; Ps 68:6; Jer 25:30) or the tabernacle/temple (1 Sam 2:29; 2 Chron 36:15; Ps 26:8). Stead (126) argues that this verse is a probable intertextual echo of Hab 2:20 וַיהוָה בְּהֵיכַל קָדְשׁוֹ הַס מִפָּנָיו כָּל־הָאָרֶץ, though the possible influence of Zeph 1:7 הַס מִפְּנֵי אֲדֹנָי יְהוִה should not be excluded.

Fourth Vision (Zechariah 3:1-10)
New High Priestly Clothes for Joshua

The fourth Night Vision is centered on Joshua the high priest and begins as he is seen standing before the angel of YHWH. To Joshua's right the prophet sees "the Satan" (הַשָּׂטָן; on the term, see below), who is rebuked by YHWH (v. 2). It is then revealed that Joshua is wearing filthy garments (v. 3), which are subsequently changed for clean ones (vv. 4-5). Although verse 7 contains some philological challenges, it appears to be a divine promise that if Joshua is faithful in the discharge of his office, he will be granted intermediaries who will "go about" in YHWH's throne room. A brief oracle begins in verse 8 in which YHWH promises to send his servant *Ṣemaḥ* (צֶמַח). Verses 9-10 contain a reference to a stone (or stones) of Joshua's high priestly garb (v. 9) with the assurance of the removal of the land's iniquity "in a single day," a statement strongly suggestive of the Day of Atonement ritual (Rogland 2013a, with references to further literature). The passage concludes with a promise of prosperity (v. 10). The basic thrust of the vision is both to encourage Joshua and to challenge him to faithful ministry, and thereby to provide the people with a hope of future blessing, brought about in part through his priestly intercession.

The figures of *Ṣemaḥ* (צֶ֫מַח) and "the Satan" (הַשָּׂטָן) have produced an enormous amount of scholarly literature, which cannot be adequately treated here, but a few brief remarks are in order. שָׂטָן/ הַשָּׂטָן is attested in the HB with and without the definite article, and there is much discussion as to whether or not it is to be understood as a proper name (cf. Wolters 2014: 91). It is widely held that the noun שָׂטָן means an "accuser" or "adversary"—often popularly likened to a "prosecuting attorney"—with the denominative verb √שׂטן understood accordingly (e.g., BDB, 966). An important study by Stokes (2014) has demonstrated the shortcomings of this understanding, however, which is based on a number of unproven assumptions. While the word group indeed conveys an adversarial notion, there is little evidence that it is juridical in nature, and a closer examination of its usage in BH indicates that it is to be understood more specifically as denoting "violent, physical attack" (Stokes, 253, 264), e.g., Num 22:22, 32-33; 1 Sam 29:4; 2 Sam 19:23 (ET: v. 22); 1 Kgs 5:18 (ET: v. 4). Even a case like Ps 109:6 וְשָׂטָן יַעֲמֹד עַל־יְמִינוֹ "and may a שָׂטָן stand at his right hand" does not need to be read in an "accusatory" legal fashion but rather in an aggressive, violent sense, befitting the imprecations of verses 8ff. A preferable rendering of הַשָּׂטָן, according to Stokes, would be "the executioner" or "the attacker." The latter term is adopted here, taking it not as a proper name but as a common noun being used as a title.

The reference to the coming of צֶ֫מַח in verse 8, also mentioned in 6:12, is typically associated intertextually with the prophecies of Jer 23:1-8; 33:1-26; and Isa 11:1-10 (Stead, 166–68), though the terminology of the latter is distinctly different as it utilizes חֹטֶר, נֵצֶר, and שֹׁרֶשׁ (Rose, 108–9). With regard to the meaning of צֶ֫מַח in verse 8 and 6:12, after an extensive lexical and comparative-philological investigation, Rose concludes that

> the Hebrew noun צֶמַח and its use in the Old Testament suggests the meaning of this word is neither "branch" nor "shoot/sprout," as is commonly thought, but (a) "vegetation, greenery, growth," and (b) "growth" (as a process). Similarly, the verb צָמַח means "to grow." Evidence from cognate languages is too scarce to either support or contradict this interpretation. (91–120, esp. 106)

The fact that צֶמַח is anarthrous but stands in apposition to the definite "my servant" (עַבְדִּי) indicates that it is functioning as a proper noun (BDB, 855, #3), and indeed the name *Ṣemaḥ* is attested in epigraphic Hebrew (Arad 49:11 *[b]n ṣmḥ* "[s]on of *Ṣemaḥ*") and hence will simply be transliterated here. The identity of *Ṣemaḥ* is a major point of contention within OT scholarship, with many suggesting that he is Zerubbabel (Boda 2001: §4.3.3.4) but others asserting that he is a figure on the more distant horizon (Rose).

[1]And he showed me Joshua the High Priest standing before the angel of YHWH, and the Attacker was standing on his right to attack him.

[2]And YHWH said to the Attacker, "May YHWH reject you, O Attacker! Yea, may YHWH, who is going to choose Jerusalem, reject you! Is this one not a brand plucked out of the fire?"

[3]And Joshua had been clothed in filthy garments, and was standing before the angel.

[4]And he responded and said to the ones standing before him: "Remove those filthy garments from him." And he said to him, "See, I hereby remove your punishment for iniquity from you; let them dress you in a sash."

[5]And I said, "Let them place a clean turban upon his head." And they placed the clean turban upon his head, and they dressed him with garments. And the angel of YHWH was waiting.

[6]And the angel of YHWH impressed upon Joshua:

[7]"Thus has YHWH Tsevaot said, If you walk in my ways and if you keep my guard, and you judge my household as well as guard my courts, then I will appoint for you those who go about among these ones standing by.

[8]Now hear, O High Priest Joshua—you and your fellow citizens who are dwelling under your oversight, for they are men receiving a miraculous sign—for behold, I am going to bring my servant, Ṣemaḥ.

[9]For behold the stone which I have set before Joshua: Upon one stone with seven surfaces I am going to engrave its engraving—oracle of YHWH Tsevaot. And I will depart with the guilt of that land in one day.

[10]In that day—oracle of YHWH Tsevaot—you will call to each other to come under one's vine and fig tree."

3:1 וַיַּרְאֵנִי אֶת־יְהוֹשֻׁעַ הַכֹּהֵן הַגָּדוֹל עֹמֵד לִפְנֵי מַלְאַךְ
יְהוָה וְהַשָּׂטָן עֹמֵד עַל־יְמִינוֹ לְשִׂטְנוֹ׃

וַיַּרְאֵנִי אֶת־יְהוֹשֻׁעַ הַכֹּהֵן הַגָּדוֹל עֹמֵד לִפְנֵי מַלְאַךְ יְהוָה. Hifil *wayyiqtol* 3 m s √ראה with 1 c s pronoun suffix, Qal ptc m s √עמד. The subject of the verb is not stated; the same verb occurs in 1:9 with the Interpreting Angel as the subject, but in 2:3 with YHWH as the subject, making it difficult to decide. On the identity of the "angel of YHWH," see the introductory remarks to 1:7-17. "To stand before" (עָמַד לִפְנֵי) someone often means "to be(come) the servant of, attend upon" (BDB, 764, #1e), but in this instance it simply refers to Joshua's physical stance or position.

וְהַשָּׂטָן עֹמֵד עַל־יְמִינוֹ לְשִׂטְנוֹ. Qal ptc m s √עמד, Qal inf cstr √שׂטן with prefixed לְ and 3 m s pronoun suffix. See the introductory remarks to this pericope for the rendering of הַשָּׂטָן as "the Attacker" and the verb לְשִׂטְנוֹ as "to attack him." Proper nouns as a rule do not take determiners such as the definite article (JM §137b), thus its occurrence with שָׂטָן in this instance indicates that it is functioning as a title rather than a name.

3:2 וַיֹּאמֶר יְהוָה אֶל־הַשָּׂטָן יִגְעַר יְהוָה בְּךָ הַשָּׂטָן
וְיִגְעַר יְהוָה בְּךָ הַבֹּחֵר בִּירוּשָׁלִָם הֲלוֹא זֶה אוּד
מֻצָּל מֵאֵשׁ׃

וַיֹּאמֶר יְהוָה אֶל־הַשָּׂטָן. Qal *wayyiqtol* 3 m s √אמר. The clause could indicate that YHWH is a distinct character in this vision, though it may be that we are to understand the מַלְאַךְ־יהוה as speaking on YHWH's behalf. Note that in verses 6-10 the angel of YHWH is speaking (v. 6 וַיָּעַד מַלְאַךְ יְהוָה בִּיהוֹשֻׁעַ לֵאמֹר), but what follows is clearly first person speech from YHWH ("my ways . . . my house . . . my courts,"). While it may seem odd to the contemporary reader for YHWH to refer to himself in the third person in the following discourse (cf. Joosten 2014: 353 n. 25), such uses are attested elsewhere in the HB (e.g., Num 32:11-12; Deut 1:36; 2 Sam 7:11; Hos 1:7; Amos 4:11).

יִגְעַר יְהוָה בְּךָ הַשָּׂטָן. Qal jussive 3 m s √גער. Sentence-initial *yiqtol* forms typically display the jussive rather than the indicative mood (see Niccacci, with further refinement by Joosten 2011). Although the verb displays jussive modality, which is often associated with wishes and prayers, the fact that it is uttered by YHWH (or his representative angel) assures its fulfillment (cf. Num 6:24-27). The definite article can serve for the vocative (JM §137g; WB §89; AC §2.1.3; MNK §24.4.3i; WO §13.5.2c), hence הַשָּׂטָן is to be rendered "O Attacker!"

The verb √גער sometimes takes an accusative object but more typically governs objects with בְּ (Hartley, 885; BDB, 172) and most often has YHWH as the subject (10 out of 15×). It is often understood as "to rebuke" (BDB, 172; *HALOT*, 199–200), but some DSS occurrences of the verb have the notion of "to reject, drive out" (*DCH* 2, 369–70): 1QM 14:10 ורוחי [ח]בלו גערתה ממ[נו "you *have driven* his spirits of destruction fr[om us]"; 1QH[a] 17:11-12 ולא גערתה חיי ושלומי לא הזנחתה ולא עזבתה תקותי "You *have not rejected* my life, and you have not spurned my well-being, and you have not forsaken my hope." Interestingly, in some broken contexts we find the verb used with בליעל and שטן as objects: 4Q463 D 2:3 ויגער בליעל "And he *drove out* Belial" and 1QH[a] 22:25 תגער בכול שטן משחית "You *will drive out* every destroying attacker." Joosten (2014) has drawn attention to analogous uses of Aramaic √גער in the exorcism of evil spirits in the *Genesis Apocryphon* from Qumran (1Q20 20:28-29), a usage which is amply attested in later Aramaic amulets. Furthermore, it is noteworthy that over time Zech 3:2 became a staple text for defense against evil spirits (cf. *b. Berachot* 51a) and was utilized in exorcisms. Joosten (2014: 354) suggests that such later usages represent a "delocutive" derivation—that is, that √גער in the sense of "to exorcize" developed from "to say 'may the Lord rebuke you' (Zech 3:2)" to "to exorcize by reciting Zech 3:2." Nevertheless, while Zech 3:2 was undoubtedly influential on later exorcistic practices, it is questionable whether all "expelling" or "rejecting" usages can be derived from it (e.g., 1QH[a] 17:11-12). Moreover, it is arguably the case that an exorcistic sense is already attested in Ketef Hinnom II:4 הגער ב־ "the one who *drives out*" (Barkay et al., 65) from the late seventh or early sixth century BCE, thus predating Zechariah, and much earlier in Ugaritic. Hence a simpler explanation is that BH √גער has a wider range of meanings than has often been noticed and can express not only "to rebuke" but also "to reject, to drive away/out," —e.g., Ruth 2:16 (*TDOT* 3, 50); Pss 9:6 (parallel to Piel √אבד); 106:9; Isa 17:13 (followed by Qal √נוס); 54:9 (parallel to Qal √קצף; quoted in 4Q176); Nah 1:4; and Mal 2:3; 3:11. The more specialized use of √גער in exorcisms can be viewed as an application of this latter sense.

וְיִגְעַר יְהוָה בְּךָ הַבֹּחֵר בִּירוּשָׁלָםִ. Qal jussive 3 m s √גער with *vav*, Qal ptc m s √בחר with def art. The form וְיִגְעַר could represent a "direct volitive" (JM §114) with a simple juxtaposing *vav*, or the *vav* could introduce a subordinate clause as an "indirect volitive" (JM §116), which can convey various nuances of purpose or consecution (cf. Muraoka 1997). The former option seems more likely here, as it is difficult to see how וְיִגְעַר would be subordinated to יִגְעַר. The verbal forms יִגְעַר . . . וְיִגְעַר may seem repetitious but in this instance the *vav* probably indicates an affirming sense of "yea" (BDB, 252, #1c; GKC §154a n.1b). On the use of Qal √בחר with בְּ, see 1:17, and on the temporal reference of substantival participles, see 1:9. The previous references to YHWH "choosing" (√בחר) Jerusalem in 1:17 and 2:16 [ET v. 12] were future oriented, and the participle הַבֹּחֵר is best understood in a similar vein.

הֲלוֹא זֶה אוּד מֻצָּל מֵאֵשׁ. Hofal ptc m s √נצל. The noun אוּד is rare in BH and the DSS (Isa 7.4; Amos 4.11; 4Q171 1+3_4 iii 7-8), but it is attested in RH (Jastrow, 22) and its meaning of "firebrand" is not in doubt.

3:3 וִיהוֹשֻׁעַ הָיָה לָבֻשׁ בְּגָדִים צוֹאִים וְעֹמֵד לִפְנֵי הַמַּלְאָךְ׃

וִיהוֹשֻׁעַ הָיָה לָבֻשׁ בְּגָדִים צוֹאִים. Qal *qatal* 3 m s √היה, Qal passive ptc m s √לבשׁ. The passive participle "mostly denotes a completed action or a state" (JM §121q; AC §3.4.3) and can occur with direct objects (JM §121o), primarily with verbs of wearing, as here: "dressed (in) filthy garments." In this case it is not immediately obvious why the periphrastic construction of √היה plus participle was employed, as it does not seem necessary since the past time frame has already been established in verses 1-2, and the situation is continuous or durative by its nature (cf. JM §121f–g). Possibly the construction was used for temporal backtracking, which is a common function of the *vav*-subject-*qatal* structure in narrative texts, often being equivalent to a pluperfect: "Now Joshua *had been clothed* with filthy garments." The narrator would thus be providing background information to explain the reason for the "aggression" of verses 1-2, which had not yet been explained. The adjective צֹאִי "filthy" is related to nouns referring to excrement, e.g., צֵאָה (Deut 23:14; Ezek 4:12) and צֹאָה (*Qere* in 2 Kgs 18:27 and Isa 36:12; Temple Scroll 46:15).

וְעֹמֵד לִפְנֵי הַמַּלְאָךְ. Qal ptc m s √עמד. The RSV has inexplicably reversed the order of the clauses: "Now Joshua was standing before the angel, clothed with filthy garments."

3:4 וַיַּעַן וַיֹּאמֶר אֶל־הָעֹמְדִים לְפָנָיו לֵאמֹר הָסִירוּ הַבְּגָדִים הַצֹּאִים מֵעָלָיו וַיֹּאמֶר אֵלָיו רְאֵה הֶעֱבַרְתִּי מֵעָלֶיךָ עֲוֺנֶךָ וְהַלְבֵּשׁ אֹתְךָ מַחֲלָצוֹת׃

וַיַּעַן וַיֹּאמֶר אֶל־הָעֹמְדִים לְפָנָיו לֵאמֹר. Qal *wayyiqtol* 3 m s √ענה, Qal *wayyiqtol* 3 m s √אמר, Qal ptc m pl √עמד with def art, Qal inf cstr √אמר with prefixed לְ. On the verb √ענה as "to respond," see 1:10. One can assume that the subject of the verb is the angel of YHWH (Tiemeyer 2015: 128). The "ones standing" are most often understood as referring to the members of the heavenly court (see v. 7).

הָסִירוּ הַבְּגָדִים הַצֹּאִים מֵעָלָיו. Hifil impv 2 m pl √סור. The def art on הַבְּגָדִים הַצֹּאִים (cp. v. 3) is anaphoric and could be translated as a demonstrative: "*those* filthy garments" (see Hag 2:3). The compound preposition מֵעַל is often used with the removal of garments or ornaments (BDB, 758, #IV2a).

וַיֹּאמֶר אֵלָיו רְאֵה הֶעֱבַרְתִּי מֵעָלֶיךָ עֲוֺנֶךָ. Qal *wayyiqtol* 3 m s √אמר, Qal impv 2 m s √ראה, Hifil *qatal* 1 c s √עבר. The angel of YHWH continues to speak, beginning with the exclamation רְאֵה, which essentially functions as a variant of הֵן and הִנֵּה "behold!" (MNK §44.3). The context of a symbolic (ritual) act makes it likely that הֶעֱבַרְתִּי is best understood as a "performative perfect" (Rogland 2003: 115–26): "I (hereby) put away." In this instance, the compound preposition מֵעַל is used for "relief from a burden or trouble" (BDB, 758, #IV2b; see also on the preceding clause). It is unlikely that עָוֺן "iniquity" is to be understood to refer to Joshua's personal sin, whether specific or general, but the noun can refer to the consequences of or punishment for iniquity (BDB, 731, #3), which is undoubtedly the intent here. In this context it would refer to the destruction of Jerusalem and the Babylonian exile as consequences of the people's sin, which uniquely affected the priesthood and Joshua as the High Priest.

וְהַלְבֵּשׁ אֹתְךָ מַחֲלָצוֹת. Hifil inf abs √לבשׁ. The infinitive absolute sometimes occurs in place of a finite verb (see Hag 1:6), which could be an indicative future tense (RSV: "I will clothe you . . ."; cf. Smith, 258) or a volitive such as a jussive or imperative (cf. LXX:

ἐνδύσατε). While either option is possible contextually, the occurrence of a jussive form in the following verse seems to favor a volitive understanding of the verb here. It is questionable, however, whether this use of the infinitve absolute can be considered more "emphatic" than an imperative (so GKC §113bb; see Muraoka 1985: 83–92). The noun מַחֲלָצוֹת only occurs in this verse and in a lengthy list of items of women's clothing in Isa 3:22 (which includes the rare word צָנִיף in v. 23, see the following verse). The word is sometimes grouped with √חלץ I "to draw off or out," understanding מַחֲלָצוֹת to refer to "robes of state" which are "taken off" in ordinary life (e.g., BDB, 322–23). On the other hand, perhaps it is to be derived from √חלץ II (so Alden, 917), which is associated with the noun חָלָץ "loins." If so, it could possibly be a functional equivalent of the high priest's אַבְנֵט "girdle" or "sash" (Exod 28:4 מִצְנֶפֶת וְאַבְנֵט). The chapter's intertextual connections with Exodus would favor the latter derivation.

3:5 וָאֹמַ֕ר יָשִׂ֛ימוּ צָנִ֥יף טָה֖וֹר עַל־רֹאשׁ֑וֹ וַיָּשִׂימוּ֩ הַצָּנִ֨יף הַטָּה֜וֹר עַל־רֹאשׁ֗וֹ וַיַּלְבִּשֻׁ֙הוּ֙ בְּגָדִ֔ים וּמַלְאַ֥ךְ יְהוָ֖ה עֹמֵֽד׃

וָאֹמַ֕ר יָשִׂ֛ימוּ צָנִ֥יף טָה֖וֹר עַל־רֹאשׁ֑וֹ. Qal *wayyiqtol* 1 c s √אמר, Qal jussive 3 m pl √שׂים. The 1 c s verb וָאֹמַר is not grammatically difficult though the change from third to first person has troubled some scholars (cf. Wolters 2014: 94–95; Stead, 158–59 n. 91). See verse 2 regarding jussive verbs in clause-initial position. The adjective טָהוֹר is closely associated with ritual purity, which suits the priestly themes of the text. The noun צָנִיף, glossed as "turban" in the lexica (see also Way), is related to the verb √צנף "to wrap, wind up." It is not common in CH, occurring only in Job 29:14; Isa 3:23; 62:3; Zech 3:5; Sir 11:5 (MsA MsB); 40:4 (MsB); 47:6 (MsB). Etymologically it is related to מִצְנֶפֶת, a term used almost exclusively for the high priestly turban (Exod 28–29, 39; Lev 8, 16; Sir 45:12 [MsB]),[6] but צָנִיף is not clearly sacral in nature (e.g., Job 29:14; Isa 3:23; there is no need to view צָנִיף in Sir 40:4 [MsB] as priestly, contrary to *HALOT*, 1038). To the contrary, צָנִיף occurs in royal contexts—e.g., Sir 47:6 (MsB) בעטותו צניף נלחם ומסביב הכניע צר

[6] The only instance of a nonsacral referent of מִצְנֶפֶת is in Ezek 21:31 הָסִיר֙ הַמִּצְנֶ֔פֶת וְהָרִ֖ים הָעֲטָרָ֑ה "remove the turban and take up the crown". Its sole occurrence in the DSS (4Q372 12:2) is too fragmentary to determine.

"when he (David) wrapped up a turban, he made war and subdued foes on every side"—and appears in parallelism with עֲטָרָה "crown" (e.g., Isa 62:3 *Qere* וּצְנִיף מְלוּכָה; Ezek 21:31) and "throne," e.g., Sir 11:5 (MsA MsB) רבים נדכאים ישבו על כסא ובל על לב עטו צניף "Many crushed ones have sat upon a throne, and those not thought of have wound up a turban"; 40:3-4 (MsB) מיושב כסא . . . מעוטה צניף "from one who sits on a throne . . . from one who wraps a turban." Thus Milgrom (511) appears to be justified in positing that the distinction between צָנִיף and מִצְנֶפֶת is that of secular versus priestly headgear (cf. Tiemeyer 2015: 130). Despite the preponderance of priestly imagery in this pericope, the narrator clearly avoided מִצְנֶפֶת, the term marked for sacred cultic headgear, in favor of the unmarked term צָנִיף. In light of its usage in royal contexts it may be that צָנִיף was intentionally employed to draw kingly overtones into the text (cf. 6:9-15).

וַיָּשִׂימוּ הַצָּנִיף הַטָּהוֹר עַל־רֹאשׁוֹ וַיַּלְבִּשֻׁהוּ בְּגָדִים. Qal *wayyiqtol* 3 m pl √שׂים, Hifil *wayyiqtol* 3 m pl √לבשׁ with 3 m s pronoun suffix. Hifil √לבשׁ usually takes a double accusative (BDB, 528, #1). The definite article on הַצָּנִיף is anaphoric (see v. 4).

וּמַלְאַךְ יְהוָה עֹמֵד. Qal ptc m s √עמד. In this instance √עמד has the sense of "to remain" (BDB, 764, #3b–c).

3:6 וַיָּעַד מַלְאַךְ יְהוָה בִּיהוֹשֻׁעַ לֵאמֹר׃

Hifil *wayyiqtol* 3 m s √עוד, Qal inf cstr √אמר. Hifil √עוד with בְּ often has the sense of "to warn or admonish," but it can have a less "threatening" nuance of "to enjoin solemnly" or "to impress upon someone" (BDB, 730, #3; *HALOT*, 795, #3c). The choice of verb speaks to the importance and solemnity of the occasion and of the charge given in verses 7-9 in response to it.

3:7 כֹּה־אָמַר יְהוָה צְבָאוֹת אִם־בִּדְרָכַי תֵּלֵךְ וְאִם אֶת־מִשְׁמַרְתִּי תִשְׁמֹר וְגַם־אַתָּה תָּדִין אֶת־בֵּיתִי וְגַם תִּשְׁמֹר אֶת־חֲצֵרָי וְנָתַתִּי לְךָ מַהְלְכִים בֵּין הָעֹמְדִים הָאֵלֶּה׃

כֹּה־אָמַר יְהוָה צְבָאוֹת. Qal *qatal* 3 m s √אמר.

אִם־בִּדְרָכַי תֵּלֵךְ וְאִם אֶת־מִשְׁמַרְתִּי תִשְׁמֹר. Qal *yiqtol* 2 m s √הלך, Qal *yiqtol* 2 m s √שׁמר. It is common for the protasis of a conditional statement to commence with the particle אִם and to utilize the *yiqtol* verbal form. The first condition, אִם־בִּדְרָכַי תֵּלֵךְ, speaks generally of a life of obedience to YHWH, but the second clause, וְאִם אֶת־מִשְׁמַרְתִּי תִשְׁמֹר, is capable of multiple interpretations. The noun מִשְׁמֶרֶת has a range of meaning, including "office" or "function," commonly associated with priestly and Levitical service, though when it occurs with the verb √שׁמר, which it does frequently (BDB, 1038, #4), it often refers to performing guard duty (Segal, 720). On the other hand, Stead (162) is correct to observe that this collocation also has a more general usage for keeping the commandments of God (e.g., Gen 26:5; Lev 18:30; Deut 11:1; 2 Chron 23:6). If this were the intent here, however, then it would seem to be largely overlapping with the first condition (אִם־בִּדְרָכַי תֵּלֵךְ) and therefore superfluous. On the whole, then, it is best to understand מִשְׁמֶרֶת as referring to Joshua's priestly office and this second conditional clause is a summons to the faithful discharge thereof.

וְגַם־אַתָּה תָּדִין אֶת־בֵּיתִי וְגַם תִּשְׁמֹר אֶת־חֲצֵרָי. Qal *yiqtol* 2 m s √דין, Qal *yiqtol* 2 m s √שׁמר. There is much disagreement over where the apodosis of the condition begins and ends (see discussion in Segal, 719–26). English translations regularly take וְגַם־אַתָּה תָּדִין as commencing the apodosis of the conditional statement—e.g., the RSV's "*If* you will walk in my ways and keep my charge, *then* you shall rule my house and have charge of my courts." The LXX renders the entire verse as two conditional statements: "*If* (ἐὰν) you should walk (πορεύῃ) in my ways and keep (φυλάξῃς) my charges *then* you will also judge (καὶ σὺ διακρινεῖς) my house, and *if* (ἐὰν) you should protect (διαφυλάξῃς) my courtyard *then* I will give to you (καὶ δώσω σοι). . . ." The use of the pronoun אַתָּה is no sure marker of the apodosis (Wolters 2014: 96) however, and in fact the use of גַּם to introduce an apodosis is uncommon (BDB, 169, #4). Syntactically it is much more likely that the shift from protasis to apodosis occurs in the next clause (see the following וְנָתַתִּי לְךָ). In other words, תָּדִין אֶת־בֵּיתִי and תִּשְׁמֹר אֶת־חֲצֵרָי are not presented as a reward resulting from Joshua's "walking in YHWH's ways" and "keeping his charge" but rather are to be understood as part and parcel of fulfilling the duties of his priestly office.

Even though תָּדִין already indicates a second masculine singular subject, it is unlikely that the pronoun אַתָּה adds an emphatic nuance here (Thomson 2012a: 51), as suggested by Meyers and Meyers (195). Some have followed Erhlich's explanation (333) that it indicates a new element such as Joshua's transition from a private life to a public ministry (cf. Wolters 2014: 96), but this is a very *ad hoc* explanation (cf. Muraoka 1985: 47, 52). It is more probable that the pronoun was triggered by syntactic factors, namely, the predilection of גַּם to be immediately followed by a personal pronoun (175×), coupled with the general avoidance of *yiqtol* immediately following the particle (cf. Van der Merwe 1990: 126, 129), which only occurs three other times in the HB besides the present verse (1 Kgs 22:22; 2 Chron 18:21; Isa 47:3). The significance of this statistic emerges when one notes that there are approximately seventy occurrences of verbal forms immediately following גַּם, among which *qatal* occurs forty-four times, the infinitive absolute eleven times, and the participle eight times. The repeated וְגַם . . . וְגַם simply adds additional conditions to the protasis and as such is best understood as epexegetical to the second condition (Thomson 2012a: 51); cf. Josh 7:11 חָטָא יִשְׂרָאֵל וְגַם עָבְרוּ אֶת־בְּרִיתִי אֲשֶׁר צִוִּיתִי אוֹתָם וְגַם לָקְחוּ מִן־הַחֵרֶם וְגַם גָּנְבוּ וְגַם כִּחֲשׁוּ וְגַם שָׂמוּ בִכְלֵיהֶם "Israel has sinned, and they have *even* transgressed my covenant which I commanded them, and they have *even* taken from the devoted things, and they have *even* stolen, and they have *even* deceived, and they have *even* placed them among their baggage" (see Delkurt, 171–12). Thus the final two conditional clauses (וְגַם־אַתָּה תָּדִין אֶת־בֵּיתִי וְגַם תִּשְׁמֹר אֶת־חֲצֵרָי) state in more detail what it means for Joshua to "keep YHWH's charge."

There has been considerable discussion concerning the interpretation of וְגַם־אַתָּה תָּדִין אֶת־בֵּיתִי. "My house" is very widely taken as a reference to the temple in light of the parallelism with "my courts" (חֲצֵרָי) in the following clause. However, the verb √דין usually governs a personal object or a cognate accusative (e.g., Jer 5:28 דִּין לֹא־דָנוּ "they have not judged a judgment"), thus making the present clause an apparent anomaly (cf. Rose, 70–73). To resolve this difficulty Segal (720–26) appeals to an analogous expression in Akkadian and argues that תָּדִין אֶת־בֵּיתִי means "to strengthen my house," but this proposal has found little acceptance. More commonly, it is suggested that the verb here means "to administer" or "govern" (e.g., Wolters 2014: 97). While this reading certainly makes sense, it nevertheless appears to be semantic special pleading for this particular instance (see BDB, 192, #5; cf. also Jastrow, 300–1), and contra Rose (72–73), the verb's frequency of occurrence (54×) is such that this lack of attestation cannot be treated as merely "coincidental." The problems associated with this interpretation lead one to question whether בֵּיתִי indeed refers to the temple structure. It should be noted that in place of "my house" Targum Jonathan reads "those who serve in my temple" (תדין לדמשמשין בבית מקדשי), which takes "my house" as a metonymy for the people present in the building (so Tiemeyer 2006: 253–54, who understands בַּ֫יִת to refer to the temple and thereby to the priesthood). Indeed, the use of בַּ֫יִת for "household, family" is extremely common in the HB (592×, according to BDB, 109, #5) and is used at times to refer to God's people (e.g., Jer 12:7; Hos 9:15; see also the examples below). Segal (721) objects to this due to the parallel structure between בֵּיתִ֫י and חֲצֵרָ֫י in the following clause, but this presses the semantic aspect of the parallelism too far, since the corresponding verbs √דין and √שׁמר are clearly distinct in meaning. It would be philologically responsible, then, to translate the clause, "and if you also judge my household." The use of household language with respect to the high priest is noteworthy, inviting comparison with a chief servant over a great house (e.g., Gen 24:2; 41:40) or, even more significantly, with Moses himself: Num 12:7 לֹא־כֵ֖ן עַבְדִּ֣י מֹשֶׁ֑ה בְּכָל־בֵּיתִ֖י נֶאֱמָ֥ן הֽוּא "Not thus is my servant Moses; he is faithful in all of my house" (cf. Heb 3:2, 5; see also 1 Chron 17:14). The verb √דין occurs several times with the noun עַם as its object (Gen 49:16; Deut 32:36; Job 36:31; Pss 7:9; 50:4; 72:2; 96:10; 135:14; Isa 3:13). It could, potentially, refer to the calling of the priests and Levites to render judgments regarding ritual matters (see Hag 2:10-19 passim), but is probably better understood from the standpoint of priestly intercession, since the verb can mean "to plead one's cause" (BDB, 192, #2; *HALOT*, 220, #1; *DCH* 2, 434, #2a). The expression speaks to the interpersonal aspects of the priestly office, while the final condition, וְגַם֙ תִּשְׁמֹ֣ר אֶת־חֲצֵרָ֑י "and if you will also guard my courts," speaks more to the upkeep and oversight of the temple complex.

וְנָתַתִּ֤י לְךָ֙ מַהְלְכִ֔ים בֵּ֥ין הָעֹמְדִ֖ים הָאֵֽלֶּה. Qal *weqatal* 1 c s √נתן, Qal ptc m pl √עמד. This clause is best analyzed syntactically as forming the apodosis of the conditional statement (on the improbability of the preceding clauses introducing the apodosis, see discussion above). The structure of the protasis and apodosis maintained here corresponds to the shift from the second person *yiqtols* (indicating the addressee's responsibilities) to the first person *weqatal* (indicating the speaker's promise): "*If* you will walk . . . keep . . . judge . . . guard . . . *then* I will give you. . . ." This syntactical analysis is reflected in the Masoretic accentuation, which places the *athnaḥ* on אֶת־חֲצֵרָ֑י, the noun phrase which immediately precedes וְנָתַתִּ֤י.

מַהְלְכִים בֵּין הָעֹמְדִים הָאֵלֶּה. The brief apodosis, indicating the reward that Joshua will receive for keeping these conditions, is a notoriously difficult interpretive problem due to the uncertainty of the word מַהְלְכִים. Most frequently this is taken as the plural form of the rare word מַהֲלָךְ ("walkway, passageway, journey"), in this case allegedly in an extended sense of "access" (BDB, 237, #3; *DCH* 5, 164, #3). This option faces both morphological and semantic problems, however: The expected plural of מַהֲלָךְ would be *מַהֲלָכִים and, moreover, the proposed meaning is not attested elsewhere. It is possible that the MT should be revocalized, though several have argued that the MT can in fact be analyzed as a variant form of the Piel masculine plural participle √הלך (see Segal, 729–31 and Rose, 88–90, with references to additional literature). As such, it can be understood as "those who go about," a notion which finds general support from the ancient versions (Segal, 730 n. 39; Rose, 74). Rendsburg (2002: 23) proposes that מַהְלְכִים is a rare Hebrew word cognate to the Phoenician noun מלך "sacrifice," but while an exegetical case can be made for this, it opens up as many problems as it solves. On the whole it appears that the simplest explanation of the MT is indeed to take מַהְלְכִים as a Piel masculine plural participle. The phrase בֵּין הָעֹמְדִים הָאֵלֶּה is generally understood to refer to the heavenly counsel chamber, though there is some debate as to whether supernatural beings or human agents are intended (cf. Rose 79–82). The preposition בֵּין can mean not only "between" but also "among" (BDB, 107, #1). Segal's proposal to repoint הָעֹמְדִים to הָעַמֻּדִים "the pillars" (727–29) is largely due to a failure to appreciate the metonymy present in the expression "my house."

The difficulties of the apodosis mean that any explanation of this problematic verse must remain fairly tentative, and a survey of interpretive options cannot be undertaken here. Taking מַהְלְכִים as a Piel masculine plural participle √הלך, the idea appears to be that if Joshua fulfills his high priestly duties faithfully YHWH will grant or appoint for him "those who go about" among the members of the heavenly court. In other words, the promise seems to refer to the appointment of special intermediaries in YHWH's throne room. As such, these intermediaries form a sharp contrast to "the Attacker," who likewise "stands" in the divine presence but with malicious intent vis-à-vis Joshua. Rendsburg (2002: 25) is probably correct to suggest that the word is intended to evoke the sounds of מַלְאָךְ, which occurs frequently in this chapter (vv. 1, 3, 5, 6) and throughout Zechariah.

3:8 שְׁמַע־נָא יְהוֹשֻׁעַ ׀ הַכֹּהֵן הַגָּדוֹל אַתָּה וְרֵעֶיךָ
הַיֹּשְׁבִים לְפָנֶיךָ כִּי־אַנְשֵׁי מוֹפֵת הֵמָּה כִּי־הִנְנִי
מֵבִיא אֶת־עַבְדִּי צֶמַח׃

שְׁמַע־נָא יְהוֹשֻׁעַ ׀ הַכֹּהֵן הַגָּדוֹל אַתָּה וְרֵעֶיךָ הַיֹּשְׁבִים לְפָנֶיךָ. Qal impv m s √שׁמע, Qal ptc m pl √ישׁב with def art. On the use of the particle נָא with an imperative, see Hag 2:2. No "colleagues" or "companions" (רֵעִים) have been mentioned in the text, and there is no reason to suppose that these are the members of the heavenly court (see v. 7), who are described in verses 4 and 7 as "standing" (√עמד) rather than "sitting." Rather, רֵעִים is to be understood as referring to Joshua's "fellow citizens" (BDB, 946, #2) who would ultimately be the recipients of Zechariah's message. We are not to think of them as particpants in the visionary scene, and the attributive participle הַיֹּשְׁבִים should be taken in the sense of "dwell, inhabit" (BDB, 434, #3) as in its earlier occurrences in Zechariah (1:11; 2:8, 11). The prepositional phrase לְפָנֶיךָ indicates "under your oversight" (BDB, 817, #II4a), thus the phrase is to be translated, "your fellow citizens, dwelling under your oversight." Joshua is being informed of a sign/portent that will need to be communicated to the populace of Judea.

כִּי־אַנְשֵׁי מוֹפֵת הֵמָּה. The particle כִּי is causal, not "emphatic" as Wolters alleges (2014: 100; see Muraoka 1985: 158–64), and explains the reason why Joshua and his fellow citizens need to "listen" to this oracle. Construct relationships can have a variety of nuances of meaning, and various analyses of this phrase have been suggested. Rather than viewing the men themselves as the "sign" (pace Stead, 167 and many others) or as agents who will perform the sign, it is best to understand the construct phrase as expressing possession: they are being given a sign, namely, the coming of *Ṣemaḥ*.

כִּי־הִנְנִי מֵבִיא אֶת־עַבְדִּי צֶמַח. Hifil ptc m s √בוא. The participle presents an event as imminent (*futurum instans*): "I am going to bring, I am about to bring" (see Hag 2:6). On the meaning of צֶמַח and its usage as a proper name, see the introductory remarks to this pericope.

3:9 כִּי ׀ הִנֵּה הָאֶבֶן אֲשֶׁר נָתַתִּי לִפְנֵי יְהוֹשֻׁעַ עַל־אֶבֶן
אַחַת שִׁבְעָה עֵינָיִם הִנְנִי מְפַתֵּחַ פִּתֻּחָהּ נְאֻם יְהוָה
צְבָאוֹת וּמַשְׁתִּי אֶת־עֲוֺן הָאָרֶץ־הַהִיא בְּיוֹם אֶחָד׃

כִּי | הִנֵּה הָאֶבֶן אֲשֶׁר נָתַתִּי לִפְנֵי יְהוֹשֻׁעַ. Qal *qatal* 1 c s √נתן. In this instance the particle הִנֵּה acquires a virtually imperatival force (cf. the interjection רְאֵה), "Behold the stone", i.e., "look at the stone!" הָאֶבֶן could be understood as singular or collective (WO §7.2.1d) and as referring to discrete stones, stone as raw material, precious stones, ore, and the like (BDB, 6). From an exegetical standpoint it is debated whether הָאֶבֶן refers to a stone or stones that decorate the priestly garments (e.g., the breastplate) or instead to a stone of the temple structure, though it would be fair to say that the former represents the majority opinion, and this is surely the correct view in light of the abundant intertextual links with the priestly directives of the Torah (cf. Stead, 169–70). The prepositional phrase לִפְנֵי יְהוֹשֻׁעַ "before/in front of Joshua" refers to the fact that the stones of the priestly breastplate were placed on Joshua's front as opposed to his back, and the verb נָתַתִּי can be understood either as "to place, set" or perhaps more specifically as "to attach" (Wolters 2014: 104–5). The verb is not infrequently rendered as a present tense, and while it could conceivably be considered a "performative perfect" (see v. 4), its occurrence in a subordinate clause and reference to Joshua in the third person speak against this, and it is best translated as a past tense.

עַל־אֶבֶן אַחַת שִׁבְעָה עֵינָיִם הִנְנִי מְפַתֵּחַ פִּתֻּחָהּ נְאֻם יְהוָה צְבָאוֹת. Piel ptc m s √פתח. Like the future-oriented verbal forms in verses 8 and 10, the participle indicates the imminent future (see Hag 2:6). The *athnach* on שִׁבְעָה עֵינָיִם makes it unlikely that this noun phrase is functioning either as an accusative object or as an indirect accusative of הִנְנִי מְפַתֵּחַ; i.e., YHWH is not engraving "seven eyes" on the אֶבֶן. Rather, all of עַל־אֶבֶן אַחַת שִׁבְעָה עֵינָיִם is to be taken as a prepositional phrase modifying הִנְנִי מְפַתֵּחַ פִּתֻּחָהּ. The noun פִּתֻּחָהּ is an "accusative of the effected object" (AC §2.3.1b; WB §52; MNK §33.2.1ib; WO §10.2.1f). As Joüon and Muraoka explain, "Whereas the *affected* object is understood as existing prior to the action, the *effected* object is produced by the action itself" (JM §125p). Typically it involves a cognate noun and verb (see 1:2) such as Gen 1:29 זֹרֵעַ זֶרַע "producing seed," but it is to be distinguished from the "internal accusative" (e.g., "he was wrathful with a great wrath") in that an "effected object is concrete, and external in relation to the action." The content of the engraving is unspecified, but the parallels in terminology make it extremely likely that this is a specific intertextual reference to the directives for the two onyx stones of the priestly breastplate, which indicate its subject matter: וּפִתַּחְתָּ עֲלֵיהֶם שְׁמוֹת בְּנֵי יִשְׂרָאֵל׃ שִׁשָּׁה מִשְּׁמֹתָם עַל

הָאֶבֶן הָאֶחָת "and you shall engrave upon them the names of the sons of Israel, six of their names upon the one stone" (Exod 28:9-10). The number "one" is capable of various nuances (BDB, 25–26). Although it can be used in the sense of an indefinite pronoun (JM §137u), the phrase אֶבֶן אַחַת does not mean "a certain stone" (as in 1 Sam 7:12), since the previous clause had already indicated הָאֶבֶן as grammatically definite. Wolters' proposal of "unique" (2014: 102–5) is unfounded, and אֶבֶן אַחַת is best understood numerically in light of Exod 28:9-10 as "one stone." The oracle's focus upon one particular stone does not deny the presence of other stones on the priestly breastplate.

The closest grammatical parallel to the prepositional object phrase אֶבֶן אַחַת שִׁבְעָה עֵינָיִם is 1 Sam 2:13 וְהַמַּזְלֵג שְׁלֹשׁ־הַשִּׁנַּיִם "and the fork (with) three teeth." In both cases a noun is followed by a noun phrase involving a number in apposition, with the latter phrase expressing an "inalienable possession" of the head noun, that is, "a possessive construction in which the possessed item cannot in principle be separated from the possessor" (Trask, 136; cf. JM §131c). Thus אֶבֶן אַחַת שִׁבְעָה עֵינָיִם means "one stone (with) seven eyes." The noun phrase שִׁבְעָה עֵינָיִם has vexed scholars both in terms of the number and the lexical meaning of עֵינָיִם. With regard to the number, it is debated whether the phrase means seven "eyes" or seven *pairs of* "eyes," since עֵינָיִם is a dual form. VanderKam, for example, opts for the latter, arguing (568) that it refers to a total of fourteen stones or jewels on the priestly breastplate. While interpreting שִׁבְעָה עֵינָיִם as seven pairs of eyes cannot be absolutely excluded, neither is it required by the grammar. It should be noted that the plural form of עַיִן is never attested in the HB—pace Thomson (2012b: 119, 122–13), the plural עֲיָנוֹת "springs" is derived from a separate lemma (cf. BDB, 744–45; *DCH* 6, 355–65)—and the form עֵינַיִם serves for the expression of either the dual or plural. This is the case for a number of dual forms, though Thomson goes even farther and argues that with body parts the dual form, without a numerical modifier, *only* indicates plurality (2012b: 121–21). Yet this presses the evidence a little too far. The dual form remained grammatically productive even in LBH, and only a distinction of number—not lexical sense—is capable of accounting for a contrasting minimal pair such as Cant 4:3 שִׂפְתֹתַיִךְ "your lips" versus Prov 5:2 שְׂפָתֶיךָ "your (two) lips" (cf. Thomson 2012b: 119 n. 28). Likewise, the dual sense is still evident in a case such as Qoh 4:6 טוֹב מְלֹא כַף נָחַת מִמְּלֹא חָפְנַיִם עָמָל

וּרְעוּת רוּחַ "Better is fullness of a peaceful hand than two handfuls with toil and a striving of wind."

The noun עַ֫יִן is typically feminine, but in this instance the usage of the feminine שִׁבְעָה indicates that the noun is being treated as masculine (on the syntax and gender of numerals 3–10, see 2:1; for possible exceptions to the pattern, see Thomson 2012b: 123 n. 57). It has been noted that such changes in a noun's gender can correspond to a concrete versus a figurative usage, in this case possibly signifying "facet" or "engraving surface" as opposed to a physical "eye." Thomson (2012b: 123 n. 57) is skeptical of this point, but sufficient examples are cited in the grammatical literature to establish the phenomenon (see WO §6.4.1e; JM §134a n. 2; MNK §24.2.2if; Gibson, 18; GKC §122u). Like most frequently occuring words, עַ֫יִן has a range of meanings (BDB, 744–45), and in addition to denoting the organ of sight it can refer to, e.g., "appearance" (Lev 13:55 וְהִנֵּה לֹא־הָפַךְ הַנֶּגַע אֶת־עֵינוֹ "and behold, if the disease has not changed its appearance . . ."), "gleam, sparkle" (Dan10:6 וּמַרְגְּלֹתָיו כְּעֵין נְחֹשֶׁת קָלָל "and his feet were as the gleam of burnished bronze"), or "surface" (Exod 10:5 וְכִסָּה אֶת־ עֵין הָאָרֶץ "and it will cover all the surface of the earth"). The last mentioned sense is often glossed as "facet" in Zech 3:9, thus referring to a "seven-sided" or "seven-faceted" stone; though some eschew this sense of the word (e.g., Wolters 2014: 105; Thomson 2012b: 123–24), it is simply an extension of the clearly attested meaning "surface."

The fact that the collocation of a "stone" with "eyes" is not attested elsewhere in CH urges caution concerning the meaning of שִׁבְעָה עֵינָיִם, and though the verse appears to be quoted in the DSS (4Q177), the context is too fragmentary to provide any interpretive assistance. Many will argue that עֵינַיִם indeed refers to the organ of sight by appealing to intratextuality, that is, to a book's reference to material within itself, since Zech 4:10 contains a reference to the "seven eyes of YHWH which range throughout the whole earth," the context of which also mentions a "stone" (4:7). Yet the connection is dubious (Wolters 2014: 104), since in that passage the "seven eyes" of 4:10 are linked with the "seven lamps" of the menorah (v. 4) and have no connection with the "stone" of 4:7, which in any event does not refer to the precious stones of the priest's breastplate. In light of the grammatical parallel between אֶבֶן אַחַת שִׁבְעָה עֵינָיִם and 1 Sam 2:13 וְהַמַּזְלֵג שְׁלֹשׁ־הַשִּׁנַּיִם discussed above, it is best to understand the phrase in question as "seven surfaces" (cf. Wolters 2014: 105–6), which are an inalienable possession of stones, in contrast to "eyes" (the organ of sight), which are not. It should be noted that if עֵינָיִם referred concretely to "eyes," then this striking detail would serve no particular purpose in its current context, in contrast to 4:10, where the significance of the "seven eyes" is made explicit. On the other hand, if שִׁבְעָה עֵינָיִם refers to "seven surfaces" then a purpose for them is immediately at hand, namely, to be inscribed upon by YHWH (הִנְנִי מְפַתֵּחַ פִּתֻּחָהּ).

Drawing together the details of the preceding discussion, the text can be best understood as follows: The first occurrence of הָאֶבֶן is to be taken as a collective noun (as it is used in, e.g., Gen 2:12; 35:14; Exod 24:12), thus referring to all of the stones that YHWH had directed to be placed "in front of" (לִפְנֵי) Joshua, that is, on the breastplate of the priestly breastplate. YHWH then declares that he will make an inscription upon "one stone with seven surfaces." As noted above, the language of "one stone" is influenced by the phrasing of Exod 28:9-10, and it need not be taken in an exclusive sense (as if there were only one stone upon the visionary breastplate).

וּמַשְׁתִּי אֶת־עֲוֺן הָאָרֶץ־הַהִיא בְּיוֹם אֶחָד. Qal *weqatal* 1 c s √מושׁ. On the noun עָוֺן, see verse 4. Qal √מושׁ means "to depart" and is used intransitively in every other instance in CH, including the HB, DSS, and Ben Sira; the transitive meaning "to remove" occurs in the Hifil *binyan*. Although this instance is treated in the lexica as an exceptional transitive usage of the Qal (so BDB, 559) or emended to Hifil (so *HALOT*, 561), the pattern of usage is consistent and sufficiently attested to exclude such a possibility (for references, see Rogland 2013b). **וּמַשְׁתִּי** must therefore be understood as intransitive here with the particle **אֶת** interpreted as the preposition "with" rather than the direct object marker: "And I will depart *with* the guilt of that land." This comports with a number of intertextual references to the Day of Atonement ritual in this text (Tiemeyer 2015: 144–15; Stead, 170). Strikingly, then, the text presents YHWH as taking on the role of the "scapegoat" (for a more expansive discussion, see Rogland 2013b).

It is often overlooked that the phrase הָאָרֶץ הַהִיא "that land" is much less common in the HB than the phrase הָאָרֶץ הַזֹּאת "this land" (ca. 14 vs. 55 occurrences). Despite the grammar, modern translations often render הָאָרֶץ הַהִיא in this instance as "this land" (e.g., RSV), in contrast to, e.g., the LXX, which uses the far demonstrative "that land" (τῆς γῆς ἐκείνης). The use of הִיא instead of זאת is indicative of the fact that there is a "distance" between the events and utterances of the visionary realm experienced by the prophet and the heavenly court (v. 7) and what will take place back in "that land,"—that is, Judah, the normal place of activity for the prophet, Joshua, and their countrymen (cf. JM §143k).

3:10 בַּיּ֣וֹם הַה֗וּא נְאֻם֙ יְהוָ֣ה צְבָא֔וֹת תִּקְרְא֖וּ אִ֣ישׁ
לְרֵעֵ֑הוּ אֶל־תַּ֥חַת גֶּ֖פֶן וְאֶל־תַּ֥חַת תְּאֵנָֽה׃

Qal *yiqtol* 2 m pl √קרא. The use of אִישׁ with either אָח or רֵעַ expresses reciprocity, e.g., "each one, one another" (see Hag 2:22), in this instance with לְ, though other prepositions occur as well (cf. 7:9). The prepositional phrases אֶל־תַּ֥חַת גֶּ֖פֶן וְאֶל־תַּ֥חַת תְּאֵנָ֑ה represent a "pregnant" use of Hebrew אֶל, that is, one that implies additional aspects of meaning beyond its semantics or the surface structure of the phrase. BDB (40, #9) notes that when אֶל is prefixed to other prepositions "it combines with them the idea of *motion* or *direction to*," and this particular collocation is specifically listed. The idea is that of "calling to someone *to come* under" one's vine and fig tree. The expression, which could be echoing texts such as 1 Kgs 5:5 [ET: 4:25], 2 Kgs 18:31, and Mic 4:4 (cf. Stead, 171) is one of prosperous security.

Fifth Vision (Zechariah 4:1-14)
The Golden Lampstand and an Oracle for Zerubbabel

The vision of Zech 4 consists of a large golden menorah with two olive trees beside it providing oil (vv. 2-3). This traditional Jewish symbol for the Divine Presence (*b. Menahot* 86b)[7] was first constructed for the tabernacle according to the Law of Moses (Exod 25:31-40; 27:20-21; 37:17-24; Num 8:1-4). Although obviously differing from it in various respects, the temple and its accoutrements were patterned significantly after those of the tabernacle (cf. *b. Menahot* 98b), and lampstands were subsequently constructed for the Solomonic temple (1 Kgs 7:49; 1 Chron 28:15; 2 Chron 4:7, 20; 13:11; Josephus, *Ant.* 8.90, 104; 10.145; *b. Menahot* 29a; *b. Shabbat* 22b) and were later taken as plunder by the Babylonians (Jer 52:19). Lampstands were present in the second temple as well (e.g., 1 Macc 1:21; 4:49; 2 Macc 10:3; Josephus,

[7] This has been a common understanding of the image, though according to Josephus (*B.J.* 5.216–17) and Philo (*Her.* 1.221, 227; *Mos.* 2.102–3), the seven lamps of the menorah signify the seven planets.

Ant. 12.318–19; 14.72; *b. Yoma* 39a), and the Maccabean revolt and temple rededication would later become famously associated with the tradition of the menorah's continuing to burn for seven days from one cruse of oil (*b. Shabbat* 21b).

In addition to the textual sources from antiquity, there is a significant amount of archaeological and iconographic data pertaining to the menorah (Meyers; Hachlili; Houtman). Nevertheless, although it would seem that we possess an impressive wealth of information concerning the ancient menorah, in reality the Mosaic directives concerning the lampstand are themselves so minimal as to make it difficult to reconstruct the device with any kind of detail (Houtman, 3; cf. *b. Menahot* 29a). According to Rabbinic tradition, even Moses was unable to craft it, and consequently threw a mass of gold into a fire in frustration, whereupon YHWH himself fashioned it (Fine, 106, 113). In a similar way, Zechariah's "architecturally complex" (Tell, 48) vision of a menorah is clear enough as to its basic subject matter, but is difficult to envision in detail due to a number of rare or lexically uncertain terms used to describe its features (e.g., גֻּלָּה, מוּצָקוֹת, שִׁיבֹּלֶת, צַנְתְּרוֹת). It is no wonder, then, that more than once the prophet himself confesses ignorance as to the meaning of various items (vv. 5, 13) and seeks clarification (vv. 4, 11-12).

Another complicating feature in this chapter is an oracle to Zerubbabel embedded within the vision of the menorah (vv. 6-10a), which is felt to be intrusive by many and judged by redaction-critical scholars to be an interpolation (see, e.g., Hallaschka 2011: 222–28). The intermingling of visionary and oracular material is common in apocalyptic literature, however, and does not necessarily indicate multiple authors or sources (J. J. Collins, 14). The oracle makes the famous proclamation that YHWH's purposes are accomplished "not by might, nor by power, but by my spirit" (v. 6), and assures Zerubbabel that he will see the temple rebuilding through to completion (v. 9). The chapter then returns to the visionary description and concludes with the mysterious explanation that what has been depicted represents "the two anointed ones who stand by the Lord of the whole earth" (v. 14), an explanation which itself has been the subject of much scholarly discussion. Both from a philological and an exegetical perspective, then, this chapter is one of the most difficult to analyze in all of the Night Visions.

[1]And the angel who was speaking with me again roused me as a man who is roused from his sleep.

[2]And he said to me, "What do you see?" And I said, "I looked, and
behold, a lampstand entirely of gold. And a bowl is on its top, and seven
are its lamps upon it, with seven liquid streams each for the lamps that are
near its top.
[3]And two olive trees are beside it, one on the right of the bowl and one
on its left."
[4]And I answered and I said to the angel who was speaking with me,
"What are these, my lord?"
[5]And the angel who was speaking with me answered and he said to me,
"Do you not know what these are?" And I said, "No, my lord."
[6]And he answered and he said to me, "This is the word of YHWH to
Zerubbabel: 'Not by power, and not by force, but rather by my spirit,' has
YHWH Tsevaot said.
[7]Who are you, O Mountain of the Great One, before Zerubabbel, for
uprightness? And he will bring forth the stone to the top, with noises of 'It
has grace, grace!'"
[8]And the word of YHWH came to me:
[9]"The hands of Zerubbabel reestablished this house, and his hands will
finish it off. And you will know that YHWH Tsevaot has sent me to you.
[10]For who has despised the day of small things? They should rejoice and
see the tin-stone in the hand of Zerubbabel. These seven are the eyes of
YHWH; they rove about in all the earth."
[11]And I answered and I said to him, "What are these two olive trees on
the right of the lampstand and on its left?"
[12]And I answered a second time and I said to him, "What are the two
flowing streams of the olive trees, which are in the hand of the two golden
centaurs, who are emptying the gold(en oil) from upon them?"
[13]And he said to me, "Do you not know what these (are)?" And I said,
"No, my lord."
[14]And he said, "These are the two sons of oil, who are standing beside
the Lord of all the earth."

4:1 וַיָּשָׁב הַמַּלְאָךְ הַדֹּבֵר בִּי וַיְעִירֵנִי כְּאִישׁ אֲשֶׁר־יֵעוֹר מִשְּׁנָתוֹ׃

וַיָּשָׁב הַמַּלְאָךְ הַדֹּבֵר בִּי. Qal *wayyiqtol* 3 m s √שׁוב, Qal ptc m s √דבר with def art. The verb √שׁוב could mean "and he returned," but elsewhere in the Night Visions it is used as an auxiliary verb to indicate "to do something again" (e.g., 5:1; see, e.g., Wolters 2014: 114).

וַיְעִירֵ֫נִי כְּאִ֫ישׁ אֲשֶׁר־יֵעֹ֫ור מִשְּׁנָתֹֽו. Hifil *wayyiqtol* 3 m s and Nifal *yiqtol* 3 m s √עור. The verb √עור can be used in the sense of "inciting someone to action" (e.g., Ezra 1:1, 5; Hag 1:14), but here refers to rousing from sleep. For analogous instances of a prophet being in a sleeplike state, see Dan 8:18 and 10:9 (cf. Num 12:6).

4:2 וַיֹּ֣אמֶר אֵלַ֔י מָ֥ה אַתָּ֖ה רֹאֶ֑ה וָאֹמַ֞ר רָאִ֣יתִי \| וְהִנֵּ֣ה
מְנֹורַ֣ת זָהָ֣ב כֻּלָּ֗הּ וְגֻלָּהּ֮ עַל־רֹאשָׁהּ֒ וְשִׁבְעָ֤ה נֵרֹתֶ֨יהָ֙
עָלֶ֔יהָ שִׁבְעָ֣ה וְשִׁבְעָ֔ה מֽוּצָקֹ֔ות לַנֵּרֹ֖ות אֲשֶׁ֥ר עַל־
רֹאשָֽׁהּ׃

וַיֹּ֣אמֶר אֵלַ֔י מָ֥ה אַתָּ֖ה רֹאֶ֑ה. Qal *wayyiqtol* 3 m s √אמר, Qal ptc m s √ראה. On the use of the participle in questions, see Hag 2:3.

וָאֹמַ֞ר רָאִ֣יתִי \| וְהִנֵּ֣ה. Qal *wayyiqtol* 1 c s √אמר (Qere), Qal *qatal* 1 c s √ראה.

מְנֹורַ֣ת זָהָ֣ב כֻּלָּ֗הּ. The term מְנֹרָה properly denotes the lampstand structure, in distinction from the lights or oil-burning lamps, which are indicated by the term נֵרֹות (Meyers 1976: 18). Genitive relationships such as מְנֹורַת זָהָב often express the material from which an item is built or out of which it consists (JM §129f5; AC §2.2.10; WB §40a; MNK §25.4.6i; WO §9.5.3d). This structure, with suffixed כֹּל standing in apposition to the noun phrase which it qualifies, is well attested in BH, and in this instance has the notion of "entirely" (JM §146j2). Fine (108) notes that solid or "pure gold" (Exod 25:31 מְנֹרַת זָהָב טָהֹור) must be a relative term, since solid gold would be too soft for the menorah's intricate craftsmanship, but the expression here simply refers to the menorah's visual appearance.

וְגֻלָּהּ עַל־רֹאשָׁהּ. The same noun גֻּלָּה occurs without *mappiq* in verse 3 but with an anaphoric definite article, indicating how this גֻּלָּהּ was understood by the Masoretes (*BHQ*, 137*). The *mappiq* in גֻּלָּהּ, which is absent in some manuscripts (Kennicott, 293), appears to be a scribal error (Bauer and Leander §74h) due to dittography from the preceding כֻּלָּהּ (Petersen, 215) and is to be omitted. Some have suggested that it is the feminine pronoun and that the feminine termination with *tav* has been omitted from גֻּלָּה (Davidson, 50), in which case the rendering would be "and *its* bowl is on its top" rather than "*a* bowl." Wolters (2014: 115–16), among others, appeals to etymology and comparative Semitics to argue that גֻּלָּה refers to the curving "branchwork" of the lampstand, but there is little evidence from the HB to support this, and the noun is reasonably well attested as a bowl or basin (BDB, 165; *HALOT*, 192; *DCH* 2, 352; Jastrow, 221). Here it stands on the top of the menorah, serving as a reservoir for fuel. The fact that no such reservoir is mentioned in the directives concerning the menorah of Exod 25 is no argument against this, given both the incomplete nature of its description there (see the introductory remarks above) as well as the visionary context, in which the addition of unusual features is not uncommon.

וְשִׁבְעָה נֵרֹתֶיהָ עָלֶיהָ. See above on the meaning of נֵר. As is regularly the case with compact verbless clauses such as this, identifying the subject and predicate can pose a challenge: Does the prepositional phrase עָלֶיהָ represent the predicate ("Its seven lamps were *upon it*"), or rather the number שִׁבְעָה ("Its lamps upon it were *seven*")? The former seems to be preferred by most translations and may find some confirmation by the conjunctive *m*^{e}*huppāḵ* accent on וְשִׁבְעָה and the disjunctive *pašṭāʾ* on נֵרֹתֶיהָ. On the other hand, when numbers 3–10 (cf. on 2:1) are utilized with nouns with pronominal suffixes, the most common pattern is for the construct form of the number to precede the noun, as in 1 Sam 17:3 שְׁלֹשֶׁת בָּנָיו "his three sons" and Ezek 14:21 אַרְבַּעַת שְׁפָטַי "my four judgments"; very occasionally the number in the absolute state follows the noun as in Exod 27:14 עַמֻּדֵיהֶם שְׁלֹשָׁה "their pillars, three" = "their three pillars" and Exod 36:38 אַדְנֵיהֶם חֲמִשָּׁה "their bases, five" = "their five bases." If the prophet had wanted unequivocally to state, "And its seven lamps were upon it," it seems most probable that he would have said *וְשִׁבְעַת נֵרוֹתֶיהָ עָלֶיהָ utilizing the construct form of the number before the suffixed noun. All things considered, then, it seems preferable to take שִׁבְעָה as the predicate of the clause: "And its lamps upon it were seven." The addressees would expect a menorah to have lamps, and while seven would have been the number of the tabernacle menorah (Exod 25:37), perhaps one could not automatically assume their number since other combinations of branches and lamps were possible (see *b. Menahot* 28b; *b. Rosh HaShanah* 24a–b; *b. Avodah Zarah* 24a). The preposition עַל can mean "beside" as well as "upon," thus various spatial configurations of the lamps could be visualized.

שִׁבְעָה וְשִׁבְעָה מוּצָקוֹת לַנֵּרוֹת אֲשֶׁר עַל־רֹאשָׁהּ. Some would argue that שִׁבְעָה וְשִׁבְעָה is to be taken as "fourteen," but a distributive sense ("seven each") seems more likely in view of examples such as 2 Sam 21:20 וְאֶצְבְּעֹת יָדָיו וְאֶצְבְּעֹת רַגְלָיו שֵׁשׁ וָשֵׁשׁ עֶשְׂרִים וְאַרְבַּע מִסְפָּר "The digits of his hands and the digits of his feet, six each, twenty-four was the number" and Gen 7:9 שְׁנַיִם שְׁנַיִם בָּאוּ אֶל־נֹחַ אֶל־הַתֵּבָה זָכָר וּנְקֵבָה "two each, they came to Noah, to the ark, male and female." Hence there are seven מוּצָקוֹת for each נֵר.

The meaning of מוּצָקוֹת has proven highly problematic due to the noun's rarity. It is derived from the root √יצק "to pour, cast, flow," which occurs as a verb fifty-three times, about fifteen of which refer to pouring or casting molten metal (Wolf and Holmstedt, 502). The only other biblical occurrence of the noun מוּצָקָה is in 2 Chron 4:3, a difficult text in which it seems to refer to cast metal: "The cattle were cast in two rows *in its casting* (בְּמֻצַקְתּוֹ)." Some suggest "casting" or "cast metal" for Zech 4:2 (*DCH* 5, 185) in the sense of "(cast) pipes" (BDB, 427) or "reeds" (*HALOT*, 559), since the context is one of oil being supplied to lamps (vv. 3, 11-14) and therefore requiring some type of machinery for that purpose. Petersen provides some interesting data from archaeological renderings suggesting that מוּצָקוֹת could refer to a "spout, indentation, lip" (see also Wolf and Holmstedt, 503). At this point, however, the vision's description of the menorah is very sparse, so that the context allows for a great many possible meanings of מוּצָקוֹת.

The discovery and publication of the DSS has brought additional attestations of this obscure word to light, however. מוצקות is found in the Qumran text 4QMMT (4Q394, with probable restorations in 4Q396 and 4Q397), where it occurs in the context of pouring and is to be understood as a "stream" or "unbroken flow of liquid" (Qimron and Strugnell, 141). Specifically, it is used in legal rulings concerning the ritual purity of liquids poured from pure vessels into impure ones (4Q394 [lines 55-58]). Contextually the meaning of "streams" for מוּצָקוֹת fits in Zech 4:2 as well: the phrase שִׁבְעָה וְשִׁבְעָה מוּצָקוֹת לַנֵּרוֹת "seven streams each for the lamps" indicates the number of streams of oil pouring from the central bowl (גֻּלָּה) to each lamp (נֵר).

The final prepositional phrase עַל־רֹאשָׁהּ could indicate various spatial relations but probably means simply that the lights were "beside" or "near" the top of the lampstand (BDB, 755–56, #II6a–c). To summarize the preceding discussion: the prophet sees a lampstand with a bowl (גֻּלָּה) on its top (עַל־רֹאשָׁהּ), and seven lamps (נֵּרוֹת) on (עָלֶיהָ) the lampstand. From this bowl, "streams of liquid" (מוּצָקוֹת) are flowing into lamps, seven streams for each lamp.

4:3 וּשְׁנַ֥יִם זֵיתִ֖ים עָלֶ֑יהָ אֶחָד֙ מִימִ֣ין הַגֻּלָּ֔ה וְאֶחָ֖ד עַל־שְׂמֹאלָֽהּ׃

וּשְׁנַ֥יִם זֵיתִ֖ים עָלֶ֑יהָ. The noun זֵיתִים can refer to groves of olive trees (e.g., Josh 24:13), not just individual olive trees, though typically just two trees are understood here. For עָלֶ֫יהָ as "beside it," see לַנֵּרוֹת אֲשֶׁר עַל־רֹאשָׁהּ in verse 2.

אֶחָד֙ מִימִ֣ין הַגֻּלָּ֔ה וְאֶחָ֖ד עַל־שְׂמֹאלָֽהּ. "Right" and "left" often occur together (BDB, 411–12), most often absolutely (Num 20:17) or with the prepositions מִן (Exod 14:22) and עַל (Gen 24:49). In verse 11 we find both occurring with עַל, but in this clause מִן is used with one and עַל with the other. The only other instances in which this occurs are Neh 8:4 and Ezek 16:46, but the data is too sparse to determine whether this might be a development of LBH.

4:4 וָאַ֙עַן֙ וָֽאֹמַ֔ר אֶל־הַמַּלְאָ֛ךְ הַדֹּבֵ֥ר בִּ֖י לֵאמֹ֑ר מָה־אֵ֖לֶּה אֲדֹנִֽי׃

Qal *wayyiqtol* 1 c s √ענה and √אמר, Qal ptc m s √דבר with def art, Qal inf cstr √אמר. On the significance of the question מָה־אֵלֶּה אֲדֹנִי, see 1:9. On √ענה as "to respond," see Hag 2:14.

4:5 וַ֠יַּעַן הַמַּלְאָ֞ךְ הַדֹּבֵ֥ר בִּי֙ וַיֹּ֣אמֶר אֵלַ֔י הֲל֥וֹא יָדַ֖עְתָּ מָה־הֵ֣מָּה אֵ֑לֶּה וָאֹמַ֖ר לֹ֥א אֲדֹנִֽי׃

וַ֠יַּעַן הַמַּלְאָ֞ךְ הַדֹּבֵ֥ר בִּי֙ וַיֹּ֣אמֶר אֵלַ֔י. Qal *wayyiqtol* 3 m s √ענה, Qal ptc m s √דבר with def art, Qal *wayyiqtol* 3 m s √אמר.

הֲל֥וֹא יָדַ֖עְתָּ מָה־הֵ֣מָּה אֵ֑לֶּה וָאֹמַ֖ר לֹ֥א אֲדֹנִֽי. Qal *qatal* 2 m s √ידע, Qal *wayyiqtol* 1 c s √אמר. The same question הֲלוֹא יָדַעְתָּ occurs in verse 13. On the syntax of the tripartite nominal clause מָה־הֵמָּה אֵלֶּה, see 1:9, which contains the identical question. As noted there, the pronoun gives some prominence to the preceding constituent, in this case the interrogative pronoun מָה, as this indirect question is not querying the *content* of the vision but rather its *significance*.

4:6 וַיַּ֜עַן וַיֹּ֤אמֶר אֵלַי֙ לֵאמֹ֔ר זֶ֚ה דְּבַר־יְהוָ֔ה אֶל־זְרֻבָּבֶ֖ל
לֵאמֹ֑ר לֹ֤א בְחַ֙יִל֙ וְלֹ֣א בְכֹ֔חַ כִּ֣י אִם־בְּרוּחִ֔י אָמַ֖ר
יְהוָ֥ה צְבָאֽוֹת׃

וַיַּ֜עַן וַיֹּ֤אמֶר אֵלַי֙ לֵאמֹ֔ר זֶ֚ה דְּבַר־יְהוָ֔ה אֶל־זְרֻבָּבֶ֖ל לֵאמֹ֑ר. Qal *wayyiqtol* 3 m s √ענה, Qal *wayyiqtol* 3 m s √אמר, Qal inf cstr √אמר (2x). Before answering the prophet's question regarding the lamps, the angel delivers an oracle concerning God's spirit and the role of Zerubbabel in the rebuilding of the temple.

לֹ֤א בְחַ֙יִל֙ וְלֹ֣א בְכֹ֔חַ כִּ֣י אִם־בְּרוּחִ֔י. The בְּ preposition could indicate "by" or "in," depending upon how the clause as a whole is interpreted. חַ֫יִל has a range of meanings, e.g., "(physical) strength; ability; wealth; military force" (BDB, 298–99), and any of these would be suitable here. For כֹּחַ and חַ֫יִל occurring together, see 2 Chron 26:13 עוֹשֵׂי מִלְחָמָה בְּכֹחַ חָיִל לַעְזֹר לַמֶּלֶךְ עַל־הָאוֹיֵב "those who could make war with power of force, to help the king against the enemy." As Wolters (2014: 120) notes, the statement represents a case of aposiopesis—that is, an incomplete sentence, and part of the thought must be supplied; contextually, the omitted element must be something along the lines of "this will happen." The rhetorical contrast employed here does not indicate one element to the exclusion of another but rather "not X so much as Y."

אָמַ֖ר יְהוָ֥ה צְבָאֽוֹת. Qal *qatal* 3 m s √אמר.

4:7 מִֽי־אַתָּ֧ה הַר־הַגָּד֛וֹל לִפְנֵ֥י זְרֻבָּבֶ֖ל לְמִישֹׁ֑ר וְהוֹצִיא֙
אֶת־הָאֶ֣בֶן הָרֹאשָׁ֔ה תְּשֻׁא֕וֹת חֵ֥ן חֵ֖ן לָֽהּ׃ פ

מִֽי־אַתָּ֧ה הַר־הַגָּד֛וֹל לִפְנֵ֥י זְרֻבָּבֶ֖ל לְמִישֹׁ֑ר. The RSV renders מִֽי־אַתָּ֧ה as "What are you?" However, while the interrogative pronoun מִי is occasionally used of things (JM §144b; BDB, 566), it much more typically refers to persons (LXX: τίς, not τί). The exegetical interpretations of the phrase הַר־הַגָּד֛וֹל are extremely varied (for a useful survey, see O'Kennedy 2008: 406–12), but it is almost universally translated as a noun with attributive adjective in the vocative case: "O great mountain." Such an understanding runs counter to the grammar, however, for if הַגָּד֛וֹל were an attributive adjective then the noun "mountain" would require the def art. Accordingly, some propose textual emendation (cf. *BHQ*, 137*), but there is no manuscript support for this. As the MT stands, it must be interpreted as a construct chain, yet if this were a "genitive of quality" (see 2:16) akin to הַר־הַקֹּדֶשׁ "mountain of holiness" (= "holy mountain") then one would expect the abstract noun גֹּדֶל "greatness" as the *nomen rectum*; it is rare to find an adjective in that position (JM §141f). Hence the adjective should be understood as substantival, and the phrase translated as "mountain of the great one." In the context of the Night Visions, this is most likely a reference to הַכֹּהֵן הַגָּדוֹל "the high (great) priest" (3:1, 8; 6:11; cf. Petersen, 239–40), speaking of the temple complex on Mount Zion. The peculiar phrase לִפְנֵי זְרֻבָּבֶל לְמִישֹׁר is frequently taken as a separate clause responding to the question מִי־אַתָּה הַר־הַגָּדוֹל, with the noun מִישֹׁר understood as a "level place" or "plain" (BDB, 449, #1–2) creating a topographical contrast to הַר "mountain" (see, e.g., 1 Kgs 20:23; Isa 40:4). לִפְנֵי זְרֻבָּבֶל לְמִישֹׁר is analyzed as one of a handful of instances of לְ in a verbless clause indicating a change of state or condition (BDB, 512, #4a), thus the RSV's "Before Zerubbabel you *shall become* a plain" is fairly representative of the majority of translations. Yet many of the examples of this usage of לְ are questionable or are in different syntactic environments than what we have here (see Rogland 2014e: 78 n. 20).

The closest syntactical parallels to verse 7a are direct and indirect questions such as Gen 33:8 מִי לְךָ כָּל־הַמַּחֲנֶה הַזֶּה אֲשֶׁר פָּגָשְׁתִּי "Who/what to you is all this company that I encountered?"; 2 Sam 16:2 מָה־אֵלֶּה לָּךְ "What are these to you?" (RSV: "Why have you brought these?"); Ezek 37:18 הֲלוֹא־תַגִּיד לָנוּ מָה־אֵלֶּה לָּךְ "Will you not tell us what these are to you?" In each case we have an interrogative pronoun, a predicate nominative, and a לְ-prepositional phrase. Such questions are asking about the significance of some entity in relation to the addressee and have the sense of "What *do these mean* to you?" To apply this syntactical analysis to Zech 4:7a, מִישׁוֹר must be understood not as topographical in nature but rather as referring to the moral quality of "uprightness" (BDB, 449, #3). As such, the clause is to be translated, "What do you signify *for uprightness* before Zerubbabel, O mountain of the Great One?" or perhaps more idiomatically, "What do you amount to before Zerubbabel, O mountain of the Great One, as far as uprightness is concerned?" The noun מִישׁוֹר is used of the reign of God in the HB (Pss 45:6; 67:5) and even of Isaiah's "shoot" (Isa 11:4), and the question is best understood as exalting the role of Zerubabbel vis-à-vis the priesthood by a kind of argument from the lesser to the greater: if the priesthood embodies the quality of מִישׁוֹר (Mal 2:6), how much more does Zerubbabel, the representative of the Davidic house! This statement (and the entire oracle to Zerubbabel) serves as an important counterbalance to the passages in the Night Visions that exalt the role of Joshua the high priest (3:1-10; 6:9-15). For an expanded treatment of this difficult text, see Rogland (2014e).

וְהוֹצִיא אֶת־הָאֶבֶן הָרֹאשָׁה תְּשֻׁאוֹת חֵן חֵן לָהּ. Hifil *weqatal* 3 m s √יצא. What is the referent of הָאֶבֶן? It is unlikely that it refers to the stones of the priestly garb as encountered earlier in 3:9. The phrase הָאֶבֶן הָרֹאשָׁה is understood by some as akin to the רֹאשׁ פִּנָּה "the chief cornerstone" of Ps 118:22 (Petterson 2015: 153), in which case it indicates Zerubbabel's involvement in a foundation laying ceremony of some sort (cf. Hag 2:15-19). Others translate הָאֶבֶן הָרֹאשָׁה as "former stone," which Petersen explains as "a building deposit which signified continuity with the earlier temple" (241). Another proposal is to translate it as "primary stonework," which Wolters argues (2014: 123–24) refers "to the still existing foundations of the temple": "It is not so much the individual 'foundation stone' . . . as the collective stonework or stone masonry which constituted the foundation walls of Solomon's temple, and which is now to serve as the foundation of the new temple as well." For a survey of other interpretations of הָאֶבֶן הָרֹאשָׁה as well as proposed textual emendations, see Petitjean (243–51).

A common weakness of most interpretations is the assumption that רֹאשָׁה is an adjective, but this is otherwise unattested in CH or RH (see *DCH* 7, 377; Jastrow, 1437–38). The significance of this lack of attestation should not be minimized. A preferable solution is to understand אֶבֶן as a collective (cf. on 3:9) referring more generally to Zerubbabel's helping to provide the stone for the rebuilding project, and to understand רֹאשָׁה as the noun רֹאשׁ, with the locative *he* (regarding the accent on the ultima, cf. JM §93c). רֹאשׁ is used a number of times with הַר (e.g., Gen 8:5; Exod 19:20; 24:17; 34:2; see BDB, 910–11, #2a), and here would refer to the "head" or "top" of the temple mount, which was mentioned in the preceding clause. Petitjean (243; cf. Schöttler, 122 n. 344) disputes this, arguing that Hifil √יצא does not utilize the locative *he* elsewhere, but this claim is clearly erroneous (see Gen 15:5; 19:17; Exod 12:46; Deut 24:11; 2 Chron 29:16; Ezek 47:2). Wolters (2014: 124) objects in part since the locative *he* is not utilized with רֹאשׁ, but such an argument is far from compelling. It should be noted that the morpheme does occur several times with the noun הַר in BH (e.g., Gen 12:8; 14:10; 19:17, 19; etc.).

תְּשֻׁאוֹת חֵן חֵן לָהּ. The substantive תְּשֻׁאוֹת functions as an indirect accusative: "He shall bring out the stone to the top *with noises* . . ." (JM §126c). The exclamation חֵן חֵן לָהּ is probably a possessive clause ("It has grace, grace!"), with the pronominal suffix referring to the feminine אֶבֶן, though the precise intent of the utterance is opaque.

4:8 וַיְהִי דְבַר־יְהוָה אֵלַי לֵאמֹר׃

Qal *wayyiqtol* 3 m s √היה, Qal inf cstr √אמר. On this "reception formula" as narrating a revelatory event, see Appendix §1.

4:9 יְדֵי זְרֻבָּבֶל יִסְּדוּ הַבַּיִת הַזֶּה וְיָדָיו תְּבַצַּעְנָה וְיָדַעְתָּ כִּי־יְהוָה צְבָאוֹת שְׁלָחַנִי אֲלֵיכֶם׃

יְדֵי זְרֻבָּבֶל יִסְּדוּ הַבַּיִת הַזֶּה וְיָדָיו תְּבַצַּעְנָה. Piel *qatal* 3 c pl √יסד, Piel *yiqtol* 3 f pl √בצע. In this instance it is possible that the verb √יסד refers to the work of repairing or reestablishing foundations rather than laying entirely new ones (see Hag 2:18). The semantic range of Piel √בצע is somewhat unusual: "to cut, sever," "to make violent gain," and "to finish, complete." It is not clear how or if the different meanings are related to each other, though the English expression "to finish something off" may provide an analogy for the meaning required by the context here (see also Isa 10:12; Lam 2:17). In contrast to its usage here, in all of its other instances the verb is transitive, that is, it takes a direct object. Hence הַבַּיִת הַזֶּה should be understood as the implied object of the verb.

וְיָדַעְתָּ כִּי־יְהוָה צְבָאוֹת שְׁלָחַנִי אֲלֵיכֶם. Qal *weqatal* 2 m s √ידע, Qal *qatal* 3 m s √שלח with 1 c s pronoun suffix. On this "validation formula," see 2:13.

4:10 כִּי מִי בַז לְיוֹם קְטַנּוֹת וְשָׂמְחוּ וְרָאוּ אֶת־הָאֶבֶן הַבְּדִיל בְּיַד זְרֻבָּבֶל שִׁבְעָה־אֵלֶּה עֵינֵי יְהוָה הֵמָּה מְשׁוֹטְטִים בְּכָל־הָאָרֶץ׃

כִּי מִי בַז לְיוֹם קְטַנּוֹת. Qal *qatal* 3 m s √בוז. Strictly speaking, בַז could be parsed as a masculine singular participle, but a finite verb would be expected following מִי. Typically the *qatal* 3 masculine singular of II-*vav* verbs is vocalized with *qameṣ*, thus *בָּז would be the expected form, but in BH some confusion of II-*vav* forms and geminate forms periodically occurs (JM §80o). The verb occasionally takes an accusative object, but most often its object is marked with לְ, as here. מִי can function as an interrogative pronoun ("who?") or as an indefinite pronoun ("whoever") introducing a "generalizing relative clause" (JM §144fa; WB §121; WO §18.2e; MNK §43.3.1vi).

BH can use the feminine adjective or participle to create abstract nouns (JM §134n), thus the feminine plural adjective קְטַנּוֹת is used to indicate "small things." The expression "day of small things" is unparalleled in the HB. Most likely it is intended as a contrast to "the day of YHWH," which is described elsewhere in the prophets as a "great" (גָּדוֹל) day, e.g., Zeph 1:14 קָרוֹב יוֹם־יְהוָה הַגָּדוֹל "for the great day of YHWH is near"; Joel 2:11 כִּי־גָדוֹל יוֹם־יְהוָה "for great is the day of YHWH" (cf. Jer 30:7; Hos 2:2); 3:4 (and Mal 3:23) לִפְנֵי בּוֹא יוֹם יְהוָה הַגָּדוֹל וְהַנּוֹרָא "before the coming of the great and fearful day of YHWH" (cf. also 1QS[a] 10:4; 4Q256 19:2; 4Q258 9:1; 4Q265 7:4). It is clear that a spirit of disappointment had infected some of the members of the Judean community (cf. Hag 1:15b–2:9).

וְשָׂמְחוּ וְרָאוּ אֶת־הָאֶבֶן הַבְּדִיל בְּיַד זְרֻבָּבֶל. Qal *weqatal* 3 c pl √שׂמח, Qal *weqatal* 3 c pl √ראה. The two *weqatal* verbs וְשָׂמְחוּ וְרָאוּ are likely a case of *hysteron proteron* ("the latter first"): in reality, the rejoicing will follow the seeing, but וְשָׂמְחוּ is placed first in order to heighten the contrast with the downcast spirit of the preceding clause.

As noted above, מִי can function as an interrogative "who?" or as an indefinite pronoun "whoever," and a number of scholars opt for the latter (e.g., Wolters 2014: 135; cf. Petersen, 238). BDB (567, g) is skeptical and maintains its interrogative nature, and claims that this instance in Zech 4:10 is "dubious" due to an anomalous construction and use of tenses. Yet is this indeed anomalous? The instances cited in the lexica often have a jussive verb in the main clause (JM §144fa), and while *weqatal* forms do not display jussive modality, they can indicate related modal nuances of obligation such as "should" or "ought." וְשָׂמְחוּ וְרָאוּ could be fittingly translated as, "they should rejoice and see." The statement is providing a directive for those who have "despised the day of small things."

The appositional noun phrase הָאֶבֶן הַבְּדִיל has proven troublesome. בְּדִיל refers to a metal in BH (BDB, 95; *HALOT*, 110; *DCH* 2, 95; etc.) and the DSS (4Q271 2:9), usually identified as tin. In this appositional structure the second noun specifies the material of the first (WO §12.3.c; Wolters 2014: 136). On the surface this appears to clash semantically with the notion of a "stone," but a comparison with 5:8 אֶ֫בֶן הָעֹפָ֫רֶת "the stone of lead" (= "the weight made of lead") indicates that these notions are not necessarily incompatible. From a lexicographical standpoint, then, the expression is best rendered either as "tin stone" or "weight of tin." Nevertheless, what the expression refers to in this context remains a matter of dispute: several lexica take the collocation הָאֶ֫בֶן הַבְּדִיל to refer to a "plummet" as a tool of the rebuilding project, potentially linked with the קָו of 1:16 or the חֶ֫בֶל מִדָּה of 2:5-6. This seems to be the most suited to the context. Others suggest that it is a building deposit (Petersen, 243) or a "completion stone" connected with the "stone" of verse 7 (Petterson 2009: 72; 2015: 149), deriving בְּדִיל from √בדל "to separate, divide," with הָאֶ֫בֶן הַבְּדִיל to be translated as "chosen stone," though this derivation is dubious in light of the general attestation of בְּדִיל.

שִׁבְעָה־אֵ֫לֶּה עֵינֵי יְהוָה. On the syntax of numbers 3–10, which can also modify pronouns, see 2:1. שִׁבְעָה־אֵ֫לֶּה means "these seven," not "these are seven"; cf. Gen 9:19 שְׁלֹשָׁה אֵ֫לֶּה בְּנֵי־נֹ֑חַ "these three were Noah's sons" and 22:23 שְׁמֹנָה אֵ֫לֶּה יָלְדָה מִלְכָּה לְנָחוֹר אֲחִי אַבְרָהָם "These eight Milcah bore to Nahor, the brother of Abraham." In the context of Zech 4, this is referring to the seven "lamps" (נֵרוֹת) of verse 2. The clause finally provides a partial answer to the prophet's question of verse 4, following the unexpected oracle to Zerubbabel. Although many scholars find it tempting to identify YHWH's "seven eyes" with the "one stone with seven עֵינָיִם" of 3:9, the similarities between the two texts are more superficial than real (see 3:9). The "eyes of YHWH" is an anthropomorphism encountered elsewhere in the HB (e.g., Prov 15:3; see BDB, 744, #1b).

הֵ֫מָּה מְשׁוֹטְטִים בְּכָל־הָאָ֫רֶץ. Polel ptc m pl √שוט. In SBH the participle in this context would probably indicate either the "actual present" or the imminent future (see Hag 2:6). It seems likely in this instance, however, that the participle expresses a "general present" indicating God's habitual activity, which is reflective of the LBH linguistic milieu (see Hag 1:6). According to 2 Chron 16:9, the prophet Hanani made a similar statement in the late tenth/early ninth century BCE by way of rebuke to King Asa (כִּי יְהוָה עֵינָיו מְשֹׁטְטוֹת בְּכָל־הָאָ֫רֶץ), which Wolters (2014: 141) suggests may have been known to Zechariah.

4:11 וַיַּ֣עַן וָאֹמַ֣ר אֵלָ֑יו מַה־שְּׁנֵ֤י הַזֵּיתִים֙ הָאֵ֔לֶּה עַל־יְמִ֥ין הַמְּנוֹרָ֖ה וְעַל־שְׂמֹאולָֽהּ׃

וָאַ֫עַן וָאֹמַ֣ר אֵלָ֑יו. Qal *wayyiqtol* 1 c s √ענה, Qal *wayyiqtol* 1 c s √אמר.

מַה־שְּׁנֵ֤י הַזֵּיתִים֙ הָאֵ֔לֶּה עַל־יְמִ֥ין הַמְּנוֹרָ֖ה וְעַל־שְׂמֹאולָֽהּ. On the intent of the question, see 1:9. In verse 3 it was stated that the two olive trees stood on the right and left of the "bowl" (אֶחָד֙ מִימִ֣ין הַגֻּלָּ֔ה וְאֶחָ֖ד עַל־שְׂמֹאלָֽהּ), but see that the bowl is "on the top" (v. 2 עַל־רֹאשָׁ֔הּ) of the lampstand. It is just as accurate to describe the trees as standing to the right and left of the lampstand itself.

4:12 וָאַ֣עַן שֵׁנִ֔ית וָאֹמַ֖ר אֵלָ֑יו מַה־שְׁתֵּ֞י שִׁבֲּלֵ֣י הַזֵּיתִ֗ים אֲשֶׁר֙ בְּיַ֗ד שְׁנֵי֙ צַנְתְּר֣וֹת הַזָּהָ֔ב הַֽמְרִיקִ֥ים מֵעֲלֵיהֶ֖ם הַזָּהָֽב׃

וָאַ֫עַן שֵׁנִ֔ית וָאֹמַ֖ר אֵלָ֑יו. Qal *wayyiqtol* 1 c s √ענה, Qal *wayyiqtol* 1 c s √אמר. On the ordinal number שֵׁנִית, see Hag 2:20. In narrative, repetition of verb of speaking (vv. 11-12 וָאַ֫עַן . . . וָאַ֫עַן) for no "apparent" reason can indicate that someone is waiting for or expecting a reply but not getting one, and hence speaks again to prompt a response (e.g., Gen 42:1-2; 1 Sam 17:8-10, 37; cf. Alter, 107; see 5:6). The implication here is that the prophet received no response to his inquiry of verse 11, and therefore is asking a follow-up question.

מַה־שְׁתֵּ֞י שִׁבֲּלֵ֣י הַזֵּיתִ֗ים אֲשֶׁר֙ בְּיַ֗ד שְׁנֵי֙ צַנְתְּר֣וֹת הַזָּהָ֔ב הַֽמְרִיקִ֥ים מֵעֲלֵיהֶ֖ם הַזָּהָֽב. This clause represents yet another *crux interpretum* in the Night Visions, as the meaning or referent of the words שִׁבֹּ֫לֶת, צַנְתְּרוֹת, and even זָהָב is much debated. As tempting as textual emendation is in this instance, a glance at the scholarly literature makes it clear that the MT is the *lectio difficilior*, which will be assumed to be correct in the following discussion.

מַה־שְׁתֵּ֞י שִׁבֲּלֵ֣י הַזֵּיתִ֗ים. See 1:9 regarding the nature of the question "What is the meaning of . . . ?" The segolate noun שִׁבֹּ֫לֶת is grammatically feminine, but the plural (absolute and construct) takes masculine endings. Unlike the numbers 3–10, in Hebrew the numbers one and two match the nouns they modify in gender (cf. on 2:1), hence the feminine שְׁתֵּי occurs with שִׁבֳּלִים. Most lexica list two homonyms for שִׁבֹּ֫לֶת (BDB, 987; *DCH* 8, 238; *HALOT*, 1394-5; Jastrow,

1557; see also Wegner, and Grisanti), the most common of which is "ear of grain" (Gen 41:5-7, 22-27; Ruth 2:2; Job 24:24; Isa 17:5; 1QM 5:9-12). The second lemma שִׁבֹּ֫לֶת is less common and means "flowing stream," "flood, current," or possibly "river" and is attested in, e.g., Ps 69:3 בָּאתִי בְמַעֲמַקֵּי־מַ֫יִם וְשִׁבֹּלֶת שְׁטָפָתְנִי "I have come into the deeps of the water, and a current has swept over me" (see also v. 16); 4Q437 2 i 10 הׅצלתני פן אטבע בו ומׅשבׅולת גוים פן [ת]שוטפני "you have delivered me lest I should sink in it, and (you delivered me) from a flood of nations lest it should flow over me"; Sir 4:26 (MsA) אל תבוש לשוב מעון ואל תעמוד לפני שבלת "Do not be ashamed to turn from iniquity, and do not stand before a current [of sin?]." Contextually, it is not easy to make sense of שִׁבֹּ֫לֶת I "ear of grain," though some have suggested extensions of this meaning such as "the top of tree," "the end of an olive bough," or "clusters of olive branches," but these are to be eschewed since the term has clear associations with grains. On the other hand, שִׁבֹּ֫לֶת II "stream, current, river" has plausibility in light of the general context of oil flowing into the lamps (Petterson 2015: 149) and particularly in view of the analysis of מוּצָקוֹת as "streams of liquid" presented here (see v. 2). The construct phrase שִׁבֲּלֵ֫י הַזֵּיתִים represents a genitive of origin (JM §129f10).

אֲשֶׁר֙ בְּיַד֙ שְׁנֵי֙ צַנְתְּר֣וֹת הַזָּהָ֔ב. The particle אֲשֶׁר and the prepositional phrase בְּיַד have a variety of functions and meanings and will be discussed below. It was noted above that numbers one and two match the nouns they modify in gender, and thus the use of שְׁנֵי (instead of the fem שְׁתֵּי) with צַנְתְּרוֹת indicates that the noun is grammatically masculine, despite the *–ot* ending (Rose, 183). Wolters, who suggests that צַנְתְּרוֹת refers to "olive pressers," argues that צַנְתְּרוֹת הַזָּהָב represents an objective genitive (2012: 5, 8-9, 12), but it is more likely that צַנְתְּרוֹת הַזָּהָב should be understood as a genitive of material (see v. 2).

It has been suggested that masculine nouns with feminine endings may have an intensive nuance (JM §89b), but this does nothing to help clarify the meaning of צַנְתְּרוֹת, which is a famous lexicographical problem, being a *hapax* in CH as well as RH. Wolters has provided a detailed survey of the history of interpretation of this troubling word and lists thirty proposed understandings of צַנְתְּרוֹת (2012: 13–15), including "nostrils" or "snouts" (LXX: μυξωτήρων; Vulg: *duo rostra*), "thighs," "beakers" (Symmachus: ἐπιχυτῆρες), "vats" or "trough" (Rashi), "lamp snuffers" (Luther: *Schneutzen*), among many others. Contemporary translations often gloss it as "pipes," a rendering based in part on the general sense of the context, which could suggest the machinery used to harvest olive oil from the trees to feed into the menorah. The etymology of צַנְתְּרוֹת is uncertain (Wolters 2014: 144), but it is often compared to other nouns that add or insert a consonant into a tri-literal root (e.g., Rose, 183; BDB, 857; cf. GKC §85w). If the phenomenon applies in this case then צַנְתְּרוֹת could be related to BH צִנּוֹר "pipe, spout, conduit." However, as Wolters points out, the meaning of this latter term is itself questionable, as is the phenomenon of nominal forms with an infixed *tav* after a second root letter in BH (2012: 4–5). We will return to the meaning of צַנְתְּרוֹת below, after discussing the remaining constituents of the verse.

הַֽמְרִיקִים מֵעֲלֵיהֶם הַזָּהָב. Hifil ptc m pl √ריק with def art. The verb means "to empty, pour" (BDB, 937–38; *HALOT*, 1227–28; Jastrow, 1463) and once occurs absolutely (Eccl 11:3) but usually takes an accusative object (e.g., Gen 14:14; 42:35; Exod 15:9; Lev 26:33; Jer 48:12). In this instance the accusative object is הַזָּהָב, lit. "the gold," which is generally understood as referring to olive oil; Petterson aptly comments that the material is "being described by its colour rather than its substance" (2009: 77). This is the only instance in which the verb √ריק is used with a form of the preposition מִן. מֵעֲלֵיהֶם could mean "from above them" or "from upon them," and the pronoun suffix could refer either to the הַזֵּיתִים or the צַנְתְּרוֹת depending on what one views as the noun being modified by the participle הַֽמְרִיקִים (see further below).

To clarify the difficulties of the verse it is necessary to "zoom out" from individual lexemes and phrases to consider its larger syntactical structure. Recall that the clause begins with a question (מַה־שְׁתֵּי שִׁבֲּלֵי הַזֵּיתִים), which is grammatically complete in itself, containing a subject and predicate. In contrast, the remaining constituents in the verse, אֲשֶׁר בְּיַד שְׁנֵי צַנְתְּרוֹת הַזָּהָב, and הַֽמְרִיקִים מֵעֲלֵיהֶם הַזָּהָב, do not form grammatically complete independent clauses, and one must therefore seek to relate both of these to this basic interrogative structure.

The first issue regarding אֲשֶׁר בְּיַד שְׁנֵי צַנְתְּרוֹת הַזָּהָב is the function of אֲשֶׁר. It hardly seems possible to interpret it as a conjunction (BDB, 83, #8) but rather appears to have its common function as a relative pronoun, thus creating a relative clause modifying שְׁתֵּי שִׁבֲּלֵי הַזֵּיתִים (while occasionally אֲשֶׁר finds its antecedent in a following substantive [BDB, 82, #6], such does not appear to be possible here). A copula can be supplied: "What are the two flowing currents of the olive trees *which are* בְּיַד שְׁנֵי צַנְתְּרוֹת הַזָּהָב?" The prepositional phrase בְּיַד has a range of meanings and is often understood here spatially as "beside." While this makes sense, it has been pointed out (e.g., Wolters 2012: 5) that this is an extremely rare meaning of בְּיַד (cf. BDB, 391). It could also mean "by means of" (instrumental) or "in(to) the hand of," i.e., to have possession of or power over something or someone, as in Gen 38:18 וּמַטְּךָ אֲשֶׁר בְּיָדֶךָ "And your staff which is in your hand"; Gen 16:6 הִנֵּה שִׁפְחָתֵךְ בְּיָדֵךְ "Behold, your maidservant is in your hand"; 2 Sam 18:2 הַשְּׁלִשִׁית בְּיַד־יוֹאָב "a third under the command of Joab." Despite the uncertainty of the term צַנְתְּרוֹת, the best translation appears to be, "What are the two flowing streams of the olive trees, which are in the hand of (i.e., in the possession/power of) the two golden צַנְתְּרוֹת?" בְּיַד typically occurs with personal rather than impersonal objects (as correctly noted by Wolters 2012: 5–7), a point to which we will return below.

Turning to the analysis of הַמְרִיקִים מֵעֲלֵיהֶם הַזָּהָב, one must identify the antecedent of the participle הַמְרִיקִים. Given that צַנְתְּרוֹת is treated as masculine (see above), the participle could modify זֵיתִים or צַנְתְּרוֹת. If the former is correct, one could translate, "What is the meaning of the two flowing streams of the olive trees, which are in the hand of the two golden צַנְתְּרוֹת, *which (trees) are emptying* the gold(en oil) from above them." This is awkward, however, partly because צַנְתְּרוֹת is the closer antecedent of the participle and also because one would not expect the olives trees to be described as doing the "emptying" of the oil but rather the "flowing streams" (שִׁבֲּלִים), in which case one would have expected the feminine participle *הַמְרִיקוֹת. Moreover, if the olive trees were the subject of the participle, then מֵעֲלֵיהֶם would be difficult: "From above them" would make little sense if referring to trees, since presumably they are at least as tall as (if not taller than) the lampstand itself, and oil must be flowing downward from them into the menorah. One would instead have to take the suffix of מֵעֲלֵיהֶם in a reflexive sense, e.g., "which (trees) are emptying the gold(en oil) from off of *themselves*," which would be awkward as well. If צַנְתְּרוֹת is understood as the head noun of הַמְרִיקִים, the translation would be, "What is the meaning of the two flowing streams of the olive trees, which are 'in the hand of' the two golden צַנְתְּרוֹת, which are emptying the gold(en oil) from above/off of them." In this case the compound preposition מֵעַל could possibly indicate a difference in height ("from above them," with the pronoun suffix of מֵעֲלֵיהֶם refering to the צַנְתְּרוֹת themselves), but it seems more natural to interpret the pronoun suffix of מֵעֲלֵיהֶם as referring to the olive trees, and thus the צַנְתְּרוֹת are emptying the oil "from off of them."

The reader is still left struggling with the meaning of צַנְתְּרוֹת. All interpretations seek to do justice to the context of removing oil from the trees in some fashion. At the same time, one must also account for the use of בְּיַד, which is indeed suggestive of personal agents as noted above. Furthermore, to anticipate the discussion of verse 14, the ultimate answer given by the Interpreting Angel indicates that these צַנְתְּרוֹת represent personal agents, namely, "two sons of oil who stand by the Lord of the whole earth" (see v. 14), a statement which is admittedly mysterious as well. Sensing the need to interpret the צַנְתְּרוֹת as personal agents, Wolters argues that they refer to "olive pressers" and translates, "What are the two spikes of the olive trees, which are in the hands of the two pressers of 'gold'—the ones who express the 'gold' from (the olives) on them?" In addition to this problematic understanding of שִׁבֲּלִים as discussed above, a critical weakness of this proposal is that the verb √ריק does not mean "to press/express out" but "to pour/empty out," which is not the same action (contra Wolters 2012: 9, who is forced to suggest revocalization to הַמֹּרִיקִים from √ירק "to spit").

The present handbook is guided by the suggestion of Zer-Kavod (83) that the צַנְתְּרוֹת are דמויות מעין כרובים, i.e., "figures like cherubim." Part of Zer-Kavod's argument is etymological in nature, appealing to Indo-Germanic *gandharvá*, a word that refers to some sort of mythical being, and thereby to Greek κένταυρος "centaur." Whether or not the suggestion of an Indo-Germanic origin can be sustained (cf. Mayrhofer, 462), it is proposed here that Hebrew צַנְתְּרוֹת is in fact best understood as a loanword derived ultimately from Greek κένταυρος. Although a full discussion will have to await a future treatment, the following factors may briefly be noted:

1. Greek κένταυρος is attested in pre–sixth-century texts (Homer, *Iliad* 11.832; *Odyssey* 21.295, 303; Hesiod, *Shield of Heracles* 184; *Fragments* 88.4; 209.5; 302.17). Hence the word was available for borrowing into the various languages coming into Hellenistic contact.
2. Greek loanwords are found on occasion in the biblical corpus (Janse; de Lange, 805–6) and abundantly in postbiblical texts (see Krauss, with the important cautions of Krivoruchko). At the very least, one can point to קִיתָרוֹס/קַתְרוֹס, פְּסַנְתֵּרִין,

and סוּמְפֹּנְיָה from the book of Daniel (Mitchell and Joyce), which has a narrative setting of sixth-century Yehud, though most scholars date the book's composition to the Hellenistic period. Regardless, Kitchen (44–50) presents abundant evidence for the possibility of Greek loanwords in Syro-Palestine at a much earlier period and demonstrates that the possibility of a Greek loanword in a sixth-century BH text cannot be excluded a priori (cf. also Tiemeyer 2011: 257–59). It may also be noted that the hypothesis of צַנְתְּרוֹת being a loanword would help to explain its lack of attestation elsewhere. As a highly specialized borrowed term, it would only be needed in very particular contexts.

3. Centaur-like creatures are well attested in iconographic sources and the material remains of the Mediterranean and ancient Levant. Numerous depictions of centaurs are found on Greek seals, pottery, statuettes, and the like, some dating from centuries before the postexilic era (Lebessi), and Greek pottery is already attested in Syro-Palestine in the eighth century BC (Kitchen, 44–45). Moreover, centaur-like creatures are famous from Assyrian palace reliefs such as those of Ashurbanipal and Sargon II. While one can quibble whether some depictions are "properly" centaurs or not (e.g., Lemos, 18 and n. 9), there can be no doubt that analogous creatures were known in a variety of traditions in and around the Levant. The fact that BH itself does not attest a term appropriate for such creatures suggests a gap in the lexicon, which could have been filled via a convenient loanword such as κένταυρος.

Naturally, the mere possibility of a loan does not require it as an explanation. What favors this proposal most heavily is its explanatory power on a phonological level, further supported by exegetical factors. In terms of phonology, it should be observed that the proposed loan of κένταυρος into BH is capable of accounting for the final three consonantal phonemes /NTR/ in their order, which is no insignificant matter, given the otherwise obscure etymology of צַנְתְּרוֹת (see above). The only difficulty lies with the initial consonantal phoneme /ts/, since Greek κ is not transcribed in Hebrew with צ but typically with ק or כ or rarely ג, whereas צ is often used for Greek σ and ζ (Krauss, 4–5,

9–10). The sibilant English pronunciation of "centaur" is misleading for the modern reader with respect to צַנְתְּרוֹת, since the English word is derived from Latin *centaurus* rather than directly from Greek, and there is no obvious reason to suppose that a sibilant pronunciation of the Greek word existed in antiquity. It is possible, of course, that Greek κ → Hebrew צ is simply to be viewed as an anomaly or as an unexplained phonetic change that occurred in the process of lexical borrowing (cf. Heijmans, 149). However, it may be more plausible to suggest that the change occurred as a result of the word being first adopted into Aramaic and then into Hebrew (cf. Tiemeyer 2011: 257–58). In light of the abundant archaeological and iconographical attestation of centaur-like creatures in ancient Assyria, it seems likely that a borrowing into Aramaic would have been useful at an early date. It is not difficult to imagine that Greek κένταυρος would have taken the consonantal form קנתר in Aramaic, given the common tendency for Greek κ to be transliterated as Hebrew/Aramaic ק. Yet, if the word then entered CH from Aramaic, it must be remembered that certain lexemes with ק in Old and Imperial Aramaic correspond to words with צ in Hebrew, e.g., Aramaic ארק "earth, land" = Hebrew אֶרֶץ, Aramaic עק "tree" = Hebrew עֵץ, Aramaic קמר "wool" = Hebrew צֶמֶר, both originating in a hypothesized Proto-Semitic voiced emphatic interdental phoneme /ḍ/ or /ḏ/ (Moscati et al., 27–28). The process of phonetic development resulting in this dual graphic representation remains somewhat obscure (cf. Segert, 118–19; Degen, 36–37; Muraoka and Porten, 8–9; Garr, 23–24; Steiner, 1499–1501). What is clear, however, is that such correspondences between Aramaic ק and Hebrew צ exist. The proposed development of Greek κένταυρος → Aramaic קנתר → Hebrew צנתר is therefore plausible and, in view of the manifold weaknesses of other proposals, deserves serious consideration.

Moreover, an exegetical case can be made for understanding צַנְתְּרוֹת as "centaurs," which in the context of the HB would more likely refer to man-horse creatures of the winged type as in Assyrian depictions and would thus, as Zer-Kavod (83) suggests, be reminiscent of cherubim. First, this vision (as the Night Visions more broadly) is obviously marked by significant use of temple imagery, and it must be recalled that the two cherubim of the Solomonic temple were constructed from olive wood covered with gold (1 Kgs 6:23-28). Second, as already indicated, the animate nature of the צַנְתְּרוֹת is suggested by the use of the prepositional phrase בְּיַד and by the explanation in verse

14 that they represent "the two sons of oil who stand by the Lord of the whole earth." While this statement is itself a famous conundrum (see below), the fact that צַנְתְּרוֹת represent people suggests that the image itself was one of living creatures.

In sum, then, the prophet inquires in verse 11 about the meaning of the olive trees but is given no answer. The Interpreting Angel's refusal to reply causes the prophet to refocus his question on the "flowing streams" coming from the trees, which are "in the hand of" (i.e., in the possession of or under the power of) two golden centaurs (i.e., angelic beings), who are the ones "emptying" the trees of oil and directing it into the menorah. The dialogue, with its questions and selective answers, is constructed so as to direct the focus on these centaurs, which will be the subject of the angel's explanation in verse 14.

4:13 וַיֹּאמֶר אֵלַי לֵאמֹר הֲלוֹא יָדַעְתָּ מָה־אֵלֶּה וָאֹמַר לֹא אֲדֹנִי׃

וַיֹּאמֶר אֵלַי לֵאמֹר הֲלוֹא יָדַעְתָּ מָה־אֵלֶּה. Qal *wayyiqtol* 3 m s √אמר, Qal inf cstr √אמר, Qal *qatal* 2 m s √ידע. The question is slightly different from the one in verse 5, which was a tripartite nominal clause that included the personal pronoun הֵמָּה. In that instance it was suggested that the addition of the pronoun placed the focus of the question on the significance of what had been seen. By the same token, the lack of the pronoun in the indirect question מָה־אֵלֶּה here could indicate that its focus is more on identifying or describing what has been seen. This is not so surprising given the fantastic nature of the creatures in view.

וָאֹמַר לֹא אֲדֹנִי. Qal *wayyiqtol* 1 c s √אמר.

4:14 וַיֹּאמֶר אֵלֶּה שְׁנֵי בְנֵי־הַיִּצְהָר הָעֹמְדִים עַל־אֲדוֹן כָּל־הָאָרֶץ׃

Qal *wayyiqtol* 3 m s √אמר, Qal ptc m pl √עמד with def art. The syngtam √עמד plus עַל simply means "to stand beside" here. Both the olive trees and the golden centaurs are positioned next to the menorah (cf. vv. 3, 11-12), but as argued above (see v. 12), this verse provides an explanation of the golden centaurs rather than the olive trees (contra

Rose, 180–81) or the two "streams/branch ends" of the olive trees (contra Wolters 2014: 153).

The great question in this verse concerns the meaning and referent of the phrase שְׁנֵי בְנֵי־הַיִּצְהָר, lit. "the two sons of oil," but often translated as "anointed ones" (e.g., RSV, JPS, etc.), a rendering which suggests a possible messianic significance of the phrase. The exact phrase שני בני היצהר occurs verbatim in the Qumran scroll 4Q254 4:2, and while the immediate context is fragmentary, the text more broadly may suggest a messianic interpretation (Høgenhaven, 115; Evans), though a good deal of caution is needed. As with other passages in the Night Visions, the phrase שְׁנֵי בְנֵי־הַיִּצְהָר is viewed as having important implications for a supposed priestly royal diarchic structure to the political leadership of postexilic Yehud (see 3:1-10 and 6:9-15, *passim*). It has been pointed out, however, that a critical weakness of the translation "anointed ones" is that the term used for "oil" (יִצְהָר) is not the one used in the anointing of people, which is always שֶׁמֶן (Rose, 191). The two terms occasionally occur in parallel utterances (Hos 2:7, 10, 24), indicating some overlap in meaning, but the claim that they are synonymous is problematic (contra, e.g., *HALOT*, 427; see Schöttler, 245–54 and Rose, 189–92). Some appeal to the noun's etymological link with צָהֳרַיִם "noon, midday" and suggest that it originally meant "shining oil" (Averbeck 2007b; cf. BDB, 244), yet this can only be considered a speculation, and in any event the term's usage is more indicative of its semantics than its etymology. Except for this instance, יִצְהָר always occurs with תִּירוֹשׁ, and just as תִּירוֹשׁ refers to freshly pressed, unprocessed juice of the grape as the first stage of winemaking, so likewise is יִצְהָר best understood as "fresh oil" or "new oil,"—that is, the raw product of pressing olives, in contrast to oil that has been prepared for use (see BDB, 844; Dalman, 255–56; Rose, 191–92 n. 41).

This understanding of יִצְהָר, coupled with the general context of oil flowing off of the olive trees and into the menorah, has led many to suggest that בֵּן is best interpreted here as the designation of a "member of a guild, order, or class" (BDB, 121, #7a; cf. also JM §129j; WO §9.5.3b). In this instance בְּנֵי־הַיִּצְהָר could refer to "oilmen" or "oil suppliers" (Rose, 195; Petterson 2009: 84) or perhaps "oil pressers" (see v. 12 on Wolters' proposal regarding the meaning of צַנְתְּרוֹת). Many different identifications have been proposed for these two "sons of oil." e.g., Joshua and Zerubbabel, Haggai and Zechariah, Aaron and David (or Moses or the Messiah), a future king and priest, the scholars of the land of Israel, and heavenly beings, to mention only some of the most prominent theories. The answer to such a question would require a full exegetical and theological analysis of the text, which goes beyond the grammatical and lexical issues treated in this handbook.

A minority view is that יִצְהָר is to be taken as a proper name (for references, see Wolters 2014: 153). The presence of the definite article on הַיִּצְהָר is not a conclusive objection to this interpretation, since such anomalies are occasionally attested (Wolters 2014: 153; GKC §125d; JM §137b). According to Num 3:19; 16:1, יִצְהָר was a Levite and a descendant of Kohath, the head of the Levitical house given the responsibility of transporting the vessels of the tabernacle, including both the ark and the menorah. Given the cultic context and paraphernalia of chapter 4 and the mention of "centaurs/cherubim" in verse 12, such a reference to tabernacle servants would not be out of place. Wolters (2014: 153) suggests that a dual reference to the Izrahites and to "oilmen" could therefore be intended.

Sixth Vision (Zechariah 5:1-11)
The Flying Scroll and the Flying Basket

The sixth vision consists of two parts: a depiction of a large flying scroll (vv. 1-4) and a depiction of a flying basket (vv. 5-11). There is no action in the first part: Zechariah simply sees a scroll, which is said to represent a divine oath of cursing (v. 3 אָלָה) that will come upon perjurers and thieves who have heretofore been (unjustly) acquitted of their crimes. The second part of the vision is more complex: the prophet sees a basket "coming out" (הָֽאֵיפָה הַיּוֹצֵאת), that is, approaching from apparently some distance away (vv. 5-6). As it draws closer, a woman is revealed to be sitting in it (v. 7), who is called הָרִשְׁעָה "Wickedness" (v. 8). An angel subsequently forces her down into the basket and seals it with a disk or weight of lead (v. 8), and it is transported to a "house" in the land of Shinar by two women with stork-like wings (vv. 9-11). The bizarre imagery is striking, but the overall message speaks unambiguously of the containment and removal of sin.

Scholars frequently separate verses 1-4 and 5-11 into two separate visions. This textual division has not always been viewed as the most natural one, however, as evidenced by the scribal placement of a *setuma* after verse 8 rather than verse 4. In fact, a number of literary features link the two visions together (Rogland 2014c: 103–4), such as the common use of the verb √יצא as a *Leitwort*, the parallel explanatory comments (v. 3 זֹאת הָאָלָה, v. 6 זֹאת הָאֵיפָה, v. 8 זֹאת הָרִשְׁעָה) and, most obviously, the subject matter: both scenes deal with airborne objects, which are so rare in the HB that their occurrence in two successive pericopae must be viewed as intentional. Other exegetical factors also serve to unite the two scenes into a coherent whole, as emerges when the philological details of the text are properly understood (see the commentary below).

[1]*And again I lifted up my eyes and I kept looking and behold: there was a scroll, flying.*

[2]*And he said to me, "What do you see?" And I said, "I see a scroll flying; its length is twenty cubits, and its width is ten cubits."*

[3]*And he said to me, "This is the oath which is going out over the surface of all the earth, for everyone who steals has been acquitted from that which is according to it, and everyone who swears [deceptively] has been acquitted from that which is according to it.*

[4]*I have brought it out"—oracle of YHWH Tsevaot—"and it will come into the house of the thief and into the house of the one who swears deceptively by my name, and it will dwell in the midst of his house, and it will destroy it, both its wood and stones."*

[5] *And the angel who was speaking with me went out, and he said to me, "Lift up your eyes and see: What is this thing that is coming forth?"*

[6] *And I said, "What is it?" And he said, "This is the ephah which is going out." And he said, "This is their spring in all the earth."*

[7]*And look there: An elevated talent of lead! And here was some woman sitting in the midst of the ephah.*

[8]*And he said, "This is their wicked behavior." And he cast her into the midst of the ephah. And he cast the weight of lead upon its opening.*

[9]*And I lifted up my eyes and I looked and behold, two women were coming out, with wind in their wings, and they had pairs of wings like the wings of a stork, and they lifted up the ephah between the earth and heaven.*

[10]*And I said to the angel who was speaking with me, "Whence are they taking the ephah?"*

[11]*And he said to me, "To build for it a house in the land of Shinar, and when [the house] is established, [the ephah] shall be deposited there upon its stand."*

5:1 וָאָשׁוּב וָאֶשָּׂא עֵינַי וָאֶרְאֶה וְהִנֵּה מְגִלָּה עָפָה׃

וָֽאָשׁ֞וּב וָאֶשָּׂ֣א עֵינַ֔י וָאֶרְאֶ֖ה. Qal *wayyiqtol* 1 c s √שׁוב, √נשׂא, and √ראה. III-*he* verbs typically drop the final root letter in the *wayyiqtol* form, but there are a considerable number of nonapocopated forms such as וָאֶרְאֶ֖ה. The phenomenon is especially prevalent with 1 c s forms (JM §79m; Bloch, 154), and even in Zechariah 1–8 itself we encounter וָאֶשָּׂ֣א עֵינַ֔י followed by both וָאֵ֕רֶא (2:1, 5; 5:9) as well as וָאֶרְאֶה (5:1; 6:1). Joüon and Muraoka (§79m) note that "in some cases the nonapocopated form with inversive Waw actually represents an iterative, durative past," and this is reflected in the translation above. The verb √שׁוב can express repetition when used with another verb (BDB, 998, #8; JM §177b; GKC §120g), which is the intent here since there have previously been references to the prophet "lifting his eyes" (2:1 [ET: 1:18], 5 [ET: 2:1]).

וְהִנֵּ֖ה מְגִלָּ֥ה עָפָֽה. Qal ptc f s √עוף. The accent on the final syllable is what distinguishes the participle feminine singular from the *qatal* third feminine singular, which has penultimate accent (עָ֫פָה). In this instance it is difficult to decide whether the participle is functioning as an attributive adjective modifying the noun ("I saw a *flying* scroll") or whether it is a verbal predicate ("I saw a scroll *flying*"). The latter seems preferable in light of 3:1; 5:9, and 6:1 and is reflected in the translation above.

The noun מְגִלָּה is only attested in Jeremiah, Ezekiel, and Ps 40:8. The evidence suggests that it entered BH at the very end of the First Temple period, probably under the influence of Aramaic (Shin, 44–47). The ancient versions (Tg, Syr, Vulg) mostly support the MT's מְגִלָּה here, though the Greek versions vary (Lowe, 49): Aquila and Theodoton render διφθέρα, Symmachus renders κεφαλίς (variant: εἴλημα), but the LXX renders it with δρέπανον "sickle," evidently misreading מַגָּל, a translation which influenced the Greek exegetical tradition (e.g., Cyril of Alexandria, Didymus the Blind).

5:2 וַיֹּ֣אמֶר אֵלַ֔י מָ֥ה אַתָּ֖ה רֹאֶ֑ה וָאֹמַ֗ר אֲנִ֤י רֹאֶה֙ מְגִלָּ֣ה
עָפָ֔ה אָרְכָּהּ֙ עֶשְׂרִ֣ים בָּֽאַמָּ֔ה וְרָחְבָּ֖הּ עֶ֥שֶׂר בָּאַמָּֽה׃

וַיֹּ֣אמֶר אֵלַ֔י מָ֥ה אַתָּ֖ה רֹאֶ֑ה. Qal *wayyiqtol* 3 m s √אמר, Qal ptc m s √ראה. On the use of the participle for the "actual present" in a question, see Hag 2:3. It is an oddity that the angel poses the question in verse 2 *after* the prophet has already provided the answer in verse 1 (cp. 4:1-2), though a similar phenomenon occurs on occasion elsewhere (Jer 24:1-3; Amos 7:7-8; 8:1-2; see Thomson 2012a: 114). Petersen suggests that the angel is saying, in effect, "I can't believe what you just said. Let's try it again. What do you see?" (246). On the other hand, it may simply be a rhetorical device to elicit further details about the scroll or to encourage the prophet to reflect upon what the scroll signifies. The prophet's response in verse 2b provides additional detail regarding the remarkable dimensions of the scroll.

וָאֹמַ֗ר אֲנִ֤י רֹאֶה֙ מְגִלָּ֣ה עָפָ֔ה אָרְכָּהּ֙ עֶשְׂרִ֣ים בָּֽאַמָּ֔ה וְרָחְבָּ֖הּ עֶ֥שֶׂר בָּֽאַמָּֽה. Qal *wayyiqtol* 1 c s √אמר, Qal ptc m s √ראה, Qal ptc f s √עוף. The participle אֲנִ֤י רֹאֶה֙ indicates the "actual present," that is, what the prophet is seeing at the moment of speaking. See verse 1 regarding the function of the participle עָפָ֔ה, and see 2:6 regarding the syntax of length and width measurements. There have been numerous speculations as to the significance of the massive and unreal dimensions of the scroll. Most often it is noted that they are the same as those of the temple porch (אוּלָם), namely twenty cubits long and ten cubits wide (1 Kgs 6:3), though Petersen (247) aptly observes that the relevance of this datum for the interpretation of the vision is unclear. The safest explanation may be that of Thomson (2012a: 115–16), who suggests that the dimensions are mentioned "simply to give an impression of the scale, rather than because the precise numbers are significant."

5:3 וַיֹּ֣אמֶר אֵלַ֔י זֹ֚את הָֽאָלָ֔ה הַיּוֹצֵ֖את עַל־פְּנֵ֣י כָל־
הָאָ֑רֶץ כִּ֣י כָל־הַגֹּנֵ֗ב מִזֶּה֙ כָּמ֣וֹהָ נִקָּ֔ה וְכָל־הַ֨נִּשְׁבָּ֔ע
מִזֶּ֖ה כָּמ֥וֹהָ נִקָּֽה׃

וַיֹּ֣אמֶר אֵלַ֔י זֹ֚את הָֽאָלָ֔ה הַיּוֹצֵ֖את עַל־פְּנֵ֣י כָל־הָאָ֑רֶץ. Qal *wayyiqtol* 3 m s √אמר, Qal ptc f s √יצא with def art. On the use of √יצא in the Night Visions, see 2:7. As Aitken (61–62) notes, the noun אָלָה is polysemous; in some instances it denotes a "(covenantal) oath" (overlapping in meaning with שְׁבֻעָה and בְּרִית) and in others, "curse" (overlapping with, e.g., קְלָלָה). Although verse 4 refers to the punishment to come upon evildoers, אָלָה is rendered more fittingly here as "oath" in light of the following clause. The temporal reference of the participle הַיּוֹצֵאת can only be determined from the context (see Hag 1:6); it could be translated as a past process to cohere with הוֹצֵאתִיהָ in the following verse (see v. 4), though either an actual present or imminent future translation would also be possible. Whether הָאָרֶץ is to be taken as referring to the entire "earth" or more specifically to "the land" is to be determined by an analysis of the exegetical context.

כִּי כָל־הַגֹּנֵב מִזֶּה כָּמוֹהָ נִקָּה וְכָל־הַנִּשְׁבָּע מִזֶּה כָּמוֹהָ נִקָּה. Qal ptc m s √גנב with def art, Nifal *qatal* 3 m s √נקה, Nifal ptc m s √שׁבע with def art. This phrase has proven exceedingly difficult to analyze (for a more extensive discussion, see Rogland 2014c: 94–97). Contextually, הַנִּשְׁבָּע is referring specifically to one who swears falsely, as evidenced by verse 4 הַנִּשְׁבָּע בִּשְׁמִי לַשָּׁקֶר "the one who swears falsely by my name." Although strictly speaking נִקָּה could be analyzed as Piel *qatal* 3 m s, a passive voice is better suited to the context and the form is therefore analyzed as Nifal *qatal* 3 m s. This has been taken by some as a "prophetic perfect" threatening future judgment, understanding the verb to have the sense of "to be purged out" (e.g., BDB, 667, #1) based on the etymological link with the adjective נָקִי "clean." It is difficult to justify the prophetic perfect in this instance, however (Rogland 2003: 109), and such a meaning of Nifal √נקה is dubious; the verb is juridical in nature, referring to being acquitted, exempted from, or held innocent of some charge.

מִזֶּה כָּמוֹהָ . . . מִזֶּה כָּמוֹהָ. The repeated use of מִזֶּה . . . מִזֶּה is perplexing. Some have sought to interpret מִזֶּה . . . מִזֶּה temporally as "henceforth" (e.g., Hanhart, 324), as "on the one hand . . . on the other" (Meyers and Meyers, 286) or as "on one side . . . on the other side" (i.e., a double-sided scroll), appealing to Exod 32:15 לֻחֹת כְּתֻבִים מִשְּׁנֵי עֶבְרֵיהֶם מִזֶּה וּמִזֶּה הֵם כְּתֻבִים "tables that were written on both sides; on the one side and on the other were they written" (Boda, 2004: 291–92; BDB, 262, #6e). However, מִזֶּה . . . מִזֶּה in the sense of "on either side" almost always refers *not* to the back and front of an object but rather to "standing/being positioned on either side" of something. Moreover, ultimately the notion of a "double-sided scroll" makes very little exegetical contribution to this brief vision; even if that were the meaning of the expression, it would seem to be an irrelevant detail.

The issue can be clarified by considering the clause in terms of verb complementation. While the verb √גנב can take מִן as a prepositional complement (to steal "from" a person), Nifal √שׁבע does not, indicating that it is best taken as a complement to the verb נִקָּה. Two examples of Nifal √נקה plus מִן are particularly noteworthy as they involve the nouns אָלָה and שְׁבוּעָה and thus form illuminating parallels to this verse: Gen 24:8 וְאִם־לֹא תֹאבֶה הָאִשָּׁה לָלֶכֶת אַחֲרֶיךָ וְנִקִּיתָ מִשְּׁבֻעָתִי זֹאת "And if the woman is not willing to come after you, *then you will be innocent from this oath of mine,*" v. 41 אָז תִּנָּקֶה מֵאָלָתִי . . . וְאִם־לֹא יִתְּנוּ לָךְ וְהָיִיתָ נָקִי מֵאָלָתִי "Then *you will be held innocent from my oath* . . . if they will not give (her) to you, then you will be innocent (נָקִי) from my oath." In this case the repeated מִזֶּה כָּמוֹהָ can be understood if זֶה is taken either as a rare relative pronoun (JM §145c; BDB, 261, #5) or simply in the neutral sense of "this (thing), this (fact)" (JM §143a) followed by an asyndetic relative clause (JM §158a–d), thus "from this (which is) according to it" (the f s pronoun suffix on כָּמוֹהָ refers to אָלָה "oath").

Putting these components together, the following translation results: "for everyone who steals has been acquitted from that which is according to it [viz., the oath of the covenant], and everyone who swears [falsely] has been acquitted from that which is according to it." The idea is that, due to the toleration of gross offenses, these blatant lawbreakers (thieves and perjurers) have not yet received the punishment that they deserve according to the terms of God's covenant.

5:4 הוֹצֵאתִ֗יהָ נְאֻם֙ יְהוָ֣ה צְבָא֔וֹת וּבָ֙אָה֙ אֶל־בֵּ֣ית הַגַּנָּ֔ב וְאֶל־בֵּ֛ית הַנִּשְׁבָּ֥ע בִּשְׁמִ֖י לַשָּׁ֑קֶר וְלָ֙נֶה֙ בְּת֣וֹךְ בֵּית֔וֹ וְכִלַּ֖תּוּ וְאֶת־עֵצָ֥יו וְאֶת־אֲבָנָֽיו׃

הוֹצֵאתִ֗יהָ נְאֻם֙ יְהוָ֣ה צְבָא֔וֹת. Hifil *qatal* 1 c s √יצא with 3 f s pronoun suffix. The angel's words have moved into first person divine discourse. There is no need to interpret the verb as a prophetic perfect (see Rogland 2003: 109). The curse is coming or has come forth, but it has not yet made its effects felt.

וּבָ֙אָה֙ אֶל־בֵּ֣ית הַגַּנָּ֔ב וְאֶל־בֵּ֛ית הַנִּשְׁבָּ֥ע בִּשְׁמִ֖י לַשָּׁ֑קֶר. Qal *weqatal* 3 f s √בוא, Nifal ptc m s √שׁבע with def art. The preposition אֶל must mean "into," since the context indicates that the "oath" takes up lodging "in the midst of" the house. As Petersen observes (250), the phrasing "the one who swears deceptively in my name" seems to combine the Decalogue's prohibitions לֹא תִשָּׂא אֶת־שֵׁם־יְהוָה אֱלֹהֶיךָ לַשָּׁוְא (Exod 20:7) and לֹא־תַעֲנֶה בְרֵעֲךָ עֵד שָׁקֶר (Exod 20:16).

וְלָ֙נֶה֙ בְּת֣וֹךְ בֵּית֔וֹ. Qal *weqatal* 3 f s √ליןׄ. One would have expected the form *וְלָנָה, but BH occasionally attests forms in which ָה has been weakened to ֶה (GKC §73d, §80i). The verb can mean "to abide, remain" (BDB, 533, #2), though most often it means "to lodge, pass the night," which is to be preferred here due to its usage with "house."

וְכִלַּתּוּ וְאֶת־עֵצָיו וְאֶת־אֲבָנָיו. Piel *weqatal* 3 f s √כלה with 3 m s object suffix. A "house" is constructed of wood and stones, and וְאֶת־עֵצָיו וְאֶת־אֲבָנָיו is best understood as a merismus for the structure. The first *vav* could be taken as explicative ("it will consume it, namely, its wood and stones") or simply as an additive, "both its wood and its stones" (Thomson 2012a: 112).

5:5 וַיֵּצֵא הַמַּלְאָךְ הַדֹּבֵר בִּי וַיֹּאמֶר אֵלַי שָׂא נָא עֵינֶיךָ
וּרְאֵה מָה הַיּוֹצֵאת הַזֹּאת׃

וַיֵּצֵא הַמַּלְאָךְ הַדֹּבֵר בִּי. Qal *wayyiqtol* 3 m s √יצא, Qal ptc m s √דבר with def art.

וַיֹּאמֶר אֵלַי שָׂא נָא עֵינֶיךָ וּרְאֵה. Qal *wayyiqtol* 3 m s √אמר, Qal impv 2 m s √נשא, Qal impv 2 m s √ראה with prefixed *vav*. The *vav* plus imperative syntagm often indicates purpose or consecution (see Hag 1:8), but in this case we are probably dealing with a simple *vav* of juxtaposition (JM §120).

מָה הַיּוֹצֵאת הַזֹּאת. Qal ptc f s √יצא with def art. The disjunctive *zaqef qaṭon* accent on the preceding וּרְאֵה suggests that the following interrogative clause is best understood as a direct question rather than an embedded one. The feminine הַיּוֹצֵאת הַזֹּאת (also v. 6 מַה־הִיא) could be anticipating the object to be described (the grammatically feminine אֵיפָה), but more likely it is simply an expression of the neuter, which is typically done with feminine forms (see 6:6). On the use of √יצא in the Night Visions, see 2:7.

5:6 וָאֹמַר מַה־הִיא וַיֹּאמֶר זֹאת הָאֵיפָה הַיּוֹצֵאת
וַיֹּאמֶר זֹאת עֵינָם בְּכָל־הָאָרֶץ׃

וָאֹמַר מַה־הִיא. Qal *wayyiqtol* 1 c s √אמר. On the use of the feminine for the neuter, see v. 5.

וַיֹּאמֶר זֹאת הָאֵיפָה הַיּוֹצֵאת וַיֹּאמֶר. Qal *wayyiqtol* 3 m s √אמר, Qal ptc f s √יצא with def art. The angel's repeated use of וַיֹּאמֶר, which would appear unnecessary, suggests that a response from the prophet (perhaps a follow up question) was expected, but presumably he was too nonplussed by the vision to speak (see 4:12). Although other meanings of אֵיפָה have been proposed here (cf. Marenof), in the HB the word refers to a unit of measurement (LXX: μέτρον), and most scholars have taken the term here as referring to a measuring basket that would have held an *ephah* of material, roughly a little less than ten gallons (dry measure).

זֹאת עֵינָם בְּכָל־הָאָרֶץ. The form עֵינָם has proven exceedingly troublesome. Many translations follow the lead of the LXX, which read the *yod* as a *vav* and translated ἡ ἀδικία αὐτῶν "their iniquity." The Vulgate's *oculus eorum* supports the MT, however, and others have sought to interpret the word in an extended sense of "resemblance" or "appearance" (KJV, NASB) as in Lev 13:55 and Num 11:7, though it is very unclear what that would signify here. Moreover, scholars have been uncertain about the antecedent of the pronoun suffix on עֵינָם; Wolters (2014: 64, etc.) argues for "enclitic *mem*" here, yet there are reasons to be wary of appealing to this phenomenon (see 1:13). עַיִן is not problematic if taken in its common meaning of "spring, source," referring to the "source" of iniquity for those mentioned in verses 1-4. As emerges in the following verses, the text using the imagery of a "spring" that is being "sealed up" by a heavy weight, a phenomenon attested elsewhere in the HB and in ANE material culture (for a discussion, see Rogland 2014c: 99–102 and 2013c).

5:7 וְהִנֵּה כִּכַּר עֹפֶרֶת נִשֵּׂאת וְזֹאת אִשָּׁה אַחַת יוֹשֶׁבֶת בְּתוֹךְ הָאֵיפָה׃

וְהִנֵּה כִּכַּר עֹפֶרֶת נִשֵּׂאת. Nifal ptc f s √נשׂא. כִּכַּר has various meanings in BH which may or may not be related to each other (cf. Thomson 2012a: 128–29), but in this instance undoubtedly refers to a unit of weight (cf. LXX's τάλαντον), here functioning as a lid for the *ephah*. נִשֵּׂאת is typically translated as a verbal clause indicating a simple past action, e.g., "the leaden cover was lifted" (so RSV), implying that the leaden weight was already lying upon the basket's opening and was then lifted to reveal its contents. This is problematic on two counts. First, in a past time frame a predicative participle expresses an action in process, not a simple past. At the very least, then, a more grammatical translation would be, "behold, a talent of lead *was being lifted up*." Second, the Nifal participle of √נשׂא appears to be used almost exclusively in BH as an adjective for "lofty" (1 Chron 14:2; Isa 2:12, 13, 14; 6:1; 30:25; 57:7, 15). Thus it is a mistake to interpret the participle as a verbal predicate in the first place, and it would be preferable to take it adjectivally as "elevated," as indicated in the translation. In the vision, then, the prophet sees a basket "coming out" (vv. 5-6), and in verse 7a spots an elevated (or floating) "talent of lead." The Hebrew text thus gives no indication that it was already lying upon the *ephah*'s opening.

וְזֹאת אִשָּׁה אַחַת יוֹשֶׁבֶת בְּתוֹךְ הָאֵיפָה. Qal ptc f s √ישׁב. If modern estimations of the biblical *ephah* are accurate (see v. 6), the basket could not have held an adult woman. Either we are to imagine the figurine of a woman or simply a woman of disproportionate measurements (cf. vv. 1-2) more akin to a "genie in a bottle." It is possible that אִשָּׁה אַחַת is intended as a contrast with שְׁתַּיִם נָשִׁים (i.e., *one* woman vs. *two*) in verse 9, though the numeral is more likely functioning as an indefinite pronoun (JM §137u; WB §94; AC §2.7.1b): "a certain woman, some woman." The syntax of the phrase is made awkward by the demonstrative זאת. This is sometimes translated as an attributive demonstrative ("this woman, this one woman"), but in that case one would expect הָאִשָּׁה הַזֹּאת (for some rare exceptions, see JM §143i). It should be noted that זֶה and זאת originated as demonstrative adverbs, and they still display this function occasionally in BH (JM §143a), which helps to explain the usage of זאת here: it serves to draw a spatial contrast between verse 7a's "elevated talent of lead," introduced with the particle הִנֵּה, and verse 7b's "here," indicated by זאת (see further Rogland 2014c: 98–99).

5:8 וַיֹּאמֶר זֹאת הָרִשְׁעָה וַיַּשְׁלֵךְ אֹתָהּ אֶל־תּוֹךְ הָאֵיפָה
וַיַּשְׁלֵךְ אֶת־אֶבֶן הָעֹפֶרֶת אֶל־פִּיהָ׃ ס

וַיֹּאמֶר זֹאת הָרִשְׁעָה. Qal *wayyiqtol* 3 m s √אמר. BH also possesses the abstract noun רֶשַׁע to indicate "wickedness" which occurs twice as frequently as רִשְׁעָה, leading one to wonder what significance, if any, lies in the choice of the one word instead of the other (cf. *HALOT*, 1296). It is true that different members of a semantic field can overlap in meaning and even be functionally synonymous in particular contexts, yet it must also be acknowledged that total synonymity is rare. Without claiming to be a complete semantic analysis, the following observations are pertinent:

1. It is clear that רֶשַׁע is a very general term and is utilized in a wide variety of contexts, being used regularly in construct phrases to create qualitative genitives (see 2:16) such as Job 34:8 אַנְשֵׁי־רֶשַׁע "men of wickedness" (= "wicked men")

and Mic 6:11 מֹאזְנֵי רֶשַׁע "scales of wickedness" (= "wicked scales"); in striking contrast, רִשְׁעָה is never used in this way.

2. רִשְׁעָה need not refer to a single wicked act, but at times it does refer to specific acts of wickedness ("offenses") as in Deut 25:2 וְהִכָּהוּ לְפָנָיו כְּדֵי רִשְׁעָתוֹ בְּמִסְפָּר "and one shall beat him in [the judge's] presence, in proportion to *his offense*, by number." In contrast to רֶשַׁע, רִשְׁעָה occurs consistently in contexts that mention punishment or destruction (Deut 9:4-5; Prov 11:5; 13.6; Isa 9:17; Ezek 5:6; 18:20, 27; 33:12, 19; Mal 1:4; 3:19 [cf. v. 15]). Perhaps it is for this reason Jastrow (1501) distinguishes רִשְׁעָה from רֶשַׁע in RH by including "indictable offense" as a gloss for the former.

Drawing these factors together, it seems fair to say that רִשְׁעָה does not indicate "wickedness" in the abstract, as רֶשַׁע does, but rather signifies wicked *behavior* that makes one liable to judgment. In light of this, Willi-Plein's comments on verse 8 are apropos: "A general 'power of sin' is not being discussed, but rather a particular expression of (social) injustice" (108).

The definite article on הָרִשְׁעָה is rarely translated since abstract nouns often take the definite article (JM §137j; WO §13.5.1g). However, if the semantic analysis of רִשְׁעָה proposed here is valid then the noun is less "abstract" and refers more properly to wicked behavior, in which case the definite article takes on a different significance. As already argued, the pronominal suffix of עֵינָם in verse 6 refers anaphorically to the stopping up of "their spring" or "their source", i.e., the source of the thieves and perjurers mentioned in verses 3-4 (see v. 6 and Rogland 2014c: 103–4). That being the case, in this instance the definite article would also have an anaphoric function, either as a weak demonstrative referring to something previously mentioned in the context ("*that* wicked behavior"; cf. JM §137f13) or as the equivalent of a possessive pronoun ("*their* wicked behavior"; cf. AC §2.6.7; WB §86; WO §13.5.1e; JM §137f12). The latter translation is offered here in view of the possessive pronoun on עֵינָם in verse 6.

וַיַּשְׁלֵךְ אֹתָהּ אֶל־תּוֹךְ הָאֵיפָה וַיַּשְׁלֵךְ אֶת־אֶבֶן הָעֹפֶרֶת אֶל־פִּיהָ. Hifil *wayyiqtol* 3 m s √שׁלך. The woman has already been described in verse 7 as "sitting in the midst" of the *ephah*. Thus the first occurrence of Hifil √שׁלך is not so much that the angel "threw" her into the basket but rather forcibly "deposited" her (cf. Gen 21:15) or "stuffed her down" into it so that he could put a lid on its opening. Regarding אֶבֶן

הָעֹפֶרֶת, it should be noted that, much like the English word "stone," the noun אֶבֶן can refer to a "weight" (BDB, 6, #5–6) and thus there is no semantic clash between כִּכַּר עֹפֶרֶת in verse 7 and אֶבֶן הָעֹפֶרֶת here (cf. on 4:10). The definite article on אֶבֶן הָעֹפֶרֶת is anaphoric, identifying it as referring to כִּכַּר עֹפֶרֶת in verse 7. The phrase אֶל־פִּיהָ seems to be one of the many instances in which אֶל is equivalent to עַל (BDB, 41, n. 2). The feminine singular pronoun suffix on פִּיהָ refers to the grammatically feminine אֵיפָה, but the LXX translators rendered εἰς τὸ στόμα αὐτῆς, which can only refer to the woman's mouth, since they translated אֵיפָה with the neuter μέτρον ("measure"), which would require αὐτοῦ. This mistranslation again affected the Greek exegetes such as Cyril and Didymus (see v. 1).

5:9 וָאֶשָּׂא עֵינַי וָאֵרֶא וְהִנֵּה שְׁתַּיִם נָשִׁים יוֹצְאוֹת וְרוּחַ בְּכַנְפֵיהֶם וְלָהֵנָּה כְנָפַיִם כְּכַנְפֵי הַחֲסִידָה וַתִּשֶּׂאנָה אֶת־הָאֵיפָה בֵּין הָאָרֶץ וּבֵין הַשָּׁמָיִם׃

וָאֶשָּׂא עֵינַי וָאֵרֶא. Qal *wayyiqtol* 1 c s √נשׂא and √ראה. See verse 1.

וְהִנֵּה שְׁתַּיִם נָשִׁים יוֹצְאוֹת וְרוּחַ בְּכַנְפֵיהֶם וְלָהֵנָּה כְנָפַיִם כְּכַנְפֵי הַחֲסִידָה. Qal ptc f pl √יצא. There is a lack of gender concord here: the possessive pronoun suffix with בְּכַנְפֵיהֶם is masculine plural even though it refers to a feminine plural antecedent (נָשִׁים). Likewise, verse 10 displays a mismatch between a masculine plural independent personal pronoun and a feminine plural participle (הֵמָּה מוֹלְכוֹת). Though irregular, the phenomenon occurs sporadically in the HB (JM §149–50; GKC §135o1). וְרוּחַ בְּכַנְפֵיהֶם indicates the attendant circumstances to the women's "going out" (JM §159) and can be translated as "with (the) wind in their wings." The third feminine plural pronoun suffix can occur both as לָהֵנָּה and as לָהֶן. On the use of the dual כְּנָפַיִם "pairs of wings," see 3:9. The phrase וְלָהֵנָּה כְנָפַיִם כְּכַנְפֵי הַחֲסִידָה represents a possessive clause (on this use of the לְ-preposition, see Hag 1:1). This clarifying remark is necessary since the term כָּנָף itself need not refer to wings but rather to the extremities of garments (e.g., Num 15:38). הַחֲסִידָה attests the so-called "generic" use of the article, occurring with classes or species of objects (see Hag 2:3), and can be omitted in translation.

וַתִּשֶּׂאנָה אֶת־הָאֵיפָה בֵּין הָאָרֶץ וּבֵין הַשָּׁמָיִם. Qal *wayyiqtol* 3 f pl √נשׂא. The phrase בֵּין הָאָרֶץ וּבֵין הַשָּׁמָיִם means "in the air" and appears to be functionally synonymous with 2 Sam 18:9 בֵּ֥ין הַשָּׁמַ֖יִם וּבֵ֣ין הָאָ֑רֶץ (Thomson 2012a: 132).

5:10 וָאֹמַ֗ר אֶל־הַמַּלְאָ֛ךְ הַדֹּבֵ֥ר בִּ֖י אָ֥נָה הֵ֛מָּה מֽוֹלִכ֖וֹת אֶת־הָאֵיפָֽה׃

וָאֹמַ֗ר אֶל־הַמַּלְאָ֛ךְ הַדֹּבֵ֥ר בִּ֖י. Qal *wayyiqtol* 1 c s √אמר, Qal ptc m s √דבר with def art.

אָ֥נָה הֵ֛מָּה מֽוֹלִכ֖וֹת אֶת־הָאֵיפָֽה. Hifil ptc f pl √הלך. On אָ֫נָה, see 2:6 [ET: v. 2]. On the use of the participle in questions, see Hag 2:3. The verb √הלך is formed in BH as if it were I-*yod*, including in the Hifil *binyan*, a phenomenon confirmed by the corresponding Ugaritic verb (JM §75f and esp. n. 12). On the incongruence between the feminine plural participle and the masculine plural pronoun הֵ֛מָּה, see verse 9.

5:11 וַיֹּ֣אמֶר אֵלַ֔י לִבְנוֹת־לָ֥הּ בַ֖יִת בְּאֶ֣רֶץ שִׁנְעָ֑ר וְהוּכַ֛ן וְהֻנִּ֥יחָה שָּׁ֖ם עַל־מְכֻנָתָֽהּ׃ ס

וַיֹּ֣אמֶר אֵלַ֔י לִבְנוֹת־לָ֥הּ בַ֖יִת בְּאֶ֣רֶץ שִׁנְעָ֑ר. Qal *wayyiqtol* 3 m s √אמר, Qal inf cstr √בנה. לָ֥הּ is marked *raphe*; normally it would have a *mappiq* indicating that the final *he* is to be pronounced, but occasionally this is lacking (JM §25a), possibly because it is followed by a word with *mil'el* accent (JM §103f). בַּ֫יִת can refer to most types of buildings, including a place of detainment such as a prison (BDB, 109, #1aε2), though given the abundance of temple imagery in Zechariah there is some plausibility to the suggestion that this vision is intended to depict a kind of "anti-temple" (cf. Petersen, 261–62). The reference to "Shinar" is probably intended to evoke the Tower of Babel narrative (Gen 11:2).

וְהוּכַ֛ן וְהֻנִּ֥יחָה שָּׁ֖ם עַל־מְכֻנָתָֽהּ. Hofal *weqatal* 3 m s √כון, Hofal *weqatal* 3 f s √נוח. There has been considerable discussion of וְהֻנִּיחָה. The *dagesh* in the *nun* is to be attributed to the influence of Aramaising forms of geminate verbs (JM §80p), but the vocalization with *ḥireq-yod* instead of *sheva* is also peculiar. The Masoretic form is typically explained on analogy of the passive Hafel stem of Aramaic, as in Dan 7:4 הֳקִימַת "it was made to stand" (GKC §72ee; Bauer and Leander, 403, though they suggest emendation to the active Hifil וְהִנִּיחֻ֫הָ). Lowe

(55–56) claims that postexilic prophets are generally free from Aramaisms and instead points to evidence in postbiblical texts that vocal *sheva* was spelled with י, postulating a development in pronunciation from *ḥunnᵉḥāh* to *ḥunnîḥāh,* but the phenomenon does not appear to be otherwise attested in the biblical corpus, and at least some possible Aramaisms are present in Haggai–Zech 1–8 (see, e.g., on הֵן in Hag 2:12). In any event, it should be borne in mind that the only other attestation in BH of a Hofal *qatal* 3 f s of a hollow verb is Gen 33:11 הֻבָאת, a form which itself is irregular (Bauer and Leander, 445, §59p). Some see gender incongruence here (as in vv. 9-10) between the two verbs וְהוּכַן וְהֻנִּיחָה, since we have a masculine verb followed immediately by a feminine one, but more likely the subject of וְהוּכַן is בַּיִת and that of וְהֻנִּיחָה is אֵיפָה (Thomson 2012a: 132; cf. RSV). The two *weqatal* forms can be understood syntactically as the protasis and apodosis of a conditional/temporal statement, as in, e.g., Gen 44:22 וְעָזַב אֶת־אָבִיו וָמֵת "And if he should leave his father, he would die"; 1 Sam 19:3 וְרָאִיתִי מָה וְהִגַּדְתִּי לָךְ "And when I learn anything, I will inform you" (JM §167b). Thus the phrase in question can be rendered: "And when it (the house) is established, it (the basket) will be placed on its stand." In RH מְכוֹנָה refers to a "place where animals are kept ready for slaughtering; stall, coop" (Jastrow, 781), but in BH it refers to a "stand" or "base," most commonly used for supporting basins in the temple or, in one instance (Ezra 3:3), for supporting the altar. The noun's usage in the DSS (4Q525 15:6 and 11Q20 36:2) is too fragmentary or contextually uncertain to clarify its meaning, and contrary to *DCH* (5, 268), its usage in Ben Sira need not be taken as "property" or "estate" but can be understood as "base, foundation": Sir 41:1 (MsB MsM) לאיש שוקט על מכונתו "for the man at peace on his foundation"; 44:6 (MsB) ושוקטים על מכונתם "and at peace on their foundation."

Seventh Vision (Zechariah 6:1-8)
Divine Chariots and God's Spirit

The seventh vision depicts four chariots pulled by teams of horses of various colors. These chariots come forth from between two hills of copper or bronze (vv. 1-3) and proceed in various directions (vv. 5-7). The unit concludes with the report that God's "spirit" has been set at rest in the northlands (v. 8). The vision is to be understood as an instance of intratextuality (Introduction §3), that is, of a text's intentional reference to itself. It is generally agreed that this scene is thematically linked with the initial vision of the rider on the horse in Zech 1 and forms an *inclusio* with it (Wolters 2014: 42). In addition, the reference to the "four רֻחוֹת of heaven" (v. 5) could possibly connect with the second vision of 2:1-4, and the reference to "spirit(s)" (vv. 5, 8) may be linked with the fifth vision (4:6).

This concise pericope moves rapidly from narrative description (vv. 1-3) to a request for clarification (v. 4), explanatory comments from the Interpreting Angel (vv. 5-6), a narrative note concerning further activities of the fourth chariot team (v. 7), and the final report (v. 8). A pattern of vision and explanation followed by additional visionary description is attested elsewhere in the Night Visions (1:7-17; 4:1-14; 5:5-11). Several aspects of the vision are puzzling. For example, that only three of the four horse teams and only two of the four compass points are mentioned in verses 6-7 makes the vision "untidy" (Wolters 2014: 176). Moreover, the meaning of some of the color terms used in this pericope is uncertain (see v. 3). Other important aspects of the vision have been obscured by poor philological analysis, as will be pointed out in the commentary below (see esp. Rogland 2014b).

[1]*And again I lifted up my eyes and kept looking, and behold: four chariots were coming out from between the two hills, and the hills were hills of bronze.*

[2-3]*And with the first chariot were copper red horses, and with the second chariot were black horses, and with the third chariot were white horses, and with the fourth chariot were speckled, strong horses.*

[4]*And I answered and said to the angel who was speaking with me, "What are these, my lord?"*

[5]*And the angel answered and said to me, "These, the four spirits of the heavens, are going out on account of rebellion against the Lord of all the earth,*

[6]*against which the black horses are going to the land of the north, and the white horses have gone out behind them, and the speckled ones have gone out to the land of the south."*

[7]*And as for the strong ones: When they went out, they sought to go to patrol about in the earth. And he said, "Go, patrol about in the earth." And they patrolled about in the earth.*

[8]*And he gave me proclamation and spoke to me, "See, the ones who went to the land of the north have vented my angry spirit upon the northland."*

6:1 וָאָשֻׁב וָאֶשָּׂא עֵינַי וָאֶרְאֶה וְהִנֵּה אַרְבַּע מַרְכָּבוֹת יֹצְאוֹת מִבֵּין שְׁנֵי הֶהָרִים וְהֶהָרִים הָרֵי נְחֹשֶׁת׃

וָאָשֻׁב וָאֶשָּׂא עֵינַי וָאֶרְאֶה וְהִנֵּה. Qal *wayyiqtol* 1 c s √שׁוב, Qal *wayyiqtol* 1 c s √נשׂא, Qal *wayyiqtol* 1 c s √ראה. On the use of √שׁוב indicating "to do again" and on the nonapocopated form וָאֶרְאֶה, see 5:1. אַרְבַּע מַרְכָּבוֹת יֹצְאוֹת מִבֵּין שְׁנֵי הֶהָרִים וְהֶהָרִים הָרֵי נְחֹשֶׁת. Qal ptc f pl √יצא. The participle indicates an action in process, which in the narrative setting of the vision should be rendered in the past tense: "four chariots *were coming out*." On the use of cardinal numbers 3–10 see 2:1. On the use of √יצא in the Night Visions, see 2:7. נְחֹשֶׁת is rendered here as "bronze," though the noun can refer either to copper ore or to bronze alloy (BDB, 638–39). The prepositional phrase מִבֵּין שְׁנֵי הֶהָרִים and the following verbless clause וְהֶהָרִים הָרֵי נְחֹשֶׁת are exegetically difficult but grammatically quite simple and are easily translated as "from between the two hills, and the hills were hills of bronze." Most likely this is a genitive of material (see 4:2), indicating what the mountains were made of (Wolters 2014: 173). The phrase שְׁנֵי הֶהָרִים is definite, suggesting that the reader/hearer was expected to know which hills the speaker had in mind, but that shared understanding has been lost to later generations of readers, for whom these two "bronze hills" have been the subject of much speculation.

6:2-3 בַּמֶּרְכָּבָה הָרִאשֹׁנָה סוּסִים אֲדֻמִּים וּבַמֶּרְכָּבָה הַשֵּׁנִית סוּסִים שְׁחֹרִים׃

וּבַמֶּרְכָּבָה הַשְּׁלִשִׁית סוּסִים לְבָנִים וּבַמֶּרְכָּבָה הָרְבִעִית סוּסִים בְּרֻדִּים אֲמֻצִּים׃

These verses are comprised of a series of verbless clauses specifying what color of horses were "with" (בְּ) the different chariots. מֶרְכָּבָה occasionally occurs as a collective (e.g., 1 Sam 8:11; Hag 2:22; possibly Mic 1:3), though more often רֶכֶב serves as the collective noun for "chariotry" (BDB, 939, #1), and the numbered order suggests simply four chariots with different types of horses. There is some overlap with the colors of the horses from chapter 1, e.g., אֲדֻמִּים and לְבָנִים (see 1:8), however 6:2-3 does not mention the "dapple-grey" (שְׂרֻקִּים) horses of 1:8 and instead mentions horses that are שְׁחֹרִים ("black") and בְּרֻדִּים

אֲמֻצִּים. The adjectives בְּרֻדִּים אֲמֻצִּים stand in apposition to each other, but some view הָאֲמֻצִּים in verse 7 as distinct from הַבְּרֻדִּים in verse 6 (cf. Wolters 2014: 173, 176), and therefore understand אֲמֻצִּים as referring to all four groups of horses and chariots, e.g., the ESV's "the third white horses, and the fourth chariot dappled horses—*all of them strong*." If this were the intent, however, then the speaker has chosen an extremely ambiguous way of putting it. The unmistakable impression of verse 3 is that the terms are appositional, and it is imprudent to allow an unnecessary interpretation of a later verse (see v. 7) to force a grammatically convoluted interpretation upon an earlier one. The adjectives בָּרֹד and אָמֹץ are both rare in BH, and neither is attested in RH, so very little can be said with certainty about the meaning of either term (see Clark 2005: 68). Apart from its occurrences in this chapter (vv. 3, 6), בָּרֹד is only found in Gen 31:10, 12, where it appears alongside עָקֹד "striped, streaked" and נָקֹד "speckled." This suggests some sort of multi-shaded hue, but beyond that little can be said. The adjective אָמֹץ is even less common, occurring only here and in verse 7 (for a survey of proposed meanings, see Wolters 2014: 173–74). All of the other terms used here (and in chap. 1) refer to colors or appearance, hence several lexica suggest different color terms such as "flesh-colored, skewbald" (*HALOT*, 65) or "dappled" (*DCH* 1, 320). Yet most of these are speculative in nature. Verbal forms of √אמץ occur frequently with various senses of "to be strong" (Qal), "to make strong" (Piel), or "to strengthen oneself" (Hitpael), which correspond to various other cognate nouns and adjectives. BDB (55) therefore glosses the adjective as "strong," and all things considered, this is probably the best option based upon the meager evidence. In the face of such lexical uncertainty, it is a relief to note that these details do not appear to play much of a role in the vision, but simply serve to distinguish the four different chariots.

6:4 וָאַ֙עַן֙ וָֽאֹמַ֔ר אֶל־הַמַּלְאָ֖ךְ הַדֹּבֵ֣ר בִּ֑י מָה־אֵ֖לֶּה אֲדֹנִֽי׃

Qal *wayyiqtol* 1 c s √ענה and √אמר, Qal ptc m s from דבר with def art. On the significance of the question, see 1:9.

6:5 וַיַּ֥עַן הַמַּלְאָ֖ךְ וַיֹּ֣אמֶר אֵלָ֑י אֵ֗לֶּה אַרְבַּע֙ רֻח֣וֹת
הַשָּׁמַ֔יִם יוֹצְא֕וֹת מֵהִתְיַצֵּ֖ב עַל־אֲד֥וֹן כָּל־הָאָֽרֶץ׃

וַיַּ֫עַן הַמַּלְאָךְ וַיֹּ֫אמֶר אֵלָי. Qal *wayyiqtol* 3 m s √ענה and √אמר.

אֵ֫לֶּה אַרְבַּע רֻחוֹת הַשָּׁמַיִם יוֹצְאוֹת. Qal ptc f pl √יצא. In response to the prophet's inquiry, the Interpreting Angel explains the meaning of what has been seen, as he has done several times previously. There is a surprising amount of syntactical confusion regarding this clause as to the subject and the grammatical function of אַרְבַּע רֻחוֹת הַשָּׁמַיִם. Most translations understand "the four רֻחוֹת of heaven" as a directional accusative or "an accusative of local determination" (see Hag 1:8): "These are going out *to* the four winds of heaven." While this is grammatically possible, it is not the most obvious syntactical analysis, and if such had been the intent it could have been more clearly expressed by the inclusion of a preposition. Lowe (58) renders אֵ֫לֶּה as the subject and אַרְבַּע רֻחוֹת הַשָּׁמַיִם as the predicate, with the participle forming a subordinate relative clause ("These are the four winds of heaven, which go forth"), yet this would require participle יוֹצְאוֹת to have the definite article. This is a verbal clause with the subject demonstrative pronoun אֵ֫לֶּה having the verbal predicate יוֹצְאוֹת, and the noun phrase אַרְבַּע רֻחוֹת הַשָּׁמַיִם is to be understood as appositional to אֵ֫לֶּה: "These, the four רֻחוֹת of heaven, are going forth. . . ." Many render אַרְבַּע רֻחוֹת הַשָּׁמַיִם as "the four winds of heaven" in light of 2:10 [ET: v. 6] כִּי כְּאַרְבַּע רוּחוֹת הַשָּׁמַיִם פֵּרַשְׂתִּי "as the four winds of heaven I have spread you out." However, verses 6-8 only mention two of the compass points (north and south), and the overall situation described seems to refer to sentient (presumably angelic) beings, and thus the translation "spirits" is preferable, particularly in light of verse 8.

מֵהִתְיַצֵּב עַל־אֲדוֹן כָּל־הָאָרֶץ. Hitpael inf cstr √יצב with prefixed מִן preposition. Most translations render מֵהִתְיַצֵּב as "*after* presenting themselves before" (so RSV and many others), yet this is lexically problematic. In the book of Zechariah, expressions of service or support are expressed with Qal √עמד plus לִפְנֵי (e.g., Zech 3:1, 3, 4) or possibly עַל (Zech 4:14). What is more, the syntagm הִתְיַצֵּב plus עַל is better understood as expressive of defiant rebellion as in Ps 2:2 יִתְיַצְּבוּ ׀ מַלְכֵי־אֶרֶץ וְרוֹזְנִים נוֹסְדוּ־יָחַד עַל־יְהוָה וְעַל־מְשִׁיחוֹ "The kings of the earth take their stand, and rulers sat together, *against* YHWH and *against* His anointed" (for further examples and discussion, see Rogland 2014b: 120–21). Rather than indicating a temporal "after," the preposition מִן in this instance has a causal force of "from, on account of" (BDB, 583, #7a): "they are going out *on account of* rebellion against the Lord of all the earth." This analysis is not only grammatically and lexically justified, it also provides a rationale for the appearance of the heavenly chariotry, which is otherwise left unexplained in the traditional interpretation of the pericope (Rogland 2014b: 122).

6:6 אֲשֶׁר־בָּ֗הּ הַסּוּסִ֤ים הַשְּׁחֹרִים֙ יֹצְאִים֙ אֶל־אֶ֣רֶץ צָפ֔וֹן וְהַלְּבָנִ֔ים יָצְא֖וּ אֶל־אַחֲרֵיהֶ֑ם וְהַבְּרֻדִּ֣ים יָצְא֖וּ אֶל־אֶ֥רֶץ הַתֵּימָֽן׃

אֲשֶׁר־בָּ֗הּ הַסּוּסִ֤ים הַשְּׁחֹרִים֙ יֹצְאִים֙ אֶל־אֶ֣רֶץ צָפ֔וֹן. Qal ptc m pl √**יצא**. The switch from the feminine plural **יוֹצְאוֹת** in verse 5 to the masculine plural **יֹצְאִים** occurs because verse 5 was referring to the מַרְכָּבוֹת, whereas verse 6 is describing the סוּסִים (Lowe, 58). The initial אֲשֶׁר־בָּהּ has perplexed scholars and some assume a text-critical problem (e.g., Petersen, 263–64). Meyers and Meyers (324) argue that the feminine singular pronoun suffix refers to the chariot (מֶרְכָּבָה), since neither רוּחַ nor אֶרֶץ would make sense as the feminine antecedent, and that אֲשֶׁר־בָּהּ expresses "with it" in a distributive sense, referring to each set of horses accompanying the different chariots. Such a proposal results in a redundancy with verses 2-3, however, which already established that the various colors of horses were "with" the different chariots (v. 2 בַּמֶּרְכָּבָה הָרִאשֹׁנָה סוּסִים אֲדֻמִּים). Given the analysis of מֵהִתְיַצֵּב עַל־אֲדוֹן כָּל־הָאָרֶץ presented above (see v. 5), the antecedent can be understood as the abstract or neuter concept of rebellion or enmity, since BH uses feminine forms to express neuter concepts (JM §152a–b; WB §25; WO §6.6d; GKC §122p–q). The collocation √**יצא** plus בְּ can have a hostile sense of "to go out *against* someone or something" (e.g., Ruth 1:13), and thus the clause in question is to be translated, "*against which* (viz., rebellion) the black horses are going toward the north. . . ." Thus, not only does verse 5 indicate the basic reason for the appearance of the divine chariotry (viz., as a response to human rebellion), verse 6 then provides details as to the chariots' mission and destinations. On the biblical theme of "the north" as being the locus of enmity against YHWH, see inter alia Reimer, and Childs.

וְהַלְּבָנִ֔ים יָצְא֖וּ אֶל־אַחֲרֵיהֶ֑ם וְהַבְּרֻדִּ֣ים יָצְא֖וּ אֶל־אֶ֥רֶץ הַתֵּימָֽן. Qal *qatal* 3 c pl √**יצא**. אֶל־אַחֲרֵיהֶם indicates "after" or "behind" (cf. 2 Sam 5:23; 2 Kgs 9:18), here most likely in a spatial rather than temporal sense: the chariot with the white horses (the third chariot) came forth following the one with the black horses (the second). The reader is left with the impression that both chariots had been dispatched to the north and the speckled, strong horses to the south. תֵּימָן can be a proper name (for a region of Edom or Edom as a whole) but it can also refer more generally to the south, which is the intent here, as אֶרֶץ הַתֵּימָן stands in contrast to אֶרֶץ צָפוֹן ("the land of north") in the preceding clause.

6:7 וְהָאֲמֻצִּים יָצְאוּ וַיְבַקְשׁוּ לָלֶכֶת לְהִתְהַלֵּךְ בָּאָרֶץ
וַיֹּאמֶר לְכוּ הִתְהַלְּכוּ בָאָרֶץ וַתִּתְהַלַּכְנָה בָּאָרֶץ׃

וְהָאֲמֻצִּים יָצְאוּ וַיְבַקְשׁוּ לָלֶכֶת לְהִתְהַלֵּךְ בָּאָרֶץ. Qal *qatal* 3 c pl √יצא, Piel *wayyiqtol* 3 m pl √בקשׁ, Qal inf cstr √הלךְ with prefixed לְ-preposition, Hitpael inf cstr √הלךְ with prefixed לְ-preposition. While verses 5-6 was the angel's explanation to the prophet, in verse 7 the prophet switches back to narrating the additional events of the vision, focusing on the fourth chariot team with "speckled, strong" horses. Since verse 3 identifies the fourth chariot as having "speckled, strong" horses, either designation is sufficient to identify it in verse 6 (הַבְּרֻדִּים) and verse 7 (הָאֲמֻצִּים), and there is no need to view these as separate chariot teams (see v. 3). וְהָאֲמֻצִּים יָצְאוּ וַיְבַקְשׁוּ can be understood as a temporal clause (see JM §166a–b): "And as for the strong (horses), *when* they went out, they sought. . . ." Thus, after completing their southerly circuit, the fourth chariot team sought permission to continue their patrol throughout the whole "earth" (taking אֶרֶץ in v. 7 in a more comprehensive sense than a specific "land"). In LBH the verb √בקשׁ can mean "to ask, request" (BDB, 135, #6): "they sought (asked) to go . . . and he said, 'Go!' " The verb √הלךְ often occurs with an infinitive construct indicating purpose (BDB, 233, #15a). On the meaning of Hitpael √הלךְ as "to patrol," see 1:10.

וַיֹּאמֶר לְכוּ הִתְהַלְּכוּ בָאָרֶץ וַתִּתְהַלַּכְנָה בָּאָרֶץ. Qal *wayyiqtol* 3 m s √אמר, Qal impv 2 m pl √הלךְ, Hitpael impv 2 m pl √הלךְ, Hitpael *wayyiqtol* 3 f pl √הלךְ. The subject of וַיֹּאמֶר is probably the Interpreting Angel, although he is speaking on YHWH's behalf (cf. v. 8: רוּחִי "my spirit").

6:8 וַיַּזְעֵק אֹתִי וַיְדַבֵּר אֵלַי לֵאמֹר רְאֵה הַיּוֹצְאִים אֶל־
אֶרֶץ צָפוֹן הֵנִיחוּ אֶת־רוּחִי בְּאֶרֶץ צָפוֹן׃ ס

וַיַּזְעֵק אֹתִי וַיְדַבֵּר אֵלַי לֵאמֹר. Hifil *wayyiqtol* 3 m s √זעק, Piel *wayyiqtol* 3 m s √דבר, Qal inf cstr √אמר. Hifil √זעק is sometimes used with the meaning, "to call out for military service" (BDB, 277, #1), e.g., in Jdg 4:10, 13; 2 Sam 20:4-5, yet the prophet does not appear here in a militaristic role. A causative notion of Hifil √זעק is discernible in Jonah 3:7 (BDB, 277, #3) and in RH (Jastrow, 408), which seems more appropriate to Zechariah's role as a messenger (cf. Wolters 2014: 177–78): YHWH is "causing Zechariah to proclaim" by giving him a message with the assumption that he will pass it on to his hearers (cf. on 1:14, 17; 2:8).

רְאֵה הַיּֽוֹצְאִים֙ אֶל־אֶ֣רֶץ צָפ֔וֹן הֵנִ֥יחוּ אֶת־רוּחִ֖י בְּאֶ֥רֶץ צָפֽוֹן. Qal impv 2 m s √ראה, Qal ptc m pl √יצא with def art, Hifil *qatal* 3 c pl √נוח. The substantival participle הַיּֽוֹצְאִים is indeterminate as to time (see Hag 1:6), and in this instance can be translated as a past tense: "the ones who *went.*" Hifil √נוח displays two forms, the regular form (Hifil I) displayed here and the second (Hifil II) with a geminated first letter, i.e., הַנִּיחַ (see וְהֻנִּיחָה in 5:11). With the verb √נוח the morphological variation corresponds to a semantic distinction, with Hifil I denoting "to give rest to" or "to cause to light upon" and Hifil II meaning "to put, place" (cf. √נתן), "to leave, let remain," or "to leave in peace" (JM §80p; BDB, 628–29, A–B). Relevant to the present verse are examples of Hifil I in which "to give rest to" refers to satisfying anger, with בְּ marking the object of wrath (Ezek 5:13; 16:42; 24:13). In this regard, one must recall that רוּחַ can indicate "temper" or "anger" (BDB, 925, #3c), a point confirmed by the LXX's rendering of רוּחִי with τὸν θυμόν μου. Given the bellicose nature of the text as discussed here it is best to understand the clause accordingly and render הֵנִ֥יחוּ אֶת־רוּחִ֖י בְּאֶ֥רֶץ צָפֽוֹן as "they have vented my angry spirit upon the northland."

An Oracle (Zechariah 6:9-15)

A Crown for Joshua, the Coming of Ṣemaḥ, *and a Temple Memorial*

In this unit the prophet is directed to receive a contribution of silver and gold from some returned exiles and to go to the house of a certain Josiah in order to make a crown (or crowns; see v. 11 and v. 14 below), which he is to place upon Joshua the high priest as a symbolic act (Stead, 135). He is then to make a proclamation to Joshua concerning the coming of *Ṣemaḥ*, the mysterious figure mentioned earlier in 3:8. This *Ṣemaḥ* will bear ruling splendor and will build the temple of

YHWH and, what is more, will also exercise priestly prerogatives (see v. 13), while the crown(s) will be kept as a memorial in the temple (v. 14). The oracle ends on a surprising note by asserting that "far-off ones" will come and assist in building the temple, which will confirm that YHWH has sent the prophet (v. 15a). The passage concludes in verse 15b with a brief citation from Deut 28:1 urging the people to listen to the voice of YHWH.

The relationship between Joshua and *Ṣemaḥ* has been a topic of much scholarly discussion, and the crowning of Joshua has contributed to the extensive debate over a possible diarchic ruling structure in Persian period Yehud—that is, a situation of shared leadership between the Davidic house and the priesthood (see the introductory remarks to 3:1-10). While the majority of scholars accept some form of Judean diarchy, some significant objections have been raised against the concept (see esp. Rose; and Boda 2001). The present pericope is clearly relevant to the debate, though this handbook will not attempt to resolve such questions.

9 *And the word of YHWH came to me:*

10 *"An offering is to be taken from the exiles, from Ḥeldai and from Tobiah and from Jedaiah. And you shall go on that day, and you shall go to the household of Josiah, son of Zephaniah, which has come from Babylon.*

11 *And you shall take silver and gold, and you shall make a royal crown, and you will place it on the head of Joshua, the son of Jehozadak, the high priest.*

12 *And you will say to him: 'Thus has YHWH Tsevaot said: Behold, a man whose name is Ṣemaḥ! For he will grow up from the ground beneath him, and he will build the temple of YHWH.*

13 *And he will build the temple of YHWH, and he will bear splendor, and he shall sit and he shall rule upon his throne. And he will be a priest upon his throne. And a counsel of peace shall be between the two of them.'*

14 *And the royal crown will be for Ḥelem, and for Tobiah, and for Jedaiah, and for Ḥen, the son of Zephaniah, for a memorial in the temple of YHWH.*

15 *And far-off ones will come and they will build in the temple of YHWH," and you will know that YHWH Tsevaot has sent me to you. "And if you will indeed listen to the voice of YHWH your God . . ."*

6:9 וַיְהִ֥י דְבַר־יְהוָ֖ה אֵלַ֥י לֵאמֹֽר׃

Qal *wayyiqtol* 3 m s √היה, Qal inf cstr √אמר. On this "reception formula" as marking the giving of divine revelation as a narrative event, see the Appendix (§1).

6:10 לָק֗וֹחַ מֵאֵ֤ת הַגּוֹלָה֙ מֵחֶלְדַּ֔י וּמֵאֵ֥ת טוֹבִיָּ֖ה וּמֵאֵ֣ת
יְדַֽעְיָ֑ה וּבָאתָ֤ אַתָּה֙ בַּיּ֣וֹם הַה֔וּא וּבָ֗אתָ בֵּ֚ית יֹאשִׁיָּ֣ה
בֶן־צְפַנְיָ֔ה אֲשֶׁר־בָּ֖אוּ מִבָּבֶֽל׃

לָק֗וֹחַ מֵאֵ֤ת הַגּוֹלָה֙ מֵחֶלְדַּ֔י וּמֵאֵ֥ת טוֹבִיָּ֖ה וּמֵאֵ֣ת יְדַֽעְיָ֑ה. Qal inf abs √לקח. The noun גּוֹלָה can refer to the abstract notion of "exile" but it can also be used as a collective noun for "exiles" (BDB, 163), which is the sense here, as the text immediately proceeds to introduce some of the returned exiles by name. Depending on the context גּוֹלָה can refer to those living in exile (e.g., Esth 2:6) or those who have returned from it (e.g., Ezra 9:4; cf. also בְּנֵי־הַגּוֹלָה in Ezra 4:1 and 6:19-21), which is a matter of the term's referent, not its lexical sense. These individuals mentioned would presumably have been familiar in the original context of the oracle but are largely unknown to later readers, and their significance for the pericope is therefore obscure. They are sometimes described as "couriers" sent from the Jews in Babylonia (e.g., Hill, 175–76), but this is not explicitly stated, and neither is it indicated that they are the craftsmen who will fashion the "crown(s)" (vv. 10b-11). Other suggestions are that they were needed as witnesses to the transaction about to take place, with its accompanying divine utterance (Mitchell, 185), or that they had some sort of priestly connection (Boda 2001: §4.2.1 n. 41). Perhaps, as Petersen (274) suggests, their significance lies merely in the fact that three of their four names are theophoric, that is, they contain the *–yah* name of God (on the spelling of such names, see 1:1). The names are all attested elsewhere in the HB, and most are attested in ancient inscriptions and bullae: "Ḥeldai" (Arad 27:5; 39:10), "Tobiah" (e.g., Lachish 3:19; 5:10), "Jedaiah" (Arad 39:4–5; Samaria 1:8; 42:2; also in the DSS, e.g., 4Q319 7:3; 4Q332 1:2), and "Zephaniah" (Avigad seal 53; 155). The name "Josiah" has not been found in material remains but occurs twice in Ben Sira (49:1, 4 [MsB]). The name "Ḥeldai" occurs as "Ḥelem" (חֵלֶם) and "Josiah" is changed to "Ḥen" in verse 14 (see below).

The compound preposition מֵאֵת is often used with verbs of acquiring or taking (BDB, 86, #4a); the meaning can be functionally equivalent to מִן alone, as evidenced by the interchange of the two in מֵאֵת הַגּוֹלָה מֵחֶלְדַּי "from the exiles, from Ḥeldai. . . ." The verb √לקח occurs without a direct object here (as in Zech 14:21), in contrast to verse 11, where the same verb occurs but with an accusative object specifying what is to be taken (וְלָקַחְתָּ כֶסֶף־וְזָהָב); verse 10 simply does not specify what sort of offering was to be received. It is often assumed that the three men mentioned are the only ones being required to contribute, but it must be emphasized that the text does not say this, for the individuals mentioned need not be coterminous with הַגּוֹלָה; they could simply be representative members of the group and are being singled out by name. In view of the common use of the infinitive absolute in injunctive laws such as the Decalogue's שָׁמוֹר/זָכוֹר אֶת־יוֹם הַשַּׁבָּת, it could be that an offering on a larger, community-wide scale is indicated by לָקוֹחַ מֵאֵת הַגּוֹלָה, with the text only then turning to focus attention on Ḥeldai, Tobiah, and Jedaiah. Wolters (2014: 183, 196–97) has noted the intertextual links between this pericope and passages such as Exod 30:16 (the half-shekel tax for the sanctuary) and Num 31:54 (the Israelites' purifying and dividing up the plunder of Midian), which mention a large-scale "taking" (√לקח) of silver (כֶּסֶף) and gold (זָהָב), which are then placed as a "memorial" (זִכָּרוֹן) in the tabernacle. An additional important intertext would be the summons of Exod 25:2, in which YHWH directed the Israelite camp to "take a contribution for me" (וְיִקְחוּ־לִי תְּרוּמָה), which included gold and silver (Exod 25:3) and affirmed in verse 8 וְעָשׂוּ לִי מִקְדָּשׁ וְשָׁכַנְתִּי בְּתוֹכָם "And they will make a sanctuary for me and I will dwell in your midst," a promise echoed earlier in the book (see 2:14-15 [ET: vv. 10-11]).

The infinitive absolute can be used in place of a finite verb (see Hag 1:6), and here it has the force of an imperative or an injunctive future (JM §123u–v; see 3:4). As an infinitive it leaves the subject unmentioned, and thus instead of simply translating לָקוֹחַ as an imperative ("Take from . . .!") one could also render it impersonally, e.g., "one shall take from" or, in a passive transformation, "an offering is to be taken." There is no reason to assume that Zechariah himself would be the one collecting the offering from the returned exiles; indeed, if it is correct that a community-wide collection is being envisioned, it is more likely that the priests would have been the ones to receive it.

וּבָאתָ֨ אַתָּ֜ה בַּיּ֣וֹם הַה֗וּא. Qal *weqatal* 2 m s √בוא. The verb וּבָאתָ displays hiatus (JM §33), that is, normally the accent would be *mil'el* (as in the following וּבָ֫אתָ), but being followed by a word commencing with a guttural, the accent becomes *mil'ra*. The *weqatal* form often assumes a similar tense or modal value of the preceding verb, and here וּבָאתָ displays deontic modality ("must go") in keeping with the volitional sense of the preceding לָקוֹחַ (for other examples of a volitional infinitive absolute-*weqatal* sequence, see Deut 1:16; 2 Sam 24:12; 2 Kgs 5:10). The use of an apparently "unnecessary" personal pronoun with a finite verbal form, as with וּבָאתָ אַתָּה, has been noted before (see 2:9 [ET: v. 5]; 3:7). It is difficult to see how the pronoun emphasizes Zechariah's role as prophet and priest in crowning Joshua (so Sweeney, 630). Given that the preceding לָקוֹחַ did not specify a subject, it seems that the pronoun אַתָּה is used for disjunction or "adversative juxtaposition" (JM §146a2) to urge upon Zechariah that he too has a duty to fulfill, not just the priests: "An offering is to be taken from the exiles . . . then *you* shall go. . . ." The phrase בַּיּוֹם הַהוּא occurs so frequently in prophetic literature that it almost becomes an eschatological formula referring to a time of future blessing or judgment, but the phrase simply means "on that day" and can be used with past narratives (e.g., Gen 48:20; Exod 5:6) or with future-oriented directives such as Exod 13:8 וְהִגַּדְתָּ לְבִנְךָ בַּיּוֹם הַהוּא "And you will declare to your son on that day" and Lev 22:30 בַּיּוֹם הַהוּא יֵאָכֵל "It must be eaten on that day" (cf. BDB, 400, #7g).

וּבָ֫אתָ בֵּית יֹאשִׁיָּה בֶן־צְפַנְיָה אֲשֶׁר־בָּאוּ מִבָּבֶל. Qal *weqatal* 2 m s and Qal *qatal* 3 c pl √בוא. The *weqatal* form וּבָאתָ has an injunctive sense, while the noun phrase בֵּית יֹאשִׁיָּה בֶן־צְפַנְיָה represents an accusative of local determination (see Hag 1:8). The repetition of the verb וּבָאתָ might strike the reader as odd, but the first occurrence indicated only the timing of the prophet's "going" while the second specifies his destination. Since the prophet is told in verse 11 to take "silver and gold" and to make a crown (or crowns), it is often assumed that Josiah is the one doing the fashioning (Petterson 2009: 105), but this too is not stated; the obscurity of the individuals mentioned makes it difficult to determine his role in the pericope (see above). אֲשֶׁר־בָּאוּ מִבָּבֶל is most often understood as modifying Ḥeldai, Tobiah, and Jedaiah, and thus in translation the relative clause is moved earlier to make this clear: "Take from the exiles Ḥeldai, Tobijah, and Jedaiah, who have arrived from Babylon" (so RSV). Wolters (2014: 184) translates אֲשֶׁר as "to which," assuming that בֵּית יֹאשִׁיָּה בֶן־צְפַנְיָה is speaking of the structure or location where Ḥeldai et al. went to stay when they returned from Babylon (cf. Demsky, 101). While this is possible, in such a case one would have expected a resumptive שָׁם as in Hag 2:14. Moreover, if the three men were already staying with Josiah, it is peculiar that Zechariah is told first that an offering is to be received from them and thereafter is directed to go to Josiah's house; presumably he would have gone to Josiah's house in the first place in order to receive it. Without a compelling reason to read the text otherwise, the relative clause is most naturally understood as modifying the "house of Josiah," with "house" referring to the household or family of Josiah (see 3:7), thus explaining the plural verb בָּאוּ.

6:11 וְלָקַחְתָּ כֶסֶף־וְזָהָב וְעָשִׂיתָ עֲטָרוֹת וְשַׂמְתָּ בְּרֹאשׁ יְהוֹשֻׁעַ בֶּן־יְהוֹצָדָק הַכֹּהֵן הַגָּדוֹל׃

וְלָקַחְתָּ כֶסֶף־וְזָהָב וְעָשִׂיתָ עֲטָרוֹת. Qal *weqatal* 2 m s √לקח, Qal *weqatal* 2 m s √עשׂה. If the "taking" of verse 10 referred to a community-wide offering from the returned exiles, presumably under the oversight of the priests, then the "taking" indicated by וְלָקַחְתָּ in verse 11 refers more specifically to Zechariah taking silver and gold from what was brought in. On the word order of כֶּסֶף preceding זָהָב, see Hag 2:8. The prophet is directed to use the "silver and gold" of the offering to fashion עֲטָרוֹת (also mentioned in v. 14). Rose argues that עֲטָרָה is the most general term in the lexical field of crowns, garlands, diadems, and the like, though his discussion is weakened by a distinction between "coronation crowns" and "royal crowns" (2000: 52–54), which is not a semantic distinction marked by different lexemes (note also that his diagram of the lexical field on p. 53 is marred by the absence of כֶּתֶר). Rather, it would be more accurate to say that not all "crowns" or "acts of crowning" represent royal investiture or inauguration into the kingship.

The plural form עֲטָרוֹת has caused much confusion, and Petterson (2009: 105) provides a concise summary of the interpretive options:

1. The noun עֲטָרוֹת is to be understood as singular and only one crown is intended. After the crown is placed on Joshua's head (v. 11), it is later placed in the temple (v. 14) where it will serve as a זִכָּרוֹן "memorial" (e.g., Wolters 2014: 197; Rose, 46–48).

2. The noun עֲטָרוֹת is plural in both instances (e.g., Petersen, 275). It is generally assumed on the basis of שְׁנֵיהֶם "the two of them" in verse 13 that two crowns are meant (e.g., Demsky, 100), but the MT does not in fact specify a number. One crown is to be placed on Joshua, and another crown is to serve as a memorial in the temple (v. 14).
3. The noun עֲטָרוֹת is plural in verse 11 and refers to two crowns, one of which is set upon Joshua's head, but the defectively spelled עֲטָרֹת in verse 14 is taken as singular (e.g., Meyers and Meyers, 336, 350–52, 362–63).

Each option involves various difficulties, some of a grammatical and others of an exegetical nature. Against the second option, for example, it may pointed out that the plural noun הָעֲטָרֹת in verse 14 takes a singular verb תִּהְיֶה, although this is not an intractable problem, since plural subjects can take singular verbs (JM §150; WB §§227–34). One of the chief difficulties for the first and third views is the ostensibly plural form עֲטָרוֹת/עֲטָרֹת, for even though some argue for the existence of a singular *–ot* ending in BH (e.g., Wolters 2014: 184; Rose, 46–48, 84–86; Lipiński, 34–35), the evidence for such is shaky. A different approach is taken by Petterson (2009: 106), who suggests that the plural form indicates that the crown is composite in some way, for example, two-tiered, which is not implausible but lacks external confirmation. It is suggested here that the best interpretive option for understanding עֲטָרוֹת is as a "plural of respect" (WB §8; MNK §24.3.3vii; WO §7.4.3), by which "a plural word may refer to a single honourable or fearful object or person." This category is also called "honorific plural," "plural of majesty," "plural of excellence," or, n.b., the "royal plural." Taking a cue from the last-mentioned label, עֲטָרוֹת is translated here as "royal crown."

וְשַׂמְתָּ בְּרֹאשׁ יְהוֹשֻׁעַ בֶּן־יְהוֹצָדָק הַכֹּהֵן הַגָּדוֹל. Qal *weqatal* 2 m s √שׂים. The verb lacks a direct object, though it is often understood to be the עֲטָרוֹת, and thus the clause is understood as directing Zechariah to place the crown on Joshua's head. Some scholars disagree, however, maintaining that the typical expressions for setting headgear on a person utilize the verb √נתן (with either עַל or בְּ) or, in Zech 3:5, שִׂים עַל רֹאשׁ. Therefore some assert that שִׂים בְּרֹאשׁ without an object has a different connotation; appealing to Akkadian, van der Woude (1988a: 247 n. 31) suggests that the expression means "to put at the disposal of someone, to entrust," but this is a doubtful reading of the Akkadian expression in the first place (Wolters 2014: 185), and furthermore its application to BH in this singular occurrence is special pleading. Wenzel (2011a: 147–48) appeals to Deut 1:13 וַאֲשִׂימֵם בְּרָאשֵׁיכֶם "and I will make them rulers over you" and argues that שִׂים בְּרֹאשׁ means "to make the head of" in the sense that Joshua is being made the "head" of his fellow priests. This results in a glaring redundancy, however, since Joshua is designated as הַכֹּהֵן הַגָּדוֹל "the chief priest," so naturally he would have a leading role already. More problematic from a grammatical standpoint, as Wolters (2014: 186) observes, is that this would require "Joshua" to occur as a direct object rather than as a prepositional phrase and the noun ראשׁ to have a pronominal suffix representing the ones being led. All things considered, the common rendering of וְשַׂמְתָּ בְּרֹאשׁ יְהוֹשֻׁעַ as "set it upon the head of Joshua" is the most straightforward; cf. 1 Kgs 20:31 נָשִׂימָה נָּא שַׂקִּים בְּמָתְנֵינוּ וַחֲבָלִים בְּרֹאשֵׁנוּ "Let us put sackcloth on our loins and ropes on our heads" and Esth 2:17 וַיָּשֶׂם כֶּתֶר־מַלְכוּת בְּרֹאשָׁהּ "and he placed a royal crown on her head." The omission of the direct object in Zech 6:11 is not problematic, as it is common for this to be omitted from a second verb (JM §125x).

6:12 וְאָמַרְתָּ אֵלָיו לֵאמֹר כֹּה אָמַר יְהוָה צְבָאוֹת לֵאמֹר הִנֵּה־אִישׁ צֶמַח שְׁמוֹ וּמִתַּחְתָּיו יִצְמָח וּבָנָה אֶת־הֵיכַל יְהוָה׃

וְאָמַרְתָּ אֵלָיו לֵאמֹר כֹּה אָמַר יְהוָה צְבָאוֹת לֵאמֹר. Qal *weqatal* 2 m s, Qal inf cstr, and Qal *qatal* 3 m s √אמר.

הִנֵּה־אִישׁ צֶמַח שְׁמוֹ. On the meaning of the name *Ṣemaḥ*, see the introductory remarks to 3:1-10. The indeterminate status of הִנֵּה־אִישׁ means that it should be rendered as "behold a man" rather than, e.g., the RSV's "Behold the man" (cf. JM §158b). The clause is spoken directly to Joshua (וְאָמַרְתָּ אֵלָיו), and the lack of a definite article weighs against understanding אִישׁ either as a vocative addressed to the high priest (see 3:2) or as pointing deictically to one of the other men present (Boda 2001: §4.3.1).

וּמִתַּחְתָּיו יִצְמָח. Qal *yiqtol* 3 m s √צמח. The verb √צמח, which has a basic meaning of "to grow" (Rose, 99–102), is clearly a wordplay on the name *Ṣemaḥ*. In this instance the *vav* probably has a logical force of "for, because" (see JM §170c) since the clause is explaining the significance of his name. מִתַּחְתָּיו may seem somewhat awkward, but the verb √צמח occurs with the מִן preposition (e.g., Exod 10:5; Job 8:19; Ps 85:12), and תַּ֫חַת can indicate "what is under one" or "the place in which one stands" (BDB, 1065, #II2). The expression here then could indicate that *Ṣemaḥ* will spring up "from his place," "from where he stands," or possibly "from (the ground) beneath him" (see the extensive discussion by Wolters 2014: 187–89). The subject of the verb is to be understood as *Ṣemaḥ* rather than taken in an impersonal sense of "(things) will grow beneath him." It is possible that the pronoun suffix on מִתַּחְתָּיו could refer to Joshua, but if this were a continuation of the direct discourse then the second person pronominal suffix would be expected: *וּמִתַּחְתֶּ֫יךָ יִצְמָח. The expression וּמִתַּחְתָּיו יִצְמָ֔ח refers either to *Ṣemaḥ*'s emergence on the scene or perhaps, in view of verse 15a, to the growth or expansion of *Ṣemaḥ*'s influence and reputation, resulting in others coming from afar to assist in the work of temple building.

וּבָנָ֖ה אֶת־הֵיכַ֥ל יְהוָֽה. Qal *weqatal* 3 m s √בנה. Remarkably, for a book so replete with temple imagery, this is the first usage of the word הֵיכַל (see also vv. 13-15; 8:9; Hag 2:15, 18).

6:13 וְ֠הוּא יִבְנֶ֞ה אֶת־הֵיכַ֣ל יְהוָ֗ה וְהֽוּא־יִשָּׂ֤א הוֹד֙ וְיָשַׁ֣ב וּמָשַׁ֣ל עַל־כִּסְא֑וֹ וְהָיָ֤ה כֹהֵן֙ עַל־כִּסְא֔וֹ וַעֲצַ֣ת שָׁל֔וֹם תִּהְיֶ֖ה בֵּ֥ין שְׁנֵיהֶֽם׃

וְ֠הוּא יִבְנֶ֞ה אֶת־הֵיכַ֣ל יְהוָ֗ה וְהֽוּא־יִשָּׂ֤א הוֹד֙. Qal *yiqtol* 3 m s √בנה, Qal *yiqtol* 3 m s √נשׂא. We encounter in quick succession two instances of a personal pronoun used with a finite verb, a phenomenon encountered previously (see v. 10). In this case both the repetition and the pronoun usage are best understood as indicative of strong emotional heightening (Muraoka 1985: 50; cf. Rose, 161). וְ֠הוּא יִבְנֶ֞ה אֶת־הֵיכַ֣ל is not philologically difficult, but its repetitive nature has been the subject of comment (Petersen, 276–77; Meyers and Meyers, 357–58; Petterson 2009: 103), as it restates the same thought of the concluding clause of verse 12 with only some grammatical variation. Van der Woude (1988b: 145) argues that this is an indication that the word of YHWH ends with verse 12 and that verses 13-15 provide explanation from the Interpreting Angel, while Baldwin (135–36) claims that it is a device intended to distinguish between Joshua and the "Shoot" (*Ṣemaḥ*). This is a very tenuous basis on which to assert a change of speaker, however. A better explanation is that verses 12b-13a stand at the center of a chiasm. The following outline is adapted slightly from Petterson (2015: 183–84, with references to additional literature):

A: The word of YHWH (v. 9)
B: Exiles come from Babylon (v. 10a, c)
C: Exiles named (v. 10b)
D: A crown to be made (v. 11a)
E: Joshua the high priest (v. 11b)
F: *Ṣemaḥ* introduced (v. 12a)
G: Build the Temple of YHWH (v. 12b)
G′: Build the Temple of YHWH (v. 13a)
F′: Bear majesty, sit and rule (v. 13b)
E′: Priestly activity (v. 13c)
D′: A crown in the temple (v. 14a)
C′: Exiles named (v. 14b)
B′: Far off ones shall come (v. 15a)
A′: The voice of YHWH (v. 15b)

The proposed chiasm does justice to the structure of the pericope and provides a convincing rationale for the "repetitiveness" of וְהוּא יִבְנֶה אֶת־הֵיכַל in verse 13. The central focus of the unit is on *Ṣemaḥ*'s role in rebuilding the temple.

The verb √נשׂא can mean "to receive, obtain" (BDB, 671, #3f; *DCH* 5, 766, #7), which is the sense in וְהוּא־יִשָּׂא הוֹד and the noun הוד chiefly occurs in poetic texts (BDB, 217), which comports with the literary structure (chiasm) of the pericope. When applied to humans, הוד is used chiefly of kings (e.g., 1 Chron 29:25; Ps 21:6) and lends royal coloring to the utterance.

וְיָשַׁב וּמָשַׁל עַל־כִּסְאוֹ. Qal *weqatal* 3 m s √ישׁב, Qal *weqatal* 3 m s √משׁל. In contrast to the preceding clauses, the oracle now reverts to *weqatal* forms without additional pronouns. While it may seem to be a trivial detail, Rose (61–64) discusses the significance of *Ṣemaḥ*'s "sitting" on a throne as opposed to "standing," and he makes the trenchant observation that one typically reads of kings "sitting" to rule, whereas priests "stand" to serve in the HB, further indicating the regal character of the utterance. The verb √משׁל occurs very frequently with reference to YHWH's "ruling" (e.g., 1 Chron 29:12; Pss 22:29; 59:14; etc.); it is not the most common one for kingly reigning, for which Qal √מלך

is more typical, though √משל is certainly attested (e.g., Josh 12:2, 5; 1 Kgs 5:1; 2 Chron 7:18; 9:26).

וְהָיָה כֹהֵן עַל־כִּסְאוֹ. Qal *weqatal* 3 m s √היה. Despite several kingly features in the foregoing, there is also a priestly flavor to the oracle. The RSV renders the *weqatal* form וְהָיָה impersonally: "There shall be a priest." A primary motivation for this reading is the interpretation of בֵּין שְׁנֵיהֶם "between the two of them" in the following clause, which many interpret as referring to a priest ruling alongside the kingly figure *Ṣemaḥ*. Yet *Ṣemaḥ* has been the subject of six third masculine singular verbal forms in succession, and it is by far more natural to understand him to be the subject of וְהָיָה as well (Jauhiainen, 509): "And he will be a priest upon his throne." Alternately, the chiastic structure discussed above could imply that the subject of וְהָיָה is Joshua, in which case the clause could be translated, "And he will be priest alongside his (viz. *Ṣemaḥ*'s) throne." The preposition עַל can indicate a range of spatial relationships, and it does not necessarily have to be understood as a second character sitting "upon" the royal throne.

וַעֲצַת שָׁלוֹם תִּהְיֶה בֵּין שְׁנֵיהֶם. Qal *yiqtol* 3 f s √היה. The verb typically agrees with the initial noun (*nomen regens*) of a construct chain, hence תִּהְיֶה agrees with the feminine עֵצָה rather than the masculine שָׁלוֹם. The term עֵצָה can mean "counsel" in the sense of advice, or "plan" in the sense of a designed strategy. The collocation עֲצַת שָׁלוֹם, however, is a "peculiar phrase" (Petersen, 278), being unique in the HB. There are a great many types of genitive relationships, and more than one possibility would be fitting here. E.g., עֲצַת שָׁלוֹם could be understood as a "genitive of purpose" (JM §129f15; AC §2.2.8; WB §44b; MNK §25.4.5i) as in Num 35:11 עָרֵי מִקְלָט "cities of (= for) refuge," thus: "And there will be counsel for (the purpose of bringing) peace between the two of them." It could also be "genitive of effect/cause" (WO §9.5.2c; AC §2.2.7; Wolters 2014: 182) as in Isa 53:5 מוּסַר שְׁלוֹמֵנוּ "punishment of (= causing) our peace," thus: "And there will be counsel effecting peace between the two of them." Finally, it could be more generally a "genitive of topic" (JM §129f14) as in Exod 12:43 חֻקַּת הַפָּסַח "statute of (= concerning) the Passover," thus: "And there will be counsel concerning peace between the two of them." A more detailed exegetical analysis would have to determine which option, if any, is the most likely.

The great conundrum of this clause is not grammatical but exegetical, and centers on the identity of שְׁנֵיהֶם "the two of them." There have been many proposals, though as a generalization it would be fair to say that they tend to fall into two main categories. First, "the two of them" are understood as two personal beings. There are many different variations on this approach depending upon the particular identification of the two individuals, e.g., *Ṣemaḥ*, the unnamed priest allegedly indicated by וְהָיָה כֹהֵן עַל־כִּסְאוֹ in verse 13, Joshua, YHWH, Zerubbabel, and so on. The second approach is to interpret "the two of them" as having more abstract or impersonal referents such as kingly and priestly roles or offices, typically with respect to *Ṣemaḥ*'s dual priestly/kingly function (so Wolters 2014: 191–92; cf. NASB's "between the two offices"). A slight variation is presented by Hill (177–78), who argues that they are two "thrones" representing "the Branch's" two roles of king and priest. Wolters (2014: 192) defends the more abstract understanding by pointing to a number of instances where שְׁנֵיהֶם is used with reference to impersonal objects. The determining issue here is not the range of usage of שְׁנֵיהֶם, however, but rather the noun עֵצָה itself: "counsel" is, both in the HB and in the DSS, closely associated with personal agents—that is, those who possess it and can give it (whether good or bad). The notion of "counsel" being attributed to an abstract concept or an impersonal entity is unparalleled in the HB and only rarely occurs in the DSS (1QS 9:9, 17 עצת התורה "the counsel of the Torah"). The general thrust of the text seems clearly to imply the personal nature of "the two of them" (cf. Rose, 60). Exegetical and theological arguments will no doubt continue to be made for various identifications of who "the two of them" are, though the two possible antecedents closest at hand would be *Ṣemaḥ* and Joshua.

6:14 וְהָעֲטָרֹת תִּהְיֶה לְחֵלֶם וּלְטוֹבִיָּה וְלִידַעְיָה וּלְחֵן בֶּן־צְפַנְיָה לְזִכָּרוֹן בְּהֵיכַל יְהוָה׃

Qal *yiqtol* 3 f s √היה. As argued above, הָעֲטָרֹת is best understood as a "plural of majesty" or "royal plural" (see v. 11). In BH the plural of majesty typically takes a singular verb (JM §150f; WB §227, §232), hence the singular תִּהְיֶה. The verb √היה can occur with two לְ-phrases (BDB, 226, #II2f), one indicating the predicate (here: לְזִכָּרוֹן) with the sense of "to fulfill the function of" or "to serve as," and the other indicating the beneficiary or recipient (here: לְחֵלֶם וּלְטוֹבִיָּה), thus: "And the royal crown will serve as a memorial for Ḥelem, Tobiah, etc." Assuming that "Ḥen" is another name for "Josiah" (see below), it is noteworthy that he appears in the same list as the other men, whereas he seemed to be somewhat distinct from them in verse 10. As noted above, however, the roles of the different characters involved in the transaction are not entirely clear to begin with.

It was observed previously that there are some changes in the names of two of the men in the passage (see v. 10): "Ḥeldai" (v. 10) appears here as "Ḥelem," and "Joshua" appears as "Ḥen," both names being unique in the HB. The reason for the change is unclear, though of course the phenomenon of a person having multiple names is by no means unusual in the HB (e.g., Jacob/Israel, Esther/Hadassah, Daniel/Belteshazzar). The name "Ḥelem" may be nothing more than a scribal misreading of "Ḥeldai," though Meyers and Meyers (340) speculate that the name had two forms and that "Ḥeldai" was the form used in Babylon, reverting to "Ḥelem" upon returning to Judea. According to Petersen (278), both "Ḥelem" and "Ḥen" were simply nicknames used by closer acquaintances. The "Ḥeldai-Ḥelem" interchange could be analogous to the frequent interchange of "Charles" and "Chuck," whereas there is no etymological connection involved in the substitution of "Ḥen" for "Josiah." It could be one of Josiah's own birth names or a nickname acquired later. Some follow the lead of the LXX's rendering of וּלְחֵן בֶּן־צְפַנְיָה as εἰς χάριτα υἱοῦ Σοφονίου and render חֵן here as "grace" or "favor." Thus, for example, Wolters (2014: 198–99) translates, "for the favor (kindness) of the son of Zephaniah." According to this interpretation, the text speaks of a commemoration not only of Ḥelem, Tobiah's, and Jedaiah's generosity (cf. v. 10) but also of the "kindness" shown by the son of Zephaniah. This requires a forced reading of אֲשֶׁר in verse 10 as "where" (see above). The testimony of the LXX is not compelling in this instance, however, as it renders several other names in verse 10 as nouns or attributes, thus in place of מֵחֶלְדַּי וּמֵאֵת טוֹבִיָּה וּמֵאֵת יְדַעְיָה in verse 10, it translates παρὰ τῶν ἀρχόντων καὶ παρὰ τῶν χρησίμων αὐτῆς καὶ παρὰ τῶν ἐπεγνωκότων αὐτὴν "from the chiefs and from her useful ones and from the ones who have understood it." Demsky (101–2) suggests that לְחֵן does not contain a personal name at all but rather is related to Aramaic *lḥn*, a term of Assyrian origin for a temple or court steward. In any event, there can be little doubt that the same group of individuals is in view in both verses (Peterson 2009: 105 n. 68; Demsky, 100).

6:15 וּרְחוֹקִים | יָבֹאוּ וּבָנוּ בְּהֵיכַל יְהוָה וִידַעְתֶּם כִּֽי־
יְהוָה צְבָאוֹת שְׁלָחַנִי אֲלֵיכֶם וְהָיָה אִם־שָׁמוֹעַ
תִּשְׁמְעוּן בְּקוֹל יְהוָה אֱלֹהֵיכֶם׃ ס

וּרְחוֹקִים | יָבֹאוּ וּבָנוּ בְּהֵיכַל יְהוָה. Qal *yiqtol* 3 m pl √בוא, Qal *weqatal* 3 c pl √בנה. The adjective רְחוֹקִים is used substantivally for "far-off ones," naturally understood in the first instance as referring to Jews of the Diaspora, thus providing a complement to the reference in verse 11 to those who "had come from Babylon." Yet it may well be that this is also intended to echo Isaiah's references to those who come "from afar" (מֵרָחוֹק: Isa 43:6; 49:12; 60:4, 9), in which case it could be applied to Gentiles as well (Stead, 152–53; cf. Wolters 2014: 199). As Wolters (2014: 200) observes, the collocation of √בנה with בְּ־ does not mean "to build *in* the temple" but rather to "participate in building" or "work on a building" (*HALOT*, 139, #5) as in Neh 4:11.

וִידַעְתֶּם כִּֽי־יְהוָה צְבָאוֹת שְׁלָחַנִי אֲלֵיכֶם. Qal *weqatal* 2 m pl √ידע, Qal *qatal* 3 m s √שׁלח with 1 c s suffix. On this recurring formula, see 2:13 [ET: v. 9].

וְהָיָה אִם־שָׁמוֹעַ תִּשְׁמְעוּן בְּקוֹל יְהוָה אֱלֹהֵיכֶם. Qal *weqatal* 3 m s √היה, Qal inf abs √שׁמע, Qal *yiqtol* 2 m pl √שׁמע. The clause consists of a nearly verbatim quotation of Deut 28:1a (cf. also 11:13a), with only minor variations in grammatical form, e.g., a 2 m pl suffix (rather than 2 m s suffix) on אֱלֹהִים and the verbal form תִּשְׁמְעוּן with "paragogic *nun*," as opposed to the singular form תִּשְׁמַע in Deut 28:1. *Yiqtol* forms with paragogic *nun* are attested in several Semitic languages (Ugaritic, Aramaic, Arabic) and occur approximately 320 times in the HB, though it decreased in usage in LBH and eventually disappeared from the language (Qimron, 45; Van Peursen, 100–101; Muraoka 2000: 198–99). The bulk of biblical occurrences are found in Deuteronomy (56×), Isaiah (37×), Job (23×), and the Psalms (15×), typically in major and intermediate pause. Its appearance can be due to "the antiquity of a text, a deliberate archaism, or metre" (JM §44e), though other factors could be involved (see Hoftijzer; WO §31.7.1; GKC §47m). Given Deuteronomy's predilection for paragogic *nun* forms, there can be no doubt that תִּשְׁמְעוּן in Zech 6:15 is a "deliberate archaism," intentionally modifying the source citation to make it sound even more "Deuteronomic" than before. Thus, the significance of its presence here should not be overstated (cp. Ehrensvärd 2006: 181–82, 184). This clause also represents one of three instances of the "paranomastic" use of the infinitive absolute in Zech 1–8 (see also 7:5; 8:21), that is, the use of an infinitive absolute with a finite form of the same root (JM §123; WO §35.3; GKC §113l–r). The infinitive absolute was on the decline in LBH (Muraoka 2000: 195–96), rare in the DSS (Qimron, 47), and disappeared entirely in RH (Pérez Fernández, 144). According to Ehrensvärd's calculations (2006: 181), the two occurrences in Zech 1–8 roughly match SBH frequency, but its presence in this verse is simply due to the text being cited, and thus the statistical frequency of usage needs significant adjustment.

The new literary setting of the citation of Deut 28:1 has led to differing syntactical analyses of the clause. In its original setting, וְהָיָה אִם־שָׁמוֹעַ תִּשְׁמְעוּן is the protasis of a conditional statement with extensive apodoses. In Zech 6:15, however, the *weqatal* form וְהָיָה is frequently rendered as the apodosis with the protasis אִם־שָׁמוֹעַ תִּשְׁמְעוּן following: "And it will happen, if you will indeed listen to my voice. . . ." As such, Ehrensvärd (2006: 179–80) takes this as further evidence of the SBH nature of Zechariah's writing, since he considers it an example of the usage of וְהָיָה, which declined in LBH, and of the use of *weqatal* in the apodosis of conditional clauses, which was likewise on the decline. Yet this syntactical analysis appears to be unparalleled (Wolters 2014: 200) and is clearly incorrect. Unless one wishes to claim that Zechariah has completely changed the syntax of the original citation, it is best to understand this as an incomplete sentence or the rhetorical device of aposiopesis in which a sentence is deliberately left unfinished, requiring the reader or hearer to fill in the gap (Wolters 2014: 200, with reference to other literature). In this case only the protasis of the condition is stated and serves as theological shorthand, affirming the Deuteronomic theme of obedience or disobedience as the instrumentality through which divine blessing or judgment is dispensed.

Concluding Exhortation (Zechariah 7–8)
The Past Judgment and Future Redemption of Zion

Chapters 7 and 8 constitute a distinct textual unit within the book of Zechariah and are introduced with a dating formula that places them almost two years subsequent to the Night Visions (7:1). These chapters do not contain visionary narrative but rather are partly retrospective and partly hortatory in nature. Notwithstanding the complex history of textual development proposed by some redaction-critical scholars (e.g., Hallaschka 2011: 291–93), these two chapters taken together display a literary coherence and unity in their canonical shape (Petersen, 122; Boda 2003b: 395). For instance, there is a literary framework to these chapters formed by repeated references to "entreating the favor of YHWH" (7:2; 8:22) and by the fact that the question regarding fasting which is posed in 7:3 is not directly addressed until 8:19 (cf. Stead, 221–22; for a different view, see Assis, 4). At the same time, numerous "intratextual" references (Introduction §3) link these chapters to the Night Visions of Zechariah 1–6 as well (see Meyers and Meyers, lii–liii, lxi; Petersen, 123; Stead, 219–31; Boda 2003b: 402–5; Assis, 9–17, 20–24). Some of the connections between Zech 1–6 and Zech 7–8 include themes and expressions such as "the earlier prophets" (1:4; 7:7, 12; 8:9), "seventy years" (1:12; 7:5), false oaths (5:3-4; 8:16-17), the inhabiting of Jerusalem and Judah (2:8; 7:7), YHWH's "wrath" (1:2, 15; 7:12; 8:14), YHWH's "jealousy" (1:14; 8:2), YHWH's "return" (1:16; 8:3), YHWH's "dwelling in the midst" of his people (2:14-15; 8:3, cf. v. 8) and, perhaps most profoundly of all, the covenantal promise "they will be my people" (2:15; 8:8). Stead (230) aptly summarizes:

> The same message which Zech 1–6 makes via a sequence of eight visions is made in a more prosaic form in Zech 7–8. The effect of the 'intratextual' connections is to bind the two sections of Zech 1–8 together. The repetition of phrases and ideas from Zech 1–6 in Zech 7–8 signals that these chapters are dealing with the same concerns as the earlier chapters.

Chapters 7–8 thus serve at least in part as a selective recapitulation and summary of a number of key themes from chapters 1–6, yet they should not be viewed merely as a prosaic appendix to the Night Visions (Petersen, 124). Rather, they explicitly summon the people to respond in ways that were only implicit in Zech 1–6. As Stead observes, these chapters play a crucial role in Zech 1–8 in that they "provide the link between the 'cultic' focus on the temple rebuilding . . . and the 'ethical' parts of the message" (219).

Zechariah 7–8 is marked by an extremely high concentration of prophetic formulae (Wolters 2014: 204–5; see the Appendix), which at times can seem unnecessary or cumbersome. Moreover, as presented in the MT, the text is broken down into very short units by the scribal markings of *setuma* (ס) and *petuḥa* (פ), which at times can help to delineate the textual structure but at other times seem oddly placed.

The following outline is based largely on an analysis of the chapters' content:

7:1-7	A question about corporate fasting and hypocritical fasts rebuked
7:8-10	A summons to faithful living
7:11-14	The people's past refusal to heed the earlier prophets and the resulting judgment
8:1-8	YHWH's return to Zion and its transforming effect
8:9-15	YHWH's future dealings not like the former days
8:16-17	Repeated summons to faithful living
8:18-23	Joyous feasting in Zion and the coming of nations to pray

[1]And it happened in the fourth year of Darius the king: the word of YHWH came to Zechariah on the fourth of the ninth month, in Chislev.

[2]And Bethel-Sarezer and Regem-melech and his men sent to supplicate YHWH,

[3]to say to the priests who belonged to the house of YHWH Tsevaot and to the prophets: "Must I weep in the fifth month, abstaining as I have done for these however many years?"

[4]And the word of YHWH Tsevaot came to me:

[5]"Say to all the people of the land and to the priests, 'When you fasted and lamented in the fifth and in the seventh month for these seventy years, did you indeed fast for me?

[6]And when you would eat and drink, were you not the ones eating and drinking?'

[7]The words that YHWH proclaimed by the earlier prophets, when Jerusalem was inhabited and at ease, with her cities surrounding her, and the Negeb and the Shephelah were inhabited—didn't . . . ?"

7:1 וַֽיְהִי֙ בִּשְׁנַ֣ת אַרְבַּ֔ע לְדָרְיָ֖וֶשׁ הַמֶּ֑לֶךְ הָיָ֤ה דְבַר־יְהוָה֙ אֶל־זְכַרְיָ֔ה בְּאַרְבָּעָ֛ה לַחֹ֥דֶשׁ הַתְּשִׁעִ֖י בְּכִסְלֵֽו׃

Qal *wayyiqtol* 3 m s and *qatal* 3 m s √היה. On the use of לְ in dating formulae, see Hag 1:1, and on such formulae more generally, see the introductory remarks to Hag 1:12-15a. On the order of "king" and a proper name, see Hag 1:1. Just like the month שְׁבָט "Shebat" in 1:7, the month כִּסְלֵו "Chislev" is the Babylonian calendrical name (Shin, 117–19), occurring only here and Neh 1:1. On the spelling of the name "Zechariah," see 1:1.

7:2 וַיִּשְׁלַח בֵּית־אֵל שַׂר־אֶצֶר וְרֶגֶם מֶלֶךְ וַאֲנָשָׁיו
לְחַלּוֹת אֶת־פְּנֵי יְהוָה׃

Qal *wayyiqtol* 3 m s √שׁלח, Piel inf cstr √חלה with לְ-preposition. Syntactically, this clause could be analyzed in various ways. An initial question is whether בֵּית־אֵל שַׂר־אֶצֶר represents two names, that is, the name of the well-known biblical location of Bethel plus the personal name "Sarezer" (Meyers and Meyers, 379, 382–83), or only one name "Bethel-sarezer" (e.g., Petersen, 281). According to the former view, "Bethel" (representing the people of the city) would be the subject of the *wayyiqtol* verb and "Sarezer and Regem-melech and his men" would be the direct object (so RSV: "Now the people of Bethel had sent Sharezer and Regemmelech and their men"). Yet if this were so then one might have expected the particle אֶת or some other means to clarify the object as Sarezer et al.; as the text currently stands there is no clear syntactic distinction between the alleged subject and object. Alternately, "Bethel" could be an accusative of local determination (see Hag 1:8), e.g., "they sent *unto* the house of God" (KJV; similarly LXX: καὶ ἐξαπέστειλεν εἰς Βαιθηλ Σαρασαρ). This is less likely because as a general rule *wayyiqtol* is followed by the subject when one is mentioned (WB §572a; JM §155k; WO §8.3b; GKC §142f; Muraoka 1985: 28–41; so also Holmstedt 2011: §3.2 [1], even though he strongly disagrees from these scholars in other fundamental respects regarding basic BH word order). In sum, every possible means of clarifying "Bethel" as a location is absent here, which would be bound to result in confusion. On the other hand, the evidence is strong for taking "Bethel-sarezer" as a single name. "Bethel" occurs as a theophoric element in neo- and late-Babylonian names, and there is attestation of the equivalent name *bīt-ili-šar-uṣur* in Babylonian sources (Hyatt). Taking "Bethel-sarezer" as a name provides the simplest syntactical analysis for the sentence. The use of a singular verb with a plural subject is not uncommon, particularly when the verb precedes the subject (JM §150j). It is also not unusual for the verb שׁלח to be used without an object; one can assume that "messengers" were sent, but they do not need to be explicitly mentioned (e.g., Gen 27:42; 38:25; Num 22:37).

לְחַלּ֖וֹת אֶת־פְּנֵ֥י יְהוָֽה. This expression occurs approximately sixteen times in the HB, and will recur in 8:21-22 to create an *inclusio*. It is often translated as "to entreat the favor of," but it must be borne in mind that this is not a term of propitiation or offering. Rather, it belongs to the semantic field of divine-human communication and refers to laying a question (Exod 32:11) or a prayer request before YHWH (1 Kgs 13:6; 2 Chron 33:12; implied in 2 Kgs 13:4; Jer 26:19; Mal 1:9). In some instances a sacred location is made explicit (Zech 8:21-22; cf. Exod 32:11) or implied (Mal 1:9). The expression is rendered here simply as "to supplicate."

7:3 לֵאמֹ֗ר אֶל־הַכֹּהֲנִים֙ אֲשֶׁ֣ר לְבֵית־יְהוָ֣ה צְבָא֔וֹת וְאֶל־הַנְּבִיאִ֖ים לֵאמֹ֑ר הַאֶבְכֶּה֙ בַּחֹ֣דֶשׁ הַחֲמִשִׁ֔י הִנָּזֵ֕ר כַּאֲשֶׁ֣ר עָשִׂ֔יתִי זֶ֖ה כַּמֶּ֥ה שָׁנִֽים׃ פ

לֵאמֹ֗ר אֶל־הַכֹּהֲנִים֙ אֲשֶׁ֣ר לְבֵית־יְהוָ֣ה צְבָא֔וֹת וְאֶל־הַנְּבִיאִ֖ים לֵאמֹ֑ר. Qal inf cstr √אמר. Wolters (2014: 213) argues that the initial לֵאמֹר is used here "in a highly unusual way," and indeed he alleges that most instances of the infinitive construct לֵאמֹר in Zech 7–8 are "unusual or redundant" and provide evidence of redactional activity (2014: 205). This evaluation is based on the unjustifiable assumption that the "regular" usage of לֵאמֹר is to introduce direct discourse after a verb of speaking. While this is undoubtedly a very common use of the form and applies to its second usage in this verse, such a reductionistic understanding is problematic (see Miller 1996: 174, 181 n. 84) because לֵאמֹר displays the more common functions of the infinitive construct as well. In this instance, the first לֵאמֹר is conjoined with לְחַלּוֹת in verse 2, both indicating the purpose of the "sending," while only the second לֵאמֹר introduces direct discourse: "(they) sent to supplicate . . . , *to say* to the priests . . ." For the same construction with a dual use of לֵאמֹר, each with a different syntactic function, see 2 Chron 32:17 וּסְפָרִים כָּתַב לְחָרֵף לַיהוָה אֱלֹהֵי יִשְׂרָאֵל וְלֵאמֹר עָלָיו לֵאמֹר כֵּאלֹהֵי גּוֹיֵ "And he wrote letters *to revile* YHWH, God of Israel, and *to say* to him: 'As the gods of the nations. . . .'" The לְ-preposition can indicate various spatial or directional nuances, and in the phrase אֲשֶׁר לְבֵית־יְהוָה צְבָאוֹת it can be rendered as "at." Alternately, it could be understood as creating a genitive relationship here: "to the priests who belonged to the house of YHWH Tsevaot" (Wolters 2014: 213).

הַאֶבְכֶּה בַּחֹדֶשׁ הַחֲמִשִׁי הִנָּזֵר. Qal *yiqtol* 1 c s √בכה, Nifal inf abs √נזר. The question is referring to corporate lamenting as a regular ritual, as indicated by the addition of a temporal adjunct ("in the fifth month") to the *yiqtol* form. The verbal form could simply refer to the future ("Shall I . . . ?"), but it can express other modal nuances as well, and in this case the general tenor of the ensuing discussion (cf. vv. 4-5) suggests that it might have more of the nuance of "must": "*Must* I . . . ?" The lexica list "to dedicate oneself" and "to separate oneself from, to abstain" as glosses for Nifal √נזר (BDB, 634; *HALOT*, 684; *DCH* 5, 651). The verb only occurs three other times in the HB (Lev 22:2; Ezek 14:7; Hos 9:10) but six times in the DSS, where the sense of "to abstain" is clear (CD 6:15 // Hifil √בדל; 8:8; 4Q183 1:ii:5; 4Q418 81:a:2 // Hifil √בדל; fragmentary context in 4Q266 1a_b:1; 4Q512 69:3). On the use of the infinitive absolute to continue a finite verb, see Hag 1:6.

כַּאֲשֶׁר עָשִׂיתִי זֶה כַּמֶּה שָׁנִים. Qal *qatal* 1 c s √עשׂה. עָשִׂיתִי is to be understood as a "global" use of the past tense (see Hag 1:2), that is, it refers to actions that would have taken place repeatedly, but it does so in a "summarizing" way (see Hag 1:2). זֶה should not be understood as the object of the verb ("I have done *this*") because for an abstract or neuter notion one would expect the feminine זאת (JM §152). Rather, זֶה occurs in temporal phrases (JM §143a) as in Num 14:22 וַיְנַסּוּ אֹתִי זֶה עֶשֶׂר פְּעָמִים "And they tested me these ten times," thus the entire phrase זֶה כַּמֶּה שָׁנִים should be taken as an adverbial accusative of time (see 1:8). The combination of זֶה with כַּמָּה "how many" (Gen 47:8; 2 Sam 19:25; 1 Kgs 22:16; 2 Chron 18:15; Job 13:18) has the idea of "these however many years." In light of the rebuke to come, one is justified in sensing a frustrated or petulant tone to the question.

7:4 וַיְהִי דְּבַר־יְהוָה צְבָאוֹת אֵלַי לֵאמֹר׃

Qal *wayyiqtol* 3 m s √היה, Qal inf cstr √אמר. On this formula as indicating the receiving of a revelation, see the Appendix (§1).

7:5 אֱמֹר֙ אֶל־כָּל־עַ֣ם הָאָ֔רֶץ וְאֶל־הַכֹּהֲנִ֖ים לֵאמֹ֑ר כִּֽי־צַמְתֶּ֨ם וְסָפ֜וֹד בַּחֲמִישִׁ֣י וּבַשְּׁבִיעִ֗י וְזֶה֙ שִׁבְעִ֣ים שָׁנָ֔ה הֲצ֥וֹם צַמְתֻּ֖נִי אָֽנִי׃

אֱמֹר֙ אֶל־כָּל־עַ֣ם הָאָ֔רֶץ וְאֶל־הַכֹּהֲנִ֖ים לֵאמֹ֑ר. Qal impv 2 m s and inf cstr √אמר. On the phrase עַם הָאָ֫רֶץ, see Hag 2:4.

כִּֽי־צַמְתֶּ֨ם וְסָפ֜וֹד בַּחֲמִישִׁ֣י וּבַשְּׁבִיעִ֗י וְזֶה֙ שִׁבְעִ֣ים שָׁנָ֔ה. Qal *qatal* 2 m pl √צום, Qal inf abs √ספד. The introductory כִּי has a temporal sense of "when" (WB §445). On the infinitive absolute continuing a finite verb, see verse 3 and Hag 1:6. Months are sometimes indicated with the ordinal number alone, omitting the noun חֹ֫דֶשׁ (see Hag 1:15a). On the use of זֶה, and the function of the phrase וְזֶה֙ שִׁבְעִ֣ים שָׁנָ֔ה as an adverbial accusative of time, see verse 3. The use of the singular noun שָׁנָה with the number "seventy" is not unusual (see 1:12).

הֲצ֥וֹם צַמְתֻּ֖נִי אָֽנִי. Qal inf abs and *qatal* 2 m pl √צום with 1 c s pronoun suffix. The interrogative *he* can introduce rhetorical questions in addition to true inquiries and in such cases can take on an exclamatory sense (JM §161b). It would be possible, then, to translate this clause as a statement ("Indeed, you did not fast for me!") rather than a question. On the "paranomastic" construction of an infinitive absolute with a finite form of the same verb root, see 6:15. This is one of only three instances in the HB of a *(we)qatal* 2 m pl form with a pronoun suffix (also הֶעֱלִיתֻנוּ in Num 20:5 and 21:5), in which the final *mem* is absent, reflecting an earlier form of the verb (JM §62a). Pronoun suffixes need not be understood as accusatives (JM §125ba; Muraoka 1979) and in some cases can have the value of a dative. In this case הֲצוֹם צַמְתֻּנִי means "Did you indeed fast *for me*?" The function of אָנִי is puzzling at first, but in fact independent pronouns do occur in apposition to a pronoun suffix, such as in Gen 27:34 בָּרְכֵנִי גַם־אָנִי "bless me too" (see further JM §146d). The question as such does not imply a criticism of the practice of fasting in general but rather questions whether the motivation for it during the previous seventy years was one of devotion to YHWH.

7:6 וְכִ֥י תֹאכְל֖וּ וְכִ֣י תִשְׁתּ֑וּ הֲל֤וֹא אַתֶּם֙ הָאֹ֣כְלִ֔ים וְאַתֶּ֖ם הַשֹּׁתִֽים׃

וְכִי תֹאכְלוּ וְכִי תִשְׁתּוּ. Qal *yiqtol* 2 m pl √אכל and √שׁתה. On כִּי as "when" and on the interrogative *he*, see verse 5. The temporal perspective of verse 5 was retrospective, hence one could translate the *yiqtols* as habitual past tenses: "When you *would eat* and *drink*."

הֲלוֹא אַתֶּם הָאֹכְלִים וְאַתֶּם הַשֹּׁתִים. Qal ptc m pl √אכל and √שׁתה. The RSV's translation is typical ("Do you not eat for yourselves and drink for yourselves?") but cannot be justified grammatically, since the phrase is nominal rather than verbal (a predicative participle is negated by אֵין, not לֹא; MNK §20.3.1ii1) and there is nothing approximating the *dativus commodi* here. The participles are to be understood substantivally (cf. JM §137l1) and the entire question is rather to be translated, "And when you would eat and drink, were you not the ones eating and drinking?" It is a rhetorical question expecting an affirmative answer but it has the nature of a riddle (Wolters 2014: 221). It affirms the people's own volitional choice in their typical behavior of eating and drinking; no one "compelled" them to do such things. By the same token, their participation in fasting rites should also have been viewed as voluntary rather than obligatory (as is implied by the question of v. 3), and should only have been freely engaged in out of devotion to YHWH (v. 5).

7:7 הֲלוֹא אֶת־הַדְּבָרִים אֲשֶׁר קָרָא יְהוָה בְּיַד הַנְּבִיאִים הָרִאשֹׁנִים בִּהְיוֹת יְרוּשָׁלִַם יֹשֶׁבֶת וּשְׁלֵוָה וְעָרֶיהָ סְבִיבֹתֶיהָ וְהַנֶּגֶב וְהַשְּׁפֵלָה יֹשֵׁב׃ פ

הֲלוֹא אֶת־הַדְּבָרִים אֲשֶׁר קָרָא יְהוָה. Qal *qatal* 3 m s √קרא. הֲ and הֲלוֹא have introduced a series of rhetorical questions in verses 5 and 6, and thus one might expect הֲלוֹא here likewise to introduce an additional rhetorical question (Wolters 2014: 222). However, the lack of a verb to govern אֶת־הַדְּבָרִים is perplexing. It is disputable whether אֶת can mark the nominative case (see Hag 2:5 and Rogland 2007b). Some suggest that the particle is functioning as a demonstrative (Wolters 2014: 223; JM §125j). Literary explanations have also been proposed, for instance that this is simply an example of anacoluthon (e.g. Muraoka 1985: 155) or aposiopesis with either a past or present tense of √שׁמע to be supplied (so GKC §117l). The last-mentioned seems the most plausible since we find אֶת־הַדְּבָרִים as the object of the verb √שׁמע in verse 12 and 8:9. Moreover, from a rhetorical standpoint this would powerfully complement the case of aposiopesis in 6:15, which dramatically trailed off: וְהָיָה אִם־שָׁמ֣וֹעַ תִּשְׁמְע֔וּן בְּק֖וֹל יְהוָ֥ה אֱלֹהֵיכֶֽם׃ "And if you will indeed listen to the voice of YHWH your God. . . ." It appears that Zech 7:7 is the follow up to 6:15's challenge: "The words which YHWH proclaimed . . . didn't (you indeed listen to them) . . . ?" The answer implied by the context is "no."

בְּיַד֙ הַנְּבִיאִ֣ים הָרִאשֹׁנִ֔ים. On the phrase הַנְּבִיאִים הָרִאשֹׁנִים "the earlier prophets," see 1:4, and on the prepositional phrase בְּיַד, see Hag 1:1.

בִּהְי֣וֹת יְרוּשָׁלַ֗͏ִם יֹשֶׁ֙בֶת֙ וּשְׁלֵוָ֔ה וְעָרֶ֖יהָ סְבִיבֹתֶ֑יהָ וְהַנֶּ֥גֶב וְהַשְּׁפֵלָ֖ה יֹשֵֽׁב. Qal inf cstr √היה with a בְּ preposition, Qal ptc f s and m s √ישׁב. On √ישׁב with the sense of "to be inhabited," see 1:11. The parallel with שְׁלֵוָה suggests that the participle יֹשֶׁבֶת is functioning adjectivally (cf. JM §121a). Wolters (2014: 224) rightly notes that the relatively rare adjective שָׁלֵו (8×) means "peaceful, at ease" rather than "prosperous" (see the BH lexica and Jastrow, 1578). The expression is parallel to וְהִנֵּה כָל־הָאָ֖רֶץ יֹשֶׁ֥בֶת וְשֹׁקָֽטֶת in 1:11, and the adjective indeed occurs with שֹׁקֶטֶת "quiet" in 1 Chron 4:40 וְהָאָ֜רֶץ רַחֲבַ֤ת יָדַ֙יִם֙ וְשֹׁקֶ֣טֶת וּשְׁלֵוָ֔ה "And the land was broad, and quiet and at ease"; cf. also Jer 49:31 אֶל־גּ֣וֹי שְׁלֵ֔יו יוֹשֵׁ֣ב לָבֶ֔טַח "to a nation at ease, dwelling securely." The question refers to the prosperous times of Israel's past when not only Jerusalem but the surrounding cities and regions were inhabited. There is no textual support for emending יֹשֵׁב to the plural יָשְׁבוּ (cf. *BHQ*). A verb following a plural subject is typically plural as well, but the verb can be singular when the subject nouns are viewed as a single concept (JM §150p); here "the Negev and the Shephelah" are viewed as one entity, viz. the surrounding territory under Jerusalem's domain.

[8]And the word of YHWH came to Zechariah:

[9]Thus YHWH Tsevaot said, "Judge true judgment, and act with faithful love and compassion for each other.

[10]Do not oppress the widow and the orphan, the resident alien and the indigent person, and do not devise evil against one another in your hearts."

7:8 וַֽיְהִי֙ דְּבַר־יְהוָ֔ה אֶל־זְכַרְיָ֖ה לֵאמֹֽר׃

Qal *wayyiqtol* 3 m s √היה, Qal inf cstr √אמר. Wolters (2014: 224) argues that the use of לֵאמֹר is "unusual" here since this "reception formula" is not followed by direct discourse but rather by the "messenger formula" in v. 9, even though he admits that this is indeed "not unusual" in Zech 1–8 (8:1-2, 18-19) and is attested in Haggai as well (1:1-2; 2:10-11). In fact, many examples of the two formulae in immediate succession can be found, particularly in the book of Jeremiah. While the "reception formula" very frequently introduces direct discourse, it displays other uses as well (see the Appendix §1).

7:9 כֹּה אָמַר יְהוָה צְבָאוֹת לֵאמֹר מִשְׁפַּט אֱמֶת שְׁפֹטוּ
וְחֶסֶד וְרַחֲמִים עֲשׂוּ אִישׁ אֶת־אָחִיו׃

כֹּה אָמַר יְהוָה צְבָאוֹת לֵאמֹר. Qal *qatal* 3 m s and inf cstr √אמר. See verse 8 regarding the successive prophetic formulae.

מִשְׁפַּט אֱמֶת שְׁפֹטוּ וְחֶסֶד וְרַחֲמִים עֲשׂוּ אִישׁ אֶת־אָחִיו. Qal impv 2 m pl √שפט (pausal form) and √עשׂה. The noun אֱמֶת is a קֶטֶלֶת form (segolized *qatilt* formation) derived from the root √אמן in which the weak *nun* of the root has been assimilated (JM §97Be). The "cognate accusative" or "accusative of the internal object," whereby a verb governs a noun derived from the same root, is a common form of Hebrew expression (see 1:2), and the collocation of the verb √שפט with the noun מִשְׁפָּט occurs a number of times (in some instances occurring as a double accusative; e.g., Deut 16:18; 1 Kgs 3:28; Lam 3:59; Ezek 16:38). The phrase מִשְׁפַּט אֱמֶת also occurs in Ezek 18:8 and in both instances has the sense of "true justice," as opposed to a legal rendering influenced by bribes or threats; the construct phrase is to be understood as an attributive genitive (see Hag 2:12). On the use of אִישׁ with רֵעַ or אָח to express reciprocity, see Hag 2:22.

7:10 וְאַלְמָנָה וְיָתוֹם גֵּר וְעָנִי אַל־תַּעֲשֹׁקוּ וְרָעַת אִישׁ
אָחִיו אַל־תַּחְשְׁבוּ בִּלְבַבְכֶם׃

וְאַלְמָנָה וְיָתוֹם גֵּר וְעָנִי אַל־תַּעֲשֹׁקוּ. Qal jussive 2 m pl √עשק (pausal form). The verb √עשק can refer both to foreign oppression of the people of Israel and to acts of social injustice perpetrated by the people of Israel themselves (Swart, 557). The trio of "widow," "orphan," and "resident alien" is highly Deuteronomic (Deut 10:18; 14:29; 16:11, 14; 24:17, 19, 20, 21; 26:12, 13; 27:19; see also Ps 94:6; Jer 7:6; 22:3; Ezek 22:7; Mal 3:5), and the verb √עשק also occurs in the injunctions of Deut 24 regarding these easily exploited social classes (Deut 24:14). Stead (232–36) makes a plausible case for the intertextual influence of Jeremiah's "temple sermon" (Jer 7) on Zech 7, and the present clause could indeed be shaped by Jer 7:6 גֵּר יָתוֹם וְאַלְמָנָה לֹא תַעֲשֹׁקוּ "You must not oppress a resident alien, orphan, or widow." However, the addition of עָנִי "poor" to the collocation is unique to this verse and is more likely influenced directly by Deut 24 itself (Deut 24:12, 14, 15).

וְרָעַת אִישׁ אָחִיו אַל־תַּחְשְׁבוּ בִּלְבַבְכֶם. Qal jussive 2 m pl √חשב. The direct object רָעַת אִישׁ אָחִיו "the evil of a man and his neighbor" must mean "evil against one another." This is an extension of the syntagm of reciprocity (see Hag 2:22).

[11]For they refused to give attention, and they set a stubborn shoulder, and their ears they made unresponsive so that they could not hear.

[12]And their heart they made flint so that they could not hear the Torah or the words that YHWH Tsevaot sent by his spirit via the earlier prophets, so that there came great wrath from YHWH Tsevaot.

[13]And just as he called and they did not listen, so they would call and I would not listen, YHWH Tsevaot said.

[14]And I kept blowing them to all the nations which they did not know, and the land was made desolate behind them, with no one crossing or returning, and they turned a desirable land into a desolation.

7:11 וַיְמָאֲנוּ לְהַקְשִׁיב וַיִּתְּנוּ כָתֵף סֹרָרֶת וְאָזְנֵיהֶם הִכְבִּידוּ מִשְּׁמוֹעַ׃

וַיְמָאֲנוּ לְהַקְשִׁיב וַיִּתְּנוּ כָתֵף סֹרָרֶת. Piel *wayyiqtol* 3 m pl √מאן, Hifil inf cstr √קשב with לְ-preposition, Qal *wayyiqtol* 3 m pl √נתן, Qal ptc f s √סרר. The exhortations of verses 9-10 take on additional urgency when set in contrast to the Israelites' past record of disobedience introduced here and discussed over the following verses. Piel √מאן almost always takes an infinitival complement. Hifil √קשב can occur with "ears" in the sense of "to cause one's ears to be attentive to," but more commonly it occurs without an accusative (e.g., 1 Sam 15:22; 2 Chron 20:15; 33:10). The identical statement וַיִּתְּנוּ כָתֵף סֹרָרֶת "and they set a stubborn shoulder" occurs in Neh 9:29. This verse provides motivation for the exhortation of verses 9-10, and thus the *wayyiqtol* form in this case seems to have an explanatory nuance of "for, because" (JM §118j).

וְאָזְנֵיהֶם הִכְבִּידוּ מִשְּׁמוֹעַ. Hifil *qatal* 3 c pl √כבד, Qal inf cstr √שמע with prefixed מִן. The preposition מִן is often attached to an infinitive construct in contexts implying cessation or prevention, indicating a negative consequence or purpose (BDB, 583, #7b; see Hag 2:16), thus: "so that (they) could not hear." Switching to a *qatal* verb after the preceding *wayyiqtol* forms allows the direct objects here and in verse 12a to be fronted, thereby placing the focus on the two entities responsible for the people's disobedient response in previous generations: "their ears" and "their heart." By making these unresponsive, the people stopped "hearing" YHWH's words, in contrast to the famous summons of the *Shema* (Deut 6:4-9).

7:12 וְלִבָּם שָׂמוּ שָׁמִיר מִשְּׁמוֹעַ אֶת־הַתּוֹרָה וְאֶת־
הַדְּבָרִים אֲשֶׁר שָׁלַח יְהוָה צְבָאוֹת בְּרוּחוֹ בְּיַד
הַנְּבִיאִים הָרִאשֹׁנִים וַיְהִי קֶצֶף גָּדוֹל מֵאֵת יְהוָה
צְבָאוֹת׃

וְלִבָּם שָׂמוּ שָׁמִיר מִשְּׁמוֹעַ אֶת־הַתּוֹרָה וְאֶת־הַדְּבָרִים. Qal *qatal* 3 c pl √שׂים, Qal inf cstr √שמע with מִן preposition. On the fronting of the direct object, see verse 11. No special significance should be placed upon the fact that לֵב is singular; out of hundreds of occurrences with pronominal suffixes the noun is almost never plural (only Ps 125:4 and Isa 44:18). The verb √שׂים can take a double accusative (BDB, 964, #5b) with the sense of "making" or "turning" one entity into something else. The rare word שָׁמִיר is typically glossed as "adamant" or "diamond," and while the precise identification of the substance may be uncertain, it is clear in any event that it refers to something hard and impenetrable (Jer 17:1; Ezek 3:9). On the use of מִן with an infinitive construct, see verse 11.

וְאֶת־הַדְּבָרִים אֲשֶׁר שָׁלַח יְהוָה צְבָאוֹת בְּרוּחוֹ בְּיַד הַנְּבִיאִים הָרִאשֹׁנִים. Qal *qatal* 3 m s √שלח. On בְּיַד, see Hag 1:1, and on הַנְּבִיאִים הָרִאשֹׁנִים, see 1:4.

וַיְהִי קֶצֶף גָּדוֹל מֵאֵת יְהוָה צְבָאוֹת. Qal *wayyiqtol* 3 m s √היה. The *wayyiqtol* form expresses logical consecution here: "So that/with the result that there came great wrath . . ." (JM §118h–i).

7:13 וַיְהִי כַאֲשֶׁר־קָרָא וְלֹא שָׁמֵעוּ כֵּן יִקְרְאוּ וְלֹא אֶשְׁמָע אָמַר יְהוָה צְבָאוֹת׃

וַיְהִי כַאֲשֶׁר־קָרָא וְלֹא שָׁמֵעוּ. Qal *wayyiqtol* 3 m s √היה, Qal *qatal* 3 m s √קרא and Qal *qatal* 3 c pl √שמע (pausal form). The *qatal* forms are to be taken as "global" past tenses summarizing multiple events that occurred over a period of time (see v. 3 and Hag 1:2). כַּאֲשֶׁר is the standard particle for introducing a comparative statement, which is often completed with a כֵּן-clause (JM §174a–b; BDB, 455, #1b, d).

כֵּן יִקְרְאוּ וְלֹא אֶשְׁמָע. Qal *yiqtol* 3 m pl √קרא, Qal *yiqtol* 1 c s √שמע. On the switch from third person references to YHWH to his speaking in the first person, see the Excursus on 2:12-13. These *yiqtol* forms are taken by some as future-referring (e.g., Meyers and Meyers, 395, 404), but the general thrust of the text is one of recounting Israel's history of disobedience. Wolters (2014: 226) seeks to resolve the apparent conundrum by translating this clause as a quotation: "And just as he called, and they did not listen, so 'they will call and I will not listen' (the LORD of armies said)." A simpler solution is to interpret the *yiqtols* as past-iterative in nature (contra Rogland 2003: 109): "so they would call and I would not listen."

אָמַר יְהוָה צְבָאוֹת. Qal *qatal* 3 m s √אמר.

7:14 וְאֵסָעֲרֵם עַל כָּל־הַגּוֹיִם אֲשֶׁר לֹא־יְדָעוּם וְהָאָרֶץ נָשַׁמָּה אַחֲרֵיהֶם מֵעֹבֵר וּמִשָּׁב וַיָּשִׂימוּ אֶרֶץ־חֶמְדָּה לְשַׁמָּה׃ פ

וְאֵסָעֲרֵם עַל כָּל־הַגּוֹיִם אֲשֶׁר לֹא־יְדָעוּם. Piel *yiqtol* 1 c s √סער with *vav* and 3 m pl pronoun suffix, Qal *qatal* 3 c pl √ידע with 3 m pl pronoun suffix. The form וְאֵסָעֲרֵם is sometimes taken as a future (e.g., LXX's καὶ ἐκβαλῶ), but the following verbal forms are past tenses. Some suggest repointing this to a *wayyiqtol* form (cf. Vulg: *et dispersi*), but a past-iterative interpretation is fitting (Rogland 2003: 109; *BHQ*, 140*), particularly in light of the preceding past-iterative *yiqtols* (see v. 13). This is the only instance of √סער in the Piel, but the related *binyanim* and noun cognates suggest a meaning related to "storming" or "blowing" (cf. Jonah 1:11 הַיָּם הוֹלֵךְ וְסֹעֵר). By itself the relative clause הַגּוֹיִם אֲשֶׁר לֹא־יְדָעוּם is ambiguous and could indicate "nations whom they (viz. the Israelites) did not know" (with the pronoun suffix on the verb referring to הַגּוֹיִם) or "nations who did not know them (viz. the Israelites)" (cf. Wolters 2014: 227). A comparison with the expression elsewhere unambiguously favors the first option, i.e., the Israelites are to be understood as the subject of the verb √ידע: Deut 28:36 אֶל־גּוֹי אֲשֶׁר לֹא־יָדַעְתָּ אַתָּה "to a nation whom you do not know"; Jer 9:15 וַהֲפִצוֹתִים בַּגּוֹיִם אֲשֶׁר לֹא יָדְעוּ הֵמָּה וַאֲבוֹתָם "And I will scatter them among the nations whom they nor their fathers have known."

וְהָאָרֶץ נָשַׁמָּה אַחֲרֵיהֶם מֵעֹבֵר וּמִשָּׁב. Nifal *qatal* 3 f s √שׁמם, Qal ptc m s √עבר and √שׁוב with מִן preposition. אֶרֶץ occurs as the subject of Nifal √שׁמם a number of times with the meaning of "to be(come) desolate" (Jer 12:11; Ezek 29:12; 30:7; 32:15; 36:14; 36:35). אַחֲרֵיהֶם "after them" is a pregnant temporal construction (cf. GKC §119gg) implying the notion of expulsion from the land; after the Israelites had been exiled, the land became desolate. The participles עֹבֵר and שָׁב are substantival, indicating "one who crosses" and "one who returns," the idea being those who "come and go," i.e., "traverse" (Ezek 35:7; Zech 9:8). The preposition מִן can have a privative sense that approximates the meaning of "without" (BDB, 578, #1b).

וַיָּשִׂימוּ אֶרֶץ־חֶמְדָּה לְשַׁמָּה. Qal *wayyiqtol* 3 m pl √שׂים. On the noun חֶמְדָּה, cf. Hag 2:7. אֶרֶץ־חֶמְדָּה is an attributive genitive (see Hag 2:12): "a desirable land." The verb √שׂים can express the transformation of one entity into something else not only with a double accusative (see v. 12) but also with an accusative and a לְ-phrase as prepositional complement (BDB, 964, #5a): "And they turned a desirable land into a desolation." The 3 m pl verb could possibly be considered a "vague personal subject" (JM §155b), that is, an impersonal construction to be translated with the passive voice ("And the desirable land was made into a desolation"), but that would create some redundancy with the preceding clause. It seems preferable to take the Israelites as the subject of the 3 m pl verb, with the purpose of the clause being to ascribe personal responsibility to them for the destruction that came upon "the desirable land."

1*And the word of YHWH Tsevaot came:*

2*Thus has YHWH Tsevaot said, "I have been zealous with great zeal for Zion, and with great rage I have been zealous for her."*

3*Thus has YHWH said: "I have returned to Zion, and I will dwell in the midst of Jerusalem, and Jerusalem will be named 'The Truthful City,' and the mountain of YHWH Tsevaot 'The Holy Mountain.'"*

[4]Thus has YHWH Tsevaot said, "Old men and old women will again sit in the plazas of Jerusalem, each one with his staff in his hand, on account of abundant days,

[5]and the plazas of the city will be filled with lads and lasses playing in her plazas."

[6]Thus has YHWH Tsevaot said, "Though it should seem impossible to the remnant of this people in those days, should it also seem impossible to me?" Oracle of YHWH Tsevaot.

[7]Thus has YHWH Tsevaot said, "Behold, I am going to save my people from the land of the east and from the land of the west.

[8]And I will bring them and they will dwell in the midst of Jerusalem, and they will be my people and I will be their God, in truth and in righteousness."

8:1 וַיְהִ֛י דְּבַר־יְהוָ֥ה צְבָא֖וֹת לֵאמֹֽר׃

Qal *wayyiqtol* 3 m s √היה, Qal inf cstr √אמר.

8:2 כֹּ֥ה אָמַ֖ר יְהוָ֣ה צְבָא֑וֹת קִנֵּ֥אתִי לְצִיּ֖וֹן קִנְאָ֣ה גְדוֹלָ֑ה וְחֵמָ֥ה גְדוֹלָ֖ה קִנֵּ֥אתִי לָֽהּ׃

כֹּ֥ה אָמַ֖ר יְהוָ֣ה צְבָא֑וֹת. Qal *qatal* 3 m s √אמר. On the use of the messenger formula immediately following the reception formula, see 7:8 and the Appendix.

קִנֵּ֥אתִי לְצִיּ֖וֹן קִנְאָ֣ה גְדוֹלָ֑ה. Piel *qatal* 1 c s √קנא. This "cognate accusative" (see 1:2) is an "intratextual" reference to 1:14 (see Introduction §3), with לְצִיּוֹן alone instead of לִירוּשָׁלַ֖ם וּלְצִיּוֹן.

וְחֵמָ֥ה גְדוֹלָ֖ה קִנֵּ֥אתִי לָֽהּ. Piel *qatal* 1 c s √קנא. The noun חֵמָה means "wrath," and one might be initially inclined to understand this to be directed toward the enemies of Zion (cf. 1:15). However, there is no mention of the nations' hostility toward Zion in Zech 7–8, and the close similarity with the preceding clause, in which YHWH's קִנְאָה גְדוֹלָה is directed toward his people, suggests that his חֵמָה גְדוֹלָה should be so understood as well. As Wolters aptly remarks (2014: 232), "paradoxical as it may seem, it is a matter of common experience that a person can be very angry with someone they deeply love, especially if the love relationship has been recently betrayed." Indeed, Zech 1–8 does not refrain from mentioning YHWH's anger against his people elsewhere (1:15; 7:12; 8:14)

8:3 כֹּ֤ה אָמַר֙ יְהוָ֔ה שַׁ֣בְתִּי אֶל־צִיּ֔וֹן וְשָׁכַנְתִּ֖י בְּת֣וֹךְ
יְרוּשָׁלָ֑͏ִם וְנִקְרְאָ֤ה יְרוּשָׁלַ֙͏ִם֙ עִ֣יר־הָֽאֱמֶ֔ת וְהַר־יְהוָ֥ה
צְבָא֖וֹת הַ֥ר הַקֹּֽדֶשׁ׃ ס

כֹּ֤ה אָמַר֙ יְהוָ֔ה. Qal *qatal* 3 m s √אמר.

שַׁ֣בְתִּי אֶל־צִיּ֔וֹן. Qal *qatal* 1 c s √שׁוב. As with the similar statement in 1:16, it is unnecessary to understand שַׁבְתִּי as a future-referring "prophetic perfect" (Rogland 2003: 108): YHWH's "return" has already taken place, but the effects of this will be realized in the progression of time.

וְשָׁכַנְתִּ֖י בְּת֣וֹךְ יְרוּשָׁלָ֑͏ִם. Qal *weqatal* 1 c s √שׁכן. On the expression, see 2:14.

וְנִקְרְאָ֤ה יְרוּשָׁלַ֙͏ִם֙ עִ֣יר־הָֽאֱמֶ֔ת וְהַר־יְהוָ֥ה צְבָא֖וֹת הַ֥ר הַקֹּֽדֶשׁ. Qal *weqatal* 3 f s √קרא. "Verb gapping," or the eliding of a verb from one colon in the next, is a common feature of BH poetry (Watson 1984: 48). According to O'Connor (124) this occurs only in poetry. If true, this would indicate a poetic character to the line. The phrase עִיר־הָאֱמֶת is a neologism in the HB. The noun אֱמֶת can indicate both "truth" and "faithfulness" (BDB, 54), and while the latter sense would certainly be fitting here (and is reflected in most renderings), the former is intended when used of people in Zech 7–8, urging the people to "speak" or "judge" truthfully (see 7:9; 8:16), and thus is to be preferred here. On עִיר־הָאֱמֶת "the Truthful City" and הַר הַקֹּדֶשׁ "the Holy Mountain" as attributive genitives, see Hag 2:12.

8:4 כֹּ֤ה אָמַר֙ יְהוָ֣ה צְבָא֔וֹת עֹ֤ד יֵֽשְׁבוּ֙ זְקֵנִ֣ים וּזְקֵנ֔וֹת
בִּרְחֹב֖וֹת יְרוּשָׁלָ֑͏ִם וְאִ֧ישׁ מִשְׁעַנְתּ֛וֹ בְּיָד֖וֹ מֵרֹ֥ב יָמִֽים׃

כֹּ֤ה אָמַר֙ יְהוָ֣ה צְבָא֔וֹת. Qal *qatal* 3 m s √אמר.

עֹ֤ד יֵֽשְׁבוּ֙ זְקֵנִ֣ים וּזְקֵנ֔וֹת בִּרְחֹב֖וֹת יְרוּשָׁלָ֑͏ִם וְאִ֧ישׁ מִשְׁעַנְתּ֛וֹ בְּיָד֖וֹ מֵרֹ֥ב יָמִֽים. Qal *yiqtol* 3 m pl √ישׁב. In contrast to several other occurrences in Zech 1–8 (1:11; 2:8, 11; 3:8; 7:7), √ישׁב is to be understood here in the sense of "to sit" rather than "to dwell, inhabit." The adjective זָקֵן "old" is used substantivally in the phrase זְקֵנִים וּזְקֵנוֹת for "old (men) and old (women)." רְחֹבוֹת is often translated as "streets," but the term indicates open spaces such as plazas or city squares (BDB, 932; *HALOT*, 1212–13) rather than a road or path for traveling akin to דֶּרֶךְ.

וְאִ֛ישׁ מִשְׁעַנְתּ֥וֹ בְּיָד֖וֹ מֵרֹ֥ב יָמִֽים. The noun אִישׁ can have a distributive sense of "each one" (BDB, 36; WB §131; JM §147d). The preposition מִן's meaning "out (of)" is often extended to indicate the origin or cause of something, and the combination מֵרֹב is particularly common for expressing "from/out of the abundance of → on account of/due to the abundance of" (BDB, 579–80, #2e–f; e.g., Gen 16:10; 1 Sam 1:16).

8:5 וּרְחֹב֤וֹת הָעִיר֙ יִמָּ֣לְא֔וּ יְלָדִ֖ים וִֽילָד֑וֹת מְשַׂחֲקִ֖ים בִּרְחֹבֹתֶֽיהָ׃ ס

Nifal *yiqtol* 3 m pl √מלא, Piel ptc m pl √שחק. On רְחוֹב, see verse 4. A verb typically agrees with the first member of a construct chain (the *nomen regens*), and thus the verb is plural, agreeing with רְחֹבוֹת rather than הָעִיר (see 6:13). A verb in the passive voice can take an accusative object (JM §128), which in the case of Nifal √מלא indicates the object with which something is "filled" (BDB, 570). The attributive participle מְשַׂחֲקִים agrees in gender with the masculine יְלָדִים rather than the feminine יְלָדוֹת, which is normal for BH (JM §148a). The final בִּרְחֹבֹתֶיהָ is redundant but is probably intended as an *inclusio* with וּרְחֹבוֹת הָעִיר (cf. Meyers and Meyers, 416).

8:6 כֹּ֥ה אָמַר֮ יְהוָ֣ה צְבָאוֹת֒ כִּ֣י יִפָּלֵ֗א בְּעֵינֵי֙ שְׁאֵרִית֙ הָעָ֣ם הַזֶּ֔ה בַּיָּמִ֖ים הָהֵ֑ם גַּם־בְּעֵינַי֙ יִפָּלֵ֔א נְאֻ֖ם יְהוָ֥ה צְבָאֽוֹת׃ פ

כֹּה אָמַר֮ יְהוָה צְבָאוֹת. Qal *qatal* 3 m s √אמר.

כִּי יִפָּלֵא בְּעֵינֵי֙ שְׁאֵרִית֙ הָעָם הַזֶּה בַּיָּמִים הָהֵם גַּם־בְּעֵינַי֙ יִפָּלֵא נְאֻם יְהוָה צְבָאוֹת. Nifal *yiqtol* 3 m s √פלא. One might possibly interpret כִּי as a conditional, but a concessive use is more widely accepted (JM §171b; WB §448; AC §4.3.4h, §5.2.12). Here Nifal √פלא with בְּעֵינַיִם has the sense of "to seem impossible," as in 2 Sam 13:2 וַיִּפָּלֵא בְּעֵינֵי אַמְנוֹן לַעֲשׂוֹת לָהּ מְאוּמָה "And it seemed impossible to Amnon to do anything to her." On the noun שְׁאֵרִית, see Hag 1:12.

8:7 כֹּ֣ה אָמַר֮ יְהוָ֣ה צְבָאוֹת֒ הִנְנִ֤י מוֹשִׁ֙יעַ֙ אֶת־עַמִּ֔י
מֵאֶ֥רֶץ מִזְרָ֖ח וּמֵאֶ֥רֶץ מְב֥וֹא הַשָּֽׁמֶשׁ׃

כֹּה אָמַר֮ יְהוָה צְבָאוֹת. Qal *qatal* 3 m s √אמר.

הִנְנִי מוֹשִׁיעַ אֶת־עַמִּי מֵאֶרֶץ מִזְרָח וּמֵאֶרֶץ מְבוֹא הַשָּׁמֶשׁ. Hifil ptc m s √ישׁע. On the participle indicating the imminent future, see Hag 2:6. The term מָבוֹא can mean "entrance" or "entering" (BDB, 99–100, #1–2), but when used of the sun it refers to the place of its setting, most typically in the phrase מְבוֹא הַשֶּׁמֶשׁ (sometimes by מָבוֹא alone as in Ps 104:19). As such it can become purely directional for "west(ward)" (Arnold, 617), as here where it stands in contrast to מִזְרָח "east." Genitive constructions such as אֶרֶץ מִזְרָח and אֶרֶץ מְבוֹא הַשֶּׁמֶשׁ can be used to refer to a place (JM §129f11).

Hifil √ישׁע occurs often with the preposition מִן, indicating salvation from one's enemies or the "hand" of one's enemies, from one's troubles, from evil men, from the sword, and so on. What is not at all common is for the object of מִן to be a location or place, which only occurs in Jer 30:10 כִּי הִנְנִי מוֹשִׁיעֲךָ מֵרָחוֹק וְאֶת־זַרְעֲךָ מֵאֶרֶץ שִׁבְיָם "for I am going to save you from afar, and your offspring from the land of their captivity" (= 46:27). This comports with Stead's observation (241–43) that Jeremiah 30–31 is an important intertext of Zechariah 8.

8:8 וְהֵבֵאתִ֣י אֹתָ֔ם וְשָׁכְנ֖וּ בְּת֣וֹךְ יְרוּשָׁלָ֑͏ִם וְהָֽיוּ־לִ֣י לְעָ֗ם
וַאֲנִ֞י אֶהְיֶ֥ה לָהֶ֛ם לֵֽאלֹהִ֖ים בֶּאֱמֶ֥ת וּבִצְדָקָֽה׃ ס

וְהֵבֵאתִי אֹתָם. Hifil *weqatal* 1 c s √בוא.

וְשָׁכְנוּ בְּתוֹךְ יְרוּשָׁלָ͏ִם. Qal *weqatal* 3 c pl √שׁכן. On the verb √שׁכן, see 2:14-15. This verse presents an interesting twist on 2:15, to which it refers intratextually, in that here the people (instead of YHWH) are said to "dwell in the midst of Jerusalem." On the covenant formula וְהָיוּ־לִי לְעָם, see 2:15.

וְהָיוּ־לִי לְעָם וַאֲנִי אֶהְיֶה לָהֶם לֵאלֹהִים בֶּאֱמֶת וּבִצְדָקָה. Qal *weqatal* 3 c pl and Qal *yiqtol* 1 c s √היה. On the syntax of √היה, see 2:15. On the "pleonastic pronoun" אֲנִי, see 2:9 [ET: v. 5]. In this instance the noun אֱמֶת probably has the sense of "faithfulness" (cf. 8:3). BH is fond of short prepositional phrases such as בֶּאֱמֶת, בִּצְדָקָה, בְּמִשְׁפָּט, בְּקֹדֶשׁ, and so on, which often serve as adverbial modifiers.

Thus when YHWH says, "I will be God to them in faithfulness and in righteousness" the meaning is: "I will be God to them *faithfully* and *justly*."

9 *Thus has YHWH Tsevaot said, "Let your hands be strong, O you who are listening in these days to these words from the mouth of the prophets: 'When the house of YHWH Tsevaot is reestablished, the temple must be built!'*

10 *For before those days there were no wages of a man, and there were no wages of a beast, and the one who went out and the one who came in had no peace from the foe, and I kept sending each and every man against his neighbor.*

11 *But now, not as former days, I belong to the remnant of this people"—oracle of YHWH Tsevaot—*

12 *"but instead, there will be a crop of peace: the vine will give its fruit and the earth will give its produce and the heavens will give their dew and I will give all these things as an inheritance to the remnant of this people.*

13 *And it will happen, just as you were a curse among the nations, O house of Judah and Israel, so I will save you, and you will be a blessing. Do not fear! Let your hands be strong."*

14 *For thus has YHWH Tsevaot said, "Just as I purposed to do harm to you when your fathers provoked me to wrath,"—YHWH Tsevaot has said—"and I did not relent,*

15 *so I have again purposed in these days to do good to Jerusalem and the house of Judah. Do not fear!"*

8:9 כֹּה־אָמַר֮ יְהוָ֣ה צְבָאוֹת֒ תֶּחֱזַ֣קְנָה יְדֵיכֶ֔ם הַשֹּׁמְעִים֙ בַּיָּמִ֣ים הָאֵ֔לֶּה אֵ֚ת הַדְּבָרִ֣ים הָאֵ֔לֶּה מִפִּי֙ הַנְּבִיאִ֔ים אֲשֶׁ֗ר בְּי֙וֹם֙ יֻסַּ֣ד בֵּית־יְהוָ֥ה צְבָא֖וֹת הַהֵיכָ֥ל לְהִבָּנֽוֹת׃

כֹּה־אָמַר֮ יְהוָ֣ה צְבָאוֹת֒. Qal *qatal* 3ms √אמר.

תֶּחֱזַ֣קְנָה יְדֵיכֶ֔ם. Qal jussive 3 f pl √חזק. The idiom means "to take courage" (*HALOT*, 303, #2).

הַשֹּׁמְעִים֙ בַּיָּמִ֣ים הָאֵ֔לֶּה. Qal ptc m pl √שמע with def art. The substantival participle הַשֹּׁמְעִים is a vocative, hence the presence of the definite article (see 3:2). References to הַיָּמִים הָהֵם and הַיָּמִים הָהֵמָּה are fairly common in the HB in speaking of either the past or the future, but occurrences of הַיָּמִים הָאֵלֶּה are rare (Esth 1:5; 9:26-28; Zech 8:15). The usage in 8:15 is strongly suggestive of a contemporary frame of reference ("these days") rather than the future or past, and hence הַשֹּׁמְעִים בַּיָּמִים הָאֵלֶּה is best rendered, "O you who are listening in these days."

אֶת הַדְּבָרִים הָאֵלֶּה מִפִּי הַנְּבִיאִים אֲשֶׁר בְּיוֹם יֻסַּד בֵּית־יְהוָה צְבָאוֹת הַהֵיכָל לְהִבָּנוֹת. Pual *qatal* 3 m s or inf cstr √יסד (cf. JM §56b), Nifal inf cstr √בנה. The noun פֶּה "mouth" is a *singulare tantum* in BH (JM §90f), that is, it always occurs in the singular except for two instances (Jdg 3:16; Prov 5:4; cf. Ps 149:6) where it is used metaphorically for a "two-edged sword." אֲשֶׁר presents a challenge since it is not easily understood either as a conjunction or a relative particle. Wolters (2014: 237–38) proposes that an error of transposition misread an original *בְּיוֹם אֲשֶׁר יֻסַּד. Most frequently a verb of existence is understood:

> ". . . from the mouths of the prophets who *were present* when the foundation was laid for the rebuilding of the temple, the house of the LORD of hosts." (NRSV)

Or the JPS is arguably even closer to the MT:

> ". . . from the mouth of the prophets that *were* in the day that the foundation of the house of the LORD of hosts was laid, even the temple, that it might be built." (JPS)

The translation of the MT proposed here is based on the following factors:

First, אֲשֶׁר is understood as the Greek ὅτι *recitativum* (BDB, 83, #8a). Hence it may be ignored in translation and the following text treated as a quotation of the words of the prophets. It is translated above as a direct quotation, but it could also be understood as an indirect citation without affecting the basic analysis offered here.

Second, though often interpreted as indicating purpose, the final infinitive construct לְהִבָּנוֹת is understood as expressing obligation (JM §124l; GKC §114h, k–l; WO §36.2.3f; WB §196), a usage typical of LBH and QH (Qimron, 70–72; for a different perspective, see Ehrensvärd 2002: 18, 33–34). Thus הַהֵיכָל לְהִבָּנוֹת is the main clause and is to be translated, "The temple must be built!"

Third, בְּיוֹם יֻסַּד בֵּית־יְהוָה is treated as a temporal clause subordinate to the following statement of obligation. Both the verbal and cognate nominal forms of √יסד are associated with the laying of foundations, with the verb sometimes referring to laying new foundations and sometimes to repairing or restoring existing ones (see Hag 2:18; cf. Meyers and Meyers, 420–21). According to the rules of Hebrew morphology, יֻסַּד could be parsed either as *qatal* or as an infinitive construct, though the only acknowledged Pual infinitive construct in BH is of a III-*he* verb (Ps 132:1 עֻנּוֹתוֹ). Nevertheless, an infinitival analysis seems preferable since the בְּיוֹם plus infinitive construct syntagm is an extremely common way of creating a subordinate temporal phrase, whereas בְּיוֹם is only occasionally followed by a *qatal* form (Exod 6:28; Lev 7:35; Num 3:1; Deut 4:15; 2 Sam 22:1; Pss 18:1; 59:17; 102:3; 138:3). On either analysis the phrase is to be interpreted as grammatically subordinate to הַהֵיכָל לְהִבָּנוֹת.

Putting these components together, it emerges that the prophets are saying, "When the house of YHWH Tsevaot is reestablished, the temple must be built!" It is to be understood as an exhortation not to rest content with the initial work of repairing the temple's foundations but to continue on to complete the rebuilding project. Occurring some two years into the renewed rebuilding efforts, these words encourage the people to persevere in what they had set out initially to accomplish.

8:10 כִּ֗י לִפְנֵי֙ הַיָּמִ֣ים הָהֵ֔ם שְׂכַ֤ר הָֽאָדָם֙ לֹ֣א נִהְיָ֔ה וּשְׂכַ֥ר הַבְּהֵמָ֖ה אֵינֶ֑נָּה וְלַיּוֹצֵ֨א וְלַבָּ֥א אֵין־שָׁל֙וֹם֙ מִן־הַצָּ֔ר וַאֲשַׁלַּ֥ח אֶת־כָּל־הָאָדָ֖ם אִ֥ישׁ בְּרֵעֵֽהוּ׃

כִּ֗י לִפְנֵי֙ הַיָּמִ֣ים הָהֵ֔ם שְׂכַ֤ר הָֽאָדָם֙ לֹ֣א נִהְיָ֔ה וּשְׂכַ֥ר הַבְּהֵמָ֖ה אֵינֶ֑נָּה. Nifal *qatal* 3 m s √היה. The compound preposition לִפְנֵי "before" has both spatial and temporal functions. "Before those days (הַיָּמִים הָהֵם)" refers to the days prior to the reestablishing of the temple mentioned in verse 9b. The Nifal לֹא נִהְיָה occurs in parallelism with the particle of nonexistence אֵין and in this context appears to be functionally equivalent (BDB, 227, #1). The phrase שְׂכַר הַבְּהֵמָה refers to the amount needed to hire out a beast of burden.

וְלַיּוֹצֵ֨א וְלַבָּ֥א אֵין־שָׁל֙וֹם֙ מִן־הַצָּ֔ר. Qal ptc m s √יצא and √בוא with לְ and def art. The collocation of √יצא and √בוא can refer to going about one's daily tasks (e.g., Deut 28:6, 19; 31:2; Ps 121:8), but in this context they are substantival participles referring probably to travelers (cf. Josh 6:1; 1 Kgs 15:17), i.e., merchants who would engage in trade. The יֵשׁ/אֵין plus לְ syntagm indicates possession or the lack thereof (cf. on Hag 2:17). צַר (here with vowel lengthening due to pause) can refer either to impersonal "distress" or to a personal "adversary, foe" (BDB, 865); either option would work, since the former suits the economic nature of the troubles in the preceding clause while the latter fits well with the following clause.

וָֽאֲשַׁלַּח אֶת־כָּל־הָאָדָם אִישׁ בְּרֵעֵהוּ. Piel *yiqtol* 1 c s √שׁלח with attached *vav*. The verb is not to be repointed as a *wayyiqtol* form (cf. *BHQ*, 140) but rather indicates a past-iterative situation: "I kept sending" (see 7:13-14). On the use of אִישׁ . . . רֵעֵהוּ as an indication of reciprocity, see Hag 2:22; in this case the expression is supplemented by כָּל־הָאָדָם "every man." In this context it probably refers to constant banditry and raiding which caused trading to cease and thus crippled the economy (cf. Petersen, 306).

8:11 וְעַתָּה לֹא כַיָּמִים הָרִאשֹׁנִים אֲנִי לִשְׁאֵרִית הָעָם הַזֶּה נְאֻם יְהוָה צְבָאוֹת׃

It is well known that וְעַתָּה is frequently used in a logical sense of "now then" or "therefore," but this verse begins to draw a contrast between the earlier times of hardship (v. 10) and better times to come (vv. 11-12), and hence וְעַתָּה is best understood as temporal in nature: "But *now* . . ." The phrase כַּיָּמִים הָרִאשֹׁנִים only occurs here and in Deut 10:10, where it has the sense of "as at the first time" (RSV). It seems to be one of several BH expressions for "as before, as formerly," e.g., כִּתְמוֹל שִׁלְשׁוֹם (Gen 31:2), כִּתְמוֹל שִׁלְשֹׁם גַּם־תְּמוֹל גַּם־הַיּוֹם (Exod 5:14), כְּאֶתְמוֹל שִׁלְשׁוֹם (1 Sam 14:21), כָּרִאשֹׁנָה (Deut 9:18), כַּאֲשֶׁר בָּרִאשֹׁנָה (Josh 8:5), בָּרִאשׁוֹן (Joel 2:23). On שְׁאֵרִית, see Hag 1:12. Wolters (2014: 241–42) finds the text difficult and proposes a radically different reading of *אַנְחִיל שְׁאֵרִית in the place of the MT's אֲנִי לִשְׁאֵרִית, but this is a highly speculative proposal lacking any kind of text-critical support. The MT is fully understandable, since the לְ often serves to create a genitive relationship of possession (see Hag 1:1): "And now, not as formerly, *I belong* to the remnant of this people" (similarly Meyers and Meyers, 422, who emphasize the covenantal nature of the expression; cf. v. 8).

8:12 כִּי־זֶרַע הַשָּׁלוֹם הַגֶּפֶן תִּתֵּן פִּרְיָהּ וְהָאָרֶץ תִּתֵּן אֶת־יְבוּלָהּ וְהַשָּׁמַיִם יִתְּנוּ טַלָּם וְהִנְחַלְתִּי אֶת־שְׁאֵרִית הָעָם הַזֶּה אֶת־כָּל־אֵלֶּה׃

כִּי־זֶרַע הַשָּׁלוֹם. Here זֶרַע refers neither to "seed" nor even to "sowing" (so many commentators) but rather to a "crop" (Ehrlich, 341; see BDB, 282, #2c–e). זֶרַע הַשָּׁלוֹם could an attributive genitive (see Hag 2:12), i.e., "crop of peace" → "peaceful crop," but it could also be a genitive of result or purpose (WB §44a–b; MNK §25.4.5i–ii; AC §2.2.8–9), i.e., "crop of peace" → "crop that brings peace." The statement stands in contrast to the economic hardships implied by וְלַיּוֹצֵא וְלַבָּא אֵין־שָׁלוֹם מִן־הַצָּר in verse 10.

The introductory כִּי is often taken as asseverative (Petersen, 306), which would be suitable if the text were implying an oath (cf. JM §165b, e): "(I surely swear) that (there will be) a crop of peace." But verses 11-12 are the first of a series of comparative-contrastive statements (n.b., כֵּן . . . כַּאֲשֶׁר in v. 13 and vv. 14-15), and it seems preferable to understand the כִּי in relation to לֹא כַיָּמִים הָרִאשֹׁנִים in verse 11; after a negative the particle occurs with the sense of "but (rather)" (JM §172c; BDB, 474, #3e), thus: "But now, not as formerly . . . but rather. . . ." Some translations such as the RSV supply a verb of being: "For *there shall be* a sowing of peace." This is legitimate since one does encounter nominal clauses in which a subject pronoun has been omitted (JM §154b–c), e.g., Esth 1:6 חוּר ׀ כַּרְפַּס וּתְכֵלֶת . . . מִטּוֹת ׀ זָהָב "*There was* white stuff of fine linen, and blue . . . *there were* couches of gold." The nominal clause is neutral as to time (JM §153), and hence it is a contextual decision whether to supply a past, present, or future tense verb; in this case it refers to the future.

הַגֶּפֶן תִּתֵּן פִּרְיָהּ וְהָאָרֶץ תִּתֵּן אֶת־יְבוּלָהּ וְהַשָּׁמַיִם יִתְּנוּ טַלָּם. Qal *yiqtol* 3 f s √נתן, Qal *yiqtol* 3 m pl √נתן. These short clauses provide details as to what the "peaceful crop" will consist of. The statement contrasts with Hag 1:10 כָּלְאוּ שָׁמַיִם מִטָּל וְהָאָרֶץ כָּלְאָה יְבוּלָהּ, which drew upon the covenant blessings and curses of Lev 26 and Deut 28. In this instance one might have expected verbal ellipsis if the text were poetic in nature (see v. 3).

וְהִנְחַלְתִּי אֶת־שְׁאֵרִית הָעָם הַזֶּה אֶת־כָּל־אֵלֶּה. Hifil *weqatal* 1 c s √נחל. The verb can take a double accusative to indicate "to give X as an inheritance to Y" (BDB, 635, #2).

8:13 וְהָיָה כַּאֲשֶׁר הֱיִיתֶם קְלָלָה בַּגּוֹיִם בֵּית יְהוּדָה וּבֵית
יִשְׂרָאֵל כֵּן אוֹשִׁיעַ אֶתְכֶם וִהְיִיתֶם בְּרָכָה אַל־
תִּירָאוּ תֶּחֱזַקְנָה יְדֵיכֶם׃ ס

וְהָיָה כַּאֲשֶׁר הֱיִיתֶם קְלָלָה בַּגּוֹיִם בֵּית יְהוּדָה וּבֵית יִשְׂרָאֵל. Qal *weqatal* 3 m s and *qatal* 2 m pl √היה. The noun קְלָלָה "curse" here (and frequently) conveys the sense of being reviled or denigrated due to one's shameful and despised state (Aitken, 248–49). בֵּית יְהוּדָה וּבֵית יִשְׂרָאֵל are to be understood as vocatives (so, e.g., RSV). The reference not only to "Judah" but to "Israel" (the northern kingdom) is not an error (cf. 2:2 [ET: 1:19]) but rather evokes an established prophetic theme of the reunification of the northern and southern kingdoms (Ezek 37:16; Amos 5:6, Obad 18; Zech 10:6).

כֵּן אוֹשִׁיעַ אֶתְכֶם וִהְיִיתֶם בְּרָכָה. Hifil *yiqtol* 1 c s √ישׁע, Qal *weqatal* 2 m pl √היה. The nouns קְלָלָה and בְּרָכָה occur together a number of times (Aitken, 129–30), and we have an intentional contrast: הֱיִיתֶם קְלָלָה . . . וִהְיִיתֶם בְּרָכָה. The noun בְּרָכָה has a range of meanings but in this instance it is to be read antithetically to קְלָלָה in the preceding clause, and as such it is not to be understood as a blessing conferred but rather as "an object of blessing," i.e., of praise, which is a semantic development of the word in LBH (Aitken, 131). The antithetical structure also suggests that the prepositional phrase בַּגּוֹיִם is to be supplied: "And you will be an object of blessing/praise *among the nations*."

אַל־תִּירָאוּ תֶּחֱזַקְנָה יְדֵיכֶם. Qal jussive 2 m pl √ירא, Qal jussive 3 f pl √חזק. On תֶּחֱזַקְנָה יְדֵיכֶם as expressing "to take courage," see verse 9.

8:14 כִּי כֹה אָמַר יְהוָה צְבָאוֹת כַּאֲשֶׁר זָמַמְתִּי לְהָרַע לָכֶם בְּהַקְצִיף אֲבֹתֵיכֶם אֹתִי אָמַר יְהוָה צְבָאוֹת וְלֹא נִחָמְתִּי׃

כִּי כֹה אָמַר יְהוָה צְבָאוֹת. Qal *qatal* 3 m s √אמר.

כַּאֲשֶׁר זָמַמְתִּי לְהָרַע לָכֶם בְּהַקְצִיף אֲבֹתֵיכֶם אֹתִי. Qal *qatal* 1 c s √זמם, Hifil inf cstr √רעע with לְ-preposition, Hifil inf cstr √קצף with בְּ-preposition. A comparative structure is frequently marked with כַּאֲשֶׁר . . . כֵּן, and the comparison begun in this verse is not completed until the following verse. On √זמם, which often takes an infinitive construct as complement, see 1:6.

אָמַר יְהוָה צְבָאוֹת. Qal *qatal* 3 m s √אמר. This is to be understood as a variant of the "messenger formula" earlier in the verse (see Appendix §2).

וְלֹא נִחָמְתִּי. Nifal *qatal* 1 c s √נחם. On the morphological ambiguity of Nifal and Piel √נחם, see 1:17. While there are some instances of Piel √נחם used absolutely (i.e., without a direct object [BDB, 638]), most often it takes an accusative, whereas the Nifal frequently does occur without an object in the sense of "to relent" or "to change one's mind" (e.g., Exod 13:17; 32:12, 14; 1 Sam 15:29; Ps 110:4; Jer 4:28; Amos 7:3), which is the sense here.

8:15 כֵּ֣ן שַׁ֣בְתִּי זָמַ֗מְתִּי בַּיָּמִ֥ים הָאֵ֛לֶּה לְהֵיטִ֥יב אֶת־
יְרוּשָׁלִַ֖ם וְאֶת־בֵּ֣ית יְהוּדָ֑ה אַל־תִּירָֽאוּ׃

Qal *qatal* 1 c s √שׁוב and √זמם, Hifil inf cstr √טוב with לְ-preposition, Qal jussive 2 m pl √ירא. The comparison begun in verse 14 is now completed. On the use of √שׁוב with another verb to mean "to do X again," see 4:1, and on √זמם, see 1:6 and 8:14. On בַּיָּמִים הָאֵלֶּה as "in these days," see verse 9. The stark contrast created in verses 14-15 (כַּאֲשֶׁר זָמַמְתִּי לְהָרַע . . . כֵּן שַׁבְתִּי זָמַמְתִּי . . . לְהֵיטִיב) is reflective of passages such as Deut 28:63 וְהָיָה כַּאֲשֶׁר־שָׂשׂ יְהוָה עֲלֵיכֶם לְהֵיטִיב אֶתְכֶם וּלְהַרְבּוֹת אֶתְכֶם כֵּן יָשִׂישׂ יְהוָה עֲלֵיכֶם לְהַאֲבִיד אֶתְכֶם "And it will be, just as YHWH delighted over you to do good to you and to multiply you, so will YHWH delight over you to destroy you . . ." (cf. Jer 31:2).

[16]These are the things that you should do: Speak truth with one another! Judge truth and peaceable judgment in your gates.

[17]And each one of you, do not devise evil against one another in your heart, and do not love a deceptive oath, for (you must not love or devise) any of these things that I hate"—oracle of YHWH.

8:16 אֵ֥לֶּה הַדְּבָרִ֖ים אֲשֶׁ֣ר תַּֽעֲשׂ֑וּ דַּבְּר֤וּ אֱמֶת֙ אִ֣ישׁ אֶת־
רֵעֵ֔הוּ אֱמֶת֙ וּמִשְׁפַּ֣ט שָׁל֔וֹם שִׁפְט֖וּ בְּשַֽׁעֲרֵיכֶֽם׃

אֵלֶּה הַדְּבָרִים אֲשֶׁר תַּֽעֲשׂוּ. Qal *yiqtol* 2 m pl √עשׂה. The *yiqtol* form has an injunctive sense (JM §113l): "These are the things that you *must do*."

דַּבְּרוּ אֱמֶת אִישׁ אֶת־רֵעֵהוּ אֱמֶת וּמִשְׁפַּט שָׁלוֹם שִׁפְטוּ בְּשַֽׁעֲרֵיכֶם. Piel impv 2 m pl √דבר, Qal impv 2 m pl √שׁפט. The similarities with 7:9 create an *inclusio*, helping to mark off Zech 7–8 as a distinct textual unit (see the introductory remarks to this pericope). On אִישׁ אֶת־רֵעֵהוּ as an expression of reciprocity, see Hag 2:22. The substantive אֱמֶת can function as an adverb "truly" (JM §102d), thus דַּבְּרוּ אֱמֶת could mean either "Speak truly!" or, taking the noun as an accusative object, "Speak truth!" The latter option is to be preferred in light of the following clause (אֱמֶת וּמִשְׁפַּט שָׁלוֹם שִׁפְטוּ) and 7:9 (מִשְׁפַּט

(אֱמֶת שִׁפְטוּ) though in either case the difference in meaning is negligible. The context here and in 7:9 is one of legal justice, indicating that the "speaking with one's neighbor" is to be understood in light of the Decalogue, particularly Exod 20:16 לֹא־תַעֲנֶה בְרֵעֲךָ עֵד שָׁקֶר "you shall not answer as a false witness against your neighbor" (cp. וּשְׁבֻעַת שֶׁקֶר אַל־תֶּאֱהָבוּ "and do not love a false oath," v. 17). The phrase מִשְׁפַּט שָׁלוֹם is best understood as a genitive of result or purpose (see v. 12), i.e., "judgment of peace" → "judgment that brings peace," much like the phrase זֶרַע הַשָּׁלוֹם "crop that brings peace" in verse 12. "Gates" (שְׁעָרִים) represent a city as the place of judgment (Deut 21:19), and the reference to them here is possibly a subtle reflection of Deuteronomy's emphasis on YHWH's "words" being memorialized in the city gates (Deut 6:9; 11:20; cf. on 7:11 for other references to Deut 6:4-9).

8:17 וְאִישׁ | אֶת־רָעַת רֵעֵהוּ אַל־תַּחְשְׁבוּ בִּלְבַבְכֶם
וּשְׁבֻעַת שֶׁקֶר אַל־תֶּאֱהָבוּ כִּי אֶת־כָּל־אֵלֶּה אֲשֶׁר
שָׂנֵאתִי נְאֻם־יְהוָה׃ ס

וְאִישׁ | אֶת־רָעַת רֵעֵהוּ אַל־תַּחְשְׁבוּ בִּלְבַבְכֶם. Qal jussive 2 m pl √חשב. On אִישׁ . . . רֵעֵהוּ as an expression of reciprocity, see Hag 2:22.

וּשְׁבֻעַת שֶׁקֶר אַל־תֶּאֱהָבוּ. Qal jussive 2 m pl √אהב. שְׁבֻעַת שֶׁקֶר "deceptive oath" is an attributive genitive (see Hag 2:12). The book has already proclaimed judgment in 5:3-4 on those "who swear deceptively in YHWH's name" (הַנִּשְׁבָּע בִּשְׁמִי לַשָּׁקֶר).

כִּי אֶת־כָּל־אֵלֶּה אֲשֶׁר שָׂנֵאתִי נְאֻם־יְהוָה. Qal *qatal* 1 c s √שׂנא. The pairing of √אהב and √שׂנא occurs elsewhere in the HB (e.g., Jdg 14:16; 2 Sam 19:7; Ps 45:8; Mal 1:2-3). The particle אֵת is difficult here because it appears to introduce an object clause, but no governing verb is stated. This is taken by some as marking the grammatical subject (e.g., Wolters 2014: 245), allegedly as an "emphatic" means of so doing (e.g., Ehrlich, 341), but the appeal to emphasis is fraught with uncertainty (cf. Muraoka 1985), and the notion that the particle marks the nominative case is problematic (cf. Rogland 2007b: 410–11). It may simply be an instance of anacoluthon (Muraoka 1985: 155), that is, a sentence with logical incoherence due to a grammatical interruption of some kind. It is suggested here that the preceding negative imperatives אַל־תַּחְשְׁבוּ and אַל־תֶּאֱהָבוּ are implied as governing the object clause: "*Do not love or devise* any of these things which I hate."

[18]And the word of YHWH Tsevaot came to me:

[19]Thus has YHWH Tsevaot said, "The fast of the fourth month and the fast of the fifth month and the fast of the seventh month and the fast of the tenth month will become exultation and joy and good appointed times for the house of Judah. But love truth and peace!"

[20]Thus has YHWH Tsevaot said, "Yet again, when peoples come, even the inhabitants of many cities,

[21]the inhabitants of one city shall go to another: 'Let us go continually to supplicate YHWH, and to seek YHWH Tsevaot.' 'Let me also go.'

[22]And many peoples and mighty nations will come to seek YHWH Tsevaot in Jerusalem and to supplicate YHWH."

[23]Thus has YHWH Tsevaot said, "In those days when ten men from all the tongues of the nations show strength, they will seize a Jewish man's garment corner, saying: 'Let us go with you, for we have heard (that) God is with you.'"

8:18 וַיְהִ֛י דְּבַר־יְהוָ֥ה צְבָא֖וֹת אֵלַ֥י לֵאמֹֽר׃

Qal *wayyiqtol* 3 m s √היה, Qal inf cstr √אמר.

8:19 כֹּֽה־אָמַ֞ר יְהוָ֣ה צְבָא֗וֹת צ֣וֹם הָרְבִיעִ֡י וְצ֣וֹם הַחֲמִישִׁ֡י
וְצ֨וֹם הַשְּׁבִיעִ֜י וְצ֣וֹם הָעֲשִׂירִ֗י יִהְיֶ֤ה לְבֵית־יְהוּדָה֙
לְשָׂשׂ֣וֹן וּלְשִׂמְחָ֔ה וּֽלְמֹעֲדִ֖ים טוֹבִ֑ים וְהָאֱמֶ֥ת
וְהַשָּׁל֖וֹם אֱהָֽבוּ׃ פ

כֹּֽה־אָמַ֞ר יְהוָ֣ה צְבָא֗וֹת. Qal *qatal* 3 m s √אמר. On the use of the messenger formula immediately following the reception formula, see 7:8 and the Appendix (§2).

צ֣וֹם הָרְבִיעִ֡י וְצ֣וֹם הַחֲמִישִׁ֡י וְצ֨וֹם הַשְּׁבִיעִ֜י וְצ֣וֹם הָעֲשִׂירִ֗י יִהְיֶ֤ה לְבֵית־יְהוּדָה֙ לְשָׂשׂ֣וֹן וּלְשִׂמְחָ֔ה וּֽלְמֹעֲדִ֖ים טוֹבִ֑ים. Qal *yiqtol* 3 m s √היה. On the use of ordinal numbers to express the month, see Hag 1:15a. The question about ritual fasting posed in 7:3 is finally addressed here, though it is not given a direct answer (Wolters 2014: 246). On possible identifications of these various "fasts" see the exegetical literature. The verb √היה can occur with two לְ-phrases, one indicating the predicate and the other the indirect object (see 2:15). The noun מוֹעֵד means "appointed (time or place)," and can be used for any agreed-upon meeting (1 Sam 20:35), but is very often used more narrowly for one of the divinely ordained festivals (BDB, 417–18).

וְהָאֱמֶת וְהַשָּׁלוֹם אֱהָבוּ. Qal impv 2 m pl √אהב (pausal form). On the morphology of אֱמֶת, see 7:9, and on its rendering as "truth," see 8:3. Abstract nouns often take the definite article, which does not always need to be rendered in translation (see 5:8). The *vav* conjunction is capable of various nuances, and most English translations render the initial *vav* as "so" or "therefore" (e.g., RSV: "Therefore love truth and peace"). But the logic of such a statement is opaque: How does the future transformation of corporate fasts logically imply or call for loving truth and peace? It seems preferable to translate the conjunction as an adversative (so Petersen, 312): "*But* love truth and peace." The adversative nuance serves to turn the focus of the discussion away from the question of ritual fasting and to redirect it to the practice of the Torah from the heart (cf. Wolters 2014: 246), as well as to shift the focus from future occurrences to the present.

8:20 כֹּה אָמַר יְהוָה צְבָאוֹת עֹד אֲשֶׁר יָבֹאוּ עַמִּים
וְיֹשְׁבֵי עָרִים רַבּוֹת׃

כֹּה אָמַר יְהוָה צְבָאוֹת. Qal *qatal* 3 m s √אמר.

עֹד אֲשֶׁר יָבֹאוּ עַמִּים וְיֹשְׁבֵי עָרִים רַבּוֹת. Qal *yiqtol* 3 m pl √בוא, Qal ptc m pl cstr √ישב. The phrase עָרִים רַבּוֹת means "many cities," not "great cities," for the adj רַב means "much, many" far more frequently than "great," and what is more, גָּדוֹל is the adjective used in the HB for describing the size or status of cities (e.g., Jonah 3:2). The feminine adjective רַבּוֹת modifies the (irregular) feminine noun עָרִים rather than the masculine plural participle יֹשְׁבֵי, and thus יֹשְׁבֵי עָרִים רַבּוֹת means "inhabitants of many cities," not "many city dwellers." The *vav* on וְיֹשְׁבֵי עָרִים רַבּוֹת is most likely explicative (WB §434; MNK §40.8.2vii; WO §39.2.4; AC §4.3.3d): "*even* inhabitants of many cities."

The combination of the two particles עֹד אֲשֶׁר has proven extremely problematic here. Some emend the text (e.g., Petersen 316–17) and some translations simply ignore אֲשֶׁר, e.g., RSV: "Thus says the LORD of hosts: Peoples shall yet come, even the inhabitants of many cities." Others supply a future tense verb before אֲשֶׁר, treating it essentially as a conjunction: "Thus says the LORD of hosts, '*It will* yet *be that* peoples will come, even the inhabitants of many cities'" (NASB;

similarly JPS, KJV, Wolters 2014: 249–50; BDB, 83, #8aα). Meyers and Meyers (432, 437–38) suggest that עֹד אֲשֶׁר forms a compound temporal expression akin to כַּאֲשֶׁר "when," though such a compound is not attested elsewhere. Lipiński (42–46), on the other hand, compares verse 20 to verse 23, where he claims that the "messenger formula" is modified adverbially by the following בַּיָּמִים הָהֵמָּה. Accordingly, he argues in verse 20 that עֹד is to be linked with the messenger formula ("Thus YHWH Tsevaot said *again*") and suggests that the following אֲשֶׁר introduces a subordinate clause (cf. Neh 13:19, 22) with *yiqtol* indicating result or purpose. The critical problem with Lipiński's proposal is that an עוֹד following the messenger formula is always syntactically linked with the following clause and never with the formula itself (Jer 33:10, 12; Ezek 20:27; 36:37; Hag 2:6; Zech 1:17; 8:4), and it is also most unlikely that בַּיָּמִים הָהֵמָּה in verse 23 modifies the preceding messenger formula rather than the following verbal clause.

There seem to be only two real possibilities for analyzing the clause as it stands in the MT. The first is to adopt a slight revocalization of the MT from עֹד אֲשֶׁר to עַד אֲשֶׁר, which is a conjunction that occurs quite frequently meaning "until" and is suggested by the Vulgate's *usquequo veniant populi*. In this case, then, verse 20a could be subordinate to the imperative of verse 19: "But love truth and peace . . . (v. 20) *until* peoples come. . . ." We encounter a number of instances elsewhere of the impv followed by עַד (e.g., Gen 38:11; Exod 24:14; Jdg 19:8; Ruth 3:18; 1 Sam 1:23; 14:9; 2 Sam 10:5 [= 1 Chron 19:5]; Ezra 8:29; Ps 110:1; Isa 26:20). The fact that verse 20 opens with the messenger formula does not necessarily speak against this analysis, since there are other instances in which the messenger formula "interrupts" a larger syntactical structure such as in verse 14 (also arguably in vv. 2-3, 11-12). According to such a reading verses 19-20 would be urging faithful living until YHWH begins to draw foreigners into the covenant community on a large scale (cf. vv. 22-23).

While revocalization is tempting, it is made less likely by the nearly identical syntactical structure in verse 4 of the chapter (כֹּה אָמַר יְהוָה צְבָאוֹת עֹד יֵשְׁבוּ זְקֵנִים וּזְקֵנוֹת בִּרְחֹבוֹת יְרוּשָׁלָםִ), where there is no doubt that עֹד has defective spelling and is functioning as an adverbial modifier to the following *yiqtol* verb. Moreover, it does feel rather forced to try and link verse 19 with verse 20 in view of the intervening prophetic formulae in verse 20a and the scribal *petuḥa* placed between the two verses. The second interpretive option for this difficult clause is to take אֲשֶׁר as a temporal conjunction denoting "when" (cf. BDB, 82, #3bα) and to translate, "*Again, when peoples come*, even the inhabitants of many cities, (v. 21) the inhabitants of one city will go to (another) one. . . ." According to this analysis וְהָלְכוּ in verse 21 would form a kind of apodosis to the dependent temporal clause (JM §119ea, §176; WB §440; MNK §21.3.3; AC §4.3.3f; WO §32.2.1b, §38.2b). On the whole, this seems to be the simplest explanation of an already challenging text. This section's theme of foreigners aligning themselves with the people of God is connected with earlier statements in 2:15.

8:21 וְֽהָלְכ֡וּ יֹשְׁבֵ֨י אַחַ֜ת אֶל־אַחַ֗ת לֵאמֹר֙ נֵלְכָ֣ה הָל֔וֹךְ
לְחַלּוֹת֙ אֶת־פְּנֵ֣י יְהוָ֔ה וּלְבַקֵּ֖שׁ אֶת־יְהוָ֣ה צְבָא֑וֹת
אֵלְכָ֖ה גַּם־אָֽנִי׃

וְֽהָלְכ֡וּ יֹשְׁבֵ֨י אַחַ֜ת אֶל־אַחַ֗ת לֵאמֹר֙. Qal *weqatal* 3 c pl √הלך, Qal ptc m pl cstr √ישׁב, Qal inf cstr √אמר. Since the noun עִיר was just mentioned in verse 20 it can be omitted in וְֽהָלְכ֡וּ יֹשְׁבֵ֨י אַחַ֜ת אֶל־אַחַ֗ת "And the dwellers of one (city) shall go to one (city)" (WO §15.2.1b). The infinitive construct לֵאמֹר can introduce discourse even when used in conjunction with a verb of motion or action rather than a verb of speaking (Miller 1996: 188–90), hence there is nothing unusual about its occurrence here with וְהָלְכוּ (contra Wolters 2014: 250).

נֵלְכָ֣ה הָל֔וֹךְ לְחַלּוֹת֙ אֶת־פְּנֵ֣י יְהוָ֔ה וּלְבַקֵּ֖שׁ אֶת־יְהוָ֣ה צְבָא֑וֹת. Qal cohortative 1 c pl and inf abs √הלך, Piel inf cstr √חלה and √בקשׁ with לְ preposition. On √חלה as "to supplicate," see 7:2. Ehrensvärd (2006: 181) appeals to נֵלְכָה הָלוֹךְ to demonstrate that Zech 1–8 makes a more frequent use of the paranomastic construction than is typical for LBH (see 6:15 and Introduction §2), but this is based on a misunderstanding of the syntax in this case: נֵלְכָה הָלוֹךְ is not to be understood here as the paranomastic construction (which does not occur elsewhere with cohortative verbal forms), for the infinitive absolute הָלוֹךְ by itself is a unique syntagm for indicating continuous action (JM §123s; WB §206; BDB, 233, #4c3): "Let us go *always/continually* to supplicate YHWH."

אֵלְכָ֖ה גַּם־אָֽנִי. Qal cohortative 1 c s √הלך. The switch to the 1 c s cohortative אֵלְכָה from the 1 c pl cohortative נֵלְכָה is noteworthy. The singular is perhaps intended to correspond to the *yiqtol* 1 c s inquiry הַאֶבְכֶּה in 7:3 (so Wolters 2014: 250). The addition of the pronoun to the finite verbal form (see 1:9) often occurs in replies to questions or invitations (JM §146a3), and this is to be interpreted as an answer to the preceding invitation, that is, it is an imagined reply from one of the Gentile fearers of YHWH (Meyers and Meyers, 439).

8:22 וּבָ֨אוּ עַמִּ֤ים רַבִּים֙ וְגוֹיִ֣ם עֲצוּמִ֔ים לְבַקֵּ֛שׁ אֶת־יְהוָ֥ה צְבָא֖וֹת בִּירוּשָׁלִָ֑ם וּלְחַלּ֖וֹת אֶת־פְּנֵ֥י יְהוָֽה׃ ס

Qal *weqatal* 3 c pl √בוא, Piel inf cstr √בקשׁ and √חלה with לְ-preposition. Wolters (2014: 250) argues that עֲצוּמִים refers to being "strong in numbers," i.e., "numerous," appealing to the LXX's πολλά. This is possible (BDB, 783, #2), but it creates an unnecessary redundancy between עַמִּים רַבִּים and גּוֹיִם עֲצוּמִים. It is potentially an intertextual reference to Mic 4:3 וְשָׁפַט בֵּין עַמִּים רַבִּים וְהוֹכִיחַ לְגוֹיִם עֲצֻמִים עַד־רָחוֹק "and he will judge between many peoples, and he will make decisions for mighty nations at a distance," the context of which is highly militaristic and would prefer the sense of "mighty." On √חלה, see 7:2.

8:23 כֹּ֣ה אָמַר֮ יְהוָ֣ה צְבָאוֹת֒ בַּיָּמִ֣ים הָהֵ֔מָּה אֲשֶׁ֤ר יַחֲזִ֨יקוּ֙ עֲשָׂרָ֣ה אֲנָשִׁ֔ים מִכֹּ֖ל לְשֹׁנ֣וֹת הַגּוֹיִ֑ם וְהֶחֱזִ֡יקוּ בִּכְנַף֩ אִ֨ישׁ יְהוּדִ֜י לֵאמֹ֗ר נֵֽלְכָה֙ עִמָּכֶ֔ם כִּ֥י שָׁמַ֖עְנוּ אֱלֹהִ֥ים עִמָּכֶֽם׃ ס

כֹּה אָמַר יְהוָה צְבָאוֹת. Qal *qatal* 3 m s √אמר.

בַּיָּמִים הָהֵמָּה אֲשֶׁר יַחֲזִיקוּ עֲשָׂרָה אֲנָשִׁים מִכֹּל לְשֹׁנוֹת הַגּוֹיִם. Hifil *yiqtol* 3 m pl √חזק. LXX renders אֲשֶׁר as "if" (ἐὰν), but BDB calls this "rare and peculiar" (83, #8d). Some simply ignore it in translation (e.g., Meyers and Meyers, 433; Petersen, 318), while others supply "it will be" (e.g., KJV: "In those days it shall come to pass, that ten men shall take hold . . ."). In its current position it is most naturally taken as a relative pronoun modifying "those days" and can be translated as "when" (see BDB, 82, #4b; cf. on the use of אֲשֶׁר in v. 20). The reference to "ten men" probably reflects the Jewish tradition that ten men were the minimum number required to establish a synagogue or to hold an official legal gathering (Lipiński, 44). On the meaning of Hifil √חזק, see the following comment.

וְהֶחֱזִ֨יקוּ בִּכְנַ֜ף אִ֤ישׁ יְהוּדִי֙ לֵאמֹ֔ר. Hifil *weqatal* 3 c pl √חזק, Qal inf cstr √אמר with לְ-preposition. כָּנָף can refer to the corners or extremities of garments (e.g., Num 15:38). Lipiński (43–44) argues that the term יְהוּדִי is best rendered as "Judean" rather than "Jew" (cf. *HALOT*, 394), as he claims that its religious and confessional sense developed much later; for a different view, see Yamauchi (415–17). The repetition of יַחֲזִ֜יקוּ . . . וְהֶחֱזִ֨יקוּ has apparently been viewed as superfluous by some translations, which render both forms with only one English verb (e.g. RSV, ESV, and NASB, though interestingly the NRSV renders both). Presumably וְהֶחֱזִ֨יקוּ is being taken as an instance of resumptive repetition (cf. JM §176b n. 2; Driver, §118 n). However, the differing syntactical constructions of Hifil √חזק correspond to two different senses of the verb (cf. Wolters 2014: 251): יַחֲזִ֜יקוּ without an object represents the LBH idiom "to display strength" (BDB, 304, #1c), whereas וְהֶחֱזִ֨יקוּ, governing an object with the בְּ preposition, means "to take hold of" or "to seize" (BDB, 305, #6). יַחֲזִ֜יקוּ belongs to a dependent relative clause serving as a temporal modifier, while וְהֶחֱזִ֨יקוּ belongs to the main verbal clause, with the *vav* of the verbal form serving as a kind of apodosis (see vv. 20-21): "In those days when ten men . . . *display strength*, they *will seize* the garment corner."

Wolters (2014: 250), who finds the use of the infinitive construct לֵאמֹ֔ר "unusual" here (cf. on 1:7; 7:3, 8; 8:21), explains it in this instance by claiming that "grasping the hem" of a garment is to be understood as a form of prayer or petition, but this is speculative. As noted above, לֵאמֹ֔ר can introduce discourse even with a verb of action (see v. 21), and Miller (1996: 194) notes its usage with verbs such as √אחז and √תפשׂ (1 Kgs 1:51; Gen 39:12; Jer 26:8; 37:13).

נֵֽלְכָה֙ עִמָּכֶ֔ם כִּ֥י שָׁמַ֖עְנוּ אֱלֹהִ֥ים עִמָּכֶֽם. Qal cohortative 1 c pl √הלך, Qal *qatal* 1 c pl √שׁמע. An object clause of the verb √שׁמע is usually introduced with a כִּי (e.g., Gen 14:14; 29:33), but it is not obligatory.

APPENDIX
Prophetic Formulae in Haggai and Zechariah 1–8

This appendix will consider three phrases (and their variants) that occur frequently in Haggai and Zech 1–8, namely דְּבַר־יהוה הָיָה אֶל־, כֹּה אָמַר יהוה, and נְאֻם־יהוה, conventionally known as the "reception formula," "messenger formula," and "oracle formula" respectively. These have been examined several times, most extensively by Meier (273–319), and in a number of studies from the perspective of discourse analysis (e.g., Parunak; Wilt 1999). One should particularly note the studies of Clark (1985, 1988, 1992, 1994), who deals specifically with Haggai and Zechariah.

All three formulae are attested to varying degrees in narrative as well as discourse and occur throughout the chronological strata of BH. Their distribution varies greatly, however. In some books they do not occur at all or only infrequently, whereas in others these formulae can be utilized so frequently as to appear "obtrusive" (Wilt 1999: 303). Although none of the expressions is of late origin, they are particularly well attested in the exilic and postexilic prophets Jeremiah, Ezekiel, Haggai, and Zechariah, and this frequency of usage may be reflective of a Persian-era literary trend (Meier, 290, 309, 313, 315, 319). Parunak (513) notes that there is significant overlap between these three formulae, though each one displays unique features as well. Here we will consider the most relevant semantic, syntactic, and pragmatic features of these formulae as they pertain to Haggai and Zech 1–8.

§1 The "Reception Formula" (RF): דְּבַר־יהוה הָיָה אֶל־

The RF is attested several times in our corpus (Hag 1:1, 3; 2:1, 10, 20; Zech 1:1, 7; 4:8; 6:9; 7:1, 4, 8; 8:1, 18). In the HB it occurs with a number of variations (discussed below), some of which have been attributed to different textual sources, dialectical differences, or diachronic developments (Meier, 314), though such explanations are generally unconvincing. Of the three formulae under discussion in this Excursus, Parunak asserts that the RF is "the one that is the most general, the unmarked one" (501). Along similar lines, Meier (317) says the combination of דָּבָר with the verb √היה is "quite underwhelming in its banality," making its semantic contribution to a text very slight. As he explains, the phrase

> simply means that a communication has occurred. The excessive ordinariness of this phrase may be grasped by inquiring of the alternatives if one wished to be as minimally descriptive as possible when observing that communication had occurred: it is precisely this phrase that would be chosen: "there was a word." (318)

In some instances, particularly in the Night Visions, this "banal" usage is nevertheless helpful, since the number of participants can at times produce confusion as to the identity of the speaker, and the use of the RF clarifies that what is being said is the דְּבַר־יהוה, "the word of YHWH."

In addition to indicating the occurrence of a communicative act, the RF often occurs at the beginning of an oracle (e.g., Hag 1:1; 2:1, 10, 20; Zech 1:1, 7; 6:9; 7:1; 8:1) and can assist in delineating the macrostructure of a text. Additionally, the RF frequently introduces direct discourse or quoted speech, though this cannot be considered an essential function, since several times it is followed by the "messenger formula" כֹּה אָמַר יהוה (e.g., Jer 13:8-9; 24:4-5; 33:1-2, 19-20; 34:12-13; 35:12-13; 37:6-7; 47:1-2; 49:34-35; Hag 1:1-2; 2:10-11; Zech 7:8-9; 8:1-2, 18-19), which can be the actual marker of discourse (see §2).

The functions of the RF just mentioned find confirmation from various semantic and grammatical features of the expression:

§1A

As Parunak (500–501) notes, the RF sometimes occurs with the adverbial use of שֵׁנִית "again" (e.g., Hag 2:20) or with other temporal markings such as date formulae (e.g., Hag 1:1). In such instances the RF corresponds with structural divisions of a text, particularly by serving as an "incipit formula" (cf. Clark 1992: 13). This occurs frequently in our corpus (Hag 1:1; 2:1, 10, 20; Zech 1:1, 7; 6:9; 7:1; 8:1).

§1B

On very rare occasions in the HB the verb √היה is omitted (e.g., Gen 15:4; 1 Kgs 19:9 וְהִנֵּה דְבַר־יְהוָה אֵלָיו "and behold, the word of YHWH [came] to him"), but in the vast majority of instances—including all of its occurrences in our corpus—it utilizes the verb √היה. Both *qatal* and *wayyiqtol* forms are attested:

> Hag 2:10 הָיָה דְּבַר־יְהוָה אֶל־חַגַּי הַנָּבִיא לֵאמֹר: "The word of YHWH came to Haggai the prophet":

> Hag 2:20 וַיְהִי דְבַר־יְהוָה׀ שֵׁנִית אֶל־חַגַּי בְּעֶשְׂרִים וְאַרְבָּעָה לַחֹדֶשׁ לֵאמֹר: "And the word of YHWH came a second time to Haggai the prophet on the twenty-fourth of the month:"

This is typically rendered as "the word of the LORD *came* to . . ." The verb √היה can indeed take on a more dynamic (fientive) sense in this expression (cf. JM §111h–i). It is important to be aware that the RF does not contain a verb of movement (cf. Meyers and Meyers, 7–8), since in the few instances in which the noun דָּבָר is the subject of a verb of motion such as √בוא (Exod 22:8; Jer 17:15; 28:9; 2 Sam 19:12 [ET v. 11] is textually problematic) or Hifil √נגע (e.g., Esth 4:3; 8:17; 9:1), the meaning is different than the RF (cf. Meier, 317).

§1C

The infinitive construct לֵאמֹר occurs in the majority of instances (in 1 Kgs 19:9 it is followed by וַיֹּאמֶר instead of the infinitive construct) in accord with its function of introducing direct discourse. Indeed, Clark (1992: 23) asserts that this is the "highest-level quotative formula" in the Haggai-Zechariah corpus. (See Hag 1:1, and for a more extensive semantic and syntactic discussion of לֵאמֹר, including some comparative Semitic data, see Miller 1996: 163–212.) In some cases the infinitive construct is lacking completely (1 Kgs 13:20; 16:7; 19:9; Jer 42:7; Ezek 1:3; Zech 7:1), since the import of the expression is often simply to mark a true narrative event. In other words, that a word came from YHWH *is* in fact the salient information in certain narratives, rather than the reporting of the content of YHWH's "word." This feature sets the RF apart from the other formulae discussed below, neither of which can be used to narrate the occurrence of a revelatory event.

§1D

Sometimes the RF occurs with no prepositional complement at all (e.g., Zech 8:1 וַיְהִי דְּבַר־יְהוָה צְבָאוֹת לֵאמֹר "And the word of YHWH of hosts came"), but typically it utilizes the preposition אֶל, as in Hag 2:10, 20 (cited above). There is a singular use of עַל in 1 Chron 22:8, indicating the addressee of YHWH's "word" and in a few cases (only 1 Kgs 16:7; Hag 1:1, 3; 2:1) we find the prepositional phrase בְּיַד, e.g., Hag 1:1 הָיָה דְבַר־יְהוָה בְּיַד־חַגַּי הַנָּבִיא "The word of YHWH came by the hand of Haggai the prophet." When בְּיַד occurs it distinguishes an addressee of prophetic revelation (indicated by אֶל) from the agent of that revelation. Although they can often serve interchangeably, particularly with verbs of motion and of speaking, the consistent use of אֶל instead of לְ in the formula is due to the fact that לְ plus the verb √היה would indicate possession (BDB, 226, #II.2.h) rather than the recipient of a communication.

In sum, the RF indicates that communication has occurred, often introduces direct discourse, and may serve to delineate the macrostructure of a text.

§2 The "Messenger Formula" (MF): כֹּה אָמַר יהוה

Meier (279) strongly objects to designating כֹּה אָמַר יהוה as MF, in part because the formula says virtually nothing about the messenger himself but rather specifies the sender of a message. While the terminology may not be the most felicitous, it is maintained here for convenience's sake. The MF occurs more frequently than RF in our corpus (at least 24× vs. 14×: Hag 1:2, 5, 7; 2:6, 11; Zech 1:3, 4, 14, 16, 17; 2:12; 3:7; 6:12; 7:9; 8:2, 3, 4, 6, 7, 9, 14, 19, 20, 23). In some cases we encounter simply אָמַר יהוה without the adverb כֹּה (e.g., Hag 1:8; 2:7, 9; Zech 4:6; 7:13; 8:14; cp. Malachi, which always omits כֹּה except for Mal 1:4), but these are treated here simply as abbreviated forms of the MF (cf. Parunak, 517 n. 26; for a different view, see Clark 1992: 13, 16, 18; 1985: 330, 334).

In general it is clear that, in terms of the formula's meaning and function, it overlaps to a considerable extent with the RF. Indeed, in many cases in Jeremiah and in our corpus the MF immediately follows the RF (Jer 13:8-9; 24:4-5; 33:1-2, 19-20; 34:12-13; 35:12-13; 37:6-7; 47:1-2; 49:34-35; Hag 1:1-2; 2:10-11; Zech 7:8-9; 8:1-2, 18-19). The constituent parts of the MF are, like the RF, fairly bland semantically, involving very common lexemes. Both formulae indicate that a communication act has occurred, identify the message sender, and frequently introduce direct discourse (Meier, 282, 284, 290; see, e.g., Hag 1:2, 5, 7; 2:6, 11; etc.), although the MF does not do so with the same consistency as the RF. Both may help to delineate the structure of a text to some extent. One potential difference between the two formulae is that the MF is sometimes alleged to be a "performative utterance" that is to be translated with a present tense ("YHWH hereby says"; so, e.g., Wagner, 156–57). However, the occasional addition of אֵלַי "to me" to the formula is decisive evidence against a performative analysis (Krispenz). The prophet is simply reporting the fact that God communicated with him, and consequently כֹּה אָמַר יהוה is to be translated with a past tense (Rogland 2003: 120 n. 27).

The following points may be noted by way of contrast between the two formulae:

§2A

The MF can function as a structuring marker at the beginning of an oracle, but it can appear anywhere in a discourse (Parunak, 505; cf. Clark 1985). Because of this, Meier (293, 297–98) rightly cautions that "its structuring value is variable, unpredictable, often dispensable." Thus, one cannot rely on the MF alone as a marker of textual structure and must look for additional factors.

§2B

In some instances the MF is preceded by inferential particles such as כִּי (Hag 2:6; Zech 2:12; 8:14), לָכֵן (Zech 1:16) or וְעַתָּה (Hag 1:5), which is not possible in most instances of the RF since it is typically verb-initial due to the use of the *wayyiqtol* form. The significance of these inferential particles for understanding the discourse functions of the MF is disputed. Clark (1992: 13–14) argues that their occurrence "overrides [the MF's] function as the opening marker of a higher level unit and causes it to be rank-shifted downward to function within a lower-level unit." On the other hand, Parunak argues that when such particles occur,

> we should analyze the discourse relations among propositions introduced by [the MF] as though the formula were not there. The function of the formula is not to participate in the discourse structure marked by conjunctions such as 'for'

> and 'therefore' (or in other such relations among the associated propositions), but rather to mark significant breaks in the oracle and to call attention to the divine origin of the expressions that they introduce. (506)

Parunak's study focuses on such usages in Jeremiah, but an examination of the data in Haggai and Zech 1–8 bears out his conclusion.

§2C

The MF occasionally attests prepositional phrases with אֶל indicating either recipient/addressee (Ezek 34:20) or the subject matter of an utterance ("concerning/about": 2 Kgs 19:32; Isa 29:22; 37:33; Jer 22:11, 18; 27:19; 29:16, 31; 32:36; Ezek 21:33). Considering the number of overall attestations of the MF, one is perhaps most impressed with how infrequently an addressee is mentioned. One factor in this regard is that the MF regularly occurs in the middle or at the conclusion of oracles, where the mention of the addressee would be unnecessary, in contrast to the RF's more regular occurrence at the beginning of an oracle, where the mention of the addressee would be salient information.

§2D

In our corpus, the RF almost always occurs with the Tetragrammaton alone, and in only three instances (Zech 7:4; 8:1, 18) adds the moniker צְבָאוֹת (on which, see Hag 1:2). In contrast, Haggai, Zechariah, and Malachi have a strong preference for using יהוה צְבָאוֹת with the MF, accounting for over a third of its total occurrences in the HB (Meyers and Meyers, 18). This general pattern of distribution between the two formulae suggests that צְבָאוֹת was not added in the MF for rhetorical purposes but rather would appear to justify Rendsburg's claim (2012: 334) that the MF with the addition of צְבָאוֹת is an LBH development (possibly influenced by Jeremiah).

§2E

The quotation-introducing function of the MF is less pronounced than the RF. Clark (1992: 23), e.g., terms it a "second-ranking quotative formula." One indication of this can be seen in that it is only occasionally followed by infinitive construct לֵאמֹר (e.g., Jer 28:2; 29:25; 30:2; 44:25; Hag 1:2; Zech 6:12; 7:9).

§2F

In some instances in our corpus the use of the MF is strikingly repetitive within a single textual unit (Hag 1:2, 5, 7; Zech 1:3, 4, 14, 16, 17; 8:2, 3, 4, 6, 7, 9, 14, 19, 20, 23; cf. Meier, 297–98). Meier suggests that there is a kind of "emphatic," "austere," "and ultimately bombastic" tone to the phrase (290–91) and that it essentially functions as an emphasizing literary device. Such a description involves a good deal of subjectivity, and a more precise analysis is given by Parunak, who says that the MF "validates the message that it introduces as a word from Yahweh" (505; cf. 515).

As Meier notes (276–77), the MF is not a grammatically necessary feature of prophetic writing; when it does occur, it often supplies redundant information. From the features discussed above it should be clear that the MF is not used exclusively—perhaps not even primarily—for marking textual structure or introducing a quotation. The highly repetitive use of the MF in some pericopae indeed suggests a rhetorically motivated usage, such as the "validating function" proposed by Parunak (see discussion above).

§3 The "Oracle Formula" (OF): נְאֻם יהוה

The OF is the most frequent of the three formulae in Haggai and Zech 1–8, occurring thirty-two times (e.g., Hag 1:9, 13; 2:4 *tris*, 8, 9, 14, 17, 23 *tris*; Zech 1:3, 4, 16; 2:9, 10 *bis*, 14; 3:9, 10; 5:4; 8:6, 11, 17). Grammatically it is also the simplest one occurring in the HB, as it consists merely of the construct noun נְאֻם followed by YHWH or another personal agent (David, Balaam, etc.). Often times it occurs simply with the Tetragrammaton (Hag 1:13; 2:4 *bis*, 14, 17, 23; Zech 1:4; 2:9-10, 14; 8:17) but in roughly a third of its occurrences with the addition of צְבָאוֹת (Hag 1:9; 2:4, 8-9, 23 *bis*; Zech 1:3, 16; 3:9-10; 5:4; 8:6, 11). Unlike the RF and MF, it is never followed by the infinitive construct לֵאמֹר and does not function as a marker of direct discourse. It has often been asserted rather casually that the primary function of the OF is to close an oracle (cf. Aune, 90), though in fact it frequently occurs mid-oracle (BDB, 610; Parunak, 510–11; Meier, 222, 225). This can happen with such frequency that it leads Wilt to observe that its use can sometimes appear "obtrusive" (1999: 303; see the introductory remarks on Zechariah 7–8 and on Hag 2:4). There is increasing scholarly acknowledgment that marking structure (whether closure or otherwise) is not the sole function of the OF. Meier judiciously summarizes : "context is the only means of discriminating when נאם יהוה functions as a marker of the close of speech, the beginning of speech, or a medial marker in the midst of speech. . . . It is a word that does not provide macrostructural significance but simply reinforces what is already present in the context" (309–10).

Regarding the morphology of נְאֻם, some have argued that it is a construct form of the passive participle from the verb √נאם, but this cannot be insisted upon in light of Jer 23:31 וַיִּנְאֲמוּ נְאֻם "and they uttered an oracle" (the only occurrence of the verb), where נְאֻם cannot be so construed. Moreover, in light of the abundant attestation of the noun (ca. 376×) versus one occurrence of the verb, it is clear that the verb is denominative (BDB, 610), that is, the verb was derived from the noun, rather than the other way around.

The meaning of נְאֻם has proven difficult to nail down. Meier (298–308) provides a thorough comparative-philological discussion of the term's etymology, which remains uncertain. The term's elusiveness can be observed in how the OF has been rendered in translation. Both in ancient versions (LXX, Tg; see Meier, 311–12) and modern translations (Wilt 1999) it is sometimes indistinguishable from other prophetic formulae. This handbook follows the proposal of Wilt (1999: 303), who advocates the rendering of "oracle" for נְאֻם, which has the advantages of being a noun like נְאֻם and of being a marked reference to religious speech "suggesting mysterious communication between God and man," though in fact it occurs with human communication as well (cf. Meyer, 312). It seems clear that it belongs to the semantic field of terms referring specifically to revelatory acts, for example, of prophetic or of divinatory communication, such as קֶסֶם "divination," מַשָּׂא "utterance," נְבוּאָה "prophecy," and the like.

Clark (1992: 21) identifies three functions, all illustrated in Haggai and Zechariah 1–8:

1. נְאֻם can mark closure on different levels (e.g., paragraph, unit, subunit).
2. נְאֻם reinforces other discourse markers, regardless of location in a unit, though there is a general tendency for it to occur "at or near the end of units" (Clark 1992: 13).
3. נְאֻם has a climax-marking function.

Parunak (508–9, 515) discusses several more (possibly overlapping) functions and characterizes נְאֻם יהוה as "a low-level focus formula and often marks a summary that is expanded either earlier or later in the same paragraph." As he explains in more detail, as a marker of focus the OF is

> a highly local highlighting of a clause or phrase that merits the recipient's special attention. It sets off the clause or phrase with which it is associated from the context, as though it were printed in italics or boldface type . . . [The OF] may be viewed as highlighting a statement that will be amplified in what follows. In other words, it marks the head of a discourse unit. (511–12)

Analogous to Parunak's discussion of the MF, Wilt suggests that the OF has a sort of "validating function":

> The expression functions not to identify the speaker of a discourse . . . but to insist on the authenticity of the words as having YHWH as their source and as being transmitted in legitimate prophetic tradition. In exilic and post-exilic texts, its use, especially its repeated use in brief passages, emphasizes the validity and importance of the prophetic word. (1999: 302)

This is a more helpful description than Clark's rather vague assertion that the OF is a possible marker of "climax" in a text. Of the three formulae discussed here, the OF appears to possess the least value as a structural marker (Meier, 225) but the greatest rhetorical force.

GLOSSARY

adversative—a constituent, phrase or clause that expresses opposition or antithesis.

allomorph—variant forms of what is presumed to be a single morpheme, such as the English prefix "*in-*" in words such as infrequent, impassible, ignoble, etc.

anacoluthon—a break or abrupt change from a grammatical construction in the middle of an utterance resulting in an incomplete or ungrammatical statement.

anaphoric—a grammatical element that refers to something previously mentioned in a text.

anarthrous—lacking a definite article.

apocopated—the shortening of a word, e.g., by dropping a final consonant or reducing vowel length.

aposiopesis—a statement left incomplete for rhetorical effect, e.g., "Why I oughta . . . !"

asyndetic—coordination of nouns or clauses without the use of coordinating conjunctions.

clause—the combination of at least two sentence constituents, one functioning as a subject and the other as a predicate.

complement—an obligatory constituent modifying the verb in a clause.

constituent—individual words or phrases that have a syntactic role in a phrase or clause.

dativus commodi/dativus ethicus—a construction (in many languages in the dative case) indicating that the subject of an action is affected by it or benefits from it in some way.

disjunction/disjunctive—a structure which establishes a contrast or choice between alternatives.

dittography—a copyist's error of accidentally writing the same word twice.

epexegetical—an additional explanation of the previous word, phrase, or clause.

hapax/hapax legomenon—a word or form occurring only once in a text corpus.

hysteron proteron—"the latter first"—i.e. the inversion of the expected or logical order of elements, typically for rhetorical effect, e.g., "Let us die, and charge into the thick of the fight!"

inclusio—a literary bracketing device consisting of an envelope or book-end structure, which places similar words or phrases at the beginning and end of unit.

injunctive—a statement of command or exhortation; a directive.

intransitive—a verb that does not take a direct object; cf. "transitive."

Leitwort—German: a "leading word,"—i.e. a word that is intentionally repeated in a text to provide literary structure or for rhetorical effect.

locative—expressing the place at or in which an action occurs or a situation exists.

mil'el—when a Hebrew word is accented on the penultimate syllable.

mil'ra—when a Hebrew word is accented on the final syllable (the ultima).

nomen rectum—Latin: "the governed noun"—i.e. the substantive (or substantives) following the initial substantive of a construct chain; compare *nomen regens.*

nomen regens—Latin: "the governing noun"—i.e. the initial substantive in a Hebrew construct chain, which is in the construct state; compare *nomen rectum.*

nominalized—a word or phrase that has acquired the syntactic status of a noun or noun phrase, such as a participle functioning as a noun, e.g., "one who kills" = "a killer."

pars pro toto—"a part for the whole"; a literary device whereby the mention of one component represents its entirety, e.g., "I bought a new set of wheels" = "I bought a new car."

phrase—a word or words that form a distinct constituent in a clause; these can consist of different types of grammatical forms, resulting in "noun/nominal phrases," "adjectival phrases," "prepositional phrases," etc.

pleonastic—grammatical elements which are unnecessary or redundant since the same information is already expressed by other clause constituents.

singulare tantum—words that only occur in their singular form.

stative verb—a verb describing a state or quality rather than an action.

substantival—see "nominalized."

transitive—a verb that takes a direct object; compare "intransitive."

vocative—a form used for direct address; in many languages this is marked by a distinct grammatical case.

volitive—a verbal mood indicating a command, request, urging, etc.

WORKS CITED

Ackroyd, Peter. 1950–1951. "Studies in the Book of Haggai." *Journal of Jewish Studies* 2: 1–13, 163–76.

———. 1968. *Exile and Restoration: A Study of Hebrew Thought of the Sixth Century B.C.* Philadelphia: Westminster.

Aitken, James K. 2007. *The Semantics of Blessing and Cursing in Ancient Hebrew.* Ancient Near Eastern Studies Supplement Series 23. Leuven: Peeters.

Alden, Robert L. 2007. מַחֲלָצוֹת. Page 917 in *NIDOTTE* 3.

Alter, Robert. 1999. *The David Story: A Translation with Commentary of 1 and 2 Samuel.* New York: Norton.

Andersen, Francis I., and David N. Freedman. 1980. *Hosea.* Anchor Bible 24. Garden City: Doubleday.

Arnold, Bill T. 2007. בוא. Pages 615–18 in *NIDOTTE* 1.

Assis, Elie. 2010. "Zechariah 8 as Revision and Digest of Zechariah 1–7." *Journal of Hebrew Scriptures* 10, no. 15.

Aune, David. 1983. *Prophecy in Early Christianity and the Ancient Mediterranean World.* Grand Rapids: Eerdmans.

Averbeck, Richard E. 2007a. טמא. Pages 365–76 in *NIDOTTE* 2.

———. 2007b. צהר. Pages 771–72 in *NIDOTTE* 3.

Barkay, Gabriel, Marilyn J. Lundberg, Andrew G. Vaughn, and Bruce Zuckerman. 2004. "The Amulets from Ketef Hinnom: A New Edition and Evaluation." *Bulletin of the American Schools of Oriental Research* 334: 41–71.

Barr, James. 1987. *Comparative Philology and the Text of the Old Testament: with Additions and Corrections.* Winona Lake, Ind.: Eisenbrauns.

Bauer, Hands, and Pontus Leander. 1922. *Historische Grammatik der hebräischen Sprache des Alten Testaments.* Halle: Max Niemeyer.

Beentjes, Pancratius, 2006. *The Book of Ben Sira in Hebrew.* Supplements to Vetus Testamentum 68. Leiden: Brill.

Ben-Ḥayyim, Ze'ev. 1973. *The Book of Ben Sira: Text, Concordance and an Analysis of the Vocabulary*. Jerusalem: The Academy of the Hebrew Language and the Shrine of the Book. [Hebrew]

Benoit, Pierre, Józef T. Milik, and Roland de Vaux. 1961. *Les grottes de Murabba'ât*. Discoveries in the Judaean Desert 2. Oxford: Clarendon.

Bloch, Yigal. 2007. "From Linguistics to Text-Criticism and Back: *Wayyiqṭōl* Constructions with Long Prefixed Verbal Forms in Biblical Hebrew." *Hebrew Studies* 48: 141–70.

Bloomhardt, Paul. 1928. "The Poems of Haggai." *Hebrew Union College Annual* 5: 153–95.

Boda, Mark J. 2001. "Oil, Crowns and Thrones: Prophet, Priest and King in Zechariah 1:7–6:15." *Journal of Hebrew Scriptures* 3, no. 10.

———. 2003b. "From Fasts to Feasts: The Literary Function of Zechariah 7–8." *Catholic Biblical Quarterly* 65: 390–407.

———. 2004. *Haggai, Zechariah*. NIV Application Commentary. Grand Rapids: Zondervan.

———. 2005. "Terrifying the Horns: Persia and Babylon in Zechariah 1:7–6:15." *Catholic Biblical Quarterly* 67: 22–41.

Broshi, Magen, et al. 1995. *Qumran Cave 4. XIV: Parabiblical Texts, Part 2*. Discoveries in the Judaean Desert 19. Oxford: Clarendon.

Childs, Brevard S. 1959. "The Enemy from the North and the Chaos Tradition." *Journal of Biblical Literature* 78, no. 3: 187–98.

Christiansen, Bent. 1999. "A Linguistic Analysis of the Biblical Hebrew Particle *nā'*: a Test Case." *Vetus Testamentum* 59: 379–93.

Christiansen, Duane. 1993. "Poetry and Prose in the Composition and Performance of the Book of Haggai." Pages 17–30 in *Verse in Ancient Near Eastern Prose*, edited by Johannes C. de Moor and Wilfred G. E. Watson. Alter Orient und Altes Testament 42. Neukirchen: Neukirchener Verlag.

Clark, David. 1982. "The Case of the Vanishing Angel." *The Bible Translator* 33, no. 2: 213–18.

———. 1983. "Problems in Haggai 2.15-19." *The Bible Translator* 34: 432–39.

———. 1985. "Discourse Structure in Zechariah 7:1–8:23." *The Bible Translator* 36, no. 3: 328–35.

———. 1988. "Discourse Structure in Zechariah 9–14: Skeleton or Phantom?" Pages 64–80 in *Issues in Bible Translation*, edited by Philip Stine. UBS Monograph Series 3. London: United Bible Societies.

———. 1992. "Discourse Structure in Haggai." *Journal of Translation and Textlinguistics* 5, no. 1: 13–24.

———. 1994. "Vision and Oracle in Zechariah 1–6". Pages 529–60 in *Biblical Hebrew and Discourse Linguistics*, edited by Robert Bergen. Dallas: Summer Institute of Linguistics.

———. 2005. "Red and Green Horses?" *The Bible Translator* 56, no. 2: 67–71.

Cohen, Ch. 2004. "The Enclitic-*Mem* in Biblical Hebrew: Its Existence and Initial Discovery." Pages 231–60 in *Sefer Moshe: The Moshe Weinfeld Jubilee Volume*, edited by Chaim Cohen, Avi Hurvitz, and Shalom M. Paul. Winona Lake, Ind.: Eisenbrauns.

Collins, C. John. 1997. כבד. Pages 577–87 in *NIDOTTE* 5.

Collins, John J. 1984. *The Apocalyptic Imagination: An Introduction to Jewish Apocalyptic Literature*. Grand Rapids: Eerdmans.

Creason, Stuart Alan. 1995. "Semantic Classes of Hebrew Verbs: A Study of Aktionsart in the Hebrew Verbal System." Ph.D. diss., University of Chicago.

Dalman, Gustaf. 1935. *Arbeit und Sitte in Palästina. IV: Brot, Öl, und Wein*. Hildesheim: G. Olms.

Davidson, Andrew Bruce. 1901. *An Introductory Hebrew Grammar with Progressive Exercises in Reading and Writing*. 17th ed. Edinburgh: T&T Clark.

Degen, Rainer. 1969. *Altaramäische Grammatik der Inschriften des 10.–8. Jh. V. Chr.* Abhandlungen für die Kunde des Morgenlandes 38(3). Wiesbaden: Franz Steiner.

De Lange, Nicholas. 2007. "Greek Influence on Hebrew." Pages 805–10 in *A History of Ancient Greek. From the Beginnings until Late Antiquity*, edited by Anastassios-Fivos Christidis. Cambridge: Cambridge University Press.

Delkurt, Holger. 2000. *Sacharjas Nachtgesichte: Zur Aufnahme und Abwandlung prophetischer Traditionen*. Beihefte zur Zeitschrift für die alttestamentliche Wissenschaft 302. Berlin: de Gruyter.

Demsky, Aaron. 1981. "The Temple Steward Josiah ben Zephaniah." *Israel Exploration Journal* 31, nos. 1–2: 100–102.

Dobbs-Allsopp, F. W. 1995. "The Syntagma of *Bat* Followed by a Geographical Name in the Hebrew Bible: A Reconsideration of Its Meaning and Grammar." *Catholic Biblical Quarterly* 57: 451–70.

———. 2009. "Daughter Zion." Pages 125–34 in *Thus says the Lord: Essays on the Former and Latter Prophets in Honor of Robert R Wilson*. Library of Hebrew Bible/Old Testament Studies 502. London: T&T Clark.

Dresher, B. Elan. 2012. "Methodological Issues in the Dating of Linguistic Forms: Considerations from the Perspective of Contemporary

Linguistic Theory." Pages 19–38 in *Diachrony in Biblical Hebrew*, edited by Cynthia. L. Miller-Naudé and Ziony Zevit. Linguistic Studies in Ancient West Semitic 8. Winona Lake, Ind.: Eisenbrauns.

Driver, Samuel Rolles. 1892. *A Treatise on the Use of the Tenses in Hebrew and Some Other Syntactical* Questions. 3rd ed. London: Oxford University Press [1998 repr. with an introductory essay by W. R. Garr; Grand Rapids: Eerdmans].

Ego, Beate, Armin Lange, Hermann Lichtenberger, and Kristin De Troyer. 2005. *Biblia Qumranica 3B: Minor Prophets*. Leiden: Brill.

Ehrensvärd, Martin. 2002. "Studies in the Syntax and the Dating of Biblical Hebrew." Ph.D. diss., University of Aarhus.

———. 2003. "Linguistic Dating of Biblical Texts." Pages 164–88 in *Biblical Hebrew: Studies in Chronology and Typology*, edited by Ian Young. Journal for the Study of the Old Testament Supplements 36. London: T&T Clark.

———. 2006. "Why Biblical Texts Cannot Be Dated Linguistically." *Hebrew Studies* 47: 177–89.

Ehrlich, Arnold B. 1912. *Randglossen zur Hebräischen Bibel: V. Ezechiel und die Kleinen Propheten*. Leipzig: J. C. Hinrichs.

Emerton, John. 1982. "New Light on Israelite Religion: the Implications of the Inscriptions from Kuntillet 'Ajrud." *Zeitschrift für die alttestamentliche Wissenschaft* 94: 2–20.

———. 1996. "Are There Examples of Enclitic *Mem* in the Hebrew Bible?" Pages 321–38 in *Texts, Temples and Traditions: A Tribute to Menahem Haran*, edited by Michael V. Fox et al. Winona Lake, Ind.: Eisenbrauns.

Eshel, Esther, et al. 1998. *Qumran Cave 4.VI: Poetical and Liturgical Texts, Part 1*. Discoveries in the Judaean Desert 11. Oxford: Clarendon.

Eskhult, Mats. 2000. "Verbal Syntax in Late Biblical Hebrew." Pages 84–93 in *Diggers at the Well: Proceedings of a Third International Symposium on the Hebrew of the Dead Sea Scrolls and Ben Sira*, edited by John F. Elwolde and Takamitsu Muraoka. Studies in the Texts of the Desert of Judea 36. Leiden: Brill.

———. 2005. "Traces of Linguistic Development in Biblical Hebrew." *Hebrew Studies* 46: 353–70.

Evans, Craig A. 1999. "'The Two Sons of Oil': Early Evidence of Messianic Interpretation of Zechariah 4:14 in 4Q254 4 2." Pages 566–73 in *The Provo International Conference on the Dead Sea Scrolls: Technological Innovations, New Texts, and Reformulated Issues*, edited by Donald Perry and Eugene Ulrich. Leiden: Brill.

Fine, Steven. 2006. "The United Colors of the Menorah: Some Byzantine and Medieval Perspectives on the Biblical Lampstand." Pages 106–13 in *Biblical Interpretation in Judaism and Christianity*, edited by Isaac Kalimi and Peter J. Haas. Library of Hebrew Bible/Old Testament Studies 439. London: T&T Clark.

Finley, Thomas J. 1988. " 'The Apple of His Eye' (*Bābat 'Ênô*) in Zechariah II 12." *Vetus Testamentum* 38: 337–38.

Fishbane, Michael. 1988. *Biblical Interpretation in Ancient Israel.* Oxford: Clarendon.

Floyd, Michael. 2008. "Welcome Back, Daughter of Zion!" *Catholic Biblical Quarterly* 70: 484–504.

Foulkes, Francis. 2007. פּוּרָה. Pages 591–92 in *NIDOTTE* 3.

Fuller, Russell. 1990. "Early Emendations of the Scribes: The Tiqqun Sopherim in Zechariah 2:12." Pages 21–28 in *Of Scribes and Scrolls: Studies in the Hebrew Bible, Intertestamental Judaism, and Christian Origins*, edited by Harold W. Attridge, John J. Collins and Thomas H. Tobin. Lanham, Md.: University Press of America.

Futato, Mark. 2001. "Sense Relations in the 'Rain' Domain of the Old Testament." Pages 81–94 in *Imagery and Imagination in Biblical Literature. Essays in Honor of Aloysius Fitzgerald, F.S.C.*, edited by Lawrence Boadt and Mark Smith. Catholic Biblical Quarterly Monograph Series 32. Washington, DC: The Catholic Biblical Association of America.

Garr, W. Randall. 2004. *Dialect Geography of Syria-Palestine 1000–586 B.C.E.* Winona Lake, Ind.: Eisenbrauns.

Good, Robert. 1982. "Zechariah's Second Night Vision (Zech 2,1-4)." *Biblica* 63: 56–59.

Grisanti, Michael. 1997. שִׁבֹּלֶת II. Pages 31–32 in *NIDOTTE* 4.

Hachlili, Rachel. 2001. *The Menorah, the Ancient Seven-armed Candelabrum.* Origin, Form and Significance: Supplements to the Journal for the Study of Judaism 68. Leiden: Brill.

Hallaschka, Martin. 2010. "Zechariah's Angels: Their Role in the Night Visions and in the Redaction History of Zech 1,7–6,8." *Scandinavian Journal of the Old Testament* 24(1): 13–27.

———. 2011. *Haggai und Sacharja 1–8. Eine Redaktionsgeschichtliche Untersuchung.* Beihefte Zur Zeitschrift Fur die Alttestamentliche Wissenschaft 411. Berlin: de Gruyter.

Hanhart, Robert. 1998. *Sacharja* (1,1–8,23). Biblische Kommentar Altes Testament XIV/7.1. Neukirchen-Vluyn: Neukirchener Verlag.

Hartley, John. גער. Pages 884–87 in *NIDOTTE* 1.

Hasel, Gerhard F. 1972. "Semantic Values of Derivatives of the Hebrew Root *Š'R*." *Andrews University Seminary Studies* 11: 152–69.

Haupt, Paul. 1917. "The Septuagintal Addition to Haggai 2:14." *Journal of Biblical Literature* 36: 148–50.

Heijmans, Shai. 2013. "Greek Loanwords." Pages 148–51 in *Encyclopedia of Hebrew Language and Linguistics*, edited by Geoffrey Khan. Leiden: Brill.

Hill, Andrew. 2012. *Haggai, Zechariah, and Malachi*. Tyndale Old Testament Commentary 28. Downers Grove, Ill.: InterVarsity.

Hoftijzer, Jacob. 1985. *The Function and Use of the Imperfect Forms with Nun Paragogicum in Classical Hebrew*. Studia Semitica Neerlandica 21. Assen: Van Gorcum.

Høgenhaven, Jesper. 2013. "The Book of Zechariah at Qumran." *Scandinavian Journal of the Old Testament* 27 no. 1: 107–17.

Holmstedt, Robert D. 2010. *Ruth: A Handbook on the Hebrew Text*. Baylor Handbook on the Hebrew Bible. Waco, Tex.: Baylor University Press.

———. 2011. "The Typological Classification fo the Hebrew of Genesis: Subject–Verb or Verb–Subject?" *Journal of Hebrew Scriptures* 11 (14).

Holmstedt, Robert D., and Andrew R. Jones. 2014. "The Pronoun in Tripartite Verbless Clauses in Biblical Hebrew: Resumption for Left-Dislocation or Pronominal Copula?" *Journal of Semitic Studies* 59, no. 1: 53–69.

Houtman, Cornelis. 2011. מְנֹרָה—lampstand. PDF downloaded from: http://www.otw–site.eu/KLY/kly.php.

Hummel, Horace D. 1957. "Enclitic *Mem* in Early Northwest Semitic, Especially Hebrew." *Journal of Biblical Literature* 76: 85–104.

Hurvitz, Avi. 1999. "Further Comments on the Linguistic Profile of Ben Sira: Syntactic Affinities with Late Biblical Hebrew." Page 132–45 in *Sirach, Scrolls, and Sages: Proceedings of a Second International Symposium on the Hebrew of the Dead Sea Scrolls, Ben Sira, and the Mishnah, held at Leiden University, 15–17 December 1997*, edited by John F. Elwolde and Takamitsu Muraoka. Studies in the Texts of the Desert of Judea 33. Leiden: Brill.

Hyatt, James Philip. 1937. "A Neo-Babylonian parallel to Bethel-Sar-Eṣer, Zech 7:2." *Journal of Biblical Literature* 56, no. 4: 387–94.

Janse, Mark. 2014. "Greek Loanwords in Hebrew and Aramaic." Pages 122–23 in *Encyclopedia of Ancient Greek Language and Linguistics*, edited by Georgios K. Giannakis. Leiden: Brill.

Jauhiainen, Marko. 2008. "Turban and Crown Lost and Regained: Ezekiel 21:29-32 and Zechariah's Zemah." *Journal of Biblical Literature* 127, no. 3: 501–11.

Joosten, Jan. 1997. "The Indicative System of the Hebrew Verb and Its Literary Exploitation." Pages 51–71 in *Narrative Syntax and the Hebrew Bible: Papers of the Tilburg Conference 1996*, edited by Ellen van Wolde. Biblical Interpretation 29. Leiden: Brill.

———. 2002. "Do the Finite Verbal Forms in Biblical Hebrew Express Aspect?" *Journal of the Ancient Near Eastern Society* 29: 49–70.

———. 2006. "The Disappearance of Iterative WEQATAL in the Biblical Hebrew Verbal System." Pages 135–47 in *Biblical Hebrew in Its Northwest Semitic Setting. Typological and Historical Perspectives*, edited by Steven Fassberg and Avi Hurvitz. Winona Lake, Ind.: Eisenbrauns.

———. 2011. "A Neglected Rule and Its Exceptions: On Non-Volitive *yiqtol* in Clause-Initial Position." Pages 213–19 in *En pāsē grammatikē kai sophiā. Saggi di linguistica ebraica in onore di Alviero Niccacci, ofm*, edited by Gregor Geiger and Massimo Pazzini. Milan: Franciscan Printing Press.

———. 2014. "The Verb גער 'to Exorcize' in Qumran Aramaic and Beyond." *Dead Sea Discoveries* 21: 347–55.

Joüon, Paul. 1929. "Notes Philologiques sur le Texte Hébreu de Osée (etc.)." *Biblica* 10: 417–20.

Kashow, Robert. 2013. "Zechariah 1–8 as a Theological Explanation for the Failure of Prophecy in Haggai 2:20-23." *Journal of Theological Studies* n.s. 64, no. 2: 385–403.

Kennicott, Benjamin. 1780. *Vetus Testamentum Hebraicum cum variis lectionibus*. Vol. 2. Oxford: Clarendon.

Kessler, John. 2002. *The Book of Haggai:. Prophecy and Society in Early Persian Yehud*. Supplements to Vetus Testamentum 91. Leiden: Brill.

Kitchen, Kenneth A. 1965. "The Aramaic of Daniel." Pages 31–79 in *Notes on Some Problems in the Book of Daniel*, edited by Donald J. Wiseman. London: Tyndale.

Kline, Meredith G. 2001. *Glory in Our Midst: A Biblical–Theological Reading of Zechariah's Night Visions*. Eugene, Ore.: Wipf & Stock.

Kloos, Carola. 1975. "Zech. II 12: Really a Crux Interpretum?" *Vetus Testamentum* 25, no. 4: 729–36.

Kotzé, Zacharias. 2004. "The Conceptualisation of Anger in the Hebrew Bible." Ph.D. diss., University of Stellenbosch.

———. 2005. "Metaphors and Metonymies for Anger in the Old Testament: A Cognitive Linguistic Approach." *Scriptura* 88: 118–25.

Krauss, Samuel. 1898–1899. *Griechische und Lateinische Lehnwörter im Talmud, Midrasch und Targum, mit Bemerkungen von Immanuel Low*. 2 vols. Berlin: S. Calvary.

Krivoruchko, Julia. 2012. "Greek Loanwords in Rabbinic Literature. Reflections on Current Research Methodology." Pages 193–216 in *Greek Scripture and the Rabbis*, edited by Timothy Michael Law and Alison Salvesen. Contributions to Biblical Exegesis and Theology 66. Leuven: Peeters.

Krispenz, J. 1998. "Grammatik und Theologie in der Botenformel." *Zeitschrift für Althebraistik* 11: 133–39.

Kropat, Arno. 1909. *Die Syntax des Autors der Chronik verglichen mit der seiner Quellen.* Beihefte Zur Zeitschrift Fur die Alttestamentliche Wissenschaft 16. Giessen: Alfred Töpelmann.

Kruger, Paul A. 2000. "A Cognitive Interpretation of the Emotion of Anger in the Hebrew Bible." *Journal of Northwest Semitic Languages* 26, no. 1: 181–93.

Kutscher, Ezekiel Y. 1959. *The Language and Linguistic Background of the Isaiah Scroll.* Jerusalem: Magnes. [Hebrew]

———. 1982. *A History of the Hebrew Language*. Jerusalem: Magnes.

Lebessi, Angeliki. 1996. "The Relations of Crete and Euboea in the Tenth and Ninth Centuries B.C. The Lefkandi Centaur and His Predecessors." Pages 146–54 in *Minotaur and Centaur: Studies in the Archaeology of Crete and Euboea Presented to Mervyn Popham*, edited by Doniert Evely, Irene S. Lemos, and Susan Sherratt. BAR International Series 638. Oxford: Tempus Reparatum.

Lemos, Irene. 2000. "Songs for Heroes: The Lack of Images in Early Greece." Pages 11–21 in *Word and Image in Ancient Greece*, edited by N. Keith Rutter and Brian A. Sparkes. Edinburgh: Edinburgh University Press.

Lipiński, Edward. 1970. "Recherches sur le livre de Zacharie." *Vetus Testamentum* 20: 25–55.

Lopez, René. 2010. "Identifying the 'Angel of the Lord' in the Book of Judges: A Model for Reconsidering the Referent in Other Old Testament Loci." *Bulletin for Biblical Research* 20, no. 1: 1–18.

Lowe, William Henry. 1882. *The Hebrew Student's Commentary on Zechariah: Hebrew and LXX.* London: MacMillan.

Luther, Martin. 1889. *Vorlesungen über die Kleinen Propheten. D. Martin Luthers Werke: Kritische Gesammtausgabe. Schriften* 13. Weimar: Böhlau.

Malessa, Michael. 2006. *Untersuchungen zur verbalen Valenz im biblischen Hebräisch.* Studia Semitica Neerdlandica 49. Assen: Van Gorcum.

Malone, Andrew. 2011. "Distinguishing the Angel of the Lord." *Bulletin for Biblical Research* 21, no. 3: 297–314.

Marenof, Shlomo. 1932. "Note concerning the Meaning of the Word 'Ephah,' Zechariah 5:5-11." *American Journal of Semitic Languages and Literatures* 48, no. 4: 264–67.

Mayrhofer, Manfred. 1992. *Etymologisches Wörterbuch des Altindoarischen.* Vol. 1. Heidelberg: Carl Winter Universitätsverlag.

McConville, J. Gordon. 2002. *Deuteronomy.* Apollos Old Testament Commentaries. Downers Grove, Ill.: InterVarsity.

Meier, Samuel. 1992. *Speaking of Speaking. Marking Direct Discourse in the Hebrew Bible.* Supplements to Vetus Testamentum 46. Leiden: Brill.

Meyers, Carol. 1976. *The Tabernacle Menorah: A Synthetic Study of a Symbol from the Biblical Cult.* Missoula: Scholars Press.

Meyers, Carol, and Eric Meyers. 1987. *Haggai, Zechariah 1–8.* Anchor Bible 25B. Garden City: Doubleday.

Milgrom, Jacob. 1991. *Leviticus 1–16.* Anchor Bible 3. New York: Doubleday.

Miller, Cynthia. 1996. *The Representation of Speech in Biblical Hebrew Narrative.* Atlanta: Scholars Press.

———. 2003. "A Linguistic Approach to Ellipsis in Biblical Poetry (Or, What to Do When Exegesis of What Is There Depends on What Isn't)." *Bulletin for Biblical Research* 13, no. 2: 251–70.

Miller-Naudé, Cynthia L., and Ziony Zevit. 2012. *Diachrony in Biblical Hebrew.* Linguistic Studies in Ancient West Semitic 8. Winona Lake, Ind.: Eisenbrauns.

Mitchell, Hinckley G. (with John M. P. Smith and Julius A. Bewer). 1912. *Haggai, Zechariah, Malachi and Jonah.* International Critical Commentary. Edinburgh: T&T Clark.

Mitchell, T. C., and R. Joyce. 1965. "The Musical Instruments in Nebuchadnezzar's Orchestra." Pages 19–27 in *Notes on Some Problems in the Book of Daniel,* edited by Donald J. Wiseman. London: Tyndale.

Moscati, Sabatino, Anton Spitaler, Edward Ullendorff, and Wolfram von Soden. 1969. *An Introduction to the Comparative Grammar of the Semitic Languages: Phonology and Morphology.* 2nd printing. Wiesbaden: Otto Harrassowitz.

Muraoka, Takamitsu. 1979. "On Verb Complementation in Biblical Hebrew." *Vetus Testamentum* 29: 425–35.

———. 1985. *Emphatic Words and Structures in Biblical Hebrew.* Jerusalem: Magnes.

———. 1997. "The Alleged Final Function of the Biblical Hebrew Syntagm <waw + a volitive verb form>." Pages 229–41 in *Narrative Syntax and the Hebrew Bible: Papers of the Tilburg Conference 1996,* edited by Ellen van Wolde. Biblical Interpretation 29. Leiden: Brill.

———. 2000. "An Approach to the Morphosyntax and the Syntax of Qumran Hebrew." Pages 193–214 in *Diggers at the Well: Proceedings of a Third International Symposium on the Hebrew of the Dead Sea Scrolls and Ben Sira*, edited by John F. Elwolde and Takamitsu Muraoka. Studies in the Texts of the Desert of Judea 36. Leiden: Brill.

———. 2009. *A Greek-English Lexicon of the Septuagint*. Leuven: Peeters.

Muraoka, Takamitsu, and Bezalel Porten. 1998. *A Grammar of Egyptian Aramaic*. Handbook of Oriental Studies: I. The Near and Middle East. Vol. 32. Leiden: Brill.

Niccacci, Alviero. 1987. "A Neglected Point of Hebrew Syntax: Yiqtol and Position in the Sentence." *Liber Annuus* 37: 7–19.

O'Connor, Michael O. 1997. *Hebrew Verse Structure: with Afterword.* Winona Lake, Ind.: Eisenbrauns.

O'Kennedy, Daniel F. 2008. "The Meaning of 'Great Mountain' in Zechariah 4:7." *Old Testament Essays* 21, no. 2: 404–21.

———. 2013. "Sagaria 2:8(12): 'n Moontlike Afrikaanse vertaling van 'n moeilike teks." *In die Skriflig/In Luce Verbi* 47, no. 1, Art #85, 6 pages. http://dx.doi.org/10.4102/ids.v47i1.85.

Park, Sang Hoon. 2007. שׁאר. Pages 11–17 in *NIDOTTE* 4.

Parunak, H. Van Dyke. 1994. "Some Discourse Functions of Prophetic Quotation Formulas in Jeremiah." Pages 489–519 in *Biblical Hebrew and Discourse Linguistics*, edited by Robert Bergen. Dallas: Summer Institute of Linguistics.

Paul, Mart-Jan. 2007. "The Identity of the Angel of the LORD." *HIPHIL Novum* 4: 1–12.

Pérez Fernández, Miguel. 1999. *An Introductory Grammar of Rabbinic Hebrew*. Translated by John Elwolde. Leiden: Brill.

Petersen, David. 1984. *Haggai and Zechariah 1–8*. Old Testament Library. Philadelphia: Westminster John Knox.

Petitjean, Albert. 1969. *Les oracles du proto-Zacharie. Un programme de restauration pour la communauté juive après l'exil.* Paris: Gabalda.

Petterson, Anthony R. 2009. *Behold Your King: The Hope for the House of David in the Book of Zechariah*. Library of Hebrew Bible/Old Testament Studies 513. London: T&T Clark.

———. 2015. *Haggai, Zechariah and Malachi*. Apollos Old Testament Commentary 25. Downers Grove, Ill.: InterVarsity.

Qimron, Elisha. 1986. *The Hebrew of the Dead Sea Scrolls.* Harvard Semitic Studies 29. Atlanta: Scholars Press.

Qimron, Elisha, and John Strugnell. 1994. *Discoveries in the Judaean Desert X, Qumran Cave 4, V: MIQṢAT MAʿAŚE HA-TORAH.* Oxford: Clarendon.

Reimer, David J. 1989. "The 'Foe' and the 'North' in Jeremiah." *Zeitschrift für die alttestamentliche Wissenschaft* 101, no. 2: 223–32.

Rendsburg, Gary. 2002. "Hebrew Philological Notes (III)." *Hebrew Studies* 43: 21–30.

———. 2012. "Late Biblical Hebrew in the Book of Haggai." Pages 329–44 in *Language and Nature: Papers Presented to John Huehnergard on the Occasion of his 60th Birthday*, edited by Rebecca Hasselbach and Na'ama Pat-El. Chicago: Oriental Institute.

Reymond, Philippe. 1957. "Un tesson pour 'ramasser' de l'eau à la mere (Esaie xxx, 14)." *Vetus Testamentum* 7, no. 2: 203–7.

Richter, Wolfgang. 1994. "Zum syntaktischen Gebrauch von Substantiven im Althebräischen am Beispiel von *'ōd*. Ein Beitrag zur Partikelforschung." *Zeitschrift für Althebraistik* 7, no. 2: 175–95.

Riffaterre, Michael. 1982. *Semiotics of Poetry*. Bloomington: Indiana University Press.

Rogland, Max. 2003. *Alleged Non-Past Uses of Qatal in Classical Hebrew*. Studia Semitica Neerlandica 44. Assen: Van Gorcum.

———. 2007a. "Haggai 2,17—A New Analysis." *Biblica* 88, no. 4: 553–57.

———. 2007b. "Text and Temple in Haggai 2,5." *Zeitschrift für die alttestamentliche Wissenschaft* 119, no. 3: 410–15.

———. 2010. "Eggs and Vipers in Isaiah 59 and the Qumran *Hodayot*." *Revue de Qumran* 25, no. 1: 3–16.

———. 2013a. "Two Philological Notes on Haggai 2:15-19." *Hebrew Studies* 54: 69–77.

———. 2013b. "Verb Transitivity and Ancient Hebrew מוש in in Zechariah 3:9." *Vetus Testamentum* 63: 497–98.

———. 2013c. "גל נעול in Canticles 4,12." *Zeitschrift für die alttestamentliche Wissenschaft* 125: 646–49.

———. 2014a. "The Horns That Scattered Judah: The Vision of Zechariah 2,1-4." *Biblische Zeitschrift* 58, no. 1: 92–7.

———. 2014b. "Heavenly Chariots and Earthly Rebellion in Zechariah 6." *Biblica* 95, no. 1: 117–23.

———. 2014c. "Flying Scrolls and Flying Baskets in Zechariah 5: Philological Observations and Literary Implications." *Journal of Northwest Semitic Languages* 40, no. 1: 93–107.

———. 2014d. "The Verbal Forms in Haggai 1:8-9." *The Bible Translator: Technical Papers* 65, no. 2: 157–64.

———. 2014e. "The 'Mountain' of Zechariah 4,7: Translation and Interpretation." *Biblische Notizen* 162: 75–82.

Rose, Wolter H. 2000. *Zemah and Zerubbabel. Messianic Expectations in the Early Postexilic Period.* Journal for the Study of the Old Testament Supplement Series 304. Sheffield: Sheffield Academic.

Russell, Brian. 2007. *The Song of the Sea: The Date of Composition and Influence of Exodus 15:1-21.* Studies in Biblical Literature 101. New York: Peter Lang.

Sáenz-Badillos, Angel. 1993. *A History of the Hebrew Language.* Translated by John Elwolde. Cambridge: Cambridge University Press.

Schöpflin, Karin. 2007. "God's Interpreter. The Interpreting Angel in Post-Exilic Prophetic Visions of the Old Testament." Pages 189–203 in *Angels: The Concept of Celestial Beings—Origins, Development and Reception,* edited by Friedrich V. Reiterer, Tobias Nickas, and Karin Schöpflin. Deuterocanonical and Cognate Literature Yearbook. Berlin: de Gruyter.

Schöttler, Heinz-Gunther. 1987. *Gott inmitten seines Volkes: Die Neuordnung des Gottesvolkes nach Sacharja 1–6.* Trierer theologische Studien 43. Trier: Paulinus-Verlag.

Schreiner, David. 2012. "The Election and Divine Choice of Zion/Jerusalem." *Journal for the Evangelical Study of the Old Testament* 1, no. 2: 147–66.

Segal, Michael. 2007. "The Responsibilities of and Rewards of Joshua the High Priest According to Zechariah 3:7." *Journal of Biblical Literature* 126, no. 4: 717–34.

Segert, Stanislav. 1997. "Old Aramaic Phonology." Pages 115–25 in *Phonologies of Asia and Africa: Volume 1,* edited by Alan S. Kaye. Winona Lake, Ind.: Eisenbrauns.

Shin, Seoung-Yun. 2007. *A Lexical Study on the Language of Haggai-Zechariah-Malachi and Its Place in the History of Biblical Hebrew.* Ph.D. diss., Hebrew University of Jerusalem.

Shulman, Ahouva. 1999. "The Particle נָא in Biblical Hebrew Prose." *Hebrew Studies* 40: 57–82.

Smith, Mark S. 2000. "The Infinitive Absolute as Predicative Verb in Ben Sira and the Dead Sea Scrolls: A Preliminary Survey." Pages 256–67 in *Diggers at the Well. Proceedings of a Third International Symposium on the Hebrew of the Dead Sea Scrolls and Ben Sira,* edited by John F. Elwolde and Takamitsu Muraoka. Studies in the Texts of the Desert of Judea 36. Leiden: Brill.

Stead, Michael. 2009. *The Intertextuality of Zechariah 1–8.* Library of Hebrew Bible/Old Testament Studies 506. New York: T&T Clark.

Steck, Odil. 1971. "Zu Haggai 1 2–11." *Zeitschrift für die Alttestamentliche Wissenschaft* 83: 355–79.

Steiner, Richard C. "Addenda to 'The Case for Fricative–Laterals in Proto–Semitic'." Pages 1499–1513 in *Semitic Studies in Honor of Wolf Leslau on the Occasion of His Eighty–Fifth Birthday*, edited by Alan S. Kaye. Vol.2. Wiesbaden: Harrassowitz.

Stinespring, William F. 1944. "A Note on Ruth 2:19." *Journal of Near Eastern Studies* 3: 101.

Stokes, Ryan. 2014. "Satan, YHWH's Executioner." *Journal of Biblical Literature* 133, no. 2: 251–70.

Swart, Ignatius. 2007. עשׁק. Pages 557–58 in *NIDOTTE* 3.

Sweeney, Marvin A. 2000. *The Twelve Prophets*. Vol. 2: *Micah, Nahum, Habakkuk, Zephaniah, Haggai, Zechariah, Malachi*. Berit Olam: Studies in Hebrew Narrative and Poetry. Collegeville, Minn.: Liturgical Press.

Taylor, Richard A., and Ray Clendenen. 2007. *Haggai, Malachi*. New American Commentary 21a. Nashville: Broadman & Holman.

Tell, Jeffrey Scott. 2011. *"By My Spirit Says the Lord": Intertextuality and a Biblical Theology of the Golden Menorah*. M.Th. thesis, Erskine Theological Seminary.

Thomson, Christopher J. 2012a. "The Removal of Sin in the Book of Zechariah." Ph.D. diss., University of Cambridge.

———. 2012b. "The "Seven Eyes" of Zech 3:9 and the Meaning of the Dual Form." *Vetus Testamentum* 62: 115–28.

Tiemeyer, Lena-Sofia. 2004. "Compelled by Honour—A New Interpretation of Zechariah ii 12a (8a)." *Vetus Testamentum* 54: 352–72.

———. 2006. *Priestly Rites and Prophetic Rage: Post-Exilic Prophetic Critique of the Priesthood*. Forschungen Zum Alten Testament 2/19. Tübingen: Mohr Siebeck.

———. 2011. "Will the Prophetic Texts from the Hellenistic Period Stand Up, Please!" Pages 255–79 in *Judah Between East and West: The Transition from Persian to Greek Rule (ca. 400–200 BCE)*, edited by Lester Grabbe and Oded Lipschits. Library of Second Temple Studies 75. London: T&T Clark.

———. 2015. *Zechariah and His Vision: An Exegetical Study of Zechariah's Vision Report*. Library of Hebrew Bible/Old Testament Studies 605. London: T&T Clark.

Tigchelaar, Eibert. 1996. *Prophets of Old and The Day of the End: Zechariah, the Book of Watchers and Apocalyptic*. Oudtestamentische Studiën 35. Leiden: Brill.

Trask, R. L. 1993. *A Dictionary of Grammatical Terms in Linguistics*. London: Routledge.

Van der Merwe, Christo. 1990. *The Old Hebrew Particle gam: A syntatic–semantic description of gam in Gn–2Kg*. Arbeiten zu Text und Sprache in Alten Testament 34. St. Ottilien: EOS Verlag.

———. 1991. "The Old Hebrew particles *'ak* and *raq* (in Genesis to 2 Kings)." Pages 29–311 in *Text, Methode und Grammatik: Wolfgang Richter zum 65. Geburtstag*, edited by Walter Gross, Hubert Irsigler and Theodor Seidl. St. Ottilien: EOS Verlag.

———. 1992. "Is There Any Difference between ירא מן, ירא מפני, and ירא את?" *Journal of Northwest Semitic Languages* 18: 177–83.

———. 2003. "Some Recent Trends in Biblical Hebrew Linguistics: A Few Pointers Towards a More Comprehensive Model of Language Use." *Hebrew Studies* 44: 7–24.

Van der Woude, A. S. 1988a. "Zion as Primeval Stone in Zechariah 3 and 4." Pages 237–48 in *Text and Context. Old Testament and Semitic Studies for F. C. Fensham*, edited by Walter Claassen. Journal for the Study of the Old Testament Supplement Series 48. Sheffield: Sheffield Academic.

———. 1988b. "Serubbabel und die messianischen Erwartungen des Propheten Sacharja." *Zeitschrift für die alttestamentliche Wissenschaft* 100, no. 1: 138–56.

Van Peursen, Wido Th. 2004. *The Verbal System in the Hebrew Text of Ben Sira*. Studies in Semitic Languages and Linguistics 41. Leiden: Brill.

VanderKam, James. 1991. "Joshua the High Priest and the Interpretation of Zechariah 3." *Catholic Biblical Quarterly* 53: 553–70.

Van Wolde, Ellen. 2008. "Sentiments as Culturally Constructed Emotions: Anger and Love in the Hebrew Bible." *Biblical Interpretation* 16: 1–24.

Verhoef, Peter A. 1987. *The Books of Haggai and Malachi*. New International Commentary on the Old Testament. Grand Rapids: Eerdmans.

———. 1988. "Notes on the Dates in the Book of Haggai." Pages 259–67 in *Text and Context: Old Testament and Semitic Studies for F. C. Fensham*, edited by Walter Claassen. Journal for the Study of the Old Testament Supplement Series 48. Sheffield: Sheffield Academic.

Von Orelli, Conrad. 1908. *Die Zwölf Kleinen Propheten*. 3rd ed. Munich: Oskar Beck.

Wagner, Andreas. 1997. *Sprechakte und Sprechaktanalyse im Alten Testament. Untersuchungen im biblischen Hebräisch an der Nahstelle zwischen Handlungsebene und Grammatik*. Beihefte Zur Zeitschrift Fur die Alttestamentliche Wissenschaf 253. Berlin: de Gruyter.

Watson, Wilfred G. E. 1984. *Classical Hebrew Poetry. A Guide to its Techniques.* Journal for the Study of the Old Testament Supplement Series 26. Sheffield: JSOT Press.

Way, Robert J. 1997. צָנִיף. Pages 820–21 in *NIDOTTE* 3.

Wegner, Paul. 1997. שִׁבֹּלֶת II. Pages 30–31 in *NIDOTTE* 4.

Wenzel, Heiko. 2011a. *Reading Zechariah with Zechariah 1:1–6 as the Introduction to the Entire Book.* Contributions to Biblical Exegesis and Theology 59. Leuven: Peeters.

———. 2011b. "Hört auf zu sein wie eure Väter" (Sach 1,4): Ein Beitrag zur Übersetzung der Verneinung mit אַל." Pages 179–201 in *Sprache lieben—Gottes Wort verstehen. Beiträge zur biblischen Exegese. Festschrift für Heinrich von Siebenthal,* edited by Walter Hilbrands. Gießen: Brunnen.

Willi-Plein, Ina. 2007. *Haggai, Sacharja, Maleachi.* Zürcher Bibelkommentare 24/4. Zürich: Theologischer Verlag Zürich.

Wilt, Timothy. 1996. "A Sociolinguistic Analysis of *NĀ*." *Vetus Testamentum* 46, no. 2: 237–55.

———. 1999. "'Oracle of Yahweh': Translating a Highly Marked Expression." *The Bible Translator: Technical Papers* 50, no. 3: 301–4.

Wolf, Herbert M., and Robert Holmstedt. 1997. יצק. Pages 502–3 in *NIDOTTE* 2.

Wolff, Hans Walter. 1988. *Haggai. A Commentary.* Translated by Margaret Kohl. Minneapolis: Augsburg.

Wolters. Al. 2012. "The Meaning of *ṣantĕrôt* (Zech 4:12)." *Journal of Hebrew Scriptures* 12, no. 1.

———. 2014. *Zechariah.* Historical Commentary on the Old Testament. Leuven: Peeters.

Yamauchi, Edwin. 2007. יְהוּדִי. Pages 415–17 in *NIDOTTE* 2.

Young, Ian. 1999. "'*Am* Construed as Singular and Plural in Hebrew Biblical Texts: Diachronic and Textual Perspectives." *Zeitschrift für Althebraistik* 12: 48–82.

———. Ed. 2003. *Biblical Hebrew: Studies in Chronology and Typology.* Library of Hebrew Bible/Old Testament Studies 369. London: T&T Clark.

Young, Ian, Robert Rezetko, and Martin Ehrensvärd. 2008a–b. *Linguistic Dating of Biblical Texts.* 2 vols. London: Equinox.

Ziegler, Joseph. 1984. *Duodecim Prophetae.* Septuaginta 13. Göttingen: Vandenhoeck & Ruprecht.

Zer-Kavod, Mordecai. 1968. *Haggai, Zechariah, Malachi.* Jerusalem: Kiryat Sefer. [Hebrew]

INDEX OF SUBJECTS

INDEX OF HEBREW WORDS

INDEX OF NAMES